How It All Got Started

Lessons in Life, Art & Entrepreneurship from Hip Hop Icons

RAMSES M

ᴏᴀ
**Purple
Circus
Production**

Copyright © 2014 Ramsey *Ramses M'* Mullaney

All rights reserved.

For More Resources, Orders and Discounts Visit:

www.HipHopTeaches.com

First Edition, 2014

ISBN-10: 1505265592
ISBN-13: 978-1505265590

'You love to hear the story, how it all got started' — Nas, Back When

TRACKLIST

Part I: Beginnings

Part II: Building

Part III: Practical Lessons

Part VI: Universal Principles

Intro

DeWitt Clinton High School, Brooklyn, is another rest stop in Jean Paul's life. He's part of the 78% of his classmates born below the poverty line, and like 46% of them he will likely die there too.[1]

Jean wakes up in a room with three other sleeping bodies, dresses his younger brother and sends him to the nearby bus stop, then walks the ten blocks to Clinton High, with his most valuable possession strapped to his head.

Songs coming from the headphones are his meditation. Stories about the harsh realities of getting by in a broken system, the struggle of overcoming obstacles through personal effort, and the rewards of living a life of independence and freedom are the common themes.

Jean enters the rusting school gate, past the metal detector and security guard, and greets friends living similar lives. Today, the first lesson is 'personal development,' taught by a lady who's spent 35 years teaching, or better said, 'caring', for teenagers who come to school for the security, routine, nourishment, and guiding hand of responsible adults they don't find at home. After a register call, some teacher-student banter and a prayer of gratitude, Jean's teacher explains some exercises to get the class thinking about their career prospects.

What does Jean's future look like? Statistics seem stacked against him.

He lives in a country where one in five children, like him, lives in poverty, (the second highest rate of any developed nation). The government-owned building he calls home is shared with hundreds of others, and his own four-person family pack into two dingy rooms – they're on the public housing waiting list hoping to find somewhere safer to sleep, (along with a quarter million others in 'the city that never sleeps'). Jean has no stable role model to show him how to take advantage of opportunities – his mother works most of the day and he has no memory of his father, extended family members have been on-and-off drugs and in-and-out of prison. Decades of research has exposed the entrapped lives children living in these conditions are likely to lead: "They grow up with less education and lower earning power. They are more likely to have drug addiction, psychological trauma and disease, or wind up in prison."[2]

Less than 30% of teens in the bottom quarter of incomes enroll in college, and less than half of those graduate – dropping out often because of the need to earn money or campus alienation.[3]

But ask Jean what his future holds and he doesn't consider the statistics: "I'm going to learn computer programming and start a company…"

A large reason for Jean's positive outlook is because of his morning meditation – the music he listens to, and the culture it comes from. Hip Hop provides him with the motivation that it *is* possible to rise above his life of struggle. He looks at someone like Sean 'Jay Z' Carter – a man bred in America's urban slums, who now texts with the President – and sees himself. Though their lives today are planets apart, Jean sees Sean and feels he can do anything.

Hip Hop is hope.

Hamada Amor set up a video camera in his bedroom, pulled his cap low, faced the homemade microphone stand connected to his laptop, and spat. He raps vicious bars over an eerie Mobb Deep *Shook Ones* type beat about life and death in Tunisia. With the passion of a civil rights leader, his poetry vents about the daily survival struggle the masses endure while corrupt officials leach on the country's crippled corpse. Like a handful of other Arab rappers, Hamada, better known as El General, speaks about things people feel but fear to express outside their homes – a fear formed from decades of authority intimidation. Against the well-meaning advice of friends, El General shares the video online in November 2010.

That song, and others like it, captured the feeling of oppressed peoples across the Arab world and became the rhythm to the extraordinary revolutions that swept across the Middle East in spring of 2011, toppling all-powerful dictators and causing colossal social change. In Tahrir Square for example, during Egypt's 2011 revolution, you'd hear rappers, drummers and DJ's motivating crowds from the main stage and you'd see graffiti murals painted on any type of wall, expressing "the people's will" through art. Hip Hop helped spark and succeed "the greatest wave of empowerment in the early 21st century."[4]

And this is not a unique example. Countless protests across the world have been attributed to Hip Hop. 'Raptavism'[5] as one artist describes it, is a global tool to engage and empower disenfranchised people. Though, like other popular movements for past generations, Hip Hop can also be used as a tool by authorities to entrench institutional power. That's why government organizations have been meticulously documenting and trying to silently influence popular culture for decades. Look at the infamous 'rap police squads' of the late-90's, or the recent news of US authorities trying to use Hip Hop as a means to overthrown the Cuban government.[6]

Hip Hop is powerful expression.

Ben Horowitz is a Berkeley raised, middle aged, Jewish, technology nerd. Without him thousands around the world would not know what Jay Z meant in N**** In Paris: '*So I ball so hard mothafuckas wanna fine me/*'

Ben is one of Silicon Valley's most respected venture capitalists – having invested in many of the world's biggest tech companies, from Twitter to Airbnb, as well as $40 million in rap lyrics website 'Genius'.

Every day he analyzes dozens of business proposals, meets with CEO's of the companies he's invested in to "figure out impossible problems,"[7] and formulates plans to reach his colossal financial goals. Intermixed with everything is Hip Hop. Lots and lots of Hip Hop. It is, he says, "The inspiration for all my thinking on leadership."[8]

Listening to artists like "Kanyeezy and Weezy" gets Ben focused in the morning and relaxed in the evening. Hip Hop is used to 'pump up' before workouts and energize before meetings. It's used to meditate on and dance to. It's used to forget some problems and solve others. Ben used Hip Hop as much when he was a struggling student as when he became a billionaire.

Hip Hop is life's supplement.

Why?

How can Hip Hop relate to people as different as Jean, Hamada and Ben?

Because the principles Hip Hop represents connect with a universal core.

Raw emotions of: self-empowerment, achievement, overcoming, and living on your own terms by not passively playing the cards society (class, race, sex) or family (repeating past generations, expectation) hand you, are the essence of Hip Hop and a fundamental part of what it means to be human.

This human connection is the reason Hip Hop grew from a derelict district of New York four decades ago to the dominant global urban culture it is today. It's why artists like Kanye West, entrepreneurs like Curtis Jackson, and executives like Russell Simmons, are mentors, even icons, to millions across the globe. It's why Hip Hop is the embodiment of the *New American Dream*.

The traditional idea of the 'American dream' is about starting at the bottom and working long and hard for other people, 'paying dues' and slowly climbing the corporate ladder, while patiently waiting for a pot of gold at the end. But in an age of job insecurity, outsourcing and increasing debts, to most this 'dream' is a far off fantasy.

The *New American Dream* isn't about spending years working for others and doesn't have suburban 'white–picket–fence' limits. It's about entrepreneurship, owning your work and seeing no bounds to your growth. The New American Dream isn't exclusive to America. It's global. It's not about possessing certain status symbols. It's a state of mind, an attitude. Hip Hop is the embodiment of this dream and its icons are leading by example.

'I'm American dreamin' – Jay Z

Entrepreneurial Generation

In the 1950's and 60's America changed drastically. The civil rights era brought about unprecedented social movements as ethnic minorities demanded equal rights. Tens of thousands boldly took part in protests and marches across the country, like the first African-Americans to attend all white schools in southern states, who endured humiliation, isolation and abuse from other students, teachers and neighbors.

September 6, 1957: Fifteen-year-old Elizabeth Eckford, one of nine black students whose admission to Little Rock's Central High School was ordered by a federal court, is threatened by a white mob on the first day of class. Credit: ©Bettmann/Corbis

Alongside these massive social movements there were huge changes in popular culture. Mass migration across the country brought new customs and music to new regions. Styles fused to create new sounds which became the drum beat to social change. As Dan Charnas writes in 'The Big Payback,' "The rhythm-and-blues/rock-and-roll revolution formed the soundtrack to the civil rights era."

Why is this relevant? Well just like RnB/RockNRoll defined an era, now it seems that Hip Hop is defining another social change, especially among youth. Hip Hop has become the soundtrack to the 'Entrepreneurial Era.'

Hip Hop is the first cultural movement to embrace entrepreneurship. Whereas, say, Rock-N-Roll icons concealed their success, Hip Hop icons strive for it. And so do the fans. "Hip Hop's truest fans want to see their heroes succeed and want to emulate them," writes one Hip Hop journalist.[9]

Research shows it's true. 54% of 'millennials' (18-34 year olds) say they would like to start or have already started their own business. The figure is even higher for young ethnic minorities (who are also more likely to identify with Hip Hop culture) – 64 percent of Latinos and 63 percent of African-Americans expressed a desire to start their own companies.[10]

"[Right now] you see an explosion of entrepreneurial energy and enthusiasm all over the world," says venture capitalist Mark Anderson.[11]

To a generation the coolest career path is one you chose for yourself. One where you are 'your own boss' and 'do what you love' – a synonym for entrepreneurship.

'I'm a writer, I'm a fighter, entrepreneur/
Fresh out the sewer, watch me maneuver, what's it to you?'
– 50 Cent, My Life

Hip Hop, or specifically the sub-category 'Entrepreneurial Hip Hop,' is a large part of the aspiration fuel for a generation to succeed. While the music doesn't offer practical entrepreneurial advice, it provides something more important; emotional energy. As Ben Horowitz says, "All the management books are like, 'This is how you set objectives, this is how you set up an org chart,' but that's all the easy part of management. The hard part is how you feel. Rap helps me connect emotionally."[12]

Listeners relate to the emotions of independence, overcoming, no-limits and doing-you, which are so pervasive in entrepreneurial rap. As Abi Noda writes: "Entrepreneurial rap inspires us to go after our dreams and have faith that if we have the fearlessness to follow our hearts, there is nothing that can stop us."[13]

How It All Got Started adds practical advice to the emotion behind the music. This is a journey through the lives and lyrics of remarkable people who have used Hip Hop as a vehicle to achieve great things, to explain what it actually means to be 'successful' from a Hip Hop point of view.

Because of Hip Hop's aspirational focus, we're accustomed to the outward signs of the icon's success – *'they got the cars the boat and the beautiful house by the shore/ and you know there's more' (Kanye West, Supernova)* – but this book is the first to look much deeper at the internal principles they live by. The character traits that have brought about their visible success.

In these pages we've organized and broken down hundreds of sources into twenty-three universally applicable life lessons, each told though the stories of how dozens of Hip Hop icons have applied them to their career and lives.

For instance we'll learn:

- How Kanye developed his 'Godly' self-belief and why it's fundamental to his success – *(pg.87)*

- Keys to longevity and how Dr. Dre has remained at the forefront of Hip Hop for thirty years – *(pg.137)*

- Where Jay Z, and dozens of other successful 'hustlers' draw the line over what's acceptable and what is not – *(pg.174)*

- Why most Hip Hop icons choose to have long-term intimate relationships with one person – *(pg.207)*

- The 'secret' of creative genius, and how Pharrell, Grandmaster Flash and others earn millions using it – *(pg.243)*

- The one thing Diddy as an intern, Drake as a rapper and Dame Dash as a CEO, all did to break into their industry – *(pg.254)*

- The power of 'celebrity' and how Eminem, Snoop and Hopsin know how to solve the problem of getting noticed – *(pg.258)*

Much of these insights come directly from the mouths (or actions) of several Hip Hop Greats, but the teachings are also supplemented with wisdom from authors, scholars and business leaders, to add weight and greater substance – all the while maintaining a Hip Hop connection.

The principles are divided into four parts. In-between each you'll find in-depth stories of how Kanye West, Kendrick Lamar, Jay Z and Eminem rose to the forefront of popular culture. In these detailed biographies you'll see exactly how each of icon 'made it,' the little known people who played pivotal parts in the journey, and how close they all came to total failure.

Everything is told through the life experiences of today's rock stars and made ready for you to take inspiration from and apply to your own journey.

'Read slow and you'll find gold mines in these lines/ '
– Kendrick Lamar, Poetic Justice

Who's this for?

How It All Got Started is made with four people in mind:

1. Those with the 'Hip Hop State of Mind,' *(pg.11)*, or, as marketing company Alloy Access labels them, 'Urban Hustlers.' People – whether preachers, plumbers, presidents or poets – who seek to empower themselves and take control of their circumstances, like the Hip Hop Greats.

   "The Urban Hustler has come to represent a specific mindset born out of the unique energy, creativity and diversity of America's urban centers – closely connected to hip-hop, ethnically diverse with aspirations to succeed and a shared set of passions."[14]

2. Entrepreneurs and artists, aspiring and established, who want to learn practical and inspirational lessons from cultural icons who've built colossal businesses from scratch and whose work has touched the lives of millions.

3. Fans of Hip Hop who want to understand the detailed back stories behind their favorite artist's rise.

4. Hip Hop haters, who regard the culture as a grimy, ignorant, 'barely-music,' that promotes all the worlds' ills. This book will demonstrate the true treasure trove of wisdom beneath Hip Hop's sometimes shallow exterior.

Why Hip Hop?

The general idea of this book (that Hip Hop is a brilliant tool for positive development) is not unique. Many organizations exist which use Hip Hop to "empower disenfranchised students [to convert] negative circumstances into positive grounds for learning."[15] The Hip Hop Education Center (at New York University) surveyed over three hundred 'Hip Hop education programs' and found Hip Hop played a huge role in promoting skills in areas like identity formation and community activism, and also in developing an understanding of academic subjects like English language, arts, entrepreneurship and ethnic studies.

Aside from direct education programs, as the world's dominant 'youth culture,' Hip Hop influences everything from college literacy programs to liquor sales – marketing experts estimate that one-quarter of all discretionary spending in America is influenced by Hip Hop.[16]

Economically, Hip Hop is a key distributor of wealth – a vehicle thousands of people have used to ascend America's wealth pyramid.

Socially, Hip Hop has done more to eradicate racial boundaries than any movement since the civil rights era. It has played a significant role in affecting elections, sparking revolutions and empowering disenfranchised and underprivileged sections of society.

Yet to many, 'Hip Hop' conjures images of ignorant, unruly, pleasure-seeking, violent, materialistic, drug-dealing dropouts. And to some extent this view is true. However, this skewed perspective does not at all represent the Hip Hop that inspires 'Urban Hustlers' around the world – just like hate-preaching religious groups do not represent the vast majority of devout believers.

Of course, I do acknowledge the less-than-admirable side of the music and culture that seems to go directly against universal principles and lessons discussed in this book. But, although the *life-imitates-art/art-imitates-life* debate continues, I do not speak of that here because this is a book about values, life lessons and principles, whose purpose is to uplift, educate and entertain, so it makes sense to focus on the positive.

At the same time this isn't a study of Hip Hop culture, but of Hip Hop icons – an exclusive group of people who've maintained their position in the upper echelon of corporate and cultural America through the vehicle of Hip Hop. As these pages reveal, they all completely renounce the negative connotations listed above. They are all positive creators who live by a universal code.

The Icons

A cultural icon is a person who represents the values of a particular culture. They are a part of the culture, but also represent the culture as a whole. They embody ideals the culture admires and represent what members want to be.

Those profiled in this book deserve to be labeled 'icons' because, to an urban hustler, they are a representation of themselves and what they could be. As writer Rob LaFranco says of Sean Combs's global lifestyle business empire, "Why did Puffy become so famous? It's because he embodies every hope and dream of underprivileged kids."[17]

'Somehow he got around the pitfalls of the system/
When he walks we watch/ When he talks we listen/ '
– Nas, Leaders

These icons started from bedrooms and basements with no special hook-ups and no prodigal talent. When they set out on their journey, others didn't regard them as 'genius,' 'gifted' or 'special.' Yet their achievements have enabled them to legitimately "live the dream of the hustler: independence, wealth, and success outside of the mainstream's rules."[18] Their example has broken the illusion of limitation for those born into similar worlds. They've made it not only seem possible but normal to have high aspirations and be an entrepreneur. As David Mays, the Harvard-educated co-founder of Hip Hop magazines 'The Source' and 'Hip Hop Weekly,' says, "People want to start their own businesses and think they can. It's one of the staples of our culture."[16]

'Cause, dreams of being Hova/
Went from bein a broke man to bein a dopeman/
To bein the President, look there's hope man/ '
– Kanye West, Crack Music

This book is an organized collection of iconic wisdom. But, although the icons presented here are impressive individuals, they are still people – people with inbuilt frailties and limitations who may do or say things counter to the principles discussed. I have tried to let the best in each icon shine through by presenting them in a way their most admiring colleagues and fans describe, while still being honest about their human limitations. So although the icons deserve respect, when you read or see something they've done which reminds you of their human weaknesses, remember to seek the message before the messenger.

'Don't follow me, young'un, follow my moves/ '
– Jay Z, Go Crazy

Who's writing this?

In short, *How It Al Got Started* represents the combination of two of my greatest interests – Entrepreneurship and Hip Hop. I've worked on several start-up ventures over the past few years while Hip Hop provided the soundtrack. There would be nights where I'd be sitting alone in a basement office after ten hours of phone rejections and feel like life was being wasted, but songs like Tupac's 'Me Against the World,' Kanye West's 'I Wonder' or Immortal Technique's 'Positive Balance' let me sleep without popping an eye socket and wake up the next day ready to go again.

Other times, when a business deal would come together and I'd be overlooking a beautiful city from a luxury hotel's penthouse, songs like Jay Z's 'What More Can I Say,' would feel like the natural accompaniment.

Through Hip Hop I've learned lessons about branding, authenticity, communication, politics, and a host of other subjects, and I decided (somewhat accidently *(pg.334)*), to try to transfer this abstract association between life lessons and Hip Hop into something more concrete.

The motives for writing this book are simple: To create a resource I, and I hope many others, will be able to learn and take inspiration from along their journey through life. This is made especially for young 'urban hustlers' who look up to Hip Hop icons and aspire to be like (or greater than) them, but don't necessarily know how to get there (like all of us to some degree). *'Shorties get the game with no instructions to assembling'* Common raps on 'The Food,' and I hope this book will be part of those instructions.

How to Read

This book is designed to entertain and educate. It holds too much information for it to be put away after reading once. To get the most benefit from the stories and principles, *How It All Got Started* should be a regular source of inspiration and guidance. When you face a problem, it's likely that one of the names in this book has faced and overcome a similar hurdle and their experience can provide motivation and practical advice.

'I hope you fools choose to listen, I drop jewels, bust it/
These are the rules I follow in my life, you gotta love it/ '
– Jay Z, Fellin It

You can read this book however you want. It might be useful to begin with the biographies of the four featured icons, as sub-stories related to them are distributed across the book, but it's not necessary. You can start at chapter two or ten, read the biographies first or skip them altogether. Take what is relevant to you now.

Roots

Mind | Control | Natural

Jean, Hamada and Ben are united by the Hip Hop state of mind. That mindset is the essence of this book and the foundation all principles are built on.

This 'urban hustler' mindset is about owning your life, and by default your work. It's about living your interests, taking calculated risks, developing a unique brand, forcefully competing, and creating wealth through sustainable enterprises, all while abiding by a code.

The Hip Hop mentality is, "Give me $10 I'll turn it into $100. Don't give me $100 cause that makes me your slave," says Hip Hop legend KRS–One.[18] "Don't pay me. I work and you compensate me according to the mastery of my work." – Just like Jay Z thought when he sat opposite Russell Simmons in 1997 to broker a deal between Roc–A–Fella and Def Jam (*pg.232*): *'I'm not looking to get paid, I'm looking to take the whole company. I don't want you to pay to me, I want to be you.'* [19]

(This is totally different from the work-for-hire/wage-slave/employee mind state, which seeks to play it safe, earn a steady salary, live inside its comfort zone and never venture into the wild.)

'Can't complain 'bout what they ain't gon' give ya/
That ain't gon' get ya shit, might as well give up/
Or get up, get out and get something n****/
– Jay Z, Say Hello

This Hip Hop, or urban hustler, mind state is nothing new. The same energy has been expressed in different ways by past generations. But Hip Hop is the first global expression of this frame of mind among young people of all races and places. That's why Hip Hop has grown into a global cipher; a culture blind to color, creed, gender, or a particular occupation. As Hip Hop executive Steve Stoute says, "The hip hop community has nothing to do with race, it's more of an attitude."[20]

Control

The essence of the attitude is control. Every principle discussed here starts with the simple idea that you are in control of your life. You are responsible for everything.

Growing up you had no control over your neighborhood, race, parents, and most circumstances, but you do have control over how you react to these. You do control your future. Like Eminem said, "The only control you have is to get out of your situation or stay in it."[21]

All people in this book are living testaments to this principle. The principle that *The World Is Yours*, if you accept total responsibility for *your* world – your current world and the world you are building.

For instance, a person totally set in this frame of mind won't say something is 'hard,' they'll say: 'I'm not strong enough to fight for this now.' They won't say, 'She makes me angry,' they'll say: 'I need to be emotionally stronger to not let others' actions affect me.' They won't say 'It's not my fault,' they'll say: 'What can I do differently so this doesn't happen again?'

Taking control of your life is the foundation everything is built on.

'Control what I hold and of course be the boss of myself/
No-one else will bring my wealth/ '
– Big Daddy Kane, A Job Ain't Nothing But Work

'All Natural Baby'

This book is about 'life lessons' or 'principles of success' learned from Hip Hop icons, but what is the goal? What is the end result supposed to be? What is success?

Every person has a different definition of success. It might be about reaching a certain stature, possessing certain things, breaking a certain record, or just feeling good.

Everyone also has their own unique way of achieving their definition of success – a spiritualist seeking enlightenment will use different methods to a salesman seeking a profit. But if you were to compress all of these 'ways' into a single theme, a single affirmation, it would read: 'If I Get My Mind Right I Will Not Lose.'[22]

IF I GET MY
MIND RIGHT
I WILL
NOT
LOSE

This statement looks inspiring, but it creates more questions. What is 'right' and how can I get my mind there?

Well, breaking down these ten words further, most people's idea of 'success' will generally fall into two categories:

- **Personal Success** – which is about having mastery and control over yourself.

- **Commercial Success** – which is about profiting from your work.

The second definition is what's visible for the world to see (the materials, the awards, the fame) but it's really a product of the first, just like the visible branch of a tree is an extension of its 'invisible' root. To develop and sell a great product that deserves to exist in the world you need, creativity, focus, and many more principles that are developed naturally though personal success.

'Third eye navigational movements are necessary/
Everything you see in videos is secondary/ '
– Immortal Technique, Positive Balance

In fact, as we'll see throughout this book, in most walks of life there are two ways of doing things: the artificial way and the natural way. The artificial way is about learning tips, tricks and techniques. It's about 'get rich quick schemes,' and chasing the money. Greatness, as the Hip Hop icons will demonstrate, can only be achieved the natural way, which is about getting the inside right, how we think, then letting the outside change flow naturally.

'How you gonna win when you ain't right within?/ '
– Lauryn Hill, Doo Woop

The Journey Summarized

"Find your path, Believe in your path, and Live it." – Common[23]

The natural way starts with embracing your uniqueness, knowing what you want and following your interests. You might have a specific goal like 'graduate from college,' or 'perform at Madison Square Garden,' or you may be unsure of specifics but want to 'be passionate about work.' Chapter 1 'The Re-Finding' look at why living your interests is fundamental to personal (and commercial) success. The next ingredient is motivation. There are many reasons *why* you might do what you do, each with its own reward path. Chapter 2 explains the motivating forces that keep Greats creating great work, while chapter 3 examines how they are able to overcome the most common obstacle we all face.

Closely related to motivation is self-belief. When the Greats start out, their belief in their ability to overcome fear and failure and achieve their goals is so strong that, through the power of auto-suggestion, it becomes a 'This Will Be Achieved' state of mind, and they believe they can get past all the challenges that will inevitably come. Because what you focus on is the reality you experience, they develop a feeling of relaxed inevitability that something will come, that "success is just around the corner," as J Cole said, (chapter 4).

With these foundations in place, a definite yet flexible plan based around clear objectives, can be naturally created, (chapter 5). Combined with the hustle to find the back entrance (chapter 8), the energy to get past frustration and failure (chapter 9), unshakable focus on only important matters (chapter 10), and the hunger to keep learning (chapter 11), whilst forming a united team all headed in the same direction, or 'Circle of Success' as Dame Dash says, (chapter 12), are the next elements on the journey.

We then get into more practical subjects, including the critical importance of a creative mind (chapter 15), the value of being a celebrity (chapter 16) and how companies and artists break in to their industry (chapter 18).

Finally Part 4 is all about the *code* – universal principles that apply to all areas of life.

We start though, with the story of a person whose remarkable journey embodies all these principles.

The Story Of

KANYE WEST

"NO NIGGERS OR DOGS AFTER SUNDOWN."

Is the sign Portswood 'Buddy' Williams Sr. walked passed everyday on his way to work, picking cotton in an Oklahoma field.

Buddy wanted to provide the best for his family. He wanted to provide his children with the resources to live a healthier, wealthier life, so he worked hard. The abuse, insults and discrimination he faced daily developed in him a tough layer of skin, an internal resilience, which drove him to do whatever it took to better his family's life prospects for generations to come.

After years of bloody hands in the cotton fields, Buddy upgraded to shoe shining in the city, where he was called 'nigger' and 'boy' less often. From there, he taught himself how to mend furniture and started an upholstery business.

Against massive odds Buddy was able to send all his children to college, and his children's children would begin life from a far higher platform.[1]

The experiences, lessons and values Buddy, and his wife Lucille, gifted their children with, who in turn gifted their children with, would form the foundation for the colossal skyscraper one of their grandchildren would go on to build.

"I was able to ascend to these heights because of the foundation my mom and pop laid…Nothing can make me past what my parents made me,"[2] said Kanye West – a man with the vision to dream big and the resilience to chase them like a stalker.

Image ©Jeff Rayner/
Coleman–Rayner

Childhood: 1977 – 1990

Kanye is creative. He was displaying that from an early age. In 1980 a three year old 'Ye would draw 'outside the box' objects, like purple bananas or blue oranges. His elementary school would hold talent shows, where Kanye's confidence was already clear. "There would be times when we was at talent shows and I would get my shit together and then help other people with their stuff, because I just knew I was going to win."[3]

As a ten year old Kanye had the unique opportunity to live in China for a year with his university lecturer mother. There he stood out like ink in water.

"At that time, a lot of Chinese had never seen a black person. They would always come up and stare at me, fishbowl me, rub my skin."[3]

For the most part Kanye loved this attention, and he'd perform one–man breakdancing shows for crowds of fascinated school children. He probably knew then that a career in the spotlight was meant for him.

Although China opened Kanye's mind to cultures beyond America's Mid-West, he couldn't speak Chinese so would spend a lot of time alone – drawing, listening to music and dreaming.

On their return from Asia, Kanye and his mother Donda resettled in their middle class Southside Chicago home. (His parents had been divorced since he was three years old, and Kanye would visit his photo-journalist father in Atlanta during summer vacation.)

In China, to make up for the language disadvantage, Kanye was put in a class with children two years younger than himself, and on his return to the Chi' he remained behind his own age group, so often felt "bored" at school. Partly to overcome this boredom, Kanye found ways to spend his time creatively. He had dreams of being an artist and video game developer, so at twelve years old tried making his own computer games – games which reflected his 'mature' interests – complete with backing music:

"First beat I did, was in seventh grade, on my computer. I got into doing beats for the video games I used to try to make. My game was very sexual. The main character was, like, a giant penis. It was like Mario Brothers, but the ghosts were, like, vaginas. You'd have to draw in and program every little step – it literally took me all night to do a step, cause the penis, y'know, had little feet and eyes."[4]

The length of time it took to program games meant he soon ditched the idea and focused on the music. He started to explore Hip Hop.

Hip Hop is inclusive. Anybody can participate and learn rap, breaking or graffiti, without expensive equipment or training. Kanye was introduced to rap in 1989, with De La Soul's 'Me Myself and I'. He was immediately captivated by the music and would go to extreme lengths to hear more.

"If I didn't have the money to get it, I'd never get to hear the music. [So] I used to steal music, literally steal the tapes. There's times I got caught in the metal detector, cuffed up or kicked out of the mall."[5]

He started spitting rhymes soon after first hearing the music, and then out of necessity begun making beats. "I never really thought about producing. No one really wanted to produce when I was young. I was trying to rap and I made beats because what else was I going to rap on?"[3]

Sitting in his 11x9ft bedroom, twelve year old Kanye would try to recreate his favorite Hip Hop tracks. "I had a [Omega] computer that I used to make beats on and tried to put together some songs. They'd be knock–offs of Brand Nubian songs that were out at the time. I was trying to make really positive raps because it was just that era." Raps like:

"I walk through the halls of the school/and it's cool to be known by many/for my rapping ability/What about the brothers who ain't got it like me/making money off the trade/you could say I had it made/death is on the rise/and that ain't no surprise/you can see your soul in a young brother's eyes/hardened by the streets cos the streets is kinda hard/but here's another factor that we wanna disregard..."[3]

"I thought I was going to get signed back when I was 13 years old, and come out with a record and take Kris Kross out,"[6] he said of the '90s teenage rap group. Really though, it would take another ten years to get to that point.

Kanye would record songs at a local $25 an hour 'studio', (a place where the microphone would dangle from a wire clothes hanger), and with borrowed equipment from a neighbor, until he could afford his own kit.

With the help of a generous Christmas gift from his mother, Kanye bought his first professional keyboard at fourteen, a $500 Ensoniq ASR 10 sampling keyboard, described as 'one of the most powerful samplers available at the time.' "She paid for a keyboard that was completely beyond what any kid should have at that age," Kanye remembers.[7] With the machine he could sample records and create more professionally sounding beats. Then later, with money saved from working odd jobs, like cutting grass and hair, he added turntables, a mixer and a drum machine. His bedroom turned into a makeshift studio, with "thousands of records lined against the wall,"[8] "TV, bed and a pile of clothes on the floor," remembers Donda,[1] and "three three–foot–high stacks of GQ magazines," says friend JB Marshall,[8] who would make music with Kanye.

Even though still a naive and inexperienced kid, in the early 90s Kanye was one of the few Hip Hop producers in Chicago. Developing his talent in this field at this time would turn out to be a very lucrative investment, because by the end of the decade Hip Hop would be the number one music genre on the planet and Kanye would be in prime position to ride its wave in the 'Super Producer Era,' where music-makers could earn millions from a 2 bar loop. Though of course he didn't know that at the time. He was just a kid devoted to learning about his interests.

The 90's

In his early teens (1991) Kanye met a high school boy, two years older than himself, named John Monopoly. They both made beats and gravitated towards one another, forming the production crew 'Numbskulls'. John was also involved in local party promotion and offered to manage Kanye, (which meant handling the 'business side' of things, like selling beats and organizing shows). John helped Kanye sell his first beats to other underground artists.

"I started making money off my beats when I was 15 or 16. Fifty dollars a beat here and there, to local acts."

The partnership would prove beneficial for both and John continued to manage Kanye 'on and off' until 2008. Kanye would later say, "John was the first person to believe in me."[10]

(Kanye also formed the group 'State of Mind' with aspiring rappers Lucine and Gene. The trio would record and perform together locally.)

Kanye loved to work. He loved feeling himself get better behind the boards and the mic, and he loved the respect his music received. In his mind he was already a superstar, so he just had to work hard enough to realize that vision. There aren't any keyboards on street corners, so Kanye wouldn't waste time idly hanging around the block. He had dreams to chase. As rapper and friend GLC remembers: "[In 1993] when we would be out chasing hoes, there was times Kanye would be with us, but majority of the time he'd be in his bedroom making beats with the same clothes on for days, no haircut or nothing. That dude was focused since he was a shorty because he knew what he wanted to do and he had a mother who supported the shit out of him."[11]

"Kanye spent hours and hours mixing, rapping, and writing. It was nonstop," remembers his mother Donda. "He became so involved that his socializing revolved around the studio in his room. When grandparents would visit, Kanye would come out of his room only to eat and go to the bathroom, they'd have to go to his room and get a few words in while Kanye made his music…There seemed to be a sound track playing perpetually in our home."[1]

Kanye was so devoted to improving his craft that at 15 he decided to break the decade long tradition of living with his father in Atlanta over the summer vacation, and instead use the time to focus on music in Chicago.

'Lock yourself in a room doing 5 beats a day for 3 summers/'
– Spaceship

Yet despite the intense practice, Kanye was still very much a work in progress. He had a tiny taste of success by selling a few beats, but he could not progress further quickly by teaching himself or with his basic production equipment. He couldn't come close to recreating his favorite songs because his drum machine was still amateur standard compared to the professionals.

"When I was learning to produce, working in a home studio in my mother's crib, I tried to make beats that sounded exactly like Timbaland's, DJ Premier's, Pete Rock's and, especially, Dr. Dre's," he told Rolling Sone.[12] "Dre productions like Tupac's 'California Love' were just so far beyond what I was doing that I couldn't even comprehend what was going on. I had no idea how to get to that point, how to layer all those instruments."

Aside from the creative aspect, the business-side of his music dream also showed slow progress. He didn't know anybody working at any established music label, and had no idea how to get-on in the industry. He needed somebody who could mentor him, provide support and teach him how to make and market quality music. Thanks to his mother he found just the person.

One morning in 1993, Donda West was in the Chicago State University staff room chatting with a fellow lecturer about raising their children. They discovered that both their sons were making music and Mrs Wilson agreed to introduce Kanye to her son Dion, aka No I.D.

'No I.D. *my mentor now let the story begin/* '
– Big Brother

19 year old Dion had taken music making much further than 15 year old Kanye. He had set up a professional studio in his mother's basement where he was producer for CDR – a group with Chicago's most established rapper 'Common' that opened shows for major artists like NWA and Big Daddy Kane, (though often unpaid). And in 1992 Dion signed with Relativity Records to produce Common's debut album, 'Can I Borrow A Dollar?'

Dion was initially hesitant to meet with Kanye (because of the age difference), but Kanye (fully aware of how beneficial Dion as a teacher would be) would do whatever it took to be around him.

"Walking in to No I.D's basement was like walking into Def Jam offices,"[13] recalls an awed Kanye.

"He was just learning how to make music, but he was the most persistent person who I've ever met,"[9] says Dion.

No matter how hard Dion tried to get away from Kanye, there he always seemed to be.

"[Dion] changed his number 100 times on me, but I found a way to get it," Kanye remembers, with a smile, "I'll be knocking on his window while he was with his girl."[15]

"Kanye would be sleeping out in No I.D's driveway waiting for him to come home," ads friend Malik Yousef.[8]

Kanye's drive paid off, and when the two eventually got together, Kanye's energy was contagious and they developed a good relationship.

"If he didn't have the drive that he had I probably wouldn't have helped him as much. But he just wouldn't take 'No'."[8]

"[When we got together] he was like an energetic kid, 'teach me everything teach me anything!' At first I gave him something to learn on his own [like how to use a sampler] then I took him more under my wing."[14]

Still in his early teens Kanye was beginning to build his team of mentors and managers who could help him improve musically and climb the industry ladder, (many of the same people still work with him today).

Finding the right people to learn from, giving and taking, "Thank You and Your Welcome" as Kanye would say, is a major reason he was able to make progress. "He was always good at getting what he needed to get from everybody around him," says No I.D.[14]

But probably the most important quality trait for the continued success of both Kanye and No I.D. (one of Hip Hop's best producers), is their hunger. As No I.D. put it: "Kanye and I worked together well because we share the same mentality. That every day is new day, what you did yesterday don't count."[14]

This mentality is shared by most people who have achieved long lasting success in any industry. It keeps a person hungry to achieve something every day and not get lazy or fully satisfied with what they've already done – (see 'The Hunger' *pg.133*).

'Rewrite history, I don't believe in yesterday/'
– Gorgeous

In between attending high school, making music and hustling to get Dion's attention, Kanye also worked at 'The Gap' to support himself. He loved clothes anyway, but would also find ways to incorporate his other passion.

"My job was to stand inside the door and welcome people to the store. But I put my own spin on it, I used to freestyle."

"Welcome to the Gap/ We got jeans in the back/ And we got some khaki slacks/ And if you like that/ You'll probably like the shirts/ Try one on, it won't hurt/ You got red socks on/ Why don't you put a red hat on?/ We've got all that/ And it's all at the Gap."[15]

At this point in Kanye, (who went by the moniker 'Kanye the Influence'), was seeing some success with music – receiving encouragement from people around him and selling a handful of beats. But there was no major success. He was struggling to get noticed and was begging rappers to produce for them. Nothing was coming to him. He needed to make a choice between the security of continuing his formal education and seeing what happens with music on the side, or burning all bridges of retreat and chasing his dreams.

College Drop-in

After graduating from West Aurora High School, Kanye was recognized for his artistic talent and received a partial scholarship ($550 for the first semester) to attend Chicago's American Academy of Art, where he studied painting. (To Kanye music and art/painting are the same as he sees sounds as colors and shapes. "Piano is blue, snare is white, baseline's are dark brown," he says[16] – see *pg.253* for more.)

But Kanye was used to working hard and found the college course slow and unsatisfying. "I don't want to be an artist," Donda remembers Kanye pleading. So after one semester he transferred to Chicago State University to major in English, (where his mother was [the first black] department head and could get a 50% discount on tuition). But again he felt out of place and was restless to work on music. Most of his time was spent "in the music room or student union."[1]

"I just didn't really want to be there. I was like, 'how do these credits apply to what I want to do in my life?' So I would take courses that I could use a little bit: piano, voice training, public speaking, poetry, especially of Maya Angelou and Gwendolyn Brooks, which all helps me now."[17]

He continued to make beats whilst at college, learning directly from No I.D, and indirectly by trying to emulate Bad Boy's Hit Men, and others, and in 1996 was making himself more noticeable in Chicago's Hip Hop scene by performing and connecting with local underground artists.

The first beats he sold to a signed artist were to a rapper called 'Grav' on Correct Records. Grav recalls his first encounter with 'Ye:

"News had spread I had a deal. I was coming out of a Fugues concert and this young kid runs up to me and is like 'Yo, I heard you got a record deal. Yo you should let me get some beats on your album. Yo I'm telling you I'm nice I got skills. Yo my name is Kanye. Yo you should just come to the car let me play some beats for you.' I was like 'ok cool,' I go to the car he pops in the cassette, and Fire! Fire off the bat!"[18]

Kanye produced eight tracks on Grav's debut album and even rapped a verse with lines like, *'kill the black on black crime'*. As well as using similar techniques to his later well-known solo work, like shortening and bending words to flow: *'In a life or death situa(tion)/I come through with the Chi representa(tion)/And bleed you pussies that be marked like ovula(tion)'*

For his work Kanye received his first check from a record label for $8,800.

"I took half the money and I bought one of those Ghostface Jesus pieces like everybody wore, and I spent the other half on Polo, because Polo was real in style," he later told Complex.[19] Though it may seem that he was squandering his money, it would turn out to be a constructive investment because the following year (97), Kanye traded his necklace with No I.D. (who was looking for a chain to wear for his solo album's music video), for No I.D.'s advanced SP1200 drum machine.

Still a teenager and still at college, Kanye was making moves.

* * *

In the mid 90's Common was Chicago's most well-known MC. He was one of the few rappers with a record deal, and had released two albums by the time Kanye started to become friendly with Dion. Kanye would often bump into Common in No I.D's basement studio.

"Kanye was the young dude who used to be in Dion's basement talking about 'My Beats is the coldest. Check these out!'…..Kanye was cocky as hell, but you had to love him," remembers Comm. "He could be like a mosquito in your ear, though – straight get on your nerves."[20]

No I.D. adds, "Kanye would beg to give Common beats, but Kanye made Puffy–style popish beats, so Common would be like, 'Nah, I ain't messing with him. Don't have him come around.' Back then, Common didn't want input. And, you know, Kanye's very 'Let me help.' When he did hang out with Common he would always want to battle him. His hunger is everywhere and almost caused fights."[14]

Though once again Kanye's persistence eventually paid off, and his request to battle Common was granted live on 'The Twilight Tone Show' on Chicago's WHPK radio station, (since Common was friends with the hosts). The freestyle battle lasted over ten minutes and the nineteen year old Kanye defiantly held his own against (an admittedly intoxicated) Common.

The pair however, wouldn't officially work together for another eight years. "His beats were good, but they weren't knocking me over…I never said, 'Yes I'm going to use his beat,'" admits Common.

Clearly Kanye was not born with any 'musical genius,' but with focus and time that is what Common and many others would come to label him as.

Also in 1996 Kanye was performing at Open Mic Nights in local clubs across Chicago. One of these was a 'freestyle showcase' at the famous Double Door Club, where he performed alongside friend Phenom. As confident as always, at the end of his performance a panting 'Ye proclaims "Kanye represent the sexy n****, fly n****."[21]

Another at this time, following the relative success of Grav's album and his relationship with No I.D, Kanye signed a management deal with No I.D. and Peter Kang, an A&R for Relativity Records (person responsible for scouting talent) – (John Monopoly was still involved in the team). Peter and Dion helped present Kanye's work to other record labels, and also gave 'Ye the opportunity to produce songs for other artists on Relativity, like the newly signed Infinite Syndicate, a Chicago female rap duo. He even spat an introspective verse on the song 'What You Do To Me'.

(See all these songs and performances at: HipHopTeaches.com)

* * *

After two semesters at Chicago State University, Kanye was feeling more and more restless. "I was working hard as hell. I wasn't just rapping. My job was producing and I was in school for art and I had a thousand different ideas of different things I wanted to do. It was taking away from me because college was slowing me down."[22]

He was building up the courage to drop-out – something that's difficult to do when your mother is Head of Department at your University and says, "I'd come from a family where getting your education was right next to believing in God."[1]

But he finally made the move when he was offered a potential record deal with the giant Colombia Records, (set up by No I.D. and Peter Kang).

"He believed so much that he was gonna get [the] record deal that he dropped out school, [fall of sophomore year 1996]" recalls No I.D. "[There was] no fall back plan."[8]

'Told 'em I finished school and I started my own business/
They say, 'Oh you graduated?' No, I decided I was finished/'
– School Spirit

Kanye believed he would drop out, sign a contract with Colombia and begin his professional music career. Simple. However, his meeting with Colombia executives to discuss the deal did not go as he hoped. When asked, 'What is your niche?' i.e. 'what would you add to the industry other than what's already out?' Kanye had no answer. He never thought about music like that, he just knew he was good. (See 'Niche' *pg.269* for more.)

On top of that, as Kanye explains, "I was just trying to pump myself up to them. I said, 'I'm going to be bigger than Michael Jackson, I'm going to bigger than Jermaine Dupri.' I said that to [Columbia executive] Michael Mauldin."

Michael Mauldin is Dupri's father.

By the time the meeting was over, "they hit me with those three words – we'll call you. They sent limos on the way up, and when I got downstairs I couldn't even catch a cab."[6]

Kanye in his bedroom studio. ©Jeff Rayner/ Coleman– Rayner

The rejection was a huge blow. "He was disappointed and hurt it didn't go through," remembers Common, "[imagine] being so close to your dream but it shatters apart."[8]

'Ye realized the 'Happy Ending' *(pg.126)* he had imagined was fantasy, and the path to his music dreams would not be as straightforward as he thought.

However he still felt that dropping out of college was the right move for him, and would eventually inspire his debut album – the theme of which was 'about having the guts to embrace who you are, rather than following the path society has carved out for you.'[1]

'My teacher said I'se a loser, I told her why don't you kill me/
I give a fuck if you feel me, I'm gonna follow/
My heart…/'
– Get Em High

Also, with the security of a college degree gone, Kanye had put himself in a 'Do or Die' *(pg.130)* position and was forced to turn up the tempo.

"I had to figure out a way to make it…I really started grinding, just trying to sell beats to people."[22]

His mother remembers the time too. "When he got back home [from the unsuccessful meeting with Colombia], Kanye did what he always did – went to work making more music. He was producing music and writing raps like the world was coming to an end."

His friends witnessed the same relentless work ethic. "Kanye didn't go to parties, all he did was sit in his room making beats," says Ibn Jasper. "He was taking no showers, no haircut, no new shoes, nothing. Just in front of the keyboard every-day, all-day," adds GLC.[8]

He took 'The Pursuit' *(pg.137)* to another level.

On condition of dropping out of college and living at home, Kanye made a deal with his mother that: A) He'd have one year to 'make it happen' or would have to go back to college. B) He had to pay $200 a month in rent "to instill responsibilities that come with manhood" Donda explained.[1]

To support himself Kanye needed work. He first landed a job as a bus boy in a Bob Evans restaurant. He walked in the first day and didn't come back the second. He realized that the job would not develop him in any meaningful way.

'Writing my rhymes, playing my mind/
This fucking job can't help him/
So I quit, y'all welcome/'
– Spaceship

After that he found a job in telemarketing – selling insurance to Montgomery Ward credit card holders – where his 'gift of the gab' was put to good use. Plus, as he says, "I could sneak and listen to the headphones. I could never be in a situation with a job where I was not allowed to listen to music all day."[24]

The jobs served as more motivation for Kanye to put himself in a position where he could work on music full time.

"I was still making ends meet by doing beats. I used to charge people $250 to $500 (per) beat. I made a way just to hustle. You know hustling doesn't mean 'Ah, you just sell drugs.' [It means] hustle any way you can to maintain a lifestyle and then also, in all your spare time, chase your dreams. So whenever I would finish work, I would be up until 4:00 in the morning…focusing on my dream and praying for the day where I could just do that all the time."[17]

It's also important to note that upon reflection of the influence his decision to leave college may have on others, Kanye would later tell young people not to follow in his dropout footsteps:

> "It is true you can be successful without [college], but this is a hard world, a real world, and you want every advantage you can have. I would suggest to people to do all that you can. When I dropped out of school I had worked in the music industry and had checks cut in my name from record labels and had a record deal on the table, and when I wasn't successful and Columbia said, 'We'll call you,' I had to go back and work a telemarketing job, go back to the real world, and that's how life is. Life is hard. Take advantage of your opportunities."[25]

'Heading Up The Stairs': 1997–2002

Kanye continued building connections with other producers, upcoming rappers and studio owners. He would often give his music away for free, in order to establish relationships and gain exposure (pg.254). In fact most of the music he was making was given away.

"I was doing beats for free 99% of the time," he later told MTV. "You don't know how many times I heard somebody say 'Yo what's gon' happen is you gon' get paid when I get paid, because my cousin know dude at this record label and they looking for Chicago acts.'

"Do you know how many times I carried my keyboard to the studio to track a beat for somebody who said they'd pay me $200 for the beat, but they only had $80 on them and would say 'don't you remember I paid for your lunch yesterday'? I paid my dues!"[13]

Also after the unsuccessful Colombia meeting No I.D. decided to stop managing Kanye (but still support him as a friend), and let someone who could devote the time 'Ye needed take over the job. "He's a hell of a personality to manage. I only have so much capacity as a creative person. That would've been a fulltime job and I'm a producer. I wouldn't cheat him by sitting in some position trying to make some money off of him when I can let capable people step in and help him get where he needed to get."[23]

After No I.D abdicated management responsibilities he introduced 'Ye to Free Maiden, who agreed to co–manage him (with Monopoly) in exchange for 50% of Kanye's publishing rights, (which means 50% of the royalty payments or commission Kanye received from sales of a song).

Free worked as A&R for Bad Boy Entertainment, so was able to land Kanye production work for some major artists (thus explaining the high 50% fee he charged). Free introduced Kanye to producer Deric 'D–Dot' Angelettie, who ran Crazy Cat Catalog Production Company and was part of Bad Boy Entertainment's famous in-house production team: The Hitmen.

D–Dot saw great potential in Kanye and negotiated with Free Maiden to give Kanye back his publishing rights, and let him work with D-Dot directly. Dot and signed Kanye to a management deal in 1997.

"I always knew he was gonna be a genius. That's why I hooked up with him," D–Dot later told XXL magazine.[26]

Kanye had been modeling his sound on The Hitmen for years, so to work directly with them seemed a perfect match.

Kanye was still working with basic equipment compared to professional studios – mostly recording on a Roland VS 1680 in his bedroom. *('While n**** had Pro Tools, I had no tools/Karaoke machine, fuck it, I'm old school' – Keep The Receipt)*, so to compensate, he would spend a lot of time at Craig Bauer's Hinge Studio, one of the best recording spots in Chicago.

Kanye would receive work from D–Dot in New York then go to Craig Bauer's studio to create the products.

Craig recalls, "Kanye and his manager [John Monopoly] came in begging me to cut them a break on studio time, or burn a few extra CD's."

"He'd bring the MPC in and we'd track it and lay it off to tape and it would get shipped off. He was doing an increasing amount of 'ghost' beat work for other artists. The number of POs [purchase orders] to the studio kept going up, even though Kanye was not getting the credit for all of that work. But that's just part of getting yourself across in that genre. When you're young and new at it, lots of guys are happy just to get a few hundred dollars for a beat."[27]

[Although D–Dot strongly rejects the 'ghost' label, as he claims Kanye received full credit and compensation for all work.]

Kanye and D–Dot made a lot of music together during their three year relationship. D–Dot got Kanye's music heard and sold to major artists like Jermaine Dupri (for his song 'Life in 1472,' "my first platinum record" says a proud Kanye), Nas, Diddy, and Eminen. Despite later friction between the two, D–Dot always praised Kanye's energy and hunger. "He deserves every accolade because he worked hard. He was a savage under me."

Kanye was grateful to D–Dot for giving him a foot in the industry and the opportunity to build relations with so many influential people. As he says on 'Last Call' form his debut album: *That's how I got in the game/If it wasn't for [D–Dot], I wouldn't be here'.*

Although grateful, Kanye was always hungry to 'move up to the next level.' He didn't want to be stuck producing for other artists. From the beginning he knew he needed to rap. D–Dot tried to support these ambitions, by encouraging Colombia records to sign him as a rapper, letting Kanye rap on his Maad Rapper mixtape, and even rapping a verse Kanye wrote when the label didn't want Kanye on the record. However they made no progress.

"Nobody wanted him to rhyme, except me," D–Dot told Hot 97. "Free, Colombia…he couldn't get anyone to believe in him. To let him put out a rap record."[28]

Kanye's hunger would mean he would soon have to leave this circle.

A proud 21 year old Kanye at Jermaine Dupri's 1998 birthday party. ©Channelzer otv.com

By now Kanye had formed the company 'Konman Productions,' which received payment for work done for D–Dot and others, as well as being a platform to produce music for other artists; like an independent label.

Rapper Mickey Halsted, who was recruited to Konman, remembers how much talent Kanye assembled:

"At one time, Kanye had everybody in his Mama's house in that little bedroom of his – whether it was Shawnna [from Infamous Syndicate], Me, Christina, GLC, Rhymefest, Twone Gabz, Boogz [who later produced 'New God Flow'], B Miller [who later produced 'Champion']. Every time I see another Chicago rapper coming out I be like 'Ahh man, he was in Kanye's bedroom too!' We had a sick, sick, sick click."[29]

Also during Kanye's 'apprenticeship' with D–Dot, his longtime friend/manager John Monopoly, John's cousin Don Crowley (later Kanye's road manager) and their friend Happy Lewis, formed the management company 'Hustle Period,' and worked to help establish Kanye as a rapper. They organized shows, promotions and put together 'The Go–Getters' in 1998, "a group of rappers that we formed around Kanye," says Monopoly.

The Go–Getters meant Kanye could start dropping his own music (as the contract with D–Dot/Colombia only prohibited him from releasing solo songs). The group consisted of Kanye and three 'street guys,' who emulated gangster rappers of the time in their style. No I.D. says that "[Kanye's] goal was to be [as] tough as possible. Some of it was over compensation for the fact that he wasn't a street guy at all and he felt like people wouldn't respect him it if it was not tough."[9]

The Go–Getters hoped to get noticed by performing across Chicago, opening for more established local acts (like Abstract Mindstate) and released their one and only album, 'World Record Holders,' distributed independently throughout the Chicagoland area.

The song 'Oh Oh Oh' was the one they hoped would cause the most disruption. Group member Really Doe remembers trying to promote it:

"We'd be down at radio stations, at performances throughout the city, and in No I.D.'s parking lot for 7–8 hours trying to present our music. Trying to get him to open his doors for us."[9]

John Monopoly even led a picket line outside WGCI radio station to get the song played.

"We were like 'oh my god they're picketing WGCI!" remembers DJ Love.

However the song achieved little commercial success.

"There was no way the station was going put the song into [regular] rotation because there was so much [good] music from everybody that was really hot at the time,"[8] DJ Mike Love adds – though he did relent to the demonstrators and played the track a few times on his show, helping to build the 'buzz' around Kanye and the group just a little more. Another baby-step up the stairs.

Most of The Go-Getters songs (between 1996–1998), were recorded at Craig Bauer's Hinge Studio and were engineered by Craig. He admits that the music was not spectacular:

"It wasn't what you'd call 'challenging'. If you listen back to the stuff now, which Kanye and I did not too long ago, it would not stand out and I doubt he'd disagree. It didn't suggest the genius you hear now on his records. It was all stuff that was sampled off of other records. He'd take a kick drum or a hi–hat where he could find them in the open on a track, sample them, and then flip them to add a little distortion. If you could route a quarter–inch cable in a patchbay you could engineer those sessions. But what was there on the tracks was an attitude in the sound, grittiness. The talent was in the process of revealing itself."[27]

Aside from the beats, Kanye's rapping talent was also in the very premature phase of revealing itself. Listening to Go-Getters tracks its clear Kanye's rhymes improved a lot in the years since, and the reason he was able to improve so dramatically was because he truly was working on his deepest interests, *(pg.58)*.

"I was always the weakest rapper out of the people in the group. But they didn't have the passion for it. I had it. Every night I was working. It was nothing that was gonna stop me."[13]

It would take thousands more hours of work and a near death experience for Kanye to develop his sound to the genre defining 'College Dropout' album, five years after this first attempt.

Making a Ruckus

After the disappointing release of the Go–Getters album, Kanye was eager to progress onwards.

No. I.D had introduced him to a friend and Roc–A–Fella A&R, Kyambo 'Hip Hop' Joshua in 1996. They built a relationship and Kanye frequently sent him beats to consider for Roc artists. Two years after first meeting, Kyambo formed an artist management company with (another Roc A&R) Gee Robertson, called 'Hip Hop Since 1973', which would represent producers for Roc–A–Fella and external artists. Impressed by his work with D–Dot, and his sky-high ambition, Kanye became their first signee.

"The level of confidence, the level of perseverance, the level of 'I'm going to show the world' — that's the Kanye West that I met [in 1998]," said Gee Roberson. "That's what excited me [and why we signed him]."[11]

D–Dot understood Kanye had to leave to progress, but 'Ye was still contractually obliged to Dot. "Kanye was so desperate to get on," recalls Dot[28], that they came to an agreement where Kanye would give 20% of his publishing to D–Dot and 20% to HHS1973. Kanye could see the bigger picture, so was not afraid to pay the price to move forward. It would be small change compared to where he is now, and even then he knew it.

This is the point Kanye describes in Last Call, *"I just needed some fresh air.*

'cause I been there for a while, I appreciated what they did for me/ but, you know there's a time in every man's life where he gotta make a change/ try to move up to the next level."

The move was another breakthrough in Kanye's career. Many more doors would now open as his new managers had the ear of many more major artists. Kanye continued sending them "a batch of beats on a daily basis," as he had been doing for some time, and in late 1999 Kyambo choose one of the beats for a track on Beanie Segal's debut album, 'The Truth.'

Kanye always intended on being a rapper, so he carried his demo tape whether he went. When he met Kyambo in the studio to play the beat, he also played his demo. Kyambo liked the music and was surprised that it was Kanye rapping, but quickly dismissed him as another 'producer–rapper' (like Pete Rock, No I.D, or Dr. Dre) who could sound good on his own records.

But Kanye insisted on promoting himself as a producer AND a rapper. Gee Roberson remembers telling him, "We going to sign you up. You gon' get the production out there, and after that we're going to get the domino effect; the beats into the raps."[11] (Whether Gee really believed what he was saying, or was just trying to appease Kanye, is a different matter.)

After the high of selling a beat to a Roc–A–Fella artist, Kanye was expecting more good news, but things moved slowly. Kanye would continue sending beats to Kyambo, whose job as his manager was to sell them, but there was little interest. *'After they picked that Truth beat, I was figuring I was gonna do some more work. But shit just wasn't poppin off like that'.* It would be several frustrating months before Kanye would sell another beat to a major artist.

Still, as determined as ever, Kanye returned to Chicago and continued producing for local acts, though now with more connections it was easier to get his beats heard. A few months after 'The Truth' he made 'This Can't Be Life,' an original mix of Dr. Dre 'XXplosive' drums and a sped up Harold Melvin soul sample, and played it for Kyambo over the phone.

"This was pre email, so I had to send him money just so he could send the beat to me," remembers Kyambo.[11]

The beat became one of the most powerful songs on Jay Z's 'The Dynasty: Roc La Familia' album and was another step forward for Kanye.

"Kymbo Hip–Hop Joshua, was definitely the one who changed my life, because he is one of Jay Z's best friends so he had the relationship. He was in a position to say 'listen to this guy right here.' So he put me in position to play. And that's the most important thing – to have an opportunity for Jay to actually hear your shit. There are people who would kill for that."[17]

While tracking 'This Can't Be Life' in the studio with Jay Z, Kanye was eager to demonstrate his rap skills. He said 'Yo Jay I can rap'" and started rapping on a table, in front of TyTy (Jay's childhood friend and road manager), John Meneilly (Jay's financial manager), Lenny S (Roc A&R), and many other strangers in the room. This total self-confidence to perform anytime anywhere is what it takes to ensure no opportunities are missed.

Although he wasn't offered a deal right then, he did receive Jay's compliments. That day was another high for Kanye, "I was so honored, [Jay had] inspired me so much."

After finishing 'This Can't Be Life' (selling it for around $7,500), Kanye returned to Chicago, to work with local artists like on Da Brat Chi Town's album 'Unrestricted', as well as selling the original version of 'Never Change' to rapper 'Payroll,' but again Kanye felt "there wasn't nothing really poppin' off the way it should have been." He went from the high of meeting Jay Z in New York to several lows back home.

The majority of Kanye's work involved producing multi-track demo tapes for $500 for what he refers to as "terrible" Chicago 'rappers,' while young producers he had met while in New York were working with established artists for infinitely more exposure and pay.

"[I would be talking to Just Blaze over the phone while working on a demo tape] and he'd say, 'I have to go, I think that's Busta [Rhymes] right behind me.' [So] I'm thinking], 'Yo, I need to get out there man, what am I doing? He out there doing beats for Busta and I'm doing [$500 demos] for bust-ers!'"[13]

At the same time, Kanye was going thorugh other problems. One of his best artists, Mikkey Halsted, left Konman to sign with Cash Money Records, he was in bitter arguments with former managers over his publishing rights, and on top of that he was evicted from his Chicago apartment, (which he'd been living in since moving out of his mother's house a few months prior), for noise complaints and the constant stream of Konman people in and out.

Kanye, like most Greats in this book, was (and is) so focused on achieving his dream, that all obstacles in his way are 'turned into possible.'[29] All potentially negative experiences only serve as fuel for the mission – (see 'Love Life' *pg.324*). So despite his best artist leaving the label and getting evicted, Kanye took the positive lessons. "[I thought] OK I see what's happening, God doesn't want me to be here anymore."[13]

So using money from beats sold to Cash Money, he decided to move to a city with a more dynamic Hip Hop scene.

(As part of Mikkey's deal with Cash Money, they agreed to buy some beats from Kanye, but almost broke their commitment. "I walked out the office. If they weren't going to let Kanye, who gave me the confidence to do what I do, produce on my album, then I was going to walk away from rapping," says Mikkey. "So they finally changed their mind, and they bought a handful of tracks from him. He used that money to move [out of Chicago]"[30])

Kanye moved first to Atlanta, because he had a relationship with Jermaine Dupi, but then decided he'd find better opportunities in the rap capital of the world: New York City.

"I didn't care if we were next to a crack house. I knew moving brought me one step closer to my dreams."

Interestingly, Kanye almost ended up living with fellow Roc–A–Fella producer Just Blaze. "He didn't have the resources to move out and was two seconds away from crashing at my crib," remembers Just.[31]

But Kanye found an $850 a month apartment with a glass ceiling to the sky in Newark, New Jersey. He was on his way to touching it.

* * *

Hungrier than ever, Kanye was making beats in his new apartment before even fully unpacking.

"In the first month he sold maybe 30 beats," recalls GLC.[8]

Managers Kyambo and Gee worked to sell Kanye's music inside Roc-A-Fella and gave him 24/7 access to Baseline Studios.

During one visit to the Manhattan studio in March 2001, Kanye played Beanie Siegel some tracks he had been working on, but because it was Beanie's birthday he was distracted and left without agreeing to use any. Then Kanye, about to leave empty handed, came upon a stroke of luck that would catapult his career.

Jay Z walked into the studio and Kyambo told Kanye to play several beats for him. Jay liked what he heard.

Two minutes into playing the 'Izzo (H.O.V.A.)' beat, Jay taps Kanye on the shoulder and with a smile mouths the chorus to the song: *'H to the izz-O, V to the izz-A/ For shizzle my nizzle used to dribble down in VA'.*

Unable to contain his excitement from Jay's reaction, Kanye, (who says he had "$10 in my pocket"), went into Baseline's bathroom and called his mother. "Mom we about to make it! We about to be on now!"[13]

Jay would end up using seven Kanye beats for 'The Blueprint' album. A monumental leap in Kanye's career.

"Jay could have easily not come to the studio that night of Beanie birthday and heard them beats for The Blueprint. No matter how good my beats is, that one moment made all the difference."[32]

Also, determined to take advantage of the opportunity of being around the number one rapper in the world, 'Ye insisted on demonstrating his rhymes. "Every second he got he'd play his demo"[8] Jay remembers. "I'm trying to make the album and he's jumping on the table rapping. I'm like 'Yo, this is not the time for that. Not now.'"[33]

The Blueprint became an instant classic, and sold 500,000 units its first week – despite being released on September 11th 2001.

Although Kanye earned relatively little from his work, because most of his fees were eaten up by sample publishing costs,[31] interest in him as a producer sky rocketed. *'I took that proudly, and built relationships with people.'*

"I'm a good producer but the opportunity to have Hov rap on your beats makes all the difference in the world."[17] "That was the turning point in my life. I can't say that I wouldn't have done it without him, but he made it easier because he gave me a stamp, he gave me the streets. The Roc–A–Fella chain helped me get my name."[6]

Jay is probably the biggest trend setter in Hip Hop. Everything he attaches his name to, from football jerseys to liquor, has quickly become adopted by the culture. "People want to do whatever he does, he's like the poster child of the industry, fashion, business, hustler, everything that people want to be," said Kanye. So when he rapped on Kanye's soul beats, everybody wanted soul beats.

'Everybody loopin up soul/
It's like you tryin to make The Blueprint 2 before Hov/ '
– Jay Z, The Bounce

After The Blueprint he continued working with Roc-A-Fella rappers, and sold beats to other major artists like Alicia Keys, Ludacris, Talib Kweli, Nas, Mos Def, Scarface, Dead Prez and southern artists like Trina (showing he had diverse production capabilities).

"Every major artist in urban music was requesting music from Kanye," says his cousin and assistant Devo Springsteen.

(Kanye was introduced to most of these, and other, artists through connections he'd built *(pg.196)*. For instance his New Jersey neighbor, producer 88 Keys, had Mos Def visit the apartment and Kanye (of course) took the opportunity to play him some beats. Mos bought five almost right away. Then when Kanye went to meet Mos in the studio, he ran into Talib Kweli, played some beats and sold three.[13])

This period was so important in Kanye's career that he got a tattoo on his arm with the titles of ten, "songs that changed my life, or mean something at a point in my career," he told MTV in 2002.[35] Songs like 'This Can't Be Life', 'Nothing Like It' and 'The Truth.' Each holds a message and reminds him where he came from and where he's going. (For more on the significance of the tats see 'Affirmation' *pg.95*.)

Kanye now had a platform to be heard, although it would take more time to find his unique voice to put on this platform.

'Shopping My Demo I Was Tryin To Shine'

Kanye's career as a producer was taking off, but he never intended on being just 'a producer'. His heart was set on rapping. The problem was nobody else felt the same way. Kanye's manager Gee recalls, "I lost track of the phone calls I used to get whenever he used to do a session and they would be like, 'Why he won't just stick to beats? Why he want to rap?'"[11]

"I remember people [I worked with] saying I was stupid for trying to rap,"[13] says 'Ye. "I would say 'I wanna rap,' [and] they'd say 'what the fuck are you gunna rap about?' I'd say 'man, I just rap what the people want to hear,' [and they'd say] 'Aright just play the beat'"[36]

Lawyer Reggie Ossé, who met Kanye at this time, recalls his own reaction:

"When [Kanye] mentioned he wanted to rap, how he was going to be 'the biggest rapper ever' I was like, 'Riiiiiiight.' There was no way I could imagine dude rapping. He wasn't very 'rapper–like,' in my opinion. Which meant that him being the next biggest rapper wasn't even in the stars."[37]

Reggie was one of the *many* to think like this. Even friends like producer 88 Keys, couldn't see what Kanye could:

"We both lived in Newark. We'd go to each other's apartments; going to the studio together for almost four years. Within eight minutes of our conversation he told me that he was going to be a star. He spit a rap at that time, and we went back and forth rapping. His raps were really good, but I didn't really think 'star' from those raps or that moment."[9]

The gap between Kanye's personal vision of himself and the reality around him was huge, and it would have been easy to let all the doubters suck-up his self-belief, to make him lose sight of his vision and accept his current reality. But although people's comments and cold attitudes did emotionally hurt him, it could not, would not, stop him.

"Man, people told me that I couldn't rap, that I couldn't sell a record, that I didn't have a chance. And it hurt me. Nobody believed in me."[38]

"People were saying what more do you want? Your producing for the biggest rapper in the world…people would laugh at me, saying 'Get the fuck out of here, you could never be a rapper. How could you possibly compete with Jay Z, Eminem? You'll never be on their level.' I named ten rappers that I'm sure [made] way more money than I had at that time, and they were like, 'Nah you'll never be on their level. You'll never be on that level.' I used that as my fuel."[39]

'Now I could let these dream killers kill my self-esteem/
Or use my arrogance as the steam to power my dreams/'
– Last Call

Kanye was able to convert all the rejections and closed doors into motivation to prove to the naysayers and to himself that he could do it. He worked hard to improve. He had set a goal to become one of the greatest MC's, and learned from, "All the people God put in my path," he says. "When I hooked up with Dead Prez [in 2000], they showed me how to make positive stuff sound cool, how to make it still sound hard."

"Before, when I wanted to rap, my raps sounded like a bit like Cam'ron; they sounded a bit like Mase; they sounded a bit like Jay Z or whoever. And it wasn't until I hung out with Dead Prez and understood how to make raps with a message sound cool that I was able to just write 'All Falls Down' in 15 minutes. That's how I discovered my style. I was just hanging out with them all the time in New York. I would produce for them."[40]

'Ye would also regularly attend cultural events and places for inspiration, from museums to poetry festivals, and remembers "begging" Mos Def, the host of Def Jam Poetry Jam, to let him perform. "I said you don't even have tape it, just let me perform for the audience." Spoken word artists are able to get a rise from their audience without a beat and Kanye took inspiration and said to himself, and the people who doubted his rhythmic ability: "What I lack in rhythm, I'll have words where every line can get a rise out of people, with or without a beat."

Aside from working to improve his rap skill, Kanye continued networking and pursuing record labels to sign him as a rapper, not just a producer. But as rapper Talib Kweli remembers, the door was always barricaded shut:

"[Kanye would hang out at Rawkus Records office to get the attention of the executives but they] didn't want to sign him as a rapper, they couldn't see his vision. They [just] wanted his beats."[41]

As Kweli says, A&R's had zero interest in hearing Kanye rap. Instead they just wanted to follow the trend of The Blueprint's success, so would only ask for similar sounding beats; *'give me a track that sounds like Jay Z.'* Even Jay admits that, "[To be honest with you] we [Roc-A-Fella] weren't interested in signing him as rapper. We just wanted his hot beats."[8]

Still, without asking for permission, *(see The Hustle pg.174)*, he played his music at every opportunity. Whenever an A&R asked for a beat, he'd say *'Yo but I rap too'* and spit a rhyme with the intensity of a stage performance. ("We went to five meetings [with record labels] where we jumped on tables [to preform]," remembers Kanye's friend Consequence.) Kanye even played finished tracks like 'Jesus Walks,' yet still he could not breakthrough.

"Every label A to Z, from Arista to Zomba, turned us down," says Gee.

Because Kanye's image was so different to the norm of what Hip Hop is 'supposed' to be, from the way he dressed to his back story, most A&R's were not looking to stick their neck out and sign him.

88 Keys remembers: "He'd perform 'Jesus Walks,' 'All Falls Down,' and

they would be like, 'The music is real good. Maybe we can use that beat for DMX, who do we contact about that?' He was like, 'This is my album that I'm playing you. I'm a rapper. Didn't you just hear my raps!?'"[9]

"One president of a label said Kanye was not a real artist," remembers Devo Springsteen,[11] [Most likely referring to L.A Reid, then president of Arista Records[39]].

The fact is, most people in large companies are not innovators. They follow trends. A 'gangster' image was popular at the time, so they were only looking for rappers that fit into that mold.

"[Kanye's music, with songs about Jesus,] was too edgy," says Rhymefest. "The industry is afraid of anything that breaks the conformity flow."[8]

Most people are not visionaries, and can't see the potential of a new star. They drive looking through the rear view mirror. That's why the best artists of our time, like Jay Z and Kanye, faced so many rejections when starting out. They challenged the status quo and eventually, with enough persistence, when they did 'make it,' they changed the face of the industry.

Of course he was disappointed, but Kanye was undaunted by the rejections – 'only made me more focused, only wrote more potent/'. "He was always saying, they gon regret it,"remembers No I.D. Since labels didn't want to sign him for fear there wouldn't be a market for his style, Kanye decided to build his own publicity buzz, to prove that people did want to hear his music and, he hoped, to make the labels come to him. For instance he visited the offices of every Hip Hop publication and played his music, shook hands and rhymed for the editors. "We'd go to offices, he'd rap and jump on the desks," remembers friend Coddie Simmons, who would follow Kanye around with a video camera. "Everyone was looking at us crazy because he'd walk in with a camera filming. They'd be like, 'Who is this?'"[11]

Journalist Noah Callahan–Bever interviewed Kanye in 2002. He writes:

"I'm standing on the sidewalk in front of Baseline on 27th Street. The door to Kanye's Benz truck is open and he's sitting in the passenger seat, half inside and half outside the car. He's cueing beats on the stereo at ground–shaking volume and rapping and rapping and rapping. At me. Pedestrians are walking by looking at both of us like we're nuts."[19]

It's important to note that during this time Kanye could have focused on making beats, followed the 'producer path' and earned a good income selling music to established artists. But he wasn't chasing the money – (pg.70).

"I've already taken a loss. I'm not selling as many beats as I used to sell because I'm sitting here trying to think of raps," he said at the time. "So it's once again at the point in my life where I have to step away from something I'm doing, or retreat, in order to follow what my dreams really are…I got to follow my heart"[13]

Kanye in 2002 visualizing and planning his way to the top.

The Reluctant Deal

After months of heavy practice, Kanye's decision to focus on rap began to pay off as people around him slowly started recognizing his evolving skill.

"Kanye kept working and getting better," remembers Rock–A–Fella in-house producer Just Blaze. "There was a massive progression in his rap technique from 2000 to 2003."[31]

Singer John Legend agrees. "I was there during the early time when Kanye was just developing a lot of the material. When I first started working with him, I honestly didn't think his [debut] album would be special. As a rapper, he wasn't that great. Kanye improved a lot. And it wasn't just his rapping, but it was the song craft, the production, the storytelling, everything about it came together so beautifully."[11]

How did Kanye get better? Just Blaze believes that his 'trick' is to simply *believe* himself into something greater: "He sets almost an unachievable goal then works to get there, and that's how he gets better."[44]

Self-belief is the solid foundation and naturally results in the energy to focus, learn and improve yourself until the goal is achieved – *(pg.88)*.

Eventually (after a lot of "begging" from Kanye) Jay Z, who was at first skeptical of Kanye as a rapper, let him spit a verse on 'The Bounce' from his 'Blueprint 2' album (2002). 'Ye also rapped on the Roc–A–Fella collective song 'Champions,' which he also produced that same year.

'Make it street but it just might pop/
Make it straight to the mountain top/'
– Champions

Eventually too, after countless knocks on the door, some A&R's begun to peep through the keyhole and take note. A&R's like Jessica Rivera from Def Jam, who met Kanye while he was working with her on some remixes.

"One day Kanye came in and told me he was working on some of his own stuff and asked if he could play it," remembers Jessica. "So he closed the office door, played some beats and started rapping – he actually performed 'Jesus Walks' right there!"

Impressed, Jessica brought in the president of the record label, and Kanye performed again. The boss was also impressed but couldn't see Kanye as a big star. At a meeting later on, he told Kanye: "If you had an artist that you were writing and producing for, I would sign that artist."[45]

'Shopping my demo I was tryin' to shine/
Every motherfucker told me that I couldn't rhyme/'
– Last Call

Kanye got even closer to inking a deal with Capital Records in the summer of 2002, thanks to a 19 year old A&R, Joe '3H' Weinberger.

"Kanye was never down on himself," says 3H. "He'd be ready to rap on the spot, ready to tell his story on the spot, ready to make a record on the spot. He was probably the hungriest dude I ever saw. Whatever it takes. He wasn't all caked up yet, but he still had his Kanye swagger. It was definite star quality the day I saw him. He played me three songs and I was like, 'What!' His flow was different, his beats were great, he was performing the whole time. The energy was there, it was some real star-quality stuff."[38]

3H convinced the bosses to sign Kanye, and he was a $500,000 advance.

Finally he was being taken seriously and was about to be given the opportunity to show his work to the world. Though before formally accepting the deal, Kanye decided to try one last time to solicit an offer from Roc–A–Fella, perhaps to potentially set up a 'bidding war.'

Many at the Roc "used to diss his raps"[49] but with the Capital offer under his belt, he felt confident enough to demonstrate his work to Roc–A–Fella CEO Dame Dash and others. He had nothing to lose.

"Dame was like, 'Oh shit! It's not even wack. It's not even wack! That shit is kind of hot. OK, OK play some more,' remembers Kanye. "So then I play Jesus Walks and he's like, 'Yo, Cam. Cam! We should sign Kanye. What you think, man? We could do like the East Coast Chronic!'"[19]

Similar to Dr. Dre's iconic 'The Chronic' album, Dame envisioned a compilation album with Kanye's beats and with other Roc artists contributing most of the raps.

Knowing Capital had offered Kanye a rapper/producer deal, Dame made a similar offer, (although Dame remembers some resistance from Jay Z, "he didn't want me to put [Kanye] out. But he was outvoted because Biggs [the other Roc–A–Fella partner] would vote with me.")

Kanye was thrilled with the offer. How quickly things seemed to change. For months he was blankly refused by all half-decent companies, and now he had a choice between to iconic labels.

Weighing up the two offers he decided that Capital was the right choice – "I told [3H] I was gonna do it, and I'm a man of my word,"[46] plus, Capital wanted Kanye for his raps, whereas Roc-A-Fella were more interested in the beats.

His excitement was uncontainable. "*The day [I was going to sign Capital's deal] I planned out everything I was gonna do. Man, I had picked out clothes, I already started booking studio sessions, I started arranging my album, thinking of marketing schemes. Man I was ready to go.*" (– Last Call)

However, at the 11th hour, as 3H says, "another person in the company got in the ear of Capitol's president and the deal was nixed. He told the president, 'He's just a producer/rapper. Those records won't do well. He'll never sell.'"[38]

That 'No' became yet another addition to the dishearteningly long list of rejection. "Talk about a knife in the heart."[8]

Record labels are run by fashion chasing 'professionals' who follow industry trends and don't take major risks. Their view was, as Kanye said, "If he could really rap, Def Jam would've signed him or he'd be on the Roc. If the Roc don't believe in him, then why should we go with him?"[19]

(Capital also rejected 50 Cent, a year before he would sell 12 million albums with Shady Records.)

But for once, Kanye had a backup. When Capital pulled out, three weeks later on August 3rd 2002, Kanye became "the newest member of the Rock–A–Fella team."

Coincidently, Kanye arrived at Roc–A–Fella at a convenient time, with Jay Z due to retire from music after 'The Black Album', and the label searching for artists to fill the massive void he would create. "I was definitely feeling a little bit of anxiety cause my man Jay Z is retiring," Dash said. "People were on me like, 'what you gonna do after this?'"[38]

Roc–A–Fella gave Kanye a $150,000 advance, with the intention of putting together a complication album with Kanye's beats.

"The only reason I was listening, was because I was going to put out a record where he was the producer. I could sell 500,000 records for the compilation with everyone on it who was on Roc–A–Fella," remembers Dame. But Kanye had other intentions. "We all thought he was making a compilation album for Roc–A–Fella," remembers Plain Pat. "But when I met with him, he's like, 'Nah, I'm rapping!' It was shocking because nobody [at Def Jam or Roc–A–Fella] knew he was going to rap on the whole album."[11]

"He fooled Dame and told him that he was doing a compilation album," adds GLC. "That's how he got his deal!"[9]

Kanye spent $100,000 to get out of his management deal with D–Dot, and with the left over money he bought a Mercedes SUV, a Rolex for his mother and a watch from Jakob the jeweler.[1]

'I went to Jacob an hour after I got my advance/
I just wanted to shine/
Jay's favorite line: "Dog, in due time"/
Now he look at me, like "Damn, dog, you where I am"/
A hip hop legend, I think I died in that accident…'

* * *

Two months after the Roc–A–Fella deal was officially announced, on a warm October night in Los Angles, Kanye was driving from the studio at 4am in a rented black Lexus, frustrated and tired, cutting through the night like a shooting star.

He'd been in Record Plant Studios, with DJ Whoo Kid, when Ludacris came in to rap over a beat Kanye had made. Luda was in a hurry to finish the song, as he was travelling soon. But Kanye, being so excited to meet one of his music influences, wanted to show off his verbal skills and was "rapping in the both for like an hour," remembers Whoo.

Ludacris was getting frustrated with the delays and said he was leaving, so Whoo rushed Kanye out of the booth. "Kanye's looking crazy, you know, trying to impress Luda, but it wasn't that time. Luda wanted to come in do his verse and get out."

Disappointed that Ludacris didn't appreciate his rap, (although he was accustomed to rejection by now), Kanye also didn't get to sell him a beat. "What made it worse was [Kanye] went out [to the studio] to play the beat. But by the time he got out there, Luda picked the 'Red Spyda' beat. So now I gotta tell Kanye 'your services are not needed,'" remembers Whoo.

So Kanye left the studio frustrated and tired. "He's in the car heated. And just peels off…"[47]

Driving back to the W Hotel, West Hollywood, Kanye turned up the radio to drown out the silence of the road and nodded his head to the beat.

With every nod his head felt heavier and heavier. Working double digit hours every day to perfect his album whilst producing for others, was now catching up with him like the inescapable hand of death. His eyelids slowly closed like fading credits and his mind shut off.

Kanye woke up with his mouth wired shut, stitches covering his face, jaw shattered in three places. He had fallen asleep behind the wheel and veered off into the oncoming lane, where he collided with another car (the driver of which suffered two broken legs), and smashed his jaw into the steering wheel. If he had hit his nose he would have been laid to rest. Instead he woke up in the hospital B.I.G had died in, attached to life support machines. This was the second car accident Kanye experienced in two years. *'Trying to be a millionaire/How I use two lifelines'.*

Lying motionless in a hospital bed, unable to smile, let alone speak or rap, it would have been easy for Kanye to say 'OK, I need to slow down a little. Maybe put the rap thing on hold for a while,' and most people would think something along those lines. Like Kanye's cousin Devo thought, "Well, that's it as far as rapping, he can barely talk!" But, Kanye is not 'most people'. His dreams, his goals, are so engrained in his conscious that *nothing*, repeated for emphasis, *nothing*, was going to hinder him.

Instead of wallowing in self-pity Kanye searched for positive lessons in the tragedy. He came to see it as God's way of preparing him for the bountiful treasures that he would soon reap.

"The accident [was God] saying, 'I am about to hand you the world, just know at any given time I can take it away from you.' To nearly lose your life, to nearly lose your mouth, your voice, your whole face, as a rapper…and I had to be on TV! My face looks crazy to me now…But I have to just thank God for the situation that I am in…"[48]

He also was thankful that the accident gave him a compelling story.

"Wait till I tell the world the story about my accident and what happened. I almost died! We out of here – you understand what I'm about to create?" was the first thing Kanye said to Gee while lying in the hospital bed after the accident. (See *pg.268* for more on stories.)

It was a story Kanye began crafting as soon as soon as he was consciously able. "In the hospital bed he was thinking of beats and raps," says friend Really Doe.[8]

"[Kanye] called me from his hospital bed with his jaw wired shut and asked for a drum machine," adds Roc–A–Fella CEO Damon Dash. "That impressed me."[17]

Two weeks after the accident, with his mouth still wired shut, Kanye recorded 'Through The Wire,' (titled that way because he was literally spitting with a metal wire in his mouth – "It sounded like it hurt when he spoke," says Ludacris.[8]) The song would be released a few months later, in early 2003, on Kanye's first mixtape 'Get Well Soon,' which was adorned with pictures of Kanye's mashed up face. It was a great marketing move to stand out from the crowd of signed and unsigned rappers with mixtapes.

(The accident was also a blessing because of what it did to Kanye's voice. As rapper Consequence said, "whatever diction issues he had, he came back with a super clear voice. The same way [50 Cent's voice changed after he was shot], Kanye's voice changed. But instead of him getting shot, he went through a windshield."[12])

Lying on a hospital bed for days also gave Kanye time to reflect on his life, his purpose, his 'Why'.

"When I had my accident, I was working on Beanie Sigel and Black Eyed Peas, and let's just say that those tracks were not my best work. If I would have passed that night, that would have been the end of my legacy."[4]

"I was keeping up with the Joneses and a certain lifestyle. I had to have this much in my account, so let me do these beats and charge n**** this. I think I was getting caught up in that."[22]

"[I decided to re-focus my priorities and] now when I go into the studio, I act like this could possibly be my last day."[4]

Kanye would use the accident as a catalyst to change the direction of his music from the tough Go–Getter, to something more authentic.

"I think from there the 'College Dropout' concept took a better form because he let go of the gangsta persona and formed a good concept," says No I.D. "Before that he would wrestle ideas, try to make it all line up but it wouldn't make sense. I think that was the moment when he put all the pieces of the puzzle [together] and the idea of College Dropout made sense."[11]

Though Tupac should also receive credit: Shortly after the accident Kanye saw the 'Tupac: Resurrection' documentary, and as manager Hip Hop remembers, "A light bulb went off for him; he realized he could be himself."[11]

With the new sense of clarity over where he was going, Kanye got to work immediately after checking out of hospital.

Unable to fly for medical reasons, Dame arranged a large suite at the W Hotel, in Los Angles for Kanye. They turned it into a studio and Kanye would live and record there for a year. "The only thing he had to do was get up out of bed, go into his living room, and create songs. That's when the whole album went to overdrive. From that point, it was just recording every day," says manager Gee.

"We'd leave [the studio] at three in the morning, he'd be back in there by 9:30 or 10 am," remembers singer Tarrey Torre.[11]

This was the fifth blessing Kanye took from the accident. "[It] gave me the chance to really focus on my music. That was the first time in my career when I could tell people, 'I can't go to the studio with you,' and people weren't trippin. But instead of resting and trying to recover, I was sneaking into the studio to work on College Dropout."[3]

The Baby Label

Just because Kanye had signed a record deal with Roc-A-Fella/Def Jam, didn't mean he was going to put out music any time soon. In fact for over a year Kanye "wasn't a priority artist." The heads of the company were simply not motivated to support Kanye's solo material. They were still not convinced that he would be a successful rapper. As Plain Pat bluntly put it, "For a while, Def Jam or Roc–A–Fella didn't give two shits about him."

"Sometimes I'll sign an artist and not put a record for years, until they're ready," Dame explains.

That meant Kanye wasn't given the resources needed to create his debut album. But by now he felt that he had done enough waiting. "So he just took his destiny in his own hands and did everything himself."[8]

He'd hustle any opportunity to work on his own music. For instance when Kanye was hired to produce for other artists "he would show up a couple hours early and stay a couple hours late, and work on his own album on their studio time," says 3H.

At the time Def Jam had placed the entire Roc–A–Fella artist's expenses budget on hold because of months of unverified expenses. Yet Kanye, with the help of Plain Pat, would still record at Record Plant Studios in L.A without the official approval of the label. That meant there were lots of hidden bills.

"Roc–A–Fella was wilding out," remembers Pat. "They had [their studio] Baseline going. It was just non–stop recording. They didn't know who was recording what; it was just open. The bill would come in and just say, like, 'Beanie Sigel Freestyle.' It was out of control."

"Meanwhile, Kanye was in L.A. I was letting him record but I wasn't supposed to. So I had all these bills from Record Plant and I was holding them, I was hoping for the budget to reopen but it never got reopened. I was so scared that I would get fired."[11]

(Later though Kanye was introduced to Def Jam CEO Lyor Cohen and played him some songs. Lyor "loved" 'Breath In, Breath Out' so agreed to reopen Kanye's budget (and pay the $50,000 in bills Pat had been concealing). The original budget for the album was around $250,000, but with Lyor's backing the budget was raised and eventually cost over $1 million to finish.)

As part of the 'I'll do it myself' drive, Kanye formed a "baby label" consisting of Don C, John Monopoly, Gee, Kyambo and Devo Springsteen, who hustled independently of Roc-A-Fella to move Kanye's career forward.

Devo, who worked as Kanye's assistant (for "$200 a week"[42]) when he moved to Newark, remembers their independent hustle: "From when he got the deal to when his album came out, there was a lot of grinding from us [the "baby label"]. It wasn't Roc–A–Fella pushing Kanye. We needed a hot record for Roc–A–Fella to put money behind [College Dropout]. There needed to be some buzz and momentum in order for there to be marketing – there needed to be a demand for it."[9]

"We would go to clubs [with some] vinyl and some hot girls, and had [the girls] give it to the DJ to play the record."[8]

Kanye would take advantage of any opportunity to perform. He would go on any radio show he could get invited on – no matter how small or local its reach, and he'd perform at as many clubs and shows as he was able.

The 'baby label' put together their first mixtape 'Get Well Soon' in early 2003. It featured Through The Wire, and other songs Kanye produced. They followed it up with several other mixtapes and 'samplers' including, The Cheat Sheet, Kon the Louis Vuitton Don, I'm Good, Jeanius Level Musik (hosted by DJ Akademiks) and Behind the Beats (with DJ's Plain Pat and Ferris Bueller, where Kanye spoke about the making of The Blueprint), for fans to get used to hearing Kanye as a rapper, and as a way to build 'momentum' around his debut album.

They pressed up most mixtapes in Devo's apartment, and would spend a lot of time on the artwork and packaging to distinguish from the low quality independent mixtapes and albums on store shelves.

Even though they were still unknown they wouldn't try and compete with other mixtapes on price. Divo remembers a British distributor telling him they pay $1 per mixtape. Devo replied "our CD's are $1.75."[42] The distributor was first taken aback that an unknown artist would price his product so much higher than others, so only bought ten copies. But the team were competing on quality not price, and after selling out quickly the distributor came back for 200 more.

(All mixtapes are available at HipHopTeaches.com)

In March 2002, still without Roc-A-Fella/Def Jam support, Kanye reached out to Talib Kweli while he was on tour with Common.

"Kanye was saying he was having trouble with labels signing him, not seeing him as a rapper," Kweli remembers. "So asked if he can go on tour with us."[41]

Kanye's friend, Plain Pat, also remembers the time. "Kanye paid his own money to go on tour with Talib Kweli, with his big–ass Roc–A–Fella chain and people looked at him like he was crazy."

Kanye used the tour as an educational crash course, honing his mic skills, and improving his stage presence. "He was really about learning the craft. It was incredible for me to watch" says Kweli. "Nobody gave Kanye nothing. He went and took it."[43]

Can't Tell Me Nothing

By 2003 Kanye was itching like a fiend to become a superstar.

July of that year saw the fastest selling concert in America, 'Rock The Mic' bring together some of the hottest rap acts of the moment. Jay Z, 50 Cent, Busta Rhymes, Snoop Dogg, and more, preformed a 20+ day cross-country tour.

The tour landed in Chicago's 'Tweeter Centre' on 16th July and Kanye woke up excited. He had been dreaming about performing on stage in front of his home crowd and felt this was his moment. He thought about how this was the perfect opportunity to prove himself alongside Hip Hop superstars as a legitimate rapper. 'Through the Wire' was already receiving radio play in Chicago, and this show was the chance, once and for all, to completely annihilate the 'producer–rapper' tag that was attached to him like an infected limb.

Backstage he could feel the energy and excitement from the roaring crowd. All other Roc–A–Fella artists were given the opportunity to perform and Kanye was ready for his turn. The song 'Champions' blasted through the speakers and fans roared the chorus. Kanye smiled hard. He had produced this track and was ready to step on stage to perform his opening verse. But. The music shifted to something else right before his part.

It was not a DJ mistake.

The previous year Jay and Dame had brought out Kanye at the same venue to announce his Roc–A–Fella deal – shown in the Through the Wire video.

"In the video we make it look so glamorous, like I got my chain and we move on," Kanye recalled. "What y'all don't realize is that as I keep on rapping, I'm rapping to a crowd, and about six bars in completely bombing in front of 20,000 people in my own city, completely embarrassing the entire Roc–A–Fella…and I know that stuck in Jay Z's memory."[22]

When 'Roc The Mic' came around the following year Jay felt Kanye wasn't ready to perform in front of such a large crowd again – *Jay favorite line, 'Dog in due time'*, so held him back.

"Kanye was pretty down on it" writes his mother, Donda, in her memoir. "It was the biggest slap in the face so far. He came to my house that night and I don't think I have ever seen him that disappointed. I don't remember seeing Kanye cry after 12, but that night he looked like he wanted to.…he was trying his best to take his music career to the next level but it seemed like there was always a block."[1]

The same block would re–emerge a few months later.

Movie
poster for
Jay Z's
'Fade To
Black'
Concert

25th November 2003 was special night in Hip Hop. Jay Z, the culture's unofficial leader, had announced his retirement from music and his farewell concert at a 'sold-out-in-minutes' Madison Square Garden was taking place: Fade to Black.

Again Kanye begged to perform. He yearend to take another step to stardom. He had rapped on songs with Jay Z like 'The Bounce,' and had a hand in producing Jay's last four albums, so preforming on stage with him seemed like the natural next step.

"The only thing I ever asked Jay Z for was to perform at the Tweeter Center at Chicago, to perform at Madison Square Garden, and to be on The Blueprint 2. I begged him. I went to [Jay's best friend] Ty–Ty and I begged Ty–Ty."[24]

But the answer again was 'no'.

"Jay was like, 'No, he ain't ready for that yet,'" remembers Kyambo.[9]

Instead Kanye received four complimentary tickets to the show, not even a backstage pass. When he asked for two more: *'Carlyn told me I could buy two tickets'.*

"I was definitely hurt. I was definitely hurt when I was not on that stage," reflects Kanye. He knew he could be great if just given the opportunity.

Of course by now Kanye was accustomed to turning 'tragedy to triumph.'

Every 'no' he received, every obstacle that was put in his path, just gave him more fuel, more determination to push harder and find a way. No one could stop him. He turned down the complementary tickets, and went back to the studio where he made 'Never Let Me Down.'

"Fuck that show!" he said. "Next year, I'll have my own show at Madison Square Garden!"[1]

"Think It, Sat It, Do It," and just 11 months later Kanye was performing a 45 minute set at a sold out Garden, supporting Usher's 'Truth Tour,' following the achievements of The College Dropout.

The Final Pieces

Since Kanye's first production credit for an artist in 1996, he intended on being a rapper and studied the industry in search of the best way in. As Consequence remembers: "We would study everything, we would study G–Unit, we would study Grafh, the Young Gunz was hot at the time, and the whole Philly movement was on fire. We were just sitting back figuring out what's going to be the point of entry for us to get in? We knew once we got in we could make a change,"[11] – (see 'Change The Game' *pg.286*).

By early 2003 Kanye had identified his way in. He announced his debut album 'The College Dropout,' whose overall theme was to "make your own decisions, don't let society tell you, 'This is what you have to do.'" He understood that his unique voice, his niche, was to blend two seemingly opposite worlds. "He was mixing Roc–A–Fella with what he was, but still speaking to Roc–A–Fella fans," said manager Hip Hop. "He was trying to find his way to blend the two worlds, to appeal to street people without doing it blatantly. These are conversations we had."

Kanye had already spent several years working on the album. According to John Monopoly, "Kanye was always producing with the intention of being a rapper. There's beats on the album he's been literally saving for himself for years."[47]

As well as beats, Kanye had been putting together raps for the album for over six years. "When I said that rap 'Mayonnaise colored Benz, I push Miracle Whips' for Jay I was about 21 years old. So you could say then [is when I started the album]. The last line you hear on College Dropout is the oldest line, so I call that the beginning."[3]

Although Kanye was focused on his debut he had a career plan that went much further. He had planned out his next three albums; naming Late Registration, Graduation and GoodAssJob (later MBDTF), and planning themes and songs for each, such as saving 'Hey Mama' for 'Late Registration.' He had been using this strategy to achieve excellence throughout his career. He would set an ultra-high goal, visualize achieving it, form a plan, then tell everyone to 'make it real' and create enough pressure to do it no matter what obstacles arise – (see 'Think it, Say it, Do it' *pg.90*). This all added to his self-belief and he always felt success was just around the corner:

"I knew when I wrote the line 'light–skinned friend look like Michael Jackson' [from the song 'Slow Jamz'] I was going to be a big star. At the time, they used to have the Virgin Music [stores], and I would go there and just go up the escalator and say to myself, 'I'm soaking in these last moments of anonymity.' I knew I was going to make it this far; I knew that this was going to happen."[40]

Kanye released 'Through The Wire' officially on September 30, 2003 – a year after first recording it. Because of the 'baby label's' promotion efforts in the months prior, it picked up mainstream radio attention across the country – Chicago's DJ Pharris being one of the first to play it and start the ball rolling.

The team kept pushing the record as a single, but still unable to get the full backing of Roc-A-Fella, they decided to step their independent hustle up another level and Kanye put up $40,000 from his own pocket to record a video for the track.

Inspired by a Polaroid snapshot type advertisement by Adidas, the video was shot by 'Coodie and Chike,' who also worked at MTV. Kanye would walk into MTV offices unnoticed and spend hours editing with the pair.

To launch the video Kanye and his team organized a lavish premier party at Jay Z's 40/40 club in New York, on November 30 2003. John Monopoly had a street team already buzzing to promote the event and had invited all press and Roc-A-Fella and Def Jam staff. The energy and anticipation in room was incredible.

The video (which would later be awarded 'Video of the Year' at the 2004 Source Hip Hop Awards) was played, then Kanye passionately preformed, and voiced his frustrations over his treatment by the label. The audience were stunned. Prior non-believers were speechless.

"That's when everything changed," recalls Kyambo.

"I was proud of him," says Dame. "At the time no one was listening so he definitely did what he had to do."

"It defiantly forced Roc-A-Fella's hand," adds Monopoly.

The event changed the perceptions of many 'doubters' at Kanye's label. As 3H remembers, "I don't think he was actually signed to Island Def Jam until 'Through the Wire' happened."

"That's when Def Jam started recognizing him," says the video director Coodie. "Everybody was blown away by the video and it just kept building from there."[11]

Still, despite the massive increase in approval from his own camp, Kanye and the team realized, "We need something with way more money behind it as a single," says Gee, if they were to be given full support from the label hierarchies. So they devised a cunning strategy to spend the money needed to get Kanye's name out.

Gee and Hip Hop had taken A&R positions at Atlantic records, and one of the artists they were assigned to was Twista, a Chicago rapper who hadn't released a single since 1997. They paired Kanye and Twist together to make the song 'Slow Jamz.' Roc–A–Fella negotiated with Atlantic to pay for the song's video, and in exchange Twista could use a version of the song for his album 'Kamikaze,' which would be released two weeks before 'The College Dropout,' which would also have a version of the song.

'Slow Jamz' was released in late 2003 and quickly blew. It got thousands of radio spins across the country and eventually reached number one on the charts. "That song was definitely the biggest thing that happened in my career," said Twista,[11] whose album sold 300,000+ its first week mainly because of the single.

Surly this was enough to prove to the record executives that Kanye had 'it'. Still, without waiting or depending on anybody (*pg.206*), the team continued their aggressive promotional campaign, visiting music magazine offices and doing free surprise concerts in schools and colleges. They were climbing one step at a time. In late 2003 Twista brought Kanye out in front of 20,000 people at Chicago's famous United Center, for WGCI's Big Jam Holiday Concert – the largest crowd Kanye preformed to since his Roc-A-Fella inauguration disaster the year before. Then a few months before College Dropout dropped, Kanye held a show at S.O.B.'s New York.

'Partyin' S.O.B.'s and we had packed a crowd' – Big Brother

This was another major turning point. Executives and major artists came to the show and saw firsthand what Kanye had believed for so long. "After that show at SOBs he was bona fide, he was popping. It was full–on Kanye season," remembers Coodie.[11]

"The night Kanye played SOBs, I knew that Hip Hop was about to change," says Common. "He was the first artist to bring together the backpack crowd along with the Roc–A–Fella ballers. I remember seeing people throwing up the Roc, but it was all underground hip hop backpackers doing it. That album, he bridged the gap."

One of the fans there was eighteen year old J Cole. "When I pulled up to the venue I saw a line down the block. I didn't know that there were other fans like me…it was legendary."[50]

The perception of Kanye changed. "That gave confidence to Def Jam and Roc–A–Fella to push Kanye all the way," says No I.D. "That was the moment we knew the machine was behind him and there was no question it was gonna work."[11]

* * *

Shortly before The College Dropout's release, at the listening session with journalists and music taste makers, most artists would play the records from a speaker and politely take questions from the audience. But again, Kanye is not 'most artists.' Just as he had been pouring his heart out in every performance for years, he performed the album live as if he were rapping for his life. The journey to this point had been so arduous that he was going to 'get props or die trying.'

"I'm asking you all not to let the future pass you by and be a part of history, cause this is history in the making, man," he pleaded with the audience, before playing the first track.[38]

One journalist attending remembers: "He'd be jumping on tables, pounding his chest, posing and flailing his arms, all with enough vim and vigor that you'd think he was ready to fight...If he thinks that he doesn't have 150 percent of your undivided attention he's going to put you on blast. A couple of times he stopped a song and started it over when he thought there might be someone in the room who was 'not getting it.'"

The intensity of this self-belief is contagious. "Songs I didn't even like, I started liking!"[51] Common remarked, *(pg.99)*.

After its release, 'The College Dropout' sold four million copies and was nominated for 10 Grammy's – a figure only Michael Jackson has topped.

Why?

It gave Hip Hop a fresh voice.

At the time rappers fell into three distinct boxes. They were either tough–guy 'gangsters,' like 50 Cent (who had just sold 12 million records), 'ballers,' like Cash Money, more concerned with style than substance, or underground 'backpackers' (meaning without much radio play or charting success) like Kweli and Common, who put lyrical content first.

The College Dropout combined all three, *first ni***r with a benz and a backpack*. It occupied the space between real conscious rap and easy listing party rap, and appealed to a cross section of Hip Hop fans.

'If the devil wear Prada, Adam Eve wear nada/
I'm in between but way more fresher/ '
– Can't Tell Me Nothing

"It was the perfect medium of street and conscious. It was backpack but it was hood. The magic of the album was that it was everything, not just west coast or east coast. It was fresh and it was hip hop," says poet J. Ivy.[9]

Advertisement for the album used in music magazines, designed by a proud 'Ye

The music resonated with so many walks of life. As Kanye said at the time, "I could spit any of my raps to a n**** on the corner, somebody in a barbershop, but I could go into a corporate office and say the same rap and they will understand what I'm talking about. It's so universal."[19]

In describing his niche, Kanye said: "Jay Z can't be anymore backpack than he is already, and Talib Kweli can't be any more commercial than he is already. Somehow I fit in the center of them both. I'm not too much either way, so I fall between everything. I'm like the 2003 of A Tribe Called Quest – I'm A Guy Called West."

'On the hottest rap label around/
But he wasn't talking about coke and birds/
It was more like spoken word/ '
– Through The Wire

The albums theme was 'Do You' *(pg.272)*. It was about doing what's right and best for you, regardless of what other think. It was honest, vulnerable and funny. It focused on the lives and struggles 'regular' people. College Dropout had songs about Kanye being frustrated with his job as a cashier, being self–conscious, overcoming racial stereotypes, free self-expression and God. Listeners relate to the lyrics, bang their head to the beats, memorize the melody and 'screwface' the quotables. The album was a mix of Dr. Dre production, Dead Prez lyrical depth and Michael Jackson catchy melodies.

Another reason for its immediate success, perhaps, was timing. Kanye had spent enough time in the music industry to understand its cyclical nature: "It's all a matter of a turning tide. Compared to movies, there's a time of mad gangsta movies, then its comedies, then its family films, then it's back to gangsta flicks, [because] we missed the gangsta flicks. I'm doing this little wave [of music], it's going to make people fiend for good gangsta music again after my wave is waving goodbye. I realize that time will happen. I enjoy it and I realize that it's all entertainment."[38]

But what really happened after the album's release might have even surprised Kanye. It marked a tipping point as other rappers adopted his alternative vibe and the entire genre of Hip Hop followed. Drake, Kendrick, Chance, Cole, and a whole generation of new artists have their foundations in 'The College Dropout.'

As the album was about to drop, Kanye saw the influence his music was having and his motives took on a greater purpose.

"My whole goal in life was to eventually be able to do nothing. Now that I see the type of impact I'm gonna make on music and the community, my responsibility is now to do everything for the fans, for the community."

On the album's 10th anniversary all the music magazines paid homage to it, (Complex devoted a whole week to celebrate it). All the hours, struggles and rejections were surly worth it to create a timeless masterpiece that affects millions of lives for years to come.

KEY LESSON

"Think It, Say It, Do It"[29]
-The Holy Trinity-

How It All
Got Started

Part I

Beginnings

'It all started with a dream…'
– Common, Blue Sky

Hundreds of successful people were interviewed for this book – either directly or indirectly, and after studying their journeys 'from nothing to something,' it becomes clear that they have all followed a similar, natural, process.

It begins with four simple principles that form the foundations for their entire lives: Knowing themselves – *the Re-finding*, and the reasons they are doing what they're doing – *the Why*, overcoming the greatest obstacle – *the Enemy*, and believing undoubtedly in the world they can create – *the Core*.

The Re-Finding

Hip Hop was created by marginalized inner city youth who needed to express their voices in a world designed to keep them quiet. Trains tore through New York City paint bombed with tags, flattened cardboard boxes were the grand stages for body poppin' duels, and neighborhood street lights were hacked to power DJ's colossal speaker sets. All these forms of expression represent Hip Hop's core principle: Self-empowerment.

Self-empowerment means living a life true to yourself, by not passively accepting what society, or those around you want or expect. It's about living, and earning a living, from the heart. This is Hip Hop's first lesson.

'If you don't leave with nothing else tonight, you will leave with knowing yourself'
– Kendrick Lamar, Section 80 Outro

Sean Carter zipped his hoodie and shuffled back into the shadowy gap between two project buildings in search of warmth. The bitter East Coast winter wind burned his exposed flesh and slapped his conscience. The dark thoughts returned.

Carter's life revolved around the street. He earned thousands of dollars a month travelling up and down the coast supplying fatally addictive drugs to barely living 'fiends'. In the silent moments between brief visits from these drug addicts – shivering from the cold and shaking from their disease, Carter contemplated his life. The dark feelings that had haunted him for months were always one quiet moment away. The rush of living on the edge of the law had long since been replaced by deep paranoia and the satisfaction of an elastic band stretched over a fat wad of bills no longer motivated. He didn't let his mind dwell on it, but Sean knew the likely future outcomes that awaited him if he continued this profession – death or jail. But still, for a long time he couldn't stop.

'We become addicted/ sort of like the fiends we accustomed to serving/ ' – Can I Live

Now winter of 1994, on a cold street corner, Sean accepted it was time to make a choice: commit to this life of material fulfillment, or give it up to follow his heart. He chose to choose himself.

"It just got to a point where it was, like, 'Make this decision, because this is something you really love. It's time to get serious about it, give it your all.' Once I did that, it was no looking back from there."[1]

Sean chose himself when he became Jay Z. Kanye chose himself when he dropped out of college to pursue his passion. Eminem chose himself when he continued performing despite the jeers and taunts from crowds. Kendrick Lamar chose himself when he stopped creating art based on other people's opinion, and made something true to himself.

Greats chose themselves. 'Others' let the world chose them. 'Others' live according to what those around them believe is right, despite feeling that it's not the life they want. 'Others' end life with a sigh, a nagging *'what if…'* feeling, deep inside. *"I wish I had lived my own life instead of how others expected me to live,"* is the most common regret the terminally ill talk of.[2]

'Some may never figure out their purpose in life, and some will/
There are a lot of us who are caught up in this hell we all live in/
Content with being blinded by rules and judgment/ '
– Common, My Dreams

The Greats profiled in this book (and the many more happy, healthy and wealthy people in the world) have taken the time to figure out what they really want to do with their limited time, and live their lives accordingly.

"Your passion is something you love to do. Something you wake up in the morning thinking about," rapper Common said in a lecture.[3] "When you are doing it you enjoy yourself. It's not even work to you. Only you know in your heart what makes you happy."

Some people's passion for their work seems to pour out of them. Take Dr. Dre. "He believes God put him here to make music," said Kanye,[4] and that's clear to see from his work ethic. Here is someone who earns hundreds of millions of dollars a year that has, "never been out of the studio for more than two weeks" in a 30+ year career. "I'd be making music if didn't get paid, if I was a plumber," Dre says,[5] "That's how much love I have for Hip Hop."

That is the definition of living your passion.

When you're doing something you love all the other principles in this book flow naturally. If you're doing something you believe in and are innately curious about, you'll naturally put in long hours (even when you're struggling) because you have a desire to learn, and so the work itself (not the promise of some end goal) is rewarding. You're naturally focused and will think about your work even when you're not working. You'll enjoy visualizing what 'could be' and coming up with creative solutions. Authentic enthusiasm shows in your voice, the way you walk, even your handshake.

"You can learn it. But in order to be good at it, to be really great at it, it has to be in you," said Dr. Dre in an interview with Esquire. "I've been listening to music for as long as I can remember. I was bred for this from birth. My mother has a picture of me in a onesie putting a needle to a turntable."[6]

Doing what you love (or better said, loving what you do[7]) is also the only way to achieve real commercial success. By living your interests you'll naturally have the discipline, focus and vision (personal success) to be able to create remarkable things that deserve to exist in the world. Doing things you're excited by means you're always 'tuned in' to the work and learn quickly. It can take years of struggle before tasting success, so doing something you're naturally interested in means you'll have the patience to put in '10 thousand hours' of learning, even doing menial tasks, because you're deeply committed. You'll develop skills to become an expert and will be able to spot opportunities others can't to put skills into practice and build wealth.

In the words of Pharrell: "You need to do things because you feel that you have something new and different that you can bring to that particular genre. It needs to make sense to you."[8]

But this is the opposite way of thinking to most people who go into careers because their parents pushed them into it or because money is the number one priority. They're not really interested in the work itself so tune out and don't learn as fast. In a few years they're 'burned out,' with a mid–life crisis to deal with, wondering, *what am I doing with my life?'*

> *'Did you improve on the design? Did you do something new?/*
> *Well your name ain't on the guest list, who brung you?/'*
> – Lupe Fiasco, Superstar

You may already know what your interests are, what you want to earn a living from and be Great at. You may love to draw, write code, design buildings, dance, knit, and so on. And so you can go on to another chapter. But if you have a questioning voice in your head, read on.

What Should I do?

Kevin Liles, former president of Def Jam, knew he wanted to be involved in Hip Hop from an early age. His first thought was to get involved on the artistic side and so formed a rap group. 'Numarx' built a strong fan base in the mid-Atlantic area. They were opening shows for legends like Run DMC, won local awards and had songs played on local radio. However, although Kevin loved the music and culture, he was feeling dissatisfied in his position as an artist.

Alongside creating songs and performing Kevin also took the lead in promoting the band and organizing shows. This led to forming a production company, which then led to working for the 'street teams' of major record labels. It was his job to promote artists coming to his city to perform and get them played on local radio stations. Through this he built good relations with regional radio DJ's and became well known in clubs and record stores in the community. He was tasting success and found the work more interesting than making music so decided to 'pivot' into the business side of the music business.

In the early 90's Def Jam was the epitome of a 'Hip Hop record label,' and Kevin dreamed of working there. Because of his experience with Numark he felt getting a job would be easy, so he drove to a Hip Hop convention in Atlanta and managed to get into a hotel party for 'industry people.' There he introduced himself to a senior vice president for Def Jam, Wes Johnson. Kevin told him who he was (thinking his name spoke for itself), and what he could do for Def Jam. Wes did not seem impressed and told him he could intern for free under a new recruit. "Take it or leave it."

If Kevin was only concerned with making as much money as possible he could have easily thought this job beneath him. But he felt passionate about working in the business side of one of the most admired Hip Hop labels, so he put his ego aside and followed his interests.

He took the position and for two years hustled hard, doing his upmost to support his boss, who often was less qualified than Kevin, and even spending his own money to make projects successful. Eventually all his work was noticed and he was offered a full time paid position. He went on to climb the corporate ladder like a jungle gym.[9]

Kevin followed his interests, his 'inner voice,' every step of the way in his prosperous career. But this isn't the norm. Many people enter careers they're not passionate about, with no connection to who they are, because their life choices are made by the 'outer voice' of what society, family or friends say is right.

Often they don't even realize because, as Robert Green (one of the most popular author in the Hip Hop community) writes, with years of external education we learn about things we're not interested in, with no connection to who we are. Curiosity is crushed and the 'inner voice' (which represents our unique DNA configuration) is drowned out by the 'outer voice.' We get to a point where we lose touch with who we are, what makes us unique and what we love to do. Many enter careers they're not passionate about and end up with the constant feeling of dissatisfaction and unhappiness. They will not achieve Greatness.

Robert suggests to get out of this trap we need to reconnect with the 'inner voice' (which others call our life's-task/purpose/calling/problem–your–meant–to–solve/bliss/destiny) to find and pursue our natural interests. We should think for ourselves, away from the expectations of others – as Kanye says we should, "wash the brain, don't brainwash."[10] We should find and follow our curiosity, learn practical skills in the subjects we're most interested in and create our own career path which reflect who we are. Then we can spend our lives "working as passionately as our heart allows," ultimately living a fulfilled life.[11]

It's very common to think, *'but there's nothing I really love to do,'* so to create some mental clarity about who we are and where we want to go, we need to ask ourselves some fundamental questions, like:

-   What activities or subjects spark a childhood curiosity in me now?
-   What topic could I willingly read one hundred books about?
-   What do I notice? Small things around me, in newspapers etc., which draw my attention.

You're not looking for a specific 'job' or even a 'passion,' but general fields of interest. For example, 'performing,' 'cars,' 'languages,' 'beauty,' 'science,' 'technology,' 'entrepreneurism.' It might take several years to know exactly what you want to do, but it starts with following your interests. Then, just like Kevin Liles did, as we learn about ourselves, what we love to do and what we don't, we make small adjustments in our life's journey. We pursue our interests in subjects that attract us, if something doesn't feel right we move on. It's all about listening to the internal compass of 'what feels right?'

Lyor Cohen, one of the most powerful exec's in music, and one of Jay Z's mentors, calls this process 'dabbling.' Robert Greene calls it a 'hacker apprenticeship' because, like a machete wielding explorer in the jungle, you 'hack' your way to what you want. You try going in this direction, try that direction, and if it doesn't work then pivot and hack again. It's not a straight road. It's about taking a path for a time then 'hacking' your way to find a better path.

Pharrell has this process mastered: "I spend 50% of my time just exploring different things to just do it because it peaks my interest. The other 50% of the time I'm influenced by what I've done and how much further I want to take it. From there I build ideas and make them more concrete."[8]

This is also how Jay Z lives his life:

> "I just try to pay attention to life and let it take me on a natural course in a natural direction."[12]
>
> "I've always believed in motion and action, in following connections wherever they take me, and in not getting entrenched. My life has been more poetry than prose, more about unpredictable leaps and links than simple steady movement, or worse, stagnation. It's allowed me to stay open to the next thing without feeling held back by a preconceived notion of what I'm supposed to be doing next...
>
> "I like my rhymes to stay loose enough to follow whatever ideas hijack my train of thought, just like I like my mind to stay loose enough to absorb everything around me."[13]

Over time one interest will lead to another and you can combine interests to create things that only you could have. For instance, Russell Simmons combined his love of music, comedy and meditation into a lifestyle brand, and Dr. Dre combined his love of 70's funk with Compton street culture to revolutionize Hip Hop in the early 90's with 'G–Funk'. This is what people mean when they reflect back on their lives and can 'connect the dots.'

'One day it'll all make sense'
– Common

It's also normal to feel like you don't have a burning passion for any specific 'thing'. Many people find that 'passion' is just a by-product of working on things they're interested in and good at. The more they work the better they get, the better they get the more 'passionate' they become, the more passionate they are the more they work. And so the cycle goes. Interest is the starting point, passion is just the eventual byproduct.

So stay disciplined, put your heart into whatever you do, keep building skills around interests, and don't waste years performing mindless tasks or aimlessly wandering around in jobs where you're not developing. In a few years you'll have a clear idea of the 'path' you will be happy in, and will have accumulated skills to such a high level, and so unique to you, that you will have dominated your own niche. You will be irreplaceable in a world where "trends show most people are made redundant in their 40's as they're replaced by younger, cheaper people."[14]

'Pardon me if I seems that I'm following my dreams/
I ain't reading off the script that they picked for me/'
– J Cole, Can I Live

Robert Green advises that if in youth you already know the career that's right for you, then there's no need for the 'dabbling' and you can go straight into it with intense focus. But many are in a hurry to 'make it.' They see the success stories of 'overnight celebrities' but don't see all the 'behind the scenes' work that has gone on to get them to that point. So they go into jobs for the money, or because they saw other people in their community become successful doing it, (like rappers and basketball players in some African-American communities). But they're shooting themselves in the foot. Not only are they missing out on opportunities to build skills around their own interests, they most likely won't have the commitment to excel in the work they are spending their time on. That's why having the right motives is critical.

Why do you do it?

The
Why

'Desire that ignites the torch to burn/
It's not rocket science this is easy to learn/'
— Pharoahe Monch, Desire

Where did MC Hammer find the solid gold toilet he purchased for his $15 million dollar home after the success of his first album in 1991? Was it difficult for the company that built his trouser-shaped home pool to get the layered 'hammer pants' effect right? How long did Hammer have to pose for the giant marble statue of himself in the image of Michelangelo's David? What was his manager's first response when he saw the receipt for two gold-plated 'Hammer Time' entrance gates, twenty one racehorses, seventeen luxury cars, two helicopters and two-hundred staff on one man's payroll?

These are questions people studying the rise and fall of promising artists or entrepreneurs, like MC Hammer, may want to know. The more essential question though is: *Why* did Hammer do it?

What was the driving motivation?

Two Ways to 'Make It'

If the journey is a board of Chutes and Ladders, Hammer went from 0 to 100 with just a couple rolls of the dice. So did Craig Mack, 2 Live Crew, and countless other people you barely remember the name of.

They rose from unknowns to the top of the charts quickly, earned a moment of fame and fortune, and then faded into irrelevance. They choose the Fast-Short career.

Typically these people followed a hot trend in the industry. A certain style was popular, in demand and was selling well. Record labels were looking for 'artists' to use the style and quickly sell a record. When it did sell the artist made some money (of course nothing compared to the amount of money the label made from them). When the trend inevitably faded, the artist had no foundation, was seen as 'over' and 'wasted' by audiences, and quickly shipped out of the label, which went in search of the next trend to chase. (This is also the reason most TV singing contest winners are unheard of a few years later).

'Playing with yourself thinking the game is just wealth/
Hot for a minute watch your name just melt/'
– Common, Aquarius

Some who went from 0 to 100 quickly used contacts and friends who had 'made it' to get them in easily. They acquired power not by self-effort. Again, although they may have had some success in the beginning through association, they did not last long because their character had not built itself through the journey, through the struggle. They didn't find their natural niche. They weren't ready, like children squandering inherited riches.

"Quick riches are more dangerous than poverty," – Napoleon Hill.[1]

In general, when analyzing the careers of the Greats compared to 'one hit wonders,' we find that nobody who goes from 0 to 100 without the numbers in between, stays around long. The best, most-consistent artists struggled to go from 0 to the top. They took time to learn the ropes, going through years of 'work experience' and learning.

Jay Z's first album came out in 1996, but he was rapping for fifteen years before that. He went on tour with Big Daddy Kane to learn how to rock a show. He spent six months recording and working with newly signed friend

Jaz–O in 1989, "not talking just learning." He released numerous mixtapes, went on underground radio shows, took part in countless battles and open mics, would perform on pool tables in crowded rooms, went on make-shift tours playing to audiences of twenty, all to learn about the industry and earn experience. He was building his brand slowly, at times feeling like he wasn't moving. But when it was time to record his first album he had built a strong foundation of experiences, learned valuable lessons through other people's successes and failures and had established a healthy roster of contacts to work with. He was ready.

On the flip side, when Roc–A–Fella established itself Jay Z and Co. signed many old friends from their neighborhood. People like Memphis Bleek and Freeway. Jay would be on many of their songs trying to push them into the mainstream, yet where are they now?

If success is handed on a plate a person will never be able to stand on their own. Jay now understands that the journey is vital. Trying and failing, mastering your craft, finding your niche through trial and error is the only way to survive independently. So now with Jay's new label ROC Nation, he appears on very few songs with new signees, J Cole and Jay Electronica. They're crafting a path for themselves and are much more successful than previous artists. Jay's learned to give hand-ups not handouts.

'Give an opportunity though, that's the plan now/'
– Nickels and Dimes.

Wealth

Hammer, and those seeking to be carried up the mountain, have the 'riches' state of mind. The icons in this book have the 'wealth' state of mind. What's the difference?

'Not rich but wealthy/'
– Kendrick Lamar, Poe Mans Dreams

"Wealth is of the heart and mind, not of the pocket," says Pharrell[1], and most of the people discussed in this book would agree. "Wealth is Wellbeing," explains 'The Teacha' KRS–One.[2] "Wealth is about not needing anything or anyone to be satisfied." Wealth is about having the power to use the unlimited potential in yourself to do anything you want. Wealth is having mastery of self, control of your mind, self-governance. Wealth is longevity and being able to provide for your children's children. Wealth is to fully 'Do You.' Wealth is about waking up with a purpose.

Rich is about buying stuff.

"The rich life is toxic," continues KRS. "Rich is close to poverty. Being entrapped by material possessions and needing higher and higher incomes to survive. If you're not satisfied with a little, you won't be satisfied with a lot."

This is a sentiment all Greats understand.

"It's funny; you drive in a Maybach past a homeless person and you ask, 'Who's more free?'" asks Kanye West.[3] "You could be trapped to your possessions. You gotta do this next deal 'cause you gotta do this with your house and you gotta get this car, [because] everybody [who] stay next to you last name is Jones, and you trying to keep up with all of them."

Even rappers accused of being overly materialistic understand the difference between wealth and riches. Rick Ross explains that, "Being a boss is much deeper than [cars and jewels]. It can be the brokest dude in the beat-up car who's the real boss. It's not about money or status. It's about heart…Even when I wasn't in the position I'm in today, I always had my ambitions, and I always took responsibility. That's who the boss is."[4]

'The richest man rocks the snatch-less necklace/'
– Chance the Rapper, Acid Rain

Those who don't understand the difference between riches and wealth may be in for hard times. Many will reach the top imagining money and fame will bring happiness and contentment, but instead find only isolation and the insecurity of 'losing it.'

For instance Soulja Boy shot to fame and riches in 2007 with 'Crank That.' By the end of the year he was making millions from record sales and touring, and was buying all the status symbols he had always dreamed of. But it wasn't fulfilling. "At first it was everything I ever expected. But soon I was like 'is this it,'" he recalls.[5]

The anticlimax is real.

'I'm pissed off, is this what success is all about?/
*A bunch of n**** acting like bitches with big mouths/*
All this stress, all I got is this big house/
Couple of cars, I don't bring half of them shits out/'
– Jay Z, Success

"I got a lot of rich friends who are very sad," says Russell Simmons. "Success is when you can be in touch with the happy thing inside you. Other than that, there's no payment, no end to the amount of junk you could acquire – the next business, next girlfriend. There's always a next, until you get in the box."[6]

"I have friends that have a hundred times more money than me," adds the very wealthy CEO of Interscope Records Jimmy Iovine.[7] "But they don't have peace. They're quick at the draw, ready to fight, ready to go."

That's precisely the reason many, just like MC Hammer, will fall as they continue searching for that elusive fulfillment by any means.

"Most of the people I ever saw in the music industry ended up broke, dysfunctional or drug addicted, with no steady family," says No I.D.[8]

Desires of want never satisfy fully and all decay with time (think of the taste of the first gourmet pizza slice compared to the fifth, or the first ride on a roller coaster compared to the tenth). We dream about having something then once we get it realize we're still the same person with the same thoughts and feelings and the high we imagined doesn't last long. *'Funny how my old highs is suddenly my new lows,'* J Cole raps. "Eventually we feel caught on a treadmill, having to run faster and faster for rewards that mean less and less."[9] (In the business world it's called the 'Law of Diminishing Return'.)

(J Cole's song 'Love Yourz' is a perfect illustration of this point.)

'Seems as though you lost sight of what's important when depositin'/
Them checks into your bank account and you up out of poverty/
Your values is in disarray, prioritizin' horribly/
Unhappy with the riches 'cause you're piss poor morally'
– T.I., Live Your Life

"Success is supposed to be about accumulation and consumption," Jay Z writes in 'Decoded'. "But the finest meal ends up as shit, which is a great metaphor for the fact that consumption's flip side is decay and waste, and what's left behind is emptiness. Empty apartments, empty stomach, unused objects. Which isn't to say I don't like buying things and eating nice meals as much as the next person (okay, maybe even more), but success has to mean something beyond that."[10]

That's why having the correct motives will determine everything about the path you'll travel down. Understanding that real "success has to mean something beyond that" will separate the MC Hammer's from the Jay Z's.

'And Hammer went broke so you know I'm more focused/
I lost thirty mil, so I spent another thirty/
Cause unlike Hammer, thirty million can't hurt me/'
– Jay Z, So Appalled

P's & You's

So back to the initial question, why do you do it?

Motives can range from wanting to '*buy 80 Gold chains and go ign'ant*' to wanting to '*save the children.*' Most of us are somewhere in-between. In general motives can be categorized by whether you put *profit* or *purpose* first.

Profit means the end result, the final outcome – the check, the award, the fame, the materials, the power, the pleasure. Purpose means the work itself – the process, the contribution, the discovery.

Research shows those motivated *only* by profit have a hard time realizing their fantasies. Why? Because the journey to create something remarkable which deserves to exist in the world is hard, painfully hard, and if motivation does not come from the work itself it's almost impossible to keep at it, to persevere and battle on when things don't go as planned.

Those motivated only by money, fame, power, or pleasure want satisfaction now and typically don't have the inner strength to say 'no' to a short term trivial reward, for a much larger long term gain.

In the words of one of Hip Hop's wealthiest men, Sean Combs:

"I loved music so I never did it to make money. I could have [done] it for 10 years [waiting] for my opportunity…if you do it for money you're not gonna' be successful. Trust me. You have to be patient when you're trying to do something that you love. It doesn't' happen that quickly, there may not be an opportunity there, [but] just don't lose hope, don't lose faith. You have to be prepared to sacrifice and put in long hours of work and master the industry…"[11]

But instead of mastering the industry, those driven only by the end result will cut corners and put out 'good enough' products for a fast buck, or will try to follow hot trends. They'll create products with no emotional connection to themselves. You 'get what you give' *(pg. 322)* and the audience will not have a meaningful connection with the work either. These folks won't create classic, timeless products and in the long-run they'll be replaced by younger, hungrier money chasers.

As Talib Kweli commented: "If you're making music to get money stop right now, cause you'll fuck up everybody. You're disrespecting yourself, disrespecting the music. It's destructive…[There's] nothing wrong with getting money, but when you place that responsibility on the music it taints what you do, and you're gon' make a product that's less worthy, that's not worth paying for. So you shooting yourself in the foot…the money is gonna' come along with it."[12]

'Soldiers of fortune ain't never no match for soldiers of culture/'
– Talib Kweli, Learn Truth

Purpose over Money over Bullshit

Part of the reason Dr. Dre is the richest man in Hip Hop is the 'riches' are not his driving force. "It's always weird," Dre says, "when people approach me for an investment I tell them, 'I don't need any more money. I'm good.' Then I wait for their expression. That part is entertaining because people look at you like you're crazy when you say you don't need more money."[13]

The same is true of Jay Z. "He's smart as hell," Neil Cole, CEO of Iconix Brand Group, the company that bought Rocawear in 2007 for more than $200 million, told Men's Health Magazine. "He understands himself as a brand, and it's incredibly well thought out. We meet every week, and there's nothing impulsive about him. He's very consistent, and he won't settle. If something's not right, he's not going to do it for more money. He'll wait to get it right."

"In meeting with superstars about potential deals, there are some who spit out 'How much can I get?' and the meeting is over, because you know you're starting out on the wrong basis," adds Michael Rapino, CEO of Live Nation. "When we sat down with Jay Z [to put together the historic $150 million '360' business deal in 2008], 'How much money are you going to pay me?' came up in maybe the seventh conversation. The first conversation was, 'Can we change the business together?'"[14]

Because money is not the primary motivation, Dre and Jay are able to make well thought out decisions uncluttered by short term material desires.

They know money is a byproduct of creating art that deserves to exist in the world and benefits the lives of others, so they focus on what matters. As Russell Simmons teaches, "Always focus on your effort, instead of the results of that effort."[15] It's a lesson which applies to all areas of life.

If you're playing a sport and you're only focused on the end goal, the final score, you will probably lose as your mind is not 'in the moment,' you're tenser and take less risk. Or, if a scientist working to discover something new is mainly motivated by the fame and awards of a discovery, their mind is distracted and they will lose out to a scientist motivated by the discovery process itself, who's focused on the details and lives and breathes their research. Or, if you're a sales-person focused *only* on commission, instead of benefiting the prospect, you probably won't sell as much as you'll feel too anxious and instinctively press too hard trying to close.

'What you base your happiness on material, women and large paper?/
That's why you inferior not major/ '
– Nas, No Ideas Original

Nature's alarm clock

The people in this book are on the right side of the profit/purpose scale, (aka the riches/wealth scale). The fruit is important to them, but it is not the one and only focus. Their motivation for working is greater than that.

They're motivated more by the creative process, by expressing themselves, by representing their culture, by leaving a legacy, by reaching people's hearts and minds, by being the 'Greatest ever,' by a 'Divine Purpose.'

Their work is their passion so they obsess over, and put their heart into, it. It's another universal law that we do something better when it's made for the benefit of others, and the Greats in this book spend more time creating great products because they know the impact they want it to have on others.

These people naturally have the patience to overcome the slow learning process on their journey. They naturally apply the "number one advice" of Rick Ross (who spent 10 years building his rep in Florida) to: "Take your time, invest in yourself as much as possible. Take time to build your value up."

But understand that nobody is an evangelical saint, doing everything for the benefit of others or for the love of the work. Everybody in this book, even KRS–One, is also motivated by being able to purchase material objects which make life more comfortable. It's not wrong to think like that. The point is it is not the one and only guiding motive. Their work has a greater purpose.

'I'd be lying if I said I didn't want millions/
More than money saved, I wanna' save children/'
– Common, 6th Sense

Having a greater purpose ingrained in your psyche is the best alarm clock to get you out of bed in the morning. These higher level motivations can be broken down into:

- **Challenge**: of Raising the Bar, overcoming an obstacle and achieving a difficult goal.
  'The motivation for me was them telling me what I couldn't be'
  – Pharrell, So Ambitions

- **Mastery**: of your craft and feeling yourself get better.

- **Contribution**: of having a positive impact on the lives of other people.

One of the most-consistent artists around is Common. His debut album was released in 1992, and he has steadily built his career since. His character is one of the most stable in Hip Hop and he continually puts out quality products to his growing fan base, while maintaining his original core fans.

In his first ten years or so, he never achieved major commercial recognition, and although he did want that, it wasn't the only goal. That wasn't the main motivation. If it was, he would have quit after the first few albums to do something more profitable, or would have changed his style to sell a gangster image that was more popular and much easier to commercialize at the time. But he didn't. Common stayed true to himself and his lengthy career compared to the 'trend chasers' stands testament.

In his own words: "I love what it takes to achieve great things. I'm not afraid to work for it. I thrive on the slow progress born of struggle. Those are vital aspects of what motivates my life and gives me a sense of purpose."[16]

The same mentality unites practically all Greats. Like Kendrick Lamar who used his Aftermath signing advance to move his parents out of Compton: "I ain't even made my first big purchase yet. I live in Los Angeles and I don't even have a car. My ends go to take care of my family," he told Spin magazine in 2012. "I thought I wanted jewelry and cars, but as soon as I got a taste, I realized it wasn't fulfillment. A thrill is being as creative as possible and supporting the people I love."[17]

Or Kanye who explained his creative motivations: "Dopeness is what I like the most – people who wanna' make things as dope as possible, and by default, make money from it. The thing that I like the least, are people who only wanna' make money from things whether they're dope or not, and especially make money from making things the least dope as possible."[3]

Or Pharrell, who revealed: "Money is something that comes with the job when there's some demand, it's not the most important part of what we do. Videos confuse kid, they send messages glorifying material items….but the most important thing is I have the ability to go in everyday to create a song. That's something you can't replace. I'm still feeling euphoria every time I make a new track. It gets no better than that. All the Rolls Royce's in the world are never gonna be able to fuck with that."[18]

'I don't care about your rims, kids ride Big Wheels/
Up until they learn balance and it's obvious you haven't/ '
– Murs, And This Is For

Here are some more examples of the greater purpose's that motivate the lives of Hip Hop Greats:

Kanye:
"I'm on a pursuit of awesomeness. Excellence is the bare minimum" (VOYR, 2011)

"I realize I'm fighting a battle not just for myself but for a generation. A generation fighting against false information of the media and the perceptions people create and the matrix society creates and the lies and jokes people tell." (Zane Lowe, 2013)

"I was thinking about my funeral a couple days ago. Who would be at the funeral? I wanna have like world leaders that were affected. That said 'Kanye gave me my shot here' or 'he pushed me' or 'he told me to believe in myself' or 'when I saw this it made me feel like that'. I wanna affect people like that when I pass away." (VOYYR, 2011)

Kendrick Lamar:
"I've got to carry on the [West Coast Hip Hop] legacy. I can't half–ass anything that I do." (2012)

*'My momma believed in me, she let me use her van to go to the studio/
Even though she know her tank is empty, that's who I do it for/'
– Wanna Be Heard*

Tupac:
"Throughout my life I just wanted to be an angel for God, where I can be of some help." (Tupac: Resurrection, 2003)

*'My mission is to be more than just a rap musician/
The elevation of today's generation if I can make em listen/'
– Unconditional Love*

Jay Z:
"My job is to widen it to show you can mature in hip hop and still be relevant and still be cool." (CNBC, The Big Idea, 2006)

*'Ain't in it for the fame that dies within weeks/
Ain't in it for the money can't take it when you leave/
I wanna be remembered long after you grieve/
Long after I breathe/
I leave all I am in the hands of history'
– History*

Eminem:

"My daughter is what I'm living for, what I'm doing everything for…to make sure she gets best love and life possible." (UGHH, 1998)

"I'd love to be remembered as one of the best to ever pick up a mic… [Also] somebody who stood up for what I believe in 'don't back down, don't take shit from no one and do you'…. [Also I want to] lessen racial tension. I want to bring people together. I feel that can be my biggest contribution to hip hop." (The Way I Am, 2008)

'From the beginning, it wasn't bout the ends/
It was bout busting raps and standing for something/ '
– Survival

Lupe Fiasco:

"I'm always in purist to create the ultimate song for me. [Like, 'double burger with cheese' and 'failure'] I've touched the bottom of rappers heaven with those songs." (2-Cent TV, 2012)

'Then he put him down and went back to the kitchen/
And put on another beat and got back to the mission/
To get his momma out the hood/ '
– Hip Hop Saved My Life

Kid Cudi:

"All these kids at the shows make me wanna live. They're a big part of me wanting to stay on this planet. That's why they show up because they know that. They know I went through hell and I survived in order to inspire so nobody else could fall. If I fail, millions of other kids will fail. I cannot fail. I cannot fail." (Complex, 2014)

Diddy:

"[My purpose is] to inspire others and to show people what is possible. I want my life to be about more than just fame or jewelry or parties. Hip Hop has the power to change the world. I am here to lead by example."

T.I:

'My movie agent Brian always ask me what I'm rapping for/
Its passion; I wouldn't trade it for all the diamonds out in Africa/ '
– Like So

Drake:

"I think every time I say I'm about to do something, people are waiting for me to fumble. That's probably one of the biggest motivations behind a lot of my raps – the amount of people that want me to fall." (Google Music, 2011)

'On a mission to shift the culture/'
– Tuscan Leather

Dr. Dre:

"Kids are the ultimate form of motivation. They're watching. They're mimicking. They're an extension of you. So you have to win." (Esquire, December 2013)

J Cole:

"I'm here to spread a message of hope. Follow your heart. Don't follow what you've been told you're supposed to do."… "I think about my legacy, I want to be on everybody's list, everybody's top five. I would love be number one." (2012)

Will Smith:

"I want to do good. I want the world to be better because I was here. I want my life, my work, my family to mean something."
"I want to represent an idea. I want to represent possibilities. Represent the idea that you really can make what you want." (2007)

Jhene Aiko:

"To me, selling out means doing anything that's compromising who you are, your integrity, your beliefs. Like doing a song because everyone at the label says, 'This is the perfect song for you,' but it's about something crazy that I've never done or something that I don't have any connection to. If I do the song, that's selling out.

"I've been asked to write for people that I felt like it would be a really good paycheck probably, but I felt like it was too much of a compromise. And in my mind, that's selling out. The money is not the motivation for what I do." (THR 2014)

Rick Ross:

'Determined to be the best, not looking back at regrets/
How many people you bless, is how you measure success/'
– Shot To The Heart

With these motivations engrained in your character, how could you not achieve greatness?

You should find yourself examining your own motives for working while reading these quotes.

What is it that ultimately drives you to create? Who do you do it for?

Why do you do it?

* * *

But even if your higher purpose is guiding you, following your heart to do what you know is right can be a frightening decision. It can often mean going against the well intentioned wishes of those closest to us. To really live our own lives we need the confidence to embrace who we are and conquer the main force holding us all back:

Fear.

The Enemy

We are all soldiers in the world's greatest war between our FEAR and our FUTURE.

Greats know exactly which side they're on.

They all feel fear no doubt, but when they feel it they fight it. They charge at it. They destroy it, by DOING–THE–THING–THAT–CAUSED–THE–FEAR.

They know if they don't, the fear will grow inside them and take control of their lives.

As Will Smith says, "I'm motivated by fear. Fear of fear. I hate being scared to do something. I developed an attitude. I stated attacking things I was afraid of."[1]

'Can't run from the pain go toward it/'
– Jay Z, Lost Ones

Apart from some evolutionary survival responses in our DNA, we're born fearless. As we go through life will acquire more and more fears.

'God did not make me a fearful person/'
– Yasiin Bey, Champion Requiem.

Social fears of embarrassment, loneliness, expectation, judgment, failure; Material fears of losing possessions; Physical fears of death or disease; Spiritual fears of the unknown, and the greatest fear people have of just being themselves. Fear dominates the lives of weak characters.

'I think that all the silence is worse than all the violence /
Fear is such a weak emotion /
That's why I despise it/'
– Lupe Fiasco, Words I Never Said

Fear is the BIGGEST enemy holding back most people from their potential. Living in fear – not major fear, but subtle silent fear – is the greatest obstacle to a happy and fulfilled life. Letting fear control us means living deep inside our comfort zone. We will never be able to create things that impact the world if we are afraid to step out onto the edge. Like 50 Cent, who wrote a book on the subject, said, "People limit themselves. Fear doesn't allow people to be what they can."[2]

The process back to fearlessness requires going through pain, and is what ultimately separates those who live their life to the fullest and those who don't. Overcoming fear is part of our job as humans.[3]

For the names mentioned in this book, and people who are achieving their potential, fear is exciting. Fear is an opportunity to grow and develop as a person. Fear is a challenge to be overcome. And there is NOTHING like the feeling of concurring it.

Like Kendrick Lamar told the Guardian Newspaper: "At first, I was scared to show fear because you can never be sure how people will perceive you. But I dared myself to do it, to stand out. Now I'll talk about being beaten up or robbed or making a stupid decision because of a girl or whatever."

Kendrick lived with a fear of failure for a long time, but he pushes himself to overcome. He doesn't forget his past defeats with the 'fear monster' and uses them as lessons to not let it win again. Like an experience in High School: "This is always in my head: There was a math question that I knew the answer to, but I was so scared to say it. Then this little chick said the answer and it

was the right answer, my answer. That bothers me still to this day, bein'
scared of failure."[4]

'My biggest fear is not feeling accomplished/
Or turning back to that same accomplice/'
– Kendrick Lamar, The Heart Part 3

Kanye appears to be one of the most fearless humans on the planet. You
can see it through his art. Each of his albums boldly ventures into new,
unexplored territories to best express himself at that moment. Even working
on his second album, which most artists who have had a successful first
album are terrified to do, he showed no interest in just emulating the success
of 'The College Dropout.'

"If ever there was a time not to mess with the formula, this would be it,"
Jon Brion who co–produced the album 'Late Registration' says. "But he's
fearless. A lot of people have a governor on themselves, usually peer pressure
or fear of not being liked. This is a guy that is truly living by his tastes and his
beliefs."[5]

Aside from music, Kanye has repeatedly forced himself to do things that
he was initially afraid of. "He will walk on the killer's block even if he's not a
killer," says Dame Dash.[6] From when he was a no-name rapper publically
battling respected MC's like Common and Mos Def, to finding the courage
to speak up in a room full of Roc–A–Fella 'gangsters' in the late 90's, and
demanding attention from strangers and journalists, to calling for an end to
homophobia in Hip Hop, and recently when he admitting to being afraid to
wear a kilt on the Chicago leg of the Watch The Throne tour. He overcomes
these fears. He fights against them and keeps on pushing the envelope, and
that's why he is where he is today.

'I'm the only thing I'm afraid of/'
– Kanye West, Amazing

Jay Z was able to make the transition from the streets to the music business
because he let go of the fear of failure he felt over the failed Jaz-O–EMI deal
(pg.217). He'd been carrying the fear for years after the incident until he spoke
openly about it to his girlfriend. Talking made him realize that the failure
didn't even belong to him. He was able to overcome the fear, stop standing
in his own way, and move fully into the life he wanted.

'I move onward, the only direction/
Can't be scared to fail, in search of perfection/'
– Jay Z, On To The Next One

The mind is at war between the Reptile brain (which wants security, comfort, food and sex) and the God brain (which wants to create, learn and evolve). When we do something new the reptile usually wins.

We, like all animals, are built to survive so fear the unknown. We fear new or 'pressured' situations like performances, so we sweat, choke, blush, and rush like we're battling in the coliseum.

The reptile fear wants to keep us comfortable, in our place. It doesn't want to work or struggle or try to grow. It keeps us afraid of the consequences of doing something 'hard,' outside of our comfort zone. That's why, like Hip Hop exec Steve Stoute says, "If you don't have fear in what you're doing, it's probably something that's too easy for you to do. There has to be some level of tension in order to rise above."[7]

Recognize the fear. Write it down. Give it a name. This is the enemy stopping you from setting out to achieve your goals. This is your arch nemesis on your journey. Draw him. Give it a costume, a mask, a catchphrase. You need to know who you're battling against.

On your journey, when you encounter a fear that threatens to stop you: breathe deeply, face it down, recognize that it's just an obstacle put here to challenge and develop you as a person, and do it anyway. Do it anyway. Do it anyway. Like Eminem raps: *'Become Friends with the Monster'*.

That is how fear is beaten. The feeling you get from doing this is indescribable. Afterwards you'll be excited to face it down again and again.

Around his first album's release in 2010 Drake remembers: "I used to have this mentality where I'd be at the Grammys or at the MTV awards, sitting at my seat, saying, 'Oh, God, I hope they cancel my performance, or maybe the stage will break and I won't have to do this tonight – I'm nervous.' Like, on tour, I'd say, 'I hope something happens where they have to clear the building, and we'll get one night off.' But now I'm just like, 'Man, I hope they give me five extra minutes.'"[8]

Manifested

When the thing that we most fear happens to us we lose the fear. Sometimes it comes without us asking. In fact, some like Dame Dash believe the mind is so powerful that it manifests the thing we continually fear most. For Dame this happened when he was fifteen.

Dame's mother taught him about the power of the mind and how 'thoughts are things.' She taught him that to think of something is to give it power. As a teen one thing he thought about a lot was his mother dying. It was an uncomfortable thought which kept intruding his brain and made him seek out distractions to silence it. One day standing idly on the block the thought was accompanied by an odd sensation. He ran home to find his mother had suffered a respiratory attack and died. The thought had manifested and Dame understood what his mother was trying to teach.

"My worst fear was losing my mom and when I lost her it was confronting my fear, and being it was at such a young age, I never had fear of anything."[9]

(Although analyzing Dame's career it might be said that he did have a fear, and again that fear did manifest itself. His fear was that the Roc-A-Fella 'Circle of Success' would break-up and that made him anxious. He saw 'outsiders' as enemies, trying to harm the circle so got defensive (which others labeled 'arrogant'). He thought Def Jam executives like Lyor Cohen and Kevin Liles were trying to steal Roc artists and reacted like a pit-bull protecting his master – (see the Hard Knock Life Tour video with Dame and Kevin). He fired people close to Jay Z, like Carline Balan and business manager John Meneilly, perhaps in part because he feared they were getting too close to Jay and trying to push him out (Jay rehired both soon after). Dame's seemingly erratic, some would say 'bullying,' behavior came from a deep place of insecurity and fear, but it is the thing which ultimately made those fears a reality when the Roc broke apart.)

For Kanye the 2009 VMA awards marked a turning point for squashing his remaining fears. Speaking about the success of his MBDTF album he said:

"I always thought I could do anything. But now I'm so fearless. To do an album after the year I had [the Taylor Swift incident, and resulting drama]. After all the 'your career's over,' 'die n**** die,' 'you'll never make music again,' 'we estimate 250K first week,' to do 600K [album sales] first week…You can't take anything away from me at this point…I completely lost everything but I gained everything because I lost the fear."[10]

The first time you stare off with fear is the hardest no doubt. But like lifting weights at the gym, the more you do it the stronger your 'courage muscle' becomes, and in time nothing inside you will stop you from doing anything out in the world.

Death

The car parked outside Jackson's grandparents' home on a side street of Jamaica Queens, where average incomes are half the average of New York, silently waited for its passengers. Jackson felt a twinge whenever he was out in the open, exposed, like a mouse caught in the spotlight. He had upset local drug bosses recently by blowing off a truce-calling meeting between him and a rival dealer, and knew that caused disrespect. But he also knew that he wouldn't be around these streets for long. He was starting to make moves in music (having just been signed to Colombia Records) and wanted to distance himself from the underground world.

After scanning the street for any dangers from his grandmother's living room window, Jackson walked over to his friend's car. He took the rear seat while his friend sat behind the wheel.

About to pull off, Jackson realized he forgot a piece of jewelry, so rushed inside to fetch it and said goodbye again to his three-year-old son in the living room, and grandmother, enjoying the afternoon sun in the front yard.

Jackson was totally unaware that a stranger was watching his every move from a distance. As he retook his seat in the rear, the stalker silently pulled his car behind Jackson's and, with a hood covering his face in shadow, strode to the rear window.

Jackson turned to look into the eyes of a masked man carrying a 9mm handgun. Within a few of seconds the gunman emptied his rounds into the car. Nine shots pierced Jackson's body.

Jackson, aka 50 Cent, was a literal inch away from death.

Though this is an extreme example it illustrates the reason many Hip Hop icons show little fear – the environment they grew up in puts 'fears' in perspective.

"On the streets, showing fear would make people lose respect for you," says 50 Cent. "You would end up being pushed around and more likely to suffer violence because of your desire to avoid it."

Many, if not most, Hip Hop icons experienced friends or family being killed when they were growing up. Some almost died themselves. Death was everywhere, so from an early age they came to terms with it and realized since death is coming anyway, fear is pointless.

"When I nearly died it made me think – this can happen again any second. I better hurry and do what I want," 50 continues. "I started to live like I never lived before. When the fear of death is gone, then nothing can bother you and nothing can stop you."[12]

And as 50's life shows, with fear beaten the world is yours. "He's so confident and calm, and so full of power...because he was inches from dying, nothing fazes him," says Robert Green, who wrote a book on fear with 50.

"What can be more powerful attitude in life, than nothing fazes you? Being around him I thought 'I wanna feel like that.'"[13]

'Whether win lose or draw, believe death is waiting for all/'
– Akon, Hustlers Story

Most people try to ignore death. They live in a delusion that it doesn't exist and they have all the time in the world. But Greats do the opposite. They acknowledge, accept and embrace death. Their life is weighed up against death and they see everything in proportion. It gives them a sense of urgency and mission. They focus on what's really important to them and ignore petty distractions that don't matter in the Grand Scheme. They adopt a fearless mentality and come to appreciate life and live it to the fullest. When the time to die comes they are at peace because they did all they could and wanted to do.

'Still giving you our all like the coffins near/'
– Pusha T, Christina Dior Denim Flow

This is what Kanye West came to realize after his near fatal car accident in 2002. "Now [after the accident] I'm just not scared of death. Everything I do is as if I already passed away. Every move I make, I live like I've already passed away – like I have nothing to lose."[14]

'To the day I die, I'm gonna touch the sky/'
– Kanye, Touch The Sky

In the documentary 'Tupac: Resurrection', 'Pac revealed that he had received a prophecy of his early death, and that became the motivation for him to record as much material as he could before the prophecy was realized.

"He was the type of guy to go in the studio and complete five songs in one day," remembers Dr. Dre.[15] Since Pac's passing, eight full albums have been released, all but one going multi-platinum.

'Death or success, is what I quest cause I'm fearless/'
– Tupac, The Streetz R Deathrow

The point is summarized by Jay Z in 'Decoded':

> "This is why we shouldn't be afraid. There are two possibilities: One is that there's more to life than the physical life, that our souls 'will find an even higher place to dwell' when this life is over. If that's true, there's no reason to fear failure or death. The other possibility

is that this life is all there is. And if that's true, then we have to really live it – we have to take it for everything it has and 'die enormous' instead of 'living dormant,' as I said way back on 'Can I Live.' Either way, fear is a waste of time."[16]

'Can you even fathom not having a fear in the world?/
I'm cool in my afterlife if I'm reading these chapters right/ '
– Jay Z, People Talkin'

And in the end, which feeling is worse: Fear just in the present moment, or regret for all life's future ones?

'Fuck what they talking, it ain't like life come often/
Only thing worse than death is a regret filled coffin/
So try before you die or always wonder what if?/ '
– J Cole, Crunch Time

One practical way to keep death and the 'bigger picture' in mind is to add your own death date to your calendar.

You can search for 'life expectancy calculator' online (livingto100.com for example) and find the statistically likely day you will stop existing on this planet. Put that date in your diary or calendar and just reflect on it for a while.

People who have done this have noted how it is strangely calming and really puts their life into perspective. 'This is me now, this is how much time I have left.' With that in mind, the fear of doing something naturally melts into irrelevance.[17]

Other Ways to Combat Fear

The Natural Way:

As mentioned in the introduction there is a natural way of living life, which is built into all our DNA's and automatically brings the results people try to teach with 'tips and techniques.' The natural way not to feel fear comes back to your 'Why?'

If you make art/product because you're motivated by getting the most sales/winning awards/being the biggest/fame/ or anything else you can't directly control, you probably will be scared of failure (and consequently won't be bold and go near the edges. Your work won't stand out, and you won't achieve your idea of success).

But if you're motivated by a higher purpose, by creating something for yourself, by feeling good about yourself, by possibly helping others, you're not worried about things you can't control (like the sales or recognition) as much, so instead of feeling fear, you will naturally feel inspired to do things that 'expand your comfort zone' and go near the edge.

The Bigger Picture:

Another method which, if practiced, will subdue fear is about getting in touch with the deepest part of *you*. If we can live outside of our body, our shell, and directly from our spirit, our conscious, all our fears become part of our body, not a part of the real us. So when we're in a situation we would normally feel fear, worry or anxiety, we can recognize it and try to distance our 'real selves' from our bodies. Like legendary Interscope CEO Jimmy Iovine says, "The thing about seeing the big picture and being self-aware is knowing that it's not about you. It's about the big picture. It's not about you. It's not. This is not about you."[18]

One way to live through our higher-selves is meditation *(pg.159)*.

The Faith:

'I hope the picture painted clear/ If your heart filled with faith then you can't fear/ '
– T.I, No Matter What

Having such strong faith in yourself, your *why*, and your future can override any emotions of fear in the present. You know that you are Greater than who you actually are right now, so the obstacle in front of you becomes minor. Nothing you can't handle. This is also an effective way to deal with the 'Fear of Success' (the third most common fear after failure and death).

But how do you develop this faith, this belief?

The
Core

"A lot of people ask me how did I get where I'm at?
It's my belief, like, I believe so strong, so crazy....
...The power to believe...
I believe in God the most, and after that myself."

— Sean Combs[1]

The cool night air blew backstage into the lungs of the two performers, carrying with it roars from 20,000 ecstatic worshipers. Kanye breathed deep. This was the, '$75,000,000 grossing,' 'sold-out-in-minutes,' 'Watch the Throne' tour at Madison Square Garden. Arguably the best Hip Hop show in history, starring the two biggest icons in urban music. A milestone in each of their careers. Although to Kanye this was always expected.

"I always knew it was gonna happen like this," he said during the 2011 tour. "This point I'm at right now is where I was when I was 4 years old."[2]

Ever since he was a child, in his mind, Kanye has been at the forefront of Hip Hop. To him the rise to global super producer/rapper/designer was inevitable. He played it out thousands of times in his head. He visualized himself as the best in the world – what is would feel, sound, taste, and smell like. With time, belief in himself and his potential for greatness became a natural part of his being, like his eyes, hair and heart. It was just a natural part of him. With that belief as his backbone it was then just about steadily bringing his vision to reality.

"You always got to see the end goal and everything else is just filling in the blanks."[2]

Without a doubt, this self-belief is the single most important trait that has enabled Kanye to overcome countless obstacles and *Touch The Sky*.

In the words of producer Jon Brion:

> "Everyone in the country is in therapy and spending all their money on self-help books so their little internal voice will be able to say, 'I am good and I am OK.' If you're going to believe all the stuff about positive thinking and self–actualization, that we affect our environment by the way we think about ourselves, do you want a better example than Kanye West? Fuck Tony Robbins. Kanye West should have infomercials!"[3]

We'll get to the practicalities of how Kanye, Diddy and others develop and maintain such strong belief, but first there are some related topics we need to address: Belief vs. Wish, Craziness, Bad Vibes, and Doubt.

Belief or Wish?

We all have dreams. The question is whether dreams come from a core self-belief (like Kanye) or whether they come from wishes (like most others).

A hope or a wish is external. It comes in the moment and is forgotten almost as quickly as it's wished for. There is a big gap between the wish and the wisher, the hope and the hoper.

'He hoped and he wished it but it didn't fall in his lap/ So he ain't even here…'
– Eminem, Airplanes

Most people can hype themselves up and 'believe' in themselves for a short amount of time; *'The world is mine'*. However, this feeling is external and vanishes quickly when obstacles get in the way; *'Life's a Bitch'*. This is why just learning 'techniques' and 'methods' on 'How To' do something is not enough. This learning will create an immediate buzz, but a belief has not been internalized and become a part of your character. The motivation you feel will soon fade away, like the sunlight gradually disappearing. Dreams that might have been beliefs become memories.

Eventually people accept their life as it is, and lose the desire to change. As they age their belief becomes 'I have no control over life,' so they believe in conspiracy theories and 'powers' holding them down. As Paulo Coelho writes in 'The Alchemist' (a book Pharrell describes as his "personal bible"[31]): "At a certain point in our lives, we lose control of what's happening to us, and our lives become controlled by fate.' That's the world's greatest lie."

'My uncle used to have all these things on his bucket list/
And now he's acting like 'oh well that's life I guess'/ '
– Drake, Too Much

But a deep seated belief in yourself, your talents, your purpose, is a part of your very being. It is the un-tearable paper that the map of your journey is printed on. Self-belief means that you are able to overcome the lows and won't quit when nobody else believes, or when things are going badly, but will just adjust the plan on the indestructible paper of belief and keep on.

There's no such thing as wishing or praying something into existence. There is definitely such a thing as believing in yourself enough to bring something into existence.

In the short term a person will be knocked around about by events and by others like a beach ball. But in the long run, it's been proven over and over again that our lives will follow our deepest held beliefs.

If you believe you'll live in the same neighborhood and work the same job till you die, that's what will happen to you. If you believe you will be the 'voice of a generation,' that is how you will see the world, act and live. In time (and in accordance with practicing other principles) that is how the world will see you, and that is what you will become.

In the words of Sean Combs: "I've never doubted myself. I go into it knowing I'm one of the baddest motherfuckers that ever lived. Not even in cocky way. I just feel I'm one of the baddest motherfuckers to ever walk the face of the earth. Just how I am. Just a fact."[1]

Once true belief is a part of you, you cannot stop it from shaping the reality you want, the world you see, and the way the world sees you.

Like the people who encounter Kanye's self-belief firsthand who can do nothing but admire and try to emulate him. As Common said to him, "We started working together, and your confidence was contagious. Your belief in yourself – and in me – brought me back in tune with my potential."[4]

Sticman from the group Dead Prez, who influenced Kanye in finding his rap style, adds: "When I met 'Ye I met a brother who believed in himself so much that it taught me some things about self-confidence. So much so that the confidence came in the room with him. He felt like 'Y'all gonna see, the world gonna see.'"[5]

The Importance of Being Crazy

'Think It, Say It, Do It' is one of Kanye's personal proverbs.

"I love saying what I think because it keeps me accountable. Once I say it, I feel like I have to do it and I love proving to everyone that I can!"[6]

Examples of this in action include, claiming in 2001 – a time when nobody (not even his closest friends) believed he could survive as a solo artist – that he would release a number one debut album. And more recently, Kanye stated that he will "spearhead the world's first trillion dollar company."[7]

These fantastically ambitious verbalized goals can seem a million miles away to some. They don't understand Kanye's belief, drive or vision so label him (at best) as 'arrogant' or 'crazy.'

For instance Talib Kweli remembers Kanye's 'verbalized prophesies' when working together in 2001. "He was never little Kanye West. He was always a legend in his mind. Kanye used to say things to me that I used to be like 'this n****'s out of his mind'. But then three years later it came true and I didn't know what I was talking about!"[8]

Looking at the lives of Greats, they will all have gone through similar skepticisms from unbelievers.

"People call me crazy," says Diddy. "You know what, I think 'yep. I was crazy enough to believe what I was saying was gonna happen. That's why I was persistent enough to exist now.'"

'Saw it all before, some of y'all thought I was crazy, maybe/'
– Jay Z, G.F.F

'Craziness' is a necessity to achieve 'remarkable' things. "There's a delusional quality that all successful people have to have," says Will Smith.[9]

You have to believe your offering to the world is valuable, especially if it is an innovation nobody else in history has done before. To most people you are crazy, and so a deep self-belief is necessary to not let this stop you.

For instance Jay Z could easily have quit when faced with the 10 years of record label rejection (from 1986 – 96):

> "I guess it's the confidence that you have in yourself. You know, you've got to have confidence to believe that you can do it. Because when the doors were shut for me as far as someone signing me to a record label and putting out my material, I could have easily said, 'that's it, I'm not good enough, this is not for me'.
>
> But I didn't do that. I did it the other way. I was like, 'OK, you're a big, multi–million dollar conglomerate, you don't know what you're talking about'. That's tough for someone to say, to look in the face of that huge company and say, 'you're wrong, and I'm going to prove your wrong.'"[10]

'Nobody believe, until I believe me/'
– Common, The People

"You have to be crazy in a positive way," Diddy continues. "You can't believe in the reality that's presented in front of you. You have to believe you can be as great as you can be. In our society we're not inspired to do that. We're not inspired to dream big"

He's right. Our society is crawling with Dream Killers.

Bad Vibes

'Could have let the dream killers kill my self-esteem/'
– Kanye, Ego

When trying to achieve 'Greatness' in average environments, many people around you won't understand.

"There are people that are projecting their fears and their shortcomings and failures on you," says Jay Z. "People telling you 'you can't do that', because they don't believe that they can do it. It's not really about you, it's about their fear. [So] you have to be strong and resilient enough to believe in whatever it is you're trying to do."[11]

These 'unbelievers' Jay speaks about live in fear of the unknown (the space between your reality and your dreams is an unknown), and will project their fears onto others. As Talib Kweli observes, "Kanye is so passionate that if you have no passion in your life you're gonna feel threatened. You're gonna feel small around him, because you [think] 'why is he so sure of himself, and I'm so unsure?'"[12]

Often the 'unbelievers' will project these fears by telling 'dreamers' around them to 'be realistic'.

'You need to get your cranium checked/
You're thinking like an alien it just aint realistic/'
– Eminem, Airplanes

Being realistic is the opposite of being Great. "Being realistic is the most commonly travelled road to mediocrity," agrees Will Smith. "What's the point in being realistic?"

Every invention, from electricity to airplanes, was once seen by most as 'unrealistic.' That means all human progress depends on the few people who think and act unrealistically, refusing to accept the reality that's presented.

This is Jay Z's "best advice" to people trying to come–up: "Have such strong belief in yourself that you can quiet down all outside noise. You need that every step of the way."[11]

When Russell Simmons and Rick Rubin founded Def Jam in 1984, people literally laughed in their face. Music execs saw Hip Hop as a cheap fad in inner city ghettos (some even saying they, "would hang themselves if Hip Hop stayed around"[13]), and the two founders were trying to make it a legitimate popular form of music through radio play and concerts. Their belief in themselves and their vision enabled them to overcome these negative voices, and Def Jam went on to impact youth culture around the world in so many ways that it deserves its own book.

Kanye was able to overcome the small thinking, mediocrity and 'realisticness' around him, when he was trying to get respected as a rapper *(pg.37)*, by not letting others shape his belief, and used the 'dream killers' as motivation.

'Somebody told me success is the best revenge/
So they going to be fucked up when you do ya thing on 'em/'
– Kanye, Gossip Files

And even once he overcame the oceans of doubters in the industry and established himself in entertainment Kanye continued to face scores of opposition. Like when he released the singing-rapping 808's & Heartbreak in 2008. At the time many said he'd "fallen off," but really 'Ye was just ahead of his time, and now those songs get the biggest response at his concerts.

'So I don't listen to the suits behind the desk no more/'
– Kanye, Last Call

Kanye said to MTV in 2005:

> "It just shows you how far you can take it when you dream and you talk it into fruition, and you don't let people kill your dreams, and you don't let people tell you, 'Why would you think that big?'
>
> What's wrong with aspiring for greatness?
>
> I want this to be five stars. I want it to be perfect. I want to take over the world. And then people say, 'It's kind of cocky to think that.' How's that?"[14]

Society's role in knocking people's self-belief is an important point to understand. Classism (prejudice against people of 'lower class' (like those who own 'inferior' products (clothes, phones, cars…) – which Kanye describes as 'Racism's cousin') is a large part of our culture. It breeds self-hate and keeps people self-consciously looking down. Kanye believes people are controlled, held back and slowed down by the perceptions of themselves, and most people's perception of themselves comes from what those around them think or expect. So when they look in the mirror, most don't see themselves through their own eyes, they see themselves through family/friends/society's eyes.

According to 'Five Percenters,' 85% of the population are in this category, akin to elephants being conditioned never to try and remove a flimsy rope from their leg. If a person is taught they can't do anything, they believe they can't do anything, and they won't do anything.

"We live in a world where we're taught to have strong self-worth, but are criticized when we really do that...we're taught to feel badly and get used to it." says Kanye's mother, the late Donda West.[15]

On his album 'Yeezus' when Kanye makes a statement like 'I am a God' what does that mean? The 'realistic' majority would brush it off as an arrogant child-like rant. But to Kanye (and other Greats like Nas who has tattooed 'God's Son' on his belly) it means taking control of your life and of your future. It means not waiting for something or somebody so save you, but working to adapt yourself and the world around you to achieve whatever goals you want.

To call oneself a 'God,' to empower yourself causes so much resentment, in part, because most people's aspirations are limited – ("grow up, get married, have a kid, drive a Volvo, do our taxes, invest in something, find a hobby," says Pharrell[31]) – and can't understand this frame of mind, *'try to dim your lights till you be humble'*. But Greats have a self-belief that allows them to think Big, Really Big – which is why they are Big, Really Big. *'You know I'm gon' shine like a million watts'* – Jay Z, F.U.T.W

Doubt

Even 'Gods,' with seemingly bulletproof self-belief will go through insecurity and doubts. 'Is this what I'm meant to be doing?' 'Can I go on?'

'Dog, I was having nervous breakdowns/
Like "Man - these n**** that much better than me?"'
– Kanye, Touch The Sky

Even Kanye admits that often his 'arrogance' is really an act to build up his self-esteem to be able to stand up to the negative forces around and inside him, in order to overcome the monstrous goals he sets himself.

"A lot of times arrogance is to combat insecurity. So in order for me to go out and do what I've done, facing insecurity and facing people telling me I couldn't do it, I had to build a force field around myself...I had to be a borderline lunatic to think that I could do what I've done. It's crazy. What I've accomplished is crazy!"[16]

For most people the forces of doubt override the forces of belief and drown their dreams. When doubt does creep in it's important not to let it dwell in the mind, but to replace the thought with a positive like, *'I Will Overcome'* and to visualize yourself already successful. Take control of your mind and convert negatives to positives. Feed the mind with positives and eventually there will be very few dark spots for doubt to lurk.

This comes naturally to people listening to their inner voice/conscience/soul/God, telling them, deep down, that 'this is right.'

'Never doubt it or allowed that shit to phase me yo/
Just switch my thoughts up like the stations on the radio/'
– J Cole, Last Call

What's more, the best performers in any industry actually like to have doubts. They often have more doubts than outsiders and constantly question themselves because they know doubts can push them to raise the bar even higher.[17] "I'm totally scared of falling off. Just imagine if I woke up one day and I was wack. What would I do then?" Kanye said in 2005.[18]

Greats can transfer their doubts into creativity and positivity (e.g. to work harder) because that's how they've programmed their minds.

'What have I learned since getting richer?/
I learned working with the negatives can make a better picture/'
– Drake, HYFR

You have achieved a true self-belief when you can say *'This is me. This is who I am. No matter what happens, what anyone says or does to me, I will achieve this.'* You have a true self-belief when you have an unshakable feeling of relaxed inevitability that something will come, or as J Cole said of his state of mind before landing a deal with ROC Nation, "I always felt that success was just around the corner."

So, how do we develop this belief?

The Affirmation

Affirmation is a technique used by successful people in every industry, from artists to executives, to build a deep, unshakable faith in themselves and their goals. It's about making the dream real and living it every day. That means always keeping your end goals in mind, and when your mind wanders bringing it back to focus. It's about believing something so strongly that it becomes part of you and in time becomes self-fulfilling.

> *'Please may these words be recorded/*
> *To serve as testimony that I saw it all before it/*
> *Came to fruition, sort of a premonition/ '*
> *– Jay Z, Grammy Family Freestyle*

The Process:

1. Decide
What do you want to achieve? What is your goal?

In 2002 Kanye decided what he was going to do. "I'm gonna release an album and come out number one. If not first album, then second album, if not second album then third album."[19] He said this at a time when 95% of the people around him would literally laugh at this seemingly 'ridiculous' statement. He decided. He claimed it.

Your decision could be anything that is meaningful to you. It could be to 'graduate from college,' 'be a loving parent,' 'lose XX pounds,' 'live through my Higher Purpose,' 'develop bulletproof confidence.' What do you want?

Experts in the subject recommend focusing on one goal at a time. It needs to be believable to you, so you shouldn't be overly impressed with it. You should also have control over it. For example, you can control the quality of your product, and to an extent the number of sales, but not necessarily winning an award.

2. Visualize

Picture yourself already successful. Picture in your mind how you will feel when the goal is achieved, and see people responding. For example your product is in stores, you're performing in stadiums, you're standing on the podium, you're receiving a certificate etc.

'I still miss being a senior/
And performing at all those open mic events/
High schools, eyes closed seeing arenas/ '
– Chance The Rapper, Acid Rain

This is one of Jay Z's biggest secrets to success. "I always used visualization the way athletes do, to conjure reality."[20]

"It's about putting that in the air and manifesting it. I felt I would manifest all these things, but I didn't [necessarily] know where it would come from."[21]

'World can't hold me, too much ambition /
Always knew it'd be like this when I was in the kitchen/ '
– Jay Z, On To The Next One

Before even releasing an album, Ab Soul had his third Grammy speech prepared. "He really sees it," says co-president of his label Punch. "He sees himself where he wants to be…you have to have a vision of what you're doing. See yourself actually doing it first, then everything will fall into place."[22]

When Kanye got braces as kid and his cousin asked why, he replied, "Because I'm going to be on TV."[15] Before he had a record deal, Kanye would blow up any magazine coverage of himself and hang it around his house to visualize himself as a star.

In 2002 Kanye tattooed on his arm the names of nine songs he produced which represent principles he tries to follow in life, like 'The Truth,' 'Nothing Like It' and 'Hey Mama'. He told MTV, in 2002 (before he had a record deal and when NOBODY saw him as a rapper): "These are songs that changed my life, or mean something at a point in my career. That's why when my family is in a million dollar home and kids say 'Dad why can't I get no tattoos but you got that' I be like, 'look, this tattoo is the reason why we here.'"

During a performance at Prospect Park, Brooklyn in 2007, KRS-One reflected back on his life:

"I hope that I am inspiring someone tonight to go after their dreams because right here, in 1980, I was homeless. I was sleeping right here. Me and a couple other guys used to visualize…I used to say, 'Yo one day we gon' rock this park'… It's so crazy because I'm in my dreams right now!"[23]

'My third eye make me shine like jewelry/ '
– Rakim, Follow the Leader

3. Write

Write your affirmation in the 1st person and in the present tense, as if you have already achieved it. For example, 'I am a first class college graduate,' 'I have a thousand customers.' 'I am a corporate partner,' 'I weigh a hundred and fifty pounds,' 'I am the owner of the most successful restaurant in town,' 'I have an open, curious mind,' 'I am the voice of a generation.'

Damien Scott, J Cole's friend, remembers Cole using this technique before being signed to Roc Nation:

"Even though he was still working a bullshit job, and money wasn't flowing as well as he'd like, he believed in his heart of hearts that he was going to make it. One day I went up to his room and saw a bank statement taped to his wall right near his bed. I took a closer look and saw his bank balance with a bunch of handwritten zeroes behind it. 'If I keep that number in mind,' he told me, 'I'm going to get it. I swear.'"[24]

You could use words or images. For instance, years before Drake became successful in music, he Googled 'biggest residential pools in California,' and used an image of a mansion as his computer desktop background. He'd see the image several times a day, visualizing that life. A few years later he's literally swimming in the exact same pool that was once a picture.[25]

4. Repeat

Repeat your affirmation throughout the day, (some set a goal of repeating it one hundred times a day, every day). While saying it run through images in your mind, imagining success. Combine visualization and affirmation. You should feel excited when repeating your affirmation, as this creative process towards achieving your goals is exciting. Many people will look in the mirror after waking up and repeat the affirmation to themselves. (Studies show its best to do one hundred 'affirmation reps' in one sitting.)

To professional athletes this is standard practice. When preparing for a race or game, they envision themselves performing perfectly over and over again in their mind. When their mind wanders, or a negative thought enters, they force it to focus on the event and repeat the movie again and again. There is astounding evidence showing the positive effect of this on the brain – it literally rewires itself.

The 'Greatest Ever,' Muhammad Ali said, "It's the repetition of affirmations that leads to belief. And once that belief becomes a deep conviction, things begin to happen."

5. Say It Loud

Say it and share it with others to make it more 'real.'

This is what Kanye is famous for. Years before he had a record deal he was telling people what he would do. He puts his dreams in the air to "bring them into fruition," he says.

This requires a large amount of confidence and belief in self. Saying dreams out loud not only creates more pressure on you to make it happen, but also opens you up to naysayers and negativity, which may disrupt your path for a while if you haven't developed the inner strength to handle it.

Nas has tattoos that read 'Gods Son' and the face of Malcom X, to reinforce his personal mission. Rick Ross has tattoos all over his body with his dreams, from 'millionaire,' which when realized was replaced with 'billionaire,' to 'boss.' "I believe in speaking shit into existence," he says.

In 2005 an unknown rapper called J Cole walked around wearing custom shirts with 'Producer for Jay Z or Die Trying' written on. Five years later he ain't dead.

'I say it then you see it, it aint only in the music/ '
– Jay Z, Illest Mothfucker Alive

Right now Greats are putting their affirmations in the air. Kanye speaks about building the "biggest brand ever" with DONDA. Dave Free of Top Dawg Entertainment was asked 'What dream do you have for the label?' and answered, "I don't have a dream, I know what's gonna happen. We gonna be the biggest ever. Period. There's not even a question in my mind." The world will witness live their affirmations turning to reality.

+   Thank

Express gratitude regularly for your life. Be grateful for every object, person, thought or situation, which enters your mind. Be grateful for all the experiences currently around you, (no matter how seemingly negative they seem), knowing they will be useful to you in the future. Be grateful that it's all part of the journey – (see 'Love Fate' *pg. 324*).

Big Sean's 'Thank you,' is an entire song devoted to expressing sincere gratitude. He even rhymes: *'thank you to the devil for trying to bring me down'*.

'Thank you for every wrong turn I made in life/
Just remember, three lefts is the same as goin' right/ '
– Big Sean, Thankyou

* * *

Understand this process is not magic. It works because of Cognitive Dissonance. The brain can't hold and believe in two contradicting facts at the same time. It can't think 'I am fat, I am thin' or 'I am an A student, I am an F student,' at the same time for very long. Having two opposing thoughts creates discomfort so the brain sticks with the thought that is easiest to accept. The person then believes that thought.

Repeating enough times 'I am...,' and visualizing success, creates cognitive dissonance at first, but eventually the brain accepts it as a fact. It can't accept its current reality and has to make that affirmation its new reality. It becomes normal to achieve the goal and anything else is unacceptable. The actual neurons in the brain change.

You know that this process is working when you begin to see your goal as extremely realistic, that 'success is just around the corner.'

The brain's default thoughts become success. These new thoughts will naturally produce the motivation, hunger, pursuit and perseverance, to ensure that you make it to the new destination your mind has been set to, and your thoughts come to fruition.

With this affirmation as the bedrock we can overcome the inevitable dips on our quest. We cultivate the strength of mind to handle slow progress and temporary failure, and it is quitting that becomes difficult.

Rick Ross, who used affirmation constantly on his come-up, said of his success: "I can't say I knew I was going to be here, but I can say I knew I would do whatever it took to be here."[26]

Similarly Kendrick Lamar says he has been "premeditating" on his 'good kid m.A.A.d city' album for several years. He was shouting out the album title since his earliest mixtape in 2003, and has been holding on to the album artwork for years. "What I think happened is I visualized that for so long, throwing that into the universe, [that] it finally comes into play."[27]

The Crown

Once your belief is affirmed as a part of you, you behave like royalty.

The Greatest people in history have crowned themselves long before anyone has given them a crown. They are successful long before anyone sees their success. They act like winners long before they officially are.

'I could tell the future of a dude how his stance is/ '
– Nas, Trust

How you carry yourself, what you say, what you do, all reflect what you think of yourself and your future. The Crown Principle[28] says 'Act like you have already achieved your goal.' Or as Russell Simmons teaches, "You have to live your life as if you are already where you want to be."[29]

In the words of Rick Ross again, "You need to know you're a boss before you even blow, you gotta feel that in your heart and carry yourself in that manner...you need to think I'm worth way more than what I got, so that's how I'm going to look at myself."

Wear a crown and carry yourself with the tranquil confidence and self-assurance of a prince who knows he was born to ascend the throne and eventually you will.

When nineteen year old Sean Combs began interning at Uptown Records he says, "I really went in there like I was gonna' be the greatest record executive of all time."[30] And just a few of years later the world witnessed what he believed.

When you believe you are destined for great things, 'Greatness' will radiate outwards, like a crown or halo creating an aura around a king or angel. This radiation will affect people around you who think you must have reason to feel so confident. Those you connect with will sense you're going to rise to the top. Like Kendrick Lamar's label mate Ab Soul commented, "When I think back, I felt like [Kendrick] was glowing. He thought he was the best, he didn't even have to say it, I just felt the energy."[26]

'Always remember that your royalty/'
– Lupe Fiasco, Heart Donor

Recap:

So first, and after considering the previous three chapters, write down what you want to achieve.

"I want to.."

To make sure these are not just wishes, they need to be internalized as beliefs, and turned into 'I Will' statements. They need to be made into definite goals, continually at the forefront of your mind. "This is what *I will* do." Then go further. Claim it. Own it. 'I will' becomes:

"I AM.."

Then we can "glow" like K-Dot.

The Story Of

Kendrick Lamar

Freshly born Kendrick Lamar Duckworth came home from the hospital in a loud rickety car. His father had Big Daddy Kane on blast through the vehicles speakers, bumping his head as he gleefully drove his first son to their home in the city of Compton. From then on rap would be part of Kendrick's life.

Kendrick's parents (along with dozens of uncles, aunts and cousins) moved from Southside Chicago to Compton, California in 1984, to get away from the destructive gang culture consuming the area. However, they found Compton wasn't much different – a cracked city flooded with drugs in the 80's cocaine epidemic and divided by Crypts, Bloods, and other gangs. Many in Kendrick's family soon relapsed into the gang life.

"I'm 6 years old, seein' my uncles playing with shotguns, sellin' dope in front of the apartment," Kendrick remembers. "My moms and pops never said nothing, 'cause they were young and living wild, too."[1]

Kendrick grew up with a close relationship to both parents – a rare thing in an environment where many are raised by, at best, one parent. Kenny Duckworth played an important role in shaping his son into the Kendrick Lamar the world knows today. Kenny would teach Kendrick life lessons from his own experiences with Chicago's 'Gangster Disciples' gang. For instance, he would cheat while playing basketball to prepare Kendrick for the realities of the world. "He wanted me to know that was what was gonna happen in life."[2]

Kendrick's parents were fairly young (father was 25, and his mother younger) when he was born in 1987, so as he was growing up, they were too. That means (like Dre and Jay), his house would host regular parties with lots and lots of music.

"My parents partied every muhfucking Friday!"[3] "I always play back those parties in my memory. Takin' off my shirt and wilin' out with my cousins, getting in trouble for riding our big wheels inside the house. They'd be playin' oldies and gangsta rap. Just drinkin' and smokin' and laughter. A young crowd enjoying themselves. They were living the lifestyle."[4]

That combination of gangsta rap and oldies soul, like Sunny Moon Band, would massively influence Kendrick's taste in music and eventually the type of music he would make – fusing the two styles in a similar way Dre fused 70's funk sounds with a 'street' attitude.

On weekends Kenny would often take his son to the Compton Swap Meet, where they could meet-up with neighbors and shop for CD's and (some questionably authentic) clothes. When Kendrick was eight his excited father rushed him to the Swap Meet, where hundreds of people had gathered to watch Dr. Dre and Tupac shoot the music video for 'California Love.' Seeing the superhero like welcome the two artists received from the star-struck crowds planted a seed in young Kendrick's mind. "I knew then consciously or subconsciously. That this is what I wanted."[5]

The Famous Compton Swap Meet/ Fashion Centre

Kendrick's mom worked in fast food, and his dad would earn money from similar low wage employment, or by hustling with his gang affiliated brothers. "My pops did whatever he could to get money. He was in the streets – you know the story."[4]

Over one third of Compton homes live below the poverty line[5] and like many in the community Kendrick's family were on-and-off welfare. "I remember always walking to the government building with mom. We got our food stamps fast because we lived across the street."

Though his parents endeavored to provide their children with a good quality of life. "I didn't know it was hard times because they always had my Christmas present under the tree and for my birthday."[4]

Contradictions defined Kendrick's early life. One day at nine years old he was watching cartoons and eating cereal in the morning, then witnessed a person get his head blown off in public that evening. As Kendrick got older he lost family and friends in murders and court convictions, yet spent most of his time like any 'normal' kid, pranking and playing. (Years later when Kendrick found his 'voice' he would be able to make sense of these contradictions as a Good Kid born into a m.A.A.d City.)

In West Compton Kendrick's family were 'poor' by general American standards, but in neighborhoods where every home is living a similar way nobody feels poor. That is until twelve year old Kendrick attended middle school and became aware of the different lifestyles that exist beyond the 10 square miles of Compton.

Children from the Valley, north of Hollywood, were bused in thirty miles to attend Kendrick's school. "I went over to some of their houses…and it was a whole 'nother world," he remembers. "Family pictures of them in suits and church clothes up everywhere. Family–oriented. Eatin' together at the table. We ate around the TV. Stuff like that – I didn't know nothin' about eatin' without your elbows on the table. I'm lookin' around like, 'What is goin' on?!' I came home and asked my mama, 'Why we don't eat 'round the table?' Then I just keep goin', always askin' questions. I think that's when I started to see the lifestyle around us."[4]

Being exposed to another, more comfortable and seemingly happier way of life made Kendrick dream. He fantasized about living with his family in these safer, wealthier neighborhoods. He wanted to be successful.

(Research has shown that children exposed to more affluent environments at a young age are more ambitious and more likely to escape a cycle of poverty. Jay Z had a similar experience when his middle school teacher took the class to her well-to-do apartment overlooking Central Park. He credits that experience with giving him a tangible goal to aim for.)

But instead of being just an abstract dream, Kendrick could see firsthand people around him who went from 'rags to riches.' He used them as mentors who provided blueprints for 'making it out.' Two people in particular, NBA player Arron Affalo and rapper The Game, he describes in the song 'Black Boy Fly'. "They did something with themselves to get out of poverty and make a better situation with their lives."[1]

'He made a dream become a reality/
Actually making it possible to swim/ '
– Black Boy Fly

By the new millennium Hip Hop was the dominant culture in L.A. and more young males aspired to be rappers than basketball players. Kendrick's friend and collaborator, MixedByAli, remembers: "Growing up, everybody wanted to be a rapper, so in high school everybody was freestyling."[1]

Kendrick was one of them. He began writing rhymes at thirteen (after listening to DMX's 'It's Dark and Hell is Hot'). Rapper Jay Rock, who would end up on the same label as Kendrick, remembers seeing him around high school "rapping like a madman."

But trying to 'make it out' in a productive way, like through rap, can be difficult in an environment enclosed in destructive energy.

Both Kendrick's parents had gang members in their families, and it was a fundamental part of his childhood. "I had cousins, my moms and pops, smoking, drinking, cussing, gangbanging, shootings outside, all type of wild shit. Being around it, it just seemed like that was what you [were] gonna do, what you [were] gonna be."[6]

Despite Kendrick being a "mellow, to self [type of] person growing up,"[3] his relations and peers sucked him into their lives, like a whirlpool at sea. "The only reason I wasn't an outcast, was I had older relatives in it."

Family connections gave him a 'tribe' to belong to but he also knows that this wasn't healthy. "Being in that crowd as a teenager, without individuality, my family rep put me in more negative circumstances than being an outsider."[7] (A family were "all my uncles are doing life sentences"[19] he says.)

'Pushing in my mama van, stop for gas on Rosecrans/
*Trust me these n**** rushed me for something my cousin probably did/*
Guilty by association story of my life…/
– P&P

Because his peers were involved in gangs, Kendrick naturally gravitated toward that street life. "For a long time, I thought going to jail was cool…all my friends and all my cousins I was comin' up with wanted to go to jail too. That's how it was in Compton."

This is the cycle of poverty children inherit form their surroundings.

'I used to want to see the penitentiary way after elementary/
Thought it was cool to look the judge in the face when he sentenced me/'
– Poe Mans Dreams

Kendrick became involved in robberies, fights, drugs, shootings. Living in a jungle means you act like an animal.

'My pops said I needed a job I thought I believed him/
Security guard for a month and ended up leaving/
In fact I got fired 'cause I was inspired by all of my friends/
To stage a robbery the third Saturday I clocked in/'
– Maad City

But what differentiated Kendrick from most of his peers was he had two loving parents at home. "That right there gave me a little bit more insight than a few of my other homeboys. My parents being there gave me a whole lot of confidence."[8]

Kendrick's father played an important role in steering him on a more positive path and making him see that there's, "something bigger than the streets out there."

"[I eventually overcame peer pressure because] I had a father in my life. That's a big part of my life. I had respect for him. He wasn't right there, he couldn't be there all the time, and he wasn't no perfect person. But at the same time, he had much love for me. He made sure I had a better life. He made sure I found that life through music."[3]

"My father said, 'I don't want you to be like me.' I said, 'What you mean you don't want me to be like you?' I couldn't really grasp the concept. He said, 'Things I have done, mistakes I've made, I never want you to make those mistakes. You can wind up out on the corner.' He knew by the company I keep what I was gettin' into. Out of respect, I really just gathered myself together."[4]

His father's teachings coincided with one fatal event that would mark a turning point in Kendrick's life.

One summer evening in 2003, outside a local burger restaurant, one of sixteen year old Kendrick's closest friends was fatally shot right beside him. He died in Kendrick's arms.

Thanks to the help of people Kendrick believes God placed in his path, this is the point he began to see life from a higher perspective.

"The same day [my homeboy got shot], I ran into an older lady who broke down what life is really about to us; the story of God, positivity, life, being free, and being real with yourself. She was letting us know what's really real. Because you have to leave this earth and speak to somebody of a higher power."[1]

He would later write the song 'Sing About Me, I'm dying of Thirst' to describe the importance of this chance encounter in changing his life.

"That song represents being baptized, getting dipped in holy water. It represents when my whole spirit changed, when my life starts – my life that you know right now, that's when it starts."[1]

Thanks to this lady, his father and indirect mentors like Arron Affalo and The Game, Kendrick began to meditate on his life with more clarity.

"I saw the same things over and over. A lot of my homeboys goin' to jail. Not, like, in and out. Sentences. And dyin' – it was a constant. It was a gift from God to be able to recognize that."[4]

"I knew something was bigger than me, something was bigger than just Compton, something was bigger than the trouble we were getting ourselves involved in, and I wanted more for myself and the people I care about."[9]

"After those long crazy nights in high school, I'd go back to my room and sit up staring at the ceiling, thinking that I could get out of this craziness if I ever found something that I loved."[10]

One 'thing' interested him more than anything: music. He had been literally listening to rap music since birth, and had been writing rhymes casually and rapping with friends at school for years, but now he began to form a serious plan to use music as an escape from the destructive life.

People around him noticed his new ambition and offered their support. At the beginning of 10th grade a mutual friend introduced Kendrick to Dave Free, a DJ and teacher at nearby Colonial High, who organized lunch time rap battles. "[He was] the first person to tell me I was good at music," Kendrick remembers.

Dave, who would later become Kendrick's manager, taught him about different styles of rap and provided the resources for Kendrick to record his first mixtape in 2003. From the first recording session at Dave's makeshift home studio (where a sock wrapped around the microphone), Kendrick knew this was the career he wanted. "The first time I heard my voice play back through the speakers I was addicted. That was it."[7]

'I used to be in the booth till four in the morning/
With school in the morning, yawning, but I was on It/ '
– Wanna Be Heard

"A mixtape is raw Hip Hop. Free verse, no structure, good beats, good rhymes. My first mixtape, I was 16 and it was called Y.H.N.I.C., Youngest Head Nigga In Charge. Kind of ignorant, right?" he later said smiling.[11]

Kendrick's strategy was to follow 50 Cent's blueprint, who in 2003 was the biggest selling rapper in the world. 50 had built a buzz locally in New York by putting out mixtapes and getting them in the hands of as many people as possible – (see 'The Break In' *pg.254*).

As part of that strategy Kendrick, Dave and friend Dasan, aimed to get the tape heard by Anthony "Top Dawg" Tiffith, who owned a local studio and independent label, 'Top Dawg Entertainment.'

"We looked at Top Dawg as the closest person to the industry. He was the one that had at least a shoestring in the door," recalls Kendrick.[20]

The team pressed up CD's and released the mixtape locally, among friends and neighbors. The buzz travelled fast.

"I started going around to different neighborhoods and people used to always talk about this young dude from Compton that's doing his shit…I didn't know I was who they were talking about. I didn't really have no pictures or nothing on the disc. It was just a bunch of blank discs rolling around…just word of mouth, people talking 'bout it at school and it got back to me, and I was like, 'Damn, my shit is really making an impact on the city [I can] go full force with this shit!'"[6]

To get into the hands of Top Dawg the team hustled. Dave remembers:

"I tried everything to get around Top Dawg. One time I posed that I can fix his computer, because he said a computer needed fixing. The whole time I was playing [Kendrick's] music while trying to fix it."[20]

Hearing Kendrick's mixtape and already feeling the buzz on the streets, Top invited the aspiring rapper to his studio.

"Aw man. I thought it was a muhfucking honor, for him to even respect my music, cause locally, in the city he was the man."[6]

Top Dawg

In 1997, using money from his 'street enterprises,' Top Dawg built a professional studio in his home. He built it excited by the hype around independent record labels like Ruthless and Death Row, and partly inspired by his wealthy independent music executive uncle, Michael Concepcion. But after the studio was built the hype died down and it went unused for several years – (see 'Happy Ending' *pg.126*).

One day Top was introduced to Demetrius Shipphe, a producer at Suge Knight's Death Row records, who was being cheated of his earnings. Top was "heavy in the street" and agreed to help Demetrius get his money back.

After that he set Demetrius up in the dusty studio and attracted some young up-n-coming rappers like Game and Juvenile to come and record.

By 2003 the studio was becoming more successful and gaining a reputation in Compton and Watts, so Top and his cousin Terrence "Punch" Henderson moved away from the streets to focus on music, and started scouting for talent.

Kendrick was invited to audition for Top Dawg. "When he came to the studio I put him in the booth and put this double time beat on, trying to throw him off. He went in there and started going off!" remembers Top.[12]

"I freestyled for, like, an hour," says Kendrick.

"So I'm trying to play like I'm not paying attention" Top continues. "He notices I'm not moving and starts going crazy. So I look up and I'm like, 'God damn. He's a monster.'"

The next day Kendrick signed a recording deal with Top Dawg Entertainment (TDE). From that time it would be another **nine** years of grind before his official debut album's release.

Top Dawg gave sixteen year old Kendrick the opportunity to be in a professional recording studio whenever he wanted. "Whatever they needed was there: food, shelter, whatever they needed," he says.

TDE had also signed local rapper Jay Rock two weeks prior to Kendrick's audition and the two MC's began working together.

The studio became Kendrick's second home. *'I used to practice early morning and then after school'* he raps on *'Wanna Be Heard'*. There he developed his understanding of the recording process and the different elements of production. He learned how songs fit together, the intricate effects of different sounds, and would hone his ear to how he wanted his own music to sound, so by the time he was ready to record his debut album he knew exactly what he wanted.

Henny aka J–Hen (of Tha Bizness) who would produce for TDE says these years of learning where the reason Kendrick was able to create such an original sound with his official debut album in 2012:

"Kendrick started out in the background working with producers and doing hooks so he already developed himself as a producer in his own right. When we got with him (in 2011), he'll tell you what sounds he likes, what vibe he's looking for. That's what inevitably made him so big. The fact that he's been able to create his own sound even with all the producers that he has worked with, he's been able to get his sound out of them."[1]

TDE gave Kendrick the opportunity to experiment and discover his unique style, his 'niche.' Top provided the access and Ken brought the attitude. He worked constantly to improve his flow, his lyrics, his tone, his subject matter, his credibility. "Years of Perfection" he says.

From early on Kendrick's focus was on creating art, not on street or battle raps. As Ab Soul says: "Kendrick was recording full songs with hooks and bridges and melodies to keep the crowd. He was not just interested in being the best rapper, he was making songs that the world could sing."[4]

He would release six mixtapes between 2003 and 2010, which he says allowed him to "figure out what to do, how to sound, what songs to use, how to deliver. It was all paying dues."[7]

At the time Kendrick's entire style on the mic was a mirror of some of his heroes. He studied artists like Jay Z and Nas, who taught him about rhyming techniques, and Tupac and DMX, who taught him how to convey emotion through song, as well as local rappers like MC Eiht, who would go on to feature on Kendrick's debut album.

"MC Eiht is a great influence on me with him being from Compton and speaking on something that was real. MC Eiht influenced me by showing me that I don't have to talk about a lifestyle that's not mine to win. He talks about his lifestyle growing up. That stuck and people still relate to that. He gave me inspiration to speak on something that was real to me."[1]

As well as giving him the resources to develop musically, Top Dawg would positively influence Kendrick's perspective on life and help keep him away from the potentially destructive streets. Top's cousin and TDE co-president 'Punch' describes Kendrick's actions on the song 'Art of Peer Pressure' (where he talks about committing robberies and using drugs) as "a prequel of him before coming over to Top Dawg Entertainment."[1]

Top became Kendrick's second father, mentoring and coaching him. As Kendrick worte in an appreciative email to him four years after meeting:

```
From: smtp.sbcglobal.net <kenny@sbcglobal.net>
To: dudedawg@tmail.com
Subject: KDOT
Date: Sat, 3 Feb 2007 17:14:33 -0800 (PST)

AY TOP..THIS DOT...I AINT NEVER GOT TO SAY I
APPRECIATED ALL YOU DONE FOR ME BIG HOMIE. I
APPRECIATE THE OPPORTUNITY YOU'VE GIVEN ME DAWG. THE
OPPORTUNITY TO BETTER ME AND MY FAMILY. FROM THE DAY I
HAD MY FIRST LABEL MEETING TO THE TIME YOU PUT UP YOUR
OWN MONEY JUST SO I CAN GO ON THE CANADA TRIP BEFORE
IT GOT CANCELLED. BUT WHATS MOST IMPORTANT. YOU THE
SECOND PERSON OTHER THAN MY POPS TO REMIND ME THAT
LIFE ITSELF IS A HUSTLE. IF U WANT SOMETHING U GOTTA
WORK FOR IT. BECAUSE IF ITS HANDED TO YOU THE
APPRECIATION VALUE LOSES IT WORTH. U BASICALLY SAY
THAT EVERY TIME U SPEAK ON YOUR HUSTLIN DAYS. I BE
LISTENIN..I LEARNED THAT IT BE SO MUCH MORE SAID THAN
JUST U REMINISING...I APPRECIATE THEM WORDS TOP..
THANX FOR EVERYTHING...
" ALWAY'S KEEP IT REAL WITH YO DAY 1 NIGGA'S " DUDE DAWG
```

As a small independent label TDE gave Kendrick access to recording facilities, linked him with talented producers and organized small local shows. But they couldn't release music on any large scale as they didn't have the distribution channels or promotional budget of a major label like Sony or Universal. So from 2003 to 2009 despite recording numerous songs and being praised by the team, Kendrick saw very little tangable success.

"I felt I was in more of a standstill than I had made it. Majority of the time I felt in a standstill," he later reflected. "A lot of integrity, heart and good people around me keep me goin."[7]

The stagnation was difficult. Some people close to him, in the streets and at home, caused Kendrick to question himself during this period. Even his father was saying he should be moving forward faster.

My pops got a different approach, yeah he believed/
But he always questioned when I'mma drop my debut CD/
*How long this gon' take n****? You still haven't ate n****/*
*At twenty–two I had two cars and my own place n****/*
It's a sacrifice I try to tell him/'
– Wanna Be Heard

Although at times he'd be frustrated and disheartened by lack of progress, the negativity didn't deter Kendrick. He knew others didn't understand his vision, and he truly believed it was his route to something better. "People around you can't understand how you feel about your art…sometimes you have to delete that [negativity] and go about what your heart says."

This determination to continue pursuing your passion despite naysayers comes from within. "Motivation [to keep going] comes from having a great amount of confidence in yourself" Kendrick says.[7]

Just like with Jay, Kanye and Em the naysayers only served as fuel.

We got some haters in this room/
What we tell 'em? I love you/
You, make, my life complete/
I wonder where would I be/
If it wasn't for you/
– Hater Love

After releasing four mixtapes with TDE (in 03, 05, 07, 09, all available at HipHopTeaches.com) as well as numerous songs deemed not good enough to put out on mixtapes, and dozens of guest verses, Kendrick was still unsure what his voice, style, his niche should be. He rapped under the moniker 'K Dot,' and would be easily influenced by people around him saying 'you should rap like this.' His music would have similar style and subject matter to that of his idols. A knowledgeable rap listener would be able to easily identify the exact flows Kendrick emulated in these early tracks.

"I basically just picked out the greats. The ones who I thought were the greatest – Jay Z, Nas, Notorious B.I.G., of course Pac, and just taking little niches from their style."[6]

But he would soon learn that he would need to find his own voice in order to become one of these 'Greats.'

In 2006, TDE took a nineteen year old Kendrick to meet with executives at a larger record label, who were impressed by his mixtapes, to create some songs, and possibly sign a joint record deal – whereby he could create music with TDE while the larger label would distribute and promote him. The experience though would show Kendrick the ugly side of the music industry and almost make him give up on his rap dreams.

"[The record label] were like, 'Take this beat, put your lyrics on it. It should sound just like this [Yung Jock, 'It's Going Down'] song. And bring it back to us.' I did that, they played it, they liked it, boom, 'Okay, we gon' move on it.' Next thing you know, another sound came out number one. They didn't move on it. Three months later, they were like, 'Okay, do this beat and let's see…'"[7]

Kendrick bit his tongue and agreed to make another clone song, but when he handed it in the trend chasing label said the same thing: "It's good but now this song is number one, so make a song similar to this."

Kendrick had enough. He had enough of trying to please record executives who were just after the next hit and didn't care about the art or culture. He had enough of false promises and he almost had enough of music entirely. "[I] felt that I would never make it," he solemnly recalls. "That made me feel I didn't meet the criteria to be a superstar."

That combined with being surrounded by negative influences in Compton made the feeling he won't make it even stronger. "Negative environments can shut out any creativity."[7] That feeling of 'not being worthy of it' would stay with him for years.

*'N**** dying, motherfuck a double entendre/'*
– The Heart Part Two

The song R.O.T.C describes Kendrick's mental state at this time. Following the rejection, lack of recognition and slow progress, he was wrestling with thoughts of quitting rap and joining family and friends on the streets where 'easy money' was alluring:

'Sometimes I wanna say fuck rapping, I need money now/
Like should I start trapping? If what I write down/
Don't collect this very moment then I'm on it, no question/'

But as the meaning of the song's title indicates, 'Right On Time Conscience,' Kendrick listened to his inner-voice and chose to 'bounce back not backwards.'

He converted the potentially destructive negativity into motivation to continue pushing forward and was able to channel the energy into his art.

"I found myself writing some of my most inspiring things at this time."[7]

Also, thanks to the experience with the major record label, Kendrick made a critical decision to stop trying to follow trends, to stop imitating other rappers, and just represent himself. He looked at his soul in the mirror and decided to totally 'Do You' (*pg.272*).

"I decided to be real and not fabricate myself to sell a gangster image. [I felt] I'mma give the people what I want and if they don't like it, fuck it. I'm doing me."[6] From then on he would only create music that he could be personally proud of.

"I basically do what I feel [now]. I was so confined in tryna have a hit record, or tryna be like 'this' artist that's winning or 'that' artist that's winning, where I really lost touch of what I really wanted to do and what I planned on doing from the jump. So, a lot of my old songs are basically me catering to the radio and whatnot. Now, I'm just doing what I feel and you'll fuck with it or you not. I'm a still be me at the end of the day. If I win or lose on it, I know you ain't take my integrity away."[6]

Part of Kendrick's transformation was a change of identity. He dropped the moniker 'K–Dot,' and embraced his real self. "When I turned around 21, 22, I figured out, You know what? It's time for me to come up with my own. First step: I want people to know who I am directly. What is an artist if you don't know them as a person? So first thing I'ma give you is Kendrick Lamar. This is me, this is my life, what my family been calling me forever, so you can have a piece of that…because the greatest artists have a story that somebody can actually relate too."[13]

'I used to wanna rap like Jay Z/
Until I finally realized that Jay wasn't me/'
– Wanna Be Heard

Thanks in part to his unique meditation practice (*pg.161*) he now understood who 'Kendrick Lamar' is, and was comfortable expressing it to the world. But he was only able to express himself in creative and sophisticated ways because of the many years he had spent developing his craft and studying the styles of Greats – (see 'Infinite Semester' *pg.167*).

"When you hear my music, you can hear a little piece I took from people I respected and just brought it to my own self and made it into my own niche."[6]

After re-finding his identity, Kendrick felt ready to release an EP (an extended mixtape with original beats), to warm up for the planned release of his debut album.

Kendrick Lamar EP, 2009

With the new 'Do You' mind-set, Kendrick was discovering his unique expression, his niche. In essence, a rounded human being with a conscious, growing up in an environment often without one. His lyrical content, tone and style changed from the aggressive, 'thuggish' previous mixtapes, to reflect a more honest, vulnerable, three-dimensional person. As he said on the newly released EP: *'I'mma close cut to Common and Gucci Mane/'*.

Another part of the new 'Do You' mentality was to not blindly follow any of the standard industry rules, and just do what felt right. For instance, the EP had 17 songs instead of the usual 7. "People were looking at me crazy for doing that. I said 'I don't give a fuck. Play it and call it whatever.'"[3]

He was beginning to differentiate himself.

TDE had planned to use this EP to build up a buzz for a debut album release shortly after, so they hustled to get the music heard by as many people as possible. Kendrick remembers, "Begging internet sites and blogs to put my music up."[6]

He would tour the country with the material, opening shows for established rappers like The Game, because Top Dawg had a relationship with him since 2002.

Kendrick also went on a 44 leg tour with Tech N9ne in 2010, all of which not only built up his buzz and earned him a good income, but he learned invaluable lessons from entertainers he performed alongside. Like Tech N9ne's ability to bring in thousands of fans every night without any major label support:

"That shit was retarded. I'm talking 'bout an independent dude, with fuckin' 4,000 people in the crowd, [every night], knowing every song line for line. Fuckin' meet and greet before the show, 300 people, $100 a pop to come see Tech N9ne and they're all there…It just took my thoughts of grinding to a whole 'nother level and I mean, made me feel like, I'm not doing enough."[6]

By this time the TDE family of rappers consisted of Kendrick, Jay Rock, Schoolboy Q and Ab Soul, together forming the 'Black Hippy' crew. The group acted like a 'Mastermind Alliance' *(pg.186)*, competing to raise one another higher. They also introduced each other to new demographics, taking inspiration from the Wu-Tang Clan in the mid 90's, who fused their different personalities to broaden the groups reach among diverse fans.

"Kendrick – he probably brings out the most ladies," says TDE co-president Punch.[14] "Jay Rock brings out the gangsters, the neighborhoods. Q and Ab–Soul, they have the whole weed culture and the druggies. So that's four different groups. And when they come together, all those fan bases intertwine. So it makes everything bigger."

The group was also able to learn from each other's success and failures. Like the time Jay Rock signed a distribution deal with Warner Brothers in 2006. When the deal was done TDE thought they could lay back. They thought Warner would handle everything and promote Jay Rock across the country. "We thought Jay Rock was signed so this is it, we good now. But that wasn't the case," remembers Punch.

Major label bureaucracy meant things moved s.l.o.w.l.y. It took almost four years for Rock to release a single. Four years. When it was eventually put out, 'All My Life,' featuring Lil' Wayne did well, with good radio play, and things seemed to be finally on the up. But in March 2009 Warner merged with Asylum Records and the album, along with Jay's future prospects were suffocated in even more bureaucracy. Eventually TDE bought back the contract and the whole team learned they had to do it themselves.

"When Jay Rock was going through his whole situation with Warner, that was Kendrick going through college," says Punch. "He was experiencing everything Jay Rock was experiencing."[15]

From then on they decided not to wait for any major label. They saw firsthand the business independent artists like Tech N9ine were doing for themselves so were inspired to step up their own hustle. "Once we got Jay Rock released [from Warner brothers], our whole goal was to never depend on anybody ever again. We were going to do everything ourselves going into Kendrick's [career],"says Punch."[1]

They decided not to meet with any more major labels but to focus on turning TDE into a forceful independent label, and make the majors come to them.

TDE's original four, (from left): Ab Soul, Kendrick Lamar, Schoolboy Q, Jay Rock

After the 'Kendrick Lamar EP,' Kendrick's name was getting more notice but he still wasn't satisfied with his popularity. So, instead of releasing an official album he decided to put out another mixtape, 'O.verly D.edicated,' to build up a stronger 'buzz' first.

'My plan be to win your hearts before I win a Grammy/'
– I Am

The goal was to get it to as many people as possible so he was reluctant to charge for it. He said at the time: "I wanted to give O.D. mixtape [away for] free, 'cause I feel everyone's not a Kendrick Lamar believer yet. I don't give a fuck about a dollar, 'cause I felt my art, my music will take me higher than that. The money, everything else, will fall in after [the people] believe."[3]

However Top Dawg urged him to charge. "My company, TDE, believed in me so much, they said 'You put in too much work, i's time. You should be getting paid for all the shit you put in.' For two weeks we had brutal arguments over it, till finally we came to compromise where I'mma put it on iTunes and still give it away free. So if you don't have the money you can get it free, if you do and love real music pay 5.99 on iTunes."

The album peaked at number 72 on the Billboard Hip Hop Albums charts in October 2010. A good accomplishment for an independent artist.

TDE used the album to embark on a nationwide tour, following the example set by Tech N9ine and Strange Music, and say they were making "a lot of money" from the album, selling it at shows and local record shops.

The team were content going down the independent route. They had seen the type of success that was possible and were earning a good income from it. They were not pursuing a deal, but they quickly realized when you depend on no one, *(pg.206)*, that's when people come to you.

The Dr. Will See You Now

Paul Rosenberg (Eminem's manager) heard 'Overly Dedicated' and told Dr. Dre about it. Dre, who is also always looking for fresh talent, watched Kendrick's video for 'Ignorance is Bliss' online and liked the music. The song was a fresh take on a young gang member's state of mind. Each verse would glorify an aspect of street life, and then end it with the phrase 'Ignorance Is Bliss.' Though it wasn't Kendrick's music that ultimately got Dre to call him, it was his interviews. Watching them on YouTube, Dre was impressed by Kendrick's character, he could sense charisma. "He liked me as a person," Kendrick explains.[16]

At the time Kendrick and his team were touring with Tech N9ne. After one show, while the crew were eating at a Denney's restaurant, Kendrick's engineer Ali received "a mysterious phone call."[17]

Dre invited Kendrick to his home studio, where the beat for 'Real' was playing. "He was testing me out, to see [what kind of artist I am]," remembers Kendrick. He passed the test.

"We just clicked."[16]

Dre asked Kendrick to work on some material for his 'Detox' album, and they put the song 'Compton' together that night. The pair worked together in the same fluid way Dre and Eminem worked together when they first met, more than ten years previously.

Kendrick with Dr. Dre in the studio[18]

Meanwhile, in July 2011 Kendrick released his first official album with TDE; 'Section 80'. It was distributed completely independently, via digital download, and CD's sold at shows. The album entered the Billboard 200 charts at number 113, and climbed to number 22 on the Billboard Hip Hop album charts. It would go on to sell 100,000 units in the first few months.

The album took Kendrick's popularity to new heights. He was invited to perform at a 2011 concert where Dr. Dre, Snoop Dogg, and The Game dubbed him, "The New King of the West Coast." This was perhaps the most pivotal moment in Kendrick's career so far. He broke down in tears on stage. "That's the moment I realized I made it."[7]

Dre had been considering signing Kendrick to his Aftermath label since meeting him, and following the success of Section 80, he made an offer.

"We weren't looking for a deal after J Rock's situation with Warner," says Kendrick's manager Dave Free. "We were making tons of money touring and selling albums independently. It was never in our mind to ever care about a deal."

But deals came. And TDE knew that partnering with a major label would provide resources and relationships to push their artists on a larger level. "Certain things we didn't understand we had to be honest with ourselves…and find out who we needed to bring on board, aligning ourselves with good people," says Dave.

The years of independent grind meant TDE came to the negotiation table with a number of cards. Their artists already had a growing fan base, they had their own recoding facilities and they had a number of labels bidding to sign Kendrick.

TDE negotiated a joint distribution deal with Interscope Records and Aftermath Entertainment for Kendrick, as well as the three other members of Black Hippy group. Under the (1.7 million dollar) deal TDE keeps creative control, publishing rights and tour revenues. Kendrick's projects are jointly released via TDE/Interscope/Aftermath while releases from the rest of Black Hippy are distributed via TDE and Interscope.

The deal was reported March 2012. It gave TDE a global distribution network for their albums, and maybe more importantly, they were able to work with and learn from music industry legends like Dr. Dre, who mentored the Black Hippy crew. Dre also executive produced Kendrick's album 'Good Kid, M.A.A.D City' and is featured on the album's lead single 'The Recipe,' which got Kendrick noticed by millions of people who follow Dre's output.

Kendrick put together the album while touring. He had been opening Drake's 'Take Care' concerts, and performing with others for two years straight. "He'll be on an airplane writing a song, get back home and lay the record, then have to fly out to do something else," remembers Punch. "It's just a testament to how focused and how strong minded he is. I don't know if a lot of artists could record that album while touring."[1]

A Decade Later

'good kid m.A.A.D city' was released in 2009. It was released in Kendrick's mind that is. That's when the concept came to him. As Punch says, "This project was in the works Kendrick's whole life. This is his life story. He had the concept before all of his mixtapes. This is the prequel to everything. He had the title for this album even before Kendrick Lamar EP had dropped. He was writing the concept the whole time."[1]

"Everything was premeditated," says Kendrick. "I already knew what I wanted to talk about, sound like, feel like, what I wanted to convey. I had that album cover for years… It's a long time coming. Everything we dwelled on is coming to light."[1]

The album was released to the world October 2012. It reflects on Kendrick's life before TDE, before he found music as a means of self-expression. The 'short film' takes place over one day in 2004.

"This is a dark movie album. I wanted to tap into that space where I was at in my teenage years. Everybody knows Kendrick Lamar, but he had to come from a certain place, a certain time, and certain experiences."

"It's as if you were to go back in time and put a microphone in the middle of Kendrick and his people," says the album's mixer Ali.[1]

It's as if his conscience is speaking through the mic. The album depicts scenes of getting beat up, shot at, set up, left heartbroken, catching STD's, struggles with alcohol, parental discipline. He talks about his life with such strong emotion that songs are relatable to people of all different backgrounds and life experiences.

The central premise of the album is the mental, spiritual and physical battle between the positive teachings parents instill at home, (the good kid) and the harsh reality of the world outside (the m.A.A.d City). It's the no makeup, no hype, true story of why kids in environments like the one Kendrick grew up in are the way they are. The story of a generation born destined to repeat the destructive lives of their predecessors. *'Babies from the late 80s wasn't born crazy, we was raised that way.'*

G.K.M.C is the type of album that can only be made when an artist has full creative control. The music holds nothing back. There is no 'trying to be like so and so,' no trend chasing, no censorship. It's just Kendrick.

The album became the biggest selling Hip Hop record of 2012 and the future looks bright for Kendrick Lamar Duckworth.

> **KEY LESSON:**
> **Be Ready To Fail Over And Over As You Find**
> **Your Unique Contribution to the World**

How It All
Got Started

Part II

Building

The foundations are set. In this section we look in-depth at the psyche of dozens of cultural icons. How they think about everything from failure to friends, from sleep to sex.

The Blueprints

*'I can't believe it's happening, no matter fact I can/
See first it was my dream then it became my plan/'*
– Nipsey Hustle, Hustlas State of Mind

In the late 80's a group of teenagers in Staten Island would regularly bunk off school to imagine living in Asia. They watched subtitled Kung Fu flicks, played chess, and studied ancient books like Sun–Tzu's 'Art of War,' where they would read lines like:

"Victorious warriors win first and then go to war, while defeated warriors go to war first and then seek to win."

They would also rap – forming ciphers, and travelling to nearby project neighborhoods to battle. All of this influenced the mindset of Robert Diggs, aka The RZA, and he began formulating the now famous 'Wu-Tang five year plan' – the strategy for a five year long game of chess that would enable nine 'hoodlums' to checkmate the rap game.

The plan was to form the ultimate rap super-group by working in harmony to build successful solo careers, then combine their stars into a Wu-Tang joint album which would top the charts within five years.

With few other options the crew put their trust in RZA to lead. "I used the bus as an analogy," he remembers. "I said, 'I want all of y'all to get on this bus and be passengers, and I'm the driver. And nobody can ask me where we going. I'm taking us to No. 1. Give me five years, and I promise that I'll get us there.'"[1]

RZA viewed the landscape like a game of chess. Each member of the crew was a piece and they needed to work together to take over the entire board. Instead of nine individuals fruitlessly fighting for the spotlight, like crabs crushing one another in a bucket, the Clan would make strategic moves to maximize rewards for everyone.

Each member contributed $100 to record their first single 'Protect Ya Neck,' which gained good radio play and sparked interest from record labels. RZA insisted not only would each Wu-Tang member sign individual contracts, but each member would sign to a different record label. The idea was to spread the groups sound as widely as possible and use the presence of each record label to market music for other Wu members.

"When Def Jam wanted to sign Method Man, they wanted to sign Method Man and Old Dirty, and Old Dirty wanted to be on Def Jam – that was like the dream label," RZA remembers. "But if I had Old Dirty and Method Man on Def Jam, that's two key pieces going in the same direction, whereas there's other labels that needed to be infiltrated."

Sure enough, a few years after the first single members of The Clan were recording for five of the six major labels, and had established allies at the record label offices to oversee the 'business side' (*pg.238*).

RZA also knew that each member brought in a different type of listener, so when the Wu combined, like Power Rangers forming the Megazord, they'd have a much larger combined fan base than any individual.

"I recall telling GZA, 'You'll get the college crowd,' Raekwon and Ghost, all the gangstas, Meth will get the women and children – and he didn't want to do women and children. He didn't know that, though. Method Man is a rough, rugged street dude, but all the girls love him. Myself, I was looking more like that I bring in rock 'n' roll."

In 1997, five years after the Wu was formed, they released their second group album 'Wu-Tang Forever.' After selling 600,000 units the first week RZA's promise was fulfilled and the Wu were number one.

The ancient Greeks believed that being able to look beyond the present and plan several steps into the future then patiently make that plan a reality, like RZA did so perfectly, was the work of Gods.[2]

Why? Because most people live their lives trapped in the moment, in their present emotions, always reacting to the world around them, unable to see past the present dangers. They go through life like a waitress in a busy restaurant, dealing with crisis and putting out fires. They are little pieces on life's chess board.

'We all seem to stumble, planning our own demise/
Forgetting the big picture and making it wallet size/ '
– Kendrick Lamar, Closer

Whereas Greats have trained themselves to step back from the busyness of everyday life and look at the larger picture – the entire chess board. They overcome the human tendency to react to immediate dangers and pleasures around them and instead form a well thought out long term vision of where they want to be, backed by realistic plans for achieving their goals.

'Standing back from situations give you the perfect view/ '
– Jay Z, A Dream

The vision is the map. Without it you're driving without direction. As co-president of Top Dog Entertainment, Punch says, "Of course it takes a lot of hard work, a lot of discipline but you have to have vision. If there's no vision you're just making songs."[3] – 'Songs' could mean any product or art you're trying to create.

In 1996 a brand new company called Roc–A–Fella Records created clear, concise plans to help them visualize the path to their goals.

"Like a lot of underground crews on a mission, we were on some real trunk–of–the–car shit," remembers Jay Z. "The difference with us was that we didn't want to get stalled at low–level hustling. We had a plan. We did more than talk about it, we wrote it down. Coming up with a business plan was the first thing the three of us did. We made short and long term projections, we kept it realistic, but the key thing is that we wrote it down, which is as important as visualization in realizing success."[7]

Knowing clearly what your goals are and having a well thought out plan to reach them is like drawing a map before you set off on a journey. It's exactly the same as an architect drawing every part of the building before shovels break the earth, or a surgeon planning the operation before slicing.

A blueprint takes the overall vision of where you want to be (like 'release a number one album in five years', or 'create the most valuable brand in Hip Hop') and breaks it down into actions based around clear goals.

Goals are stepping stones to your vision. The 'short and long term projections' as Jay says, each with a deadline that makes the 'dream' real, creates urgency. Urgency gets stuff done. Instead of wasting energy and time moving sporadically in different directions and falling into 'distraction traps', a well-defined plan creates efficient focused action. Action creates results.

'We all get distracted/
The question is, would you bounce back or bounce backwards?/ '
— Kendrick Lamar, Cut You Off

"I'm working with a plan before I sit at the board. That's the reason I can do a beat in three minutes," Kanye said in 2004.[4]

Years before he secured a record deal, Kanye had already planned the themes and songs for four albums. Despite practically all (ALL) people around him telling him he wouldn't be able, Kanye kept his self-belief intact, backed up by a clear plan, to eventually achieve all he had predicted.

Importantly, these plans were not vague and abstract. Kanye had studied the game "like a boxing coach," for six years, between the release of his first major hit with Jermaine Dupri and his debut album's release. "I sat back and peeped the game. If I rap like this, fans will react like this…I would say a lot of my success is because of that."[5]

And just like in ancient times, others see this quality as remarkable. Like DJ Hi Tek commented: "That's one guy there who I can say is a genius. When I first met Kanye he was very aggressive with it. He had it all planned out. The industry did not make Kanye. Kanye made Kanye."[6]

Similarly, the Roc–A–Fella team's clear plan focused them on their goals and kept them grinding despite facing rejection and little support in the early years. For instance, for their first single 'In My Lifetime,' Jay and Dame negotiated a deal where Payday Records would market and distribute the song. They thought Payday would spend money promoting them through high level mediums, like magazines and radio. Instead Payday gave them "a box of flyers" to hand out themselves. The team weren't put off though. "Some cats would've been derailed by lack of support from their label, but we had a plan," Jay says.[7] They hustled their own way, using connections to shoot a video in the Caribbean, and promoted the song without Payday's support.

*While n****s are shootin stupid, I'm carefully plottin/*
Ways to make it rotten, well-planned hits until you're long forgotten/
— Jay Z, In My Lifetime

First step in building the blueprint: what is your vision? What will the end goal look like? If your plan is to release a product, you need to see in your mind exactly how it will look and work with as much detail as possible. If your plan is about self-development, you need to see yourself in some future date (one or five years from now for example) with as much clarity as possible – what do you look like, who do you spend time with, what do you do and earn?

Practice visualizing this end goal frequently. You can then work backwards and break it down into smaller target 'chunks' that must be hit to reach that ultimate vision. You need to be able to see all the steps that lead to the vision, and say to yourself: 'I need to achieve this by the end of the month', or 'this by Tuesday', or 'this by 11am.'

Each week take time to plan the results you are going to achieve by the end of that week. Then every night write targets that you will achieve the following day to get to that weekly goal. As you're writing targets, visualize yourself 24 hours later with a great feeling of accomplishment. What will you have achieved to get this feeling? This exercise will help you focus on the most important activities – the '20%' (*pg.155*) – then you can schedule your day into a focused plan of attack by breaking down these daily goals into specific actions.[15]

Make sure in these daily plans you're scheduling high priority and vital 'housekeeping' activities first. Also allow yourself contingency time to deal with unexpectancies and emergencies, that way you shouldn't stress out about tying yourself down to a set of bullet points, but have room to flow with the events of the day.

Finally, every night take time to analyze the day that you just lived. Ask yourself: What worked? What didn't work? What lessons did I take away from today that I can apply to tomorrow? What activities can I delegate or cut altogether? Consistently doing this is one of the best ways to remain focused on the big picture and not fall into traps that distract from what's important. Every day you're laying down a brick until you've built your castle.

But beware. There is a fine line between realistic plans and fantasies that lead to failure.

The Happy Ending

Most people are deluded. Most people think they have good plans that will lead to their 'Happy Ending.' Really though their plans are vague and based on their imagination of what they want to happen, not on the reality of the world around them. They focus on the 'Happy Ending' but they don't really know what it actually takes to get there, and they don't see the obstacles and dangers that will come up in their path.[8]

They hurriedly start a project with a lot of excitement. They think it will bring riches and power quickly so they jump in head first without taking enough time to think and plan for potential future dangers. Soon they realize that everything is not how they expected and find they don't have the enthusiasm to keep going. They end up losing a lot of time and/or money. Many will start but few will finish.

For example, they think 'I want to start a business' and set off excitedly doing all the fun, easy things like choosing a company name and logo color, but they have no real concept of how to build a successful business. They should be doing the less 'fun' but more important tasks like researching the market place, competitors, and where they fit, talking to potential customers, getting detailed cost and revenue estimates and planning how to communicate their value proposition most effectively. This is a big reason why 80% of new businesses fail within 18 months.[16]

Birdman (CEO of Cash Money Records) liked the idea of starting an oil company. He fantasized about the riches and fame such a business would bring and excitedly set up a website with vague plans, and even tattooed an oil pump on his head. All he could see was the potential glory and not the dangers that lay ahead. Suffice to say the business never took off and probably cost him a lot of money. He's since covered his head tattoo.

J Cole had a plan to get signed by Jay Z. It revolved around the belief that if he could just get his beat-tape to Jay his career would be launched. In 2007 Cole read in a website interview that Jay was recording for his 'American Gangster' album, so he excitedly took a train to Manhattan and waited outside Baseline Studios for several hours in the pouring rain. He had the scenario pictured in his mind: "Maybe we could just slide [Jay] the CD and if we slide him the CD, he'll go upstairs and listen to it, and if he listens to it, he's gonna love it and he's gonna send down for me to come upstairs and he's probably going to sign me," Cole told ABC news.[9]

When Jay Z finally rolled up in his Rolls, Cole tried to pass on his CD but instead of taking it like he expected, Jay said, "I don't want that shit," and walked into the building.

Cole's plan was naive. He was hyped by the 'Happy Ending' he had played out in his mind, that he would just hand Jay the CD and everything would be taken care of. In reality this is not how getting signed works.

Note: Cole is also the exception here because there are hundreds of people we've never heard of who try to give Jay and other major artists their CD's, but Cole came back from this rejection to still make it happen.

'I made it to the Roc, even though they tried to box me out/
I got the key to the game, they tried to lock me out/
But what they don't understand is this is all planned/'
– J Cole, Sideline Story

Bosses like Jay Z begin gently and always stay in control by making and following plans. They don't let the project control and sweep them along.

They plan to the end and anticipate many possible crises that tempt others to improvise. They see remote dangers as they form and plan possible coping strategies in advance.

As Kevin Liles, who worked closely with Jay Z for many years, says:

> "Jay never does anything without going back and forth a few times, canvassing the judgments of people he trusts and weighing up the pros and cons. He routinely draws up a list of the positives and negatives to help him decide. I asked him how his mind works, this is what he said:
>
> 'At the end of the day this is business, and emotional decisions are bad for business. I have been able, through God's grace, to step outside of my body and ask myself: 'What does Jay Z the artist need to do? What do I, Shawn Carter, need to do? Is this about the business or the BS?'" [10]

Well thought out plans bring clarity. Clarity kills the vagueness (and ensuing anxiety) which are the reasons so many fail to reach their end goals.

'Never make choices out of desperation I think through it/'
– Nas, Wouldn't Understand

Of course nobody can plan every detail of their journey and a lot of the time plans will fail as we don't have perfect experience or foresight to plan for every possible circumstance.

'You can plan a pretty picnic/But you can't predict the weather/'
– Outkast, Ms. Jackson

That's why plans are not made in stone, they are flexible. They are open to alternative ways to achieve that goal.

We don't rigidly tie ourselves to our plans because as the world changes plans will soon become outdated. Surprises along the way may also provide opportunities for something better than we planned. That's why planning isn't about micro-managing the future, but preparing for eventualities, doing homework and feeling equipped for what might happen. Feeling prepared means feeling secure and in control. You're in a much better position to achieve your goals than someone constantly reacting to the world around them. We over-prepare, then go with the flow.

'Proper preparation prevents poor performance/'
– GLC, Poe Mans Dreams

See It Through

Most people who only focus on the 'Happy Ending' without making long term plans are quick to quit when shit hits. When a plan fails they'll say, 'Oh well, I guess it wasn't meant to be.' They'll move on and do something else, accepting their failure and living the rest of their life wondering, 'What if?'

But if your goals are ingrained in your heart, failed plans are not the end.

You will always have to put in more hours than planned. "Success happens on God's schedule, not yours" says Russell Simmons. If your first plan does not work (which it most likely won't), accept that as a signal there are flaws in your plan, sweep up the learning gold dust, adapt the plan and go again towards your goal. Then if that plan doesn't work take the learning gold dust, tweak and go on.

This comes naturally to someone with an internalized belief in themselves and their mission. Affirmation has created a commitment, so when plans turn out faulty they won't quit, but will just adjust and continue on. They understand that the first ten failures are just part of the journey and provide the experiences they will need later on.

"No. Never. Not one time," J Cole responded when asked if there was ever a moment where he thought of quitting. "For some reason I just always thought it was close, like I'll just be discovered soon."[17]

'Formulated my plan, motivated by dreams/'
– J Cole, Return of Simba

Importantly, this doesn't mean persistently trying to do the same thing over and over, and failing the same way over and over. It means always adapting to the reality of your environment, rolling with the punches and adapting the blueprint, but not quitting on that dream – (see 'The Guarantee' *pg.145* for more).

Do or Die

'Thinkin' of a master plan/
Cause ain't nothin' but sweat inside my hand/'
– Rakim, Paid in Full

Many Greats have such a strong self-belief and are so confident and secure in the knowledge that, 'I will fulfill my dream,' that they have the strength to burn all bridges and make retreat impossible. There's no option for turning back, no saying 'If this doesn't work, I will fall back on this…'

Like Will Smith said, "There's no reason to have a plan B because it distracts from plan A." (Again by 'plan' he means the target, the goal. It's likely original plans will have to change, but the dream remains.)

Legendary movie director Quentin Tarantino (who Jaime Fox and others describe as "a Hip Hop artist"[19]) faced this when he started on his quest. "I figured I couldn't have a fall back plan. I couldn't allow myself to fall back. I had to go all or nothing. I had to keep going on. I would give up everything to make it. I questioned myself 'do I have it?' but I tried not to entertain the thought 'I'm not gonna make it.'"[11]

"When you can't go back the only thing you have to worry about is the best way of moving forward." – Paulo Coelho, The Alchemist

Look at KRS-One, one of the most influential emcees of all time. At 14 he decided he was going to be a rapper and left home to pursue that goal – living in subway stations and homeless shelters. He would study in libraries by day and hustle by night (networking and performing) until he 'made it.' To him there was no going back.

Kanye dropped out of college because he knew there would be no alternatives to his dreams of a career in music. *That comfortable corporate job can't come for me'*. His mother, Donda, was initially dismayed at Kanye's decision but later came to understand. She writes:

"From the time I was making my own decisions about what I'd major in and what profession I'd enter, I never thought of falling back. I was so convinced that the only option was to achieve whatever it was that I set out to do; it would only be natural if Kanye felt the same way. Never would I argue about having plan B. But once you're truly sure of what you want in life, if your passionate about it, perhaps it's better to spend that falling–back energy concentrating solely on getting what you want."[12]

Jay Z made a similar decision when he decided to stop street hustling and instead focus on his passion. "I felt deep down, that whatever success I had on the street, I would be a failure if I didn't follow my dreams of music." So he made a clean break from the street, [allegedly] not using the money he made selling drugs to form Roc–A–Fella. There was no going back to the streets so everything channeled that energy. For example, to sell their first records the team would work with record stores on consignment and split takings, (around $150 a week), Jay and Co would be politicking with retailers and building relations with DJ's, "it was Do or Die" he remembers.[7]

After Eminem's first album 'Infinite' flopped, Marshall returned to working minimum wage jobs – sweeping floors, cleaning pots etc. He realized that music was literally the only way he could escape life in poverty and provide his daughter a better life. For the first two years of his daughter's life Marsh was sickened that he could not afford to put anything under the Christmas tree. His biggest fear was, and is, that he won't be able to provide for Hailie, and that he'd become like his own father (who abandoned him), or mother (who he says abused him). In his mind music became the only way out.

So he went in. Hard. Developing his craft and creating some of the sharpest lines rap has ever heard. He lost his inhibitions, and formed a 'Don't Give A Fuck,' 'Nothing To Lose' attitude (literally he had nothing, no possessions, after a number of burglaries). He turned into a force of energy exploding on the industry like an atomic bomb.

Refuse to quit, fuse is lit, can't defuse the wick.'
– Eminem, Survival

Some of today's best known emcees came from a background where music represented the only means of escape from impoverished environments, where death or jail is often around the corner.

For instance members of the Wu-Tang Clan lived in inner-city project housing with few legal job opportunities, or chances to develop. Their only options were to 'get on the bus' with RZA, or continue the cycle of self-destruction around them.

Similarly, 50 Cent came from a world where his single mother gave birth to him at 15 and was killed by rival drug dealers a few years later. 50 himself was heading down the same path of self-destruction. After narrowly escaping death with nine bullet holes to the body he came to see music as the only way out of the ghetto. "I ain't have a plan B. It absolutely had to work. If I don't make music I'm going back to the hood [to sell crack]. So I stayed focused and made it happen."[13]

From 1997 50 worked full time to fulfilling his goals, doing whatever it took to make it happen. What was the belief he internalized?

"GET RICH OR DIE TRYING"

A single minded affirmation that he deeply believed and lived.

Some people don't like the materialism of this statement. But it's exactly the same as:

"GIVE ME LIBERTY OR GIVE ME DEATH"

The 56 men who signed the Declaration of Independence knew there would only be two outcomes for them: execution by the British for treason, or freedom and birth of the United States.

What does this 'Do or Die' affirmation do to a person's state of mind?

From 1997 to 2002, 50 Cent was writing 'full time all the time,' and felt he was ready to come-up but could not land a major record deal. He had to run off of his own energy, and it's that belief in self, which came from the realization rap was the only 'way out,' that kept him disciplined and focused, improving his craft till his moment.

Now, after proving to himself how powerful this belief can be, he sees no limits. "At this point I tell them 'good luck' if they tell me I can't do something I set my mind on. I already come so far it's impossible to discourage me."[14]

There are several ways to put yourself in this 'Do or Die' frame of mind.

At the extreme you could completely withhold all gratification and pleasures (food, entertainment, sex) from yourself until you achieve certain milestones towards your goals.

You can make 'retreat' impossible by making your plans and goals as public as possible. For example if you want to deliver a product three months from now, then send out a press release with the launch party details now. If you want to organize an event six weeks from now, then you could pay the deposit on the venue now.

Anything to put more 'positive pressure' on yourself to make it happen. Anything to put yourself in a, *'Success is my only motherfucking option/'* (*Eminem, Lose Yourself*) state of mind.

Overall, and once again, the 'Do or Die' mentality comes naturally to people with the right motives. How hungry are you?

The Hunger

"If you know in this hotel room they have food every day, and I knock on the door. Every day they open the door to let me see the party, let me see that they throwin salami, throwin food around telling me 'there's no food'.

Every day I'm standing outside tryin to sing my way in – 'We are weak, please let us in. We're week, please let us in.'

After about a week the song is gonna change to, 'We're hungry, we need some food!'

After two, three weeks it's like 'Give me some of the food! I'm breakin down the door!'

After a year it's like, 'I'm pickin the lock, comin through the door blastin...I'm hungry.'"

– Tupac Shakur[1]

How can we channel the same hunger, to create the 'I–WILL–NOT–LOSE' state of mind?

'These dreams be waking me up at night'
– Kanye, I Wonder

The RZA would never have been able to form the Wu-Tang Clan if he had not been dropped by another record label a few years earlier. He used the rejection to fuel his hunger. "Making Wu-Tang I was determined. Nobody could stop me. I was determined, I was bitter and angry."[2]

If it were not for J Cole's hunger he wouldn't have endured the years of rejections and struggle after graduating college. His hunger was so obvious that it infected others around him, like his landlord Mohamed, who would let Cole's rent slide as he believed Cole would eventually 'make it'.

'I take advantage of the opportunities I'm handed before they vanish/
Yeah your man is so hungry I'm famished/ '
– Talib Kweli, Never Can Say Goodbye

No doubt the success of Roc–A–Fella, going from an unknown crew in 1996 to the number one Hip Hop label five years later, came from its hunger. "Entrepreneurial, hustler, say whatever you want to say – it's just that hunger to make money, and to make your situation better,"[3] said CEO at the time Dame Dash. "My main objective was to take over the whole entire planet. I made a conscious decision to take over the world."[4]

Dame had that ambition long before forming Roc-A-Fella. His insistence on playing by his own rules and a 'F the system' mentality got him expelled from four different schools, before he attended Westside High, a school "for everybody that got kicked out of the place you went when you got kicked out of someplace else,"[5] he says. But he was eventually expelled from there too for parking his car in the principal's space. Even as a teen he was hungry for the top spot.

Interviewed in 2002, Roc–A–Fella had achieved the goals they set out in 1996. They were Hip Hop's number one record label. They had diversified into films, clothing and liquor, and were pulling in hundreds of millions of dollars annually. But Dame and Co. still carried the same hunger as when they began building the empire – a "Kamikaze attitude" as Dame calls it.

"Even at this point and time, my attitude is that I am still starving…I'm a cakeaholic. If there's money out there it may be a problem because I want it. Everybody better get on top of their game cause if you leave anything I'm going to get it."[6]

Although some might question his motives, and his ultra-capitalist obsession with money, (which probably led to his ultimate downfall, as he neglected relationships, only focusing on the end result, but that's another story), there is no doubt this drive led to the Roc's initial success.

Communities like the ones Jay & Dame grew up in breed this mentality. Living in places that have little compared to the 'America' they see everywhere else, creates a *'nothing to lose, nothing to fear'* state of mind. They look around at the crowded housing, with 500 people to a building, the poor schools and minimal public services, and think *"if this is all I have to lose, then I'm going for everything. I'm going for the world."* So they take ruthless advantage of opportunities in front of them.

As Jay Z writes in Decoded:

"We came from a generation of black people that finally got the point: no one is going to help us…So we went for self, for family, for block, for crew…Success could only mean self-sufficiency, being a boss, not a dependent. The competition wasn't about greed – or not just about greed. It was about survival."

It's the Scarface mentality and the reason the movie is a Hip Hop staple – but that's also another story.

'Close your eyes see the darkness/
That's what it's like where I'm from/
No lawyers no doctors/
So either I go the hardest/
Or I can just call this a night/ '
– Jay Z, Go Hard

Most people dream of being successful but they don't want it strongly enough, they 'sort of want it.' They don't want it as much as they want to hang out with friends, surf the net or sleep. Hunger embedded in one's character differentiates the few from the many.

Hunger comes from your 'Why?' your deepest motivations. Why do you do it? Eminem did it because he felt he had to provide a better life for his daughters. Kanye, because he had to bring his ideas to the world. Part of Jay Z does it to be an example for how far people with his background can go.

'I do it to be the best monies nothing to me/
Got it all and want more how hungry are we?'
– CL Smooth, Back On the Block

Staying Hungry After Dinner

The hunger is a large part of what brought Greats to the top, but maintaining that level of hunger as they become successful is essential to continue growing.

For instance, despite all of 50 Cent's success he doesn't let it fill his appetite. "Every day I wake up in the [former] home of Mike Tyson, who earned over 500 million in his career. It makes me conscious."[8]

Referring to his $100 million payout from the famous Coca-Cola–VitaminWater deal in 2007, 50 said: "People were talking about how much money I made, but I was focused on the fact that $4.1 billion was made. I think I can do a bigger deal in the future."[9]

Eminem drives through the poor neighborhoods he grew up in to reminisce on the driving hunger he felt to get out. "I'll go back and remember, like, fuck, man, how life was back then. How much of a struggle it was. As time goes by, you might get content and forget things."[10]

Dr. Dre never gets content with his achievements by never listening to his records after they come out. "It's outlawed in my house. My wife and my kids can't play any of my music around me. Once it comes out, for me, it's just business."[11]

Similarly Kanye told Fader in 2008: "I never dwell on accolades… the thing that's most important to me is what I'm doing next."…"[Despite my success] I would think it's not quite conquered yet – I think there's still a way to go, there are levels. Like, did you see the Michael Jackson in Budapest concert [with 500,000 in the audience] yet? It's like, if it's not on that level, it's not conquered yet…maybe this is a beginning point, a starting point."[12]

Kanye has won more Grammy's than any musician his age. What does he do with the golden statues? His wife Kim Kardashian explains: "Kanye's not big on putting his Grammy's up, they're literally in the laundry room, like just randomly – or a sock drawer… He's not into awards being all around the house – he's not a show-off person."[13]

The first thing Lil Wayne said when his manager told him that 'The Carter III' sold one million copies the first week was: "Next album first week [sales] five million."[14]

Summed up in the words of Pharrell: "I'm never gunna be happy no matter how big I get… I always think I could be better"[15]

The hunger keeps Greats on the pursuit.

The Pursuit

'The greats weren't great because at birth they could paint/
The greats were great 'cause they paint a lot/'
— Macklemore, 10 Thousand Hours

When Kanye creates an album that becomes the soundtrack to your life, when Apple creates products people can't live without, when Scorsese creates a film that becomes a piece of modern culture, we define it neatly as 'Genius,' or 'Greatness.'

What it really is though, is best described by Ben Affleck, as he went from actor to director and understood what creating something 'Great' really means. "It looks like 'greatness' from the outside. From the inside, to me, it just looks like really hard work."[1]

Or in the words of Pharrell: "I don't want anybody to think I have something that's more phenomenal than anybody else. It's just I have honed in on something and cultivated it for a very long time – and it pays off."[2]

All the names mentioned in this book have cultivated something 'for a very long time.' They have a work ethic way above that of the average person.

"Every word has to be perfect or I'll trip," said Eminem. "To this day if I do a show and fuck up a word or two, I will sit and dwell on it the entire night and the next day, until I perform again."[3]

"[Eminem's] always writing, he always carries notebooks," adds legendary producer Rick Rubin, "and he knows 99% of it will never be used for anything. But he wants his facility to be there so when he needs to write something it's like practice – master level practice all the time."[4]

Jay Z begun writing lyrics at nine years of age and from then on he would, "practice from the time I woke in the morning till I went to sleep. I filled every blank space on every page of a binder with rhymes…everywhere I went I'd write…I'd spend my free time reading the dictionary, building my vocabulary for battles."[5]

Hours are the only way to go from Bad to Okay to Good to Great.

"I've never viewed myself as particularly talented," says Will Smith. "Where I excel is ridiculous, sickening work ethic. While the other guy's sleeping I'm working. While other guy's eating I'm working…there's no easy way around it. [You have to] dedicate yourself to being better every single day."[6]

We could take any name in this book and they would say exactly the same as the Fresh Prince. For instance Kanye: "My whole life I've never really been that talented at anything except for working at something to the point where it was good. And then after I've done it a few times, then I'm just good at it. When people first heard me rap, it sucked, and now I'm arguably the best in the world."[7]

Or Rick Ross: "Whatever I was lacking I made up on my grind…all you got to do is outwork people around you. I feel I haven't slept in 15 years."[8]

Or Dame Dash: "[Initial Success with Roc–A–Fella] made me believe no one's better than me at anything it's just effort. And no one's better than anybody it's just how much you work at something."

'Far from being God, but I work god dam hard/ '
– Jay Z, Blueprint MLM

There is so much junk in the world – *products, books, music, films, services –* especially in the internet age, where creation equipment is available to anyone. That means it takes a lot of work to stand out from the ocean of mediocrity and create something that deserves to exist, something remarkable – worth making a 'remark' about – something Great.

Take Dr. Dre. He will keep working on a record for however long it takes to meet his uncompromisingly great targets.

"I don't take any shorts. I don't say, 'Okay, it's good enough.' I try to get exactly what I'm hearing in my head to the tape, and I won't let it move until then. In my opinion, some of the hip hop records that come out, people are willing to compromise. I'm not."[9]

Dre sees each 'thing' he produces (songs or products) as carrying his name, his reputation, his brand. He is obsessed with ensuring his name represents excellence and nothing less.

'If it's not a classic when it's done, we trash it' – 50 Cent, Places To Go

Despite producing countless classic albums, Dre feels his best work is yet to come and he'll keep at it till he achieves what he believes is his best.

"I don't feel like I've made my best record yet. The Marshall Mathers LP got the closest, but I don't feel like I've hit that thing just 100 percent perfect, from the first note to the last note. I always use Quincy Jones as an example– he didn't make his biggest record until he was 50 and he started when he was 14. So I feel like I have a lot of room to get that thing done."

Although he admits that 100% may not be achievable, the struggle to reach it is the reason he still pushes himself everyday: "It's definitely going to be a fun ride trying."

The most successful athlete of all time, Michael Jordan, felt the same way. He said, at the peak of his illustrious career: "I never feel I'm at my best. I feel there's room to improve. I'm never complacent with what I've achieved. I still feel I have a lot to prove as a player, a father, a role model…when I get to a point I feel I can't improve as a player I'll walk away from the game."[10]

So how does Dre know when a track meets his expectations? "It's a feeling I get when it's right, so I just keep going until I get that feeling. It's like a butterfly type feeling. When I hit it, that's when it's time to come out. Nothing leaves this studio until I get that feeling."[11]

No matter how long it takes, he will not stop till he has the feeling that it's the very best it can be. "Usually I get to the studio around 3.00 pm and my hours can vary anywhere from two hours to, I mean, my record is 79 hours nonstop. As long as the ideas are flowing, I'm in here…I feel when I come to the studio I have the same energy today as I did when I started."

'Taking my time to perfect the beat…' – Still Dre

This relentless pursuit of excellence makes a mark on all people around him. Like Dre's latest signing Kendrick Lamar, who commented: "What I've learned from Dre is how to continue getting better. It can never be that's it, just good. He always wants to get better. He's always working, always trying get better."

When Dre was working with TDE and Kendrick Lamar in 2011 on the song 'Compton,' Kendrick's manager, Punch, remembers:

"Kendrick is such a perfectionist that sometimes I'll just leave the studio [because] I think he got it good the first 20 times. I think he got a lot of that from Dr. Dre because when Dre first worked with him on Detox, Dre really made an impression on us.

"We were at Dre's house recording at four in the morning. We were working on this one song for hours. Dre's like, 'I'm tired. I'm going to go to sleep. Y'all can continue working if you want to.' He goes up to his room, maybe 10 minutes later you hear the same song we was working on blasting in his room. He runs downstairs and worked until eight in the morning. And Dre, he's set, he doesn't have to work another day in his life. So to see his work ethic, it really made an impression on us.

"It trickled right down. So Kendrick is not going to budge or compromise on his art. If he's not pronouncing something right, he's going to make sure he's got it before the public hears it. Because Dre came down and worked for four more hours and he don't have to do none of that – he's set forever. That definitely trickled down."[12]

And that explains why Dre is a billionaire today.

Getting Practical

Scientists have shown that after about 10,000 hours of 'practice' the brain operates at a different level and its actual structure changes. It's at this point you become one of the very best in the world in your field – an 'expert'.

But it's not just about putting in the time and passively absorbing information. It's about being intensely absorbed in the work, actively searching for connections, learning from every experience and finding ways to put knowledge into practical use. This is how the brain learns best, like how Ali would reflect for three seconds on each successful punch he landed.

'I bully myself 'cause I force myself to do what I put my mind too/'
– Eminem, Rap God

Then when you continue to work and reach 20,000 hours, the brain changes remarkably. It reaches a state of ultimate intelligence. A person at this level can work without even thinking. For everyone else the senses perceive a stimulus and then send a message to the brain, which analyzes the stimulus, based on previous experience, and then tells the body to act. But those with this amount of experience do something else. They bypass the normal cognitive loop and the body responds to stimulus without the brain getting in the way. Like Dr. Dre knowing 'instinctly' where a sound belongs on a record, or Jay Z being able to spit a classic verse a few minutes after hearing a beat. This is when people look at them in awe and label them a 'Genius' who can produce 'magic.'

"The 'magic' of being in the zone and coming up with hits instantly comes from all the work put in beforehand," said Jay Z. "It comes from "adding dead serious discipline to whatever talent you have."[5]

But only by working on something you're genuinely interested in are you able to push past the frustration and boredom others feel at learning the basics early on. If you're doing something you love, you love feeling yourself getting better; evolving. You don't quit, but keep working and naturally put in the hours to become an expert – (see 'The Re-Finding' *pg.58*).

Though very few other artists can match Dr. Dre's hours, Lil Wayne, who started rapping around 1991, comes close. Producer Mannie Fresh, who has worked with Wayne for over a decade, points to his work ethic as the reason for his success:

"From the very beginning Wayne's always been first one [in the studio] and the last one to leave. He knows 'I have to put work in', and that's what's lacking with a whole lot of new cats. They just think 'I just wanna get my chain, get my little money and I'm moving on.' It's so much more than that. It's hard work. Dedication."[13]

"I have to tell him to sleep," adds Cash Money CEO, Birdman.[14]

Wayne has released dozens of albums and mixtapes, as well as over 200 official singles, compared to say Jay Z's one-hundred fifteen singles. Whenever Wayne travels he takes a big black bag with portable recording equipment so he can keep working away from the studio. He's been recording and touring since turning 11, so it's become a habit. Like a smoker going without a puff for too long, he has developed cravings to work. And like Dre, that is the reason for his remarkable longevity.

'My name is Weezy, I'm almost perfect/
And I work harder than hard workin/ '
– Lil Wayne, Unstoppable

Kanye too works brutally hard to push his work to 'almost perfect'.
'Lock yourself in a room doing 5 beats a day for 3 summers' – Spaceship
In making 'College Dropout' every line was scrutinized, re-edited and improved upon. Lyrics could take months to finish to ensure they fit the music as perfectly as possible. "I [continually] went back and line for line tried to improve on it. I'm really meticulous with my lyrics."

In total the album took six years to write. No shortcuts were taken, both on the lyric front (for instance the second verse of 'Jesus Walks' took four months, and 'We Don't Care' took eight months to finish writing), and the production front (like how he insisted, despite label objections, on the Harlem Boys Choir for the 'Two Words' chorus, spent $10,000 to hire them and drove to their summer camp to record in a barn).

No matter how long the process, Kanye and the team keep working till the project was as good as they could get. For instance the ten seconds of strings in the middle of 'Jesus Walks' contain 100 separate tracks of sampled strings. Producer Damon Ranger remembers, "You'll spend four to eight hours, however long it takes to weave together a saxophone sound, but it has to sound like a saxophone mixed with like a viola."[15]

For the single 'Jesus Walks' Kanye created three different music videos, spending around $1.2million because the visuals for that song meant so much to him, (he originally wanted five videos but financially wasn't able).

Kanye would play songs for others and they'd be impressed but he'd say "It's not even done yet," and then spends months improving it so it sounded completely different to the original.

"I listen to Red Hot Chili Peppers and I listen to one of my songs, and if I don't give you the same emotion that Anthony Kiedis does, then I go back and re-spit," he told Fader Magazine.[7]

Kanye wants Greatness so badly he told The Source magazine before College Dropout's release that a rating of 4.5 mics out of 5 would, "crush me."

The same is true for his next album, 'Late Registration.' After performing on tour with Usher in late 2004, he would sit alone for hours in his dressing room replaying beats and searching for the perfect words to fit. "Each line is really important to me and I can't rush the process."[7]

Kanye spends so much time on his work because it represents a part of him. It's his brand. "The biggest thing I have going is a history of excellence. So I'd be more apt to really keep on working on it until it's excellent than to put it out and hinder that in anyway. I don't wanna put my name on something that's not excellent. If you see my name on something that's not excellent, it was a favor or some political bullshit. Just know, feel it in your heart, know when you know it's really a Kanye West stamp."

And despite all this work and all his success, he knows he still has not accomplished his goals in music. "I go to Starbucks every day, listen, look at the CD rack, and I'm like, I'm not here. I could easily give up and be like, 'Well, I'm black, and I'm a rapper, and I'm a....' all this type of shit. Or, I could be like, 'Man, what could I do to get here? I mean, you only got one life and shit, who's to say what you can and can't do?'"

"I'll be in Paris, at clubs and shit, and they'll play Jimi Hendrix, Rolling Stones. I'll be like, 'I have no songs that fuck with this. That's better than what I do. It's better than what I've done up to this point. I need to make music on this level.'"[7]

Kanye's relentless purist pays off. He's one of the most awarded, bestselling, and most influential artists of all time. "He's the most consistently great person in music today," says Rick Rubin[4] (– who himself says will always "keeps working on [a project] until it's magnificent"[16])

If these artists, who are already legends in the industry, spend hours and hours a day working on their craft, how can aspiring artists expect to 'make it' if they don't at least match this work ethic? – This applies to anyone aspiring to make it in any industry.

There are only a handful of people who will dedicate their lives to the 'Pursuit of Greatness'. People who do whatever is necessary to create work that deserve to exist in the world. Their names will love for centuries.

Maintaining

How do Greats maintain the pursuit with success (or failure) and age?

It comes back to your motives and what you want.

It's not possible to work that many hours (let alone 30 years) if your job is not your passion, your joy and love.

If the work seems a huge struggle, like a painful effort, then you need to check your motives. Why are you really doing this?

As we saw in 'The Why' (*pg.65*), once you become successful at what you're doing, once you become recognized and receive the spoils of your toils, (comfort, security, luxury), it is very easy to lose focus on the craft and become lazy, if you don't have an innate desire to continue raising the bar. The early rap groups, like Run DMC, could be said to have fallen for this. The group were living the high life in 'penthouse suites with penthouse freaks,' while younger, hungrier artists were spending hours honing their craft and eventually surpassing them.

Whereas for truly successful people who have long careers at the top of their game, from Dre to Michael Jordan to Warren Buffet, the motivation comes from the work itself, comes from the impact they want to have and the legacy they want to create. It means the hunger they have at day one remains at day 1000.

In one way or another Greats live by The Notorious B.I.G.'s words:

"The key to this joint. The key to staying on top of things is to treat everything like it's your first project. Like it's your first day like back when you was an intern…Just stay hungry." (My First Song)

As No I.D. explains: "My motto, and it's a real motto that I go by that keeps me in a good place, is I treat everything as if I've never done anything. When I sit down to work on something I don't think about what I did [and] I'm absolutely not going to name what I did.

"I view myself every day as someone who's trying to make some good music to impress this year's 17 year old or 27 year old or 37 year old or 47 year old – who isn't yesterday's 47 year old and so on. So it's just always a new, fresh challenge. You get caught up into what you did and you're out of here. I've seen it.

"That longevity is priceless, and it comes from not dancing in the end zone after you finally score a touchdown."[17]

'I made it but still playing like I'm scouted till I'm out it/'
– Drake, You Know

Greatness vs. Perfection

This chapter was originally titled 'Pursuit of Perfection.' It was changed because 'perfection' is actually a negative state of mind. There is a huge difference between a person striving for Greatness and one striving for perfection.

'When you strive for perfection/
Desire get confused and you could lose your direction/'
– Wale, The Number Won

The former will be satisfied in doing a good job and getting as far as possible, even if they didn't hit all their ambitious targets. Perfectionists will accept nothing less than some ideal dream. Nothing is ever good enough and they are never satisfied. Their mind is often clouded with negativity as they ignore all the successes they've had and dwell on the few misses.

Perfectionists can also often be the biggest 'losers'. They fear making errors so often won't even start. They keep procrastinating and planning, trying to perfect every detail and never launch their offering to the world. For most companies this is the worst attitude possible. It's the exact opposite mindset to most high growth, innovative companies, whose strategy is to create a 'minimum viable product' (MVP) and get it to potential customers, so they can test it, learn, adjust, then test again, then learn and adjust (and keep repeating). Holding back till the product is perfect means holding back forever. The world changes and what you perceived as being perfect last month is now outdated.

Being a perfectionist also means you're more anxious, tense and take less risks with your work. You don't dare to go near 'the edge' (*pg.276*) and so are unlikely to create anything deserving to exist.[18]

So instead, aim for Greatness and, *'Reach for the stars so if you fall, you land on a cloud'* (*– Kanye, Homecoming*)

The
Guarantee

'Fell on my face and woke up with a scar/
Another mistake living deep in my heart/'
– Kendrick Lamar, Bitch Don't Kill My Vibe

Practically all the artists featured in this book were rejected dozens of times by record labels because they weren't 'good enough.' Jay Z had to shut down his Las Vegas nightclub and aborted plans for a casino, racetrack and own-brand car. Kanye lost 13 million dollars on his defunct clothing line Pastelle. Russell Simmons folded his advertising company, modeling agency, magazine, TV show and more. The list of failures by the icons profiled in this book could continue for pages.

In-fact a total of 108 billion people have lived on this earth. Name one who has risen to the top of any industry without failing and the author will gladly refund the cost of this book.

It's the only impossible question because on any quest it's impossible not to fail, unless you live so cautiously that you never try – in which case you fail by default. So really the only people who don't fail are losers.

'To never try is the ultimate fail/'
– J Cole, Knock The Hustle

We face two choices. One, be consistently mediocre and never fail. Or two, be prepared to fail over and over and over again on the journey above mediocrity to Greatness.

In the words of Seth Godin: "If you're not prepared to get boo'ed of the stage you're not going near the edge, and if you're not going near the edge you're boring, and if you're boring no one is gonna talk about you."

So because failure is so common among Greats why is it seen by most people as the worst thing that could happen, like some infectious disease?

Maybe because in our society mediocrity is the standard and fear of failure (criticism, looking foolish, being wrong, losing money, offending, confronting…) is the silent norm.

This is not the Hip Hop mentality. Hip Hop does not place all the heaviness on 'failure' that the world does. As Pharrell explains, "There is no such thing as a failure. Only R&D [Research and Development] like companies have."[1]

Just like companies spend millions of dollars to fail, aka R&D, failing teaches us essential things we cannot learn in any other way. The 'Greats,' the 'Geniuses,' understand that the string of failures before the break makes them who they are. So they study their failures in search of the knowledge that will eventually lead to success.

'I was taught that mistakes made with great intentions/
Were never sins but where life lessons begin/'
– Brother Ali, The Puzzle

How?

There is an art in converting defeat into the blueprints for success and it begins with PMA.[2]

A 'Positive Mental Attitude' means you can flip a potentially negative experience into something useful to you. It means you can find the seeds of opportunity in all 'mistakes'.

Part of a PMA is being able to see yourself as if you're looking at another person; totally self-aware.

Most people get emotional when they make a mistake or 'fail'. They play the victim, complain, blame and get angry. "It's his fault," or "They screwed me over." Their ego defends itself by hiding behind emotions.

'It seems that if you're going through somethin' and life is feeling uncomfortable/
The immediate place you go is to your ego to comfort you/'
– Macklemore, Ego

Although it may make a person feel better about their mistake in the short term, what a waste it is that emotive responses stop lessons from being learnt, so mistakes get continually repeated and the person never grows. That is the definition of failure.

The Greats might also get angry in the heat of the moment, but they consciously try to take a step back and analyze themselves objectively. "Maybe I need to change this," "maybe this happened because that happened in the past." Every 'mistake' is taken as a blessing and an opportunity to learn and build a better person.

'Some people learn from mistakes and don't repeat them/
Others try to block the memories and just delete them/
But I keep up as a reminder they not killing me/'
– Immortal Technique, Mistakes

As Jay wrote in Decoded: "Let's say you're Jay Z and your album flops. Are you going to keep promoting it? No you're going to reflect on the feedback you were given, practice your flow, get new beats and go back into the studio and make a better album."

It's the chess law RZA learned from a Master mentor. "I learned to invest in my loss. If I lose and live to fight another day, I learn from loss."[3]

This is also another principle which comes naturally to Kanye: "If you [need to] learn from your mistakes, then I'm a fucking genius!"[4]

Persistence and the Impossible

One of the worst things about the way we are brought up – our schools, communities, influences – is the ease in which the word 'impossible' is thrown about.

Greats who live by Hip Hop's principles have no definition of 'impossible'. It's a foreign sound with no meaning.

'Difficult takes a day, impossible takes a week/ '
– Jay Z, Diamonds from Sierra Leone

People who claim your goals are impossible are narrow minded and blinded by their own limitations of what they think they can achieve. Life has been difficult and the lessons they have taken from difficulties is, 'there's no point trying to do something great. If I never try I never fail.'

As we saw in 'The Core' chapter what you believe is how you see the world, so to these people anybody else who is trying to do anything great, 'won't be able,' 'they're gonna' fail.' Our lives reflect our intentions and people with these thoughts will find that they are right. They won't be able. They are gonna' fail.

Great minds are so aware that 'nothing is impossible' that persistence to overcome failure comes naturally. Their journey ahead, from nothing to something, is exciting. They know they will get knocked back, and they look forward to that happening so that they can learn the lessons needed to strengthen their character and develop their experiences. They are also so confident in themselves, have so much belief in themselves and their ability to improve their situation soon, that any 'hard times' are enjoyed and appreciated. They know they'll be 'living good' soon enough, so take time to appreciate the struggle and every step of the journey – (see 'Love Life' *pg.324* for more examples).

'Had to lay way in the cut, til I finally got my turn/
Now I'm on top in the spot that I earned/ '
– Jay, My 1st Song

Looking at Kanye, in his struggle going from producer to rapper, he faced scores of opposition from music insiders calling him 'just a producer rapper' and he received countless rejections from not only record labels, but colleagues and friends.

But his hustle was to 'do whatever it takes,' so he would jump on tables to rap whenever there was an audience. He paid to tour the country supporting Talib Kweli. He took every opportunity to play his music until finally achieving that 'Yes' which gave him the opportunity to create his first album and prove to the world he was right.

'I knew on the Electric Circus tour he'd get it by any means like Malcolm/'
– Talib Kweli, Right About Now

The key is not being afraid to try even if it leads to failure. As Producer Jeff Bhasker says about Kanye:

> "A lot of times, we'll try something before a show and it wouldn't necessarily come off and you think, 'Oh, he's going to be mad because I messed up.' But he's always been quite forgiving. I get the feeling through working with him that he'd rather we try and fall down than not try. He's quite comfortable with taking a risk that might fail.
>
> It's that old saying, 'You have to be willing to fall in order to succeed.' Not being willing to fail, or accepting that you might fail, holds a lot of people back from trying something. I think he's aware of that. Even if we didn't deliver, as long as we keep trying we will eventually deliver. But if we don't try, that's more upsetting to him than not being able to deliver.
>
> It's funny to ask, 'Have you ever not been able to deliver?' Sure, we fail all the time, but eventually we succeed. We try again and we keep trying until we get it."[5]

'I took the T out the word can't'
– Kanye, Welcome Back

J Cole says "the most important lessons" he's learned so far in his career are patience, persistence and, "how to stick with it despite not moving as fast as hoped."

After graduating college, Cole was so confident with his music (he'd just released his first official mixtape 'The Warm Up') that he didn't apply for jobs like all his friends, as he felt he'd get signed in "three weeks". This didn't happen. "Two months after I graduated I was on rock bottom – broke, no food, no rent. I went back to get an $8 an hour job."[6]

Some might see this as a failure and give up on any dreams of breaking into music, and for a time Cole felt like moving back to his Mom's house in North Carolina. But instead, with support from his team, he "went harder," grinding for two years, using money from his jobs to pay for studio time and keep improving. Just before releasing his second mixtape he landed the deal he'd been dreaming of.

'I'm a firm believer if you never quit you never fail/
If I slip I grab the rail I'll get a grip and never fail/'
– J Cole, Funkmaster Flex Freestyle (Part 2)

So before starting out on the journey, know that failure is guaranteed. Therefore, instead of wondering 'How can I not fail?' ask 'What will I do after I fail?'[7]

When you go through temporary defeat will you say 'Oh well, I tried. Time to move on and do something else,' or will you recognize the valuable gems of learning, let the mistakes build your character, adapt your plans, pivot and go again? Will you change your dreams and adapt to failure, or change yourself on the road to your dream?

'If at first you fail, try, try, try, try again/'
– 50 Cent, Places to Go

Persistence comes naturally when a person wants something so much it turns into a burning desire. Once again it all goes back to the beginning of living your passions. If someone lacks persistence it's often because they're putting energy into a goal they're not truly passionate about, so they don't have a huge desire to push forward.

Whereas people who pursue their passions find it natural to immerse themselves in their work. They live it and naturally develop the mental strength to overcome obstacles and keep going till they get to 'Yes'.

The world has a funny way of testing people to the limit when success is around the corner. Most people give up at this point, not knowing that the 'Yes' was close. But those who refuse to quit will pass this 'persistence test' and get their reward. (See Pahrrell's story *pg.249* for an example).

To stay persistent and overcome the dips:

• Practice 'The Affirmation' *(pg.95)*, and visualize yourself accomplishing the clearly defined end goal.
• Have a clear plan with constant action to keep moving forward, *(pg.122)*.
• Rise above the events that can distract by remaining locked into the ultimate objective with Tunnel Vision Focus.

The Headlights

TUNNEL VISION FOCUS

*'You can get the money you can get the power/
Keep your eye on the final hour/'*
– Lauryn Hill, Final Hour

The mind is a sporadic noisy creature. It's racing in a million directions like Kanye's beat 'On Sight'. Psychologists estimate the average person can focus intently on one thing for around 10 minutes, before the mind darts around in a spiral of unorganized thought. What if we could train the mind to mute the noise and focus stronger for longer? How much more effectively would we be able to learn?

"Once you focus your mind, money will follow," says the global face of Hip Hop 'kulture' KRS–One. "Success is about a mental exercise in controlling the mind. Controlling the wants, desires and temptations that govern life and send the mind in hundreds of circles. Controlling and focusing the mind leads to wealth."[1]

The ability to intensely focus on a goal until it's realized is maybe Kanye's greatest hidden asset. He told The Source in 2003:

> "When I was focused on basketball I was actually kind of cold but now I'm mad mediocre. I was an artist ever since I was little. When I was focusing on that, I won every contest and got a scholarship for my first year of college, but now, if I sit down and try to draw, it's going to be decent, but it's not going to be like, 'Yo, dog, you won a scholarship?'
>
> So now, look, I said, 'I'm going to focus on beats fully.' And then I ended up doing the most beats on the first classic album of the century, [The Blueprint]. Now, I'm partially responsible for the most classic albums this century because I focused on that.
>
> Now, is he going to be a good rapper? We got Grammy nominated for 'H to the Izzo' and I said, 'Look, I'm going to focus on rap,' and I ended up on the hottest rap label in the world. What the fuck I look like rapping? How did I end up on Roc–A–Fella? I never had a good voice. I never had a good rapper story. I wasn't ever that much of a pimp where I just had mad girls. I never was shooting at n****, so what was it? It was just focus. I decided I want to do this."[2]

(*I decided I want to do this.*' The power in those words is extraordinary.)

Most people can focus on an important task, on their 'dreams,' and follow the inner-voice/conscious/higher-self/third-eye to feel inspired for a short while. But the world around us seems to be naturally inclined to distract and bring a person down from the higher self.

Where focus goes energy flows, and if we can block all the bullshit around us to develop tunnel vision focus on our mission, like a sniper in combat, nothing outside our world will come in to disturb the flow. Whatever does come in is dealt with quickly and if it's not important isn't dealt with at all.

Jay Z learned this from The Notorious B.I.G. Before BIG's death, the two rappers and their right hand men, (TyTy and D.Roc), would often go out to dinner followed by nightclubs. On one occasion, after pulling up in front of the club 'Exit' in Manhattan, BIG saw some adversaries from his hustling days and said he wasn't going in the club. Jay initially thought BIG was afraid, but upon reflection realized that BIG was focused on the bigger picture and did not want to get caught up in petty bullshit, which wouldn't contribute to his goals. BIG was focused on Greatness.[3]

'Forever petty minds stay petty / Mines thinkin longevity until I'm seventy'
– Jay Z, 22Twos

Of course this is hard. Most lack the attention span to maintain nonstop focus. Most can't sustain a willful blindness to the unimportant, minor distractions going on around them. But having your mission firmly ingrained in your mind means focus comes more naturally. You say to self:

"I am ....therefore I WILL NOT bite the distraction."

Sean Combs, aka Diddy, has developed a tunnel vision focus that few can rival. It's something those who work with him are often shocked by. Like, some of Diddy's co-stars in the movie 'A Raisin in the Sun' commented: "He has a work ethic unlike anything I've ever seen. He is tireless, and he is a cheerleader and a clown." "He's a real mascot. He has an infectious enthusiasm that I've never seen before."[4]

Diddy lives by a series of positive terms, which he says "keep us focused, keep us grinding and moving forward."[5] Terms like:

Let's go:

"Let's go is a constant reminder to stop daydreaming and go," he says. "To make sure I'm staying focused. To keep going forward. Let's be positive. Let's take it up another notch. Let's make these hits. Let's spend time with our kids. Let's pray to God. Let's stop procrastinating. Let's go!"

Lock in:

"Lock in on your dream. Lock in. That means turn off Twitter, stop gossiping, put the blunt down. Lock in. If someone says 'you wanna go out?' [You say] 'No I gotta go to the library to do research.' Lock In."

Diddy didn't develop this relentless focus on the important when he became successful. It-Is-The-Thing-That-Made-Him-Successful. "I didn't have money to eat, but I stayed focused. I was gonna make it one day."[6]

'I looked back and saw the cat focus took notice / Stayed away from the bogus / '
– Puff Daddy, Do You Know

As already mentioned, Kanye embodies this principle well. "I'm like a machine, a robot. I'm so focused. You can't stop a robot. There's nothing anybody can say or do to me to stop the product I'm going to put out," he declared in the famous 2013 Zane Lowe interview.

When recording his masterpiece MBDTF and his collaborative 'Cruel Summer' albums from 2009–2012, Kanye set up a recoding environment in Hawaii, away from all the distractions of the world. A place where a team of producers and rappers could all focus on creating the best product possible.

Pusha T remembers it well. "As soon as you walk in the studio, there were signs saying '*no Twitter, no Instagram*'. You can't talk about anything but the album. Then you have questions on the wall like '*What would Mob Deep do?*' or '*Would this belong on 'The Blueprint' album?*' The bar is set, without anybody speaking a word [because] that's the first thing you see."[7]

Common, who was also part of that team, reflects on the benefit of the environment. "The signs create a certain team comradery. Everybody has to be focused. You know the mentality: we're here to make some great music and we ain't getting caught up in the outside world."

Comedian Chris Rock spent a few weeks in Hawaii with Kanye working on MBDTF and was amazed at the environment 'Ye had set up: "He was living it. First of all everybody in the studio had suits on – all engineers in black suits. He set up a mood. When you walked in you felt a mood. When you talk to him he's living it. He's immersed in it. And when he does fashion he's immersed in it."[8]

Focusing on our mission is easier when our entire environment is also focused on that goal. That's also the reason why businesses develop best in 'clusters' with other similar businesses. Like Silicon Valley for technology companies, Hollywood for film, Wall Street for finance firms. When people around us are focused on similar goals we keep one another on track.

Routines

'Dedication, hard work, routine builds character/'
– Nas, You Wouldn't Understand

Setting up a routine is another good way to keep focused and avoid external distractions. RZA, who was also in awe of Kanye's work ethic and focus, broke down the team's daily routine while creating MBDTF, (this is also a great example of 'Balance' – *pg.241*):

> "They get up every morning and eat breakfast together – his whole crew. Over breakfast, they plan, talk about what they're gunna do, what they did, and how to make the music better. Then they go exercise together. They go to the YMCA and play basketball, lift weights. They focus and get the energy up, get the chi up. Then they do some charity work. Invite kids – doing good deed for day, good karma. Then they go to the studio from 4pm – when I was there we stayed there till 4am; 12 hours studio work. Then they go to bed and do it again the next day….The way everything happened was focused energy and I've never seen that from a rapper before. It's not only his talent that took him to the top. It's his focus y'alll."[9]

The 20%

Jay Z has released more number one albums than any solo artist in history. On top of that he's involved in numerous businesses, from clothing to sports management, advertising and nightclubs.

> *'Write 16's while running 16 businesses/'*
> *– Reminder*

How does he find time to create so much quality work?
Constant focus on only the most important things.

Effective focus is about using time wisely to do whatever is most important first – 'put first things first' as Stephen Covey writes[10] – and spending as little time as possible on low value, unimportant, activities.

It means living the 80:20 principle, which, according to management consultant Joseph Juran and others, states that in most areas of life 80% of results come from 20% of activities. For example:

80% of income comes from 20% of clients/jobs

80% of the value comes from 20% of the product

80% of work is completed by 20% of a team.

By putting the 20% first productivity sky rockets.

What's your 20%?

Identify your 20% at the start of each day. Ask yourself: What's the top priority? What's the one thing I could do that will have the most impact on my professional or personal life?

Then, plan *the first* two, three or four hours of the work day around doing that one thing.

When 50 Cent was starting out in the late 90's he committed himself to creating two songs per day, every day, because having products to put on mixtapes was the most important thing for him.

For most businesses the top priority is S&M – sales and marketing. So the first part of everyday should be spent thinking of better ways to market your product, making sales calls, or some other related activity.

Until that number one priority thing is done, everything else (meetings, email, web browsing (even meals)) is a distraction. The work day does not end (no matter what time it is) till that most important thing has been done. (If you want to have a balanced personal life it needs to be done first thing in the day.)[11,12]

One tool to focus on the 20% every day is The Chain Game.[13]

Get a calendar. Set a goal. When you achieve the goal for that day put a big cross on the calendar. Do that every day and sees how long a chain you can create. If the chain is broken, start again and try to beat the last chain.

Goals should be 20% activities. For example: 'Write as much as you can for three hours,' or 'Make as many sales calls as you can for two hours.'

For extra motivation say to yourself that if you don't complete the goal today it gets added onto tomorrows work. So you might have six hours of writing to face tomorrow instead of three today.

(The Habit List App (habitlist.com) and www.tde.me use this 'streaking' principle to help achieve goals and form habits.)

As the day progresses, it's easy to lose sight of the 20% and get taken in by the easy but low value 80% activity traps. So we have to remember to *always question why we're doing things*. Always ask yourself 'Is This Useful?' 'Is going to this event/reading this/talking to this person really essential?'

80% of our time is typically spent on low priority activities like checking emails, phone calls, or 'researching' things that won't help us achieve results but are easy and fun to do. The idea is to eliminate these low value activities that take up 80% of our time so we can give more time and focus to the activities that generate most value.

As well as always asking yourself *'Is This Really Useful?'* you can use tools to help stay away from the tempting 80% distractions online like the customizable website blocking services 'Leechblock' and 'K9 software'.

'Hov had to get the shallow shit up off him/'
– Jay Z, Lost Ones

Putting the 20% first often means doing things that you don't enjoy doing. 20% activities don't provide immediate satisfaction like other 80% activities. Their benefit becomes apparent in the long run, so it takes more motivation to focus on them.

Interestingly, a study found that *the* most important factor separating success from failure (more than talent or skill) is: *Successful people do the things failures don't like to do.*[14] They don't necessarily like to do them either, but they do them anyway. And how are they able to tolerate unpleasant '20%' work? It's because they have such strong belief in themselves that they truly believe doing unpleasant work now allows them to master their craft and do whatever they want in the future. Their 'Higher Purpose,' allows them to sacrifice short term pleasure for a far greater long time reward.

'I'mma stack paper, hustle just to relax later/'
– J Cole, Grew Up Fast

The Why

As with most of these principles, if the 'Why?' (the motivation) is correct, focus will naturally flow.

Curtis Jackson (aka 50 Cent) wasn't necessarily a special or gifted person growing up. After dropping out of High School he sold drugs while living with his grandma in a poor area of Queens, and then back and forth with his baby momma's mother. Life was tough and his job was dangerous. After narrowly escaping death (literally 2cm from death), he laid off dealing and with a minuscule income found it hard raising his son alone. He'd wait for the bus with his baby in a stroller, while former 'colleagues' laughed.

But Curtis had a mission. He was sick of hiding and constantly watching his back for the people that wanted him dead, sick of being unable to support his family, sick of feeling powerless. He had a 'Why,' he had a mission, and all his energy became focused on the goal of making it big in music, (then venturing into other areas). He developed well thought-out, step–by–step plans to reach his goals and focused on them religiously.

Former music attorney Reggie Ossé remembers his first meeting with Curtis in 2002: "[He] was incredibly focused. Perhaps the most focused person I had ever met during my time on this planet. The man spoke calmly, with incredible clarity as to his immediate and future plans, how he was going to get his family out the hood, put together an album that wouldn't just shock the world but would also make him very rich."[15]

Crunch Time

If a boss sets a project to be handed in by 12:00 pm Tuesday, 80% of employees (or students) will send it Tuesday morning. It's called Parkinson's Law when work expands to fit the time it's given. The cure is deadlines. Set deadlines and work to beat them.

Kanye calls it Crunch Time:

> "So many people do good in crunch time, so why not do everything in crunch time? So, when we were in Hawaii I would go to the studio every day and be like, 'We're gonna finish the fucking album today.' It would be like there are some songs that aren't even done yet, mad shit that need to be filled in, and I be like, Let's attack this like we're gonna finish the album today.
>
> Because people are always like, I got time; the label had my release date in February. But why? I'm like, No, push my release date up to the closest possible thing, and if you tell me we have to have this shit mastered by next week. I will get it done."[16]

Vices

The 20% also means not getting distracted by temptations that take you away from your focus. For many successful people that means drugs.

"I could count the number of times I smoked trees," Jay Z says. "I liked to stay sober, the better to stay focused on making money. I come from that class of hustlers who looked at smoking as counterproductive. We used to judge [people] who smoked as slackers, or workers."[17]

'I don't pop moly, I rock Tom Ford/'

Partner at Roc-A-Fella, Dame Dash lived to a similar philosophy. "My rule is don't start smoking till you make your first million."

In fact the list of names featured in this book that don't drink or smoke (or do only on rare occasion) is surprisingly long: 50 Cent *('success is my drug of choice, I'm high off life' – Outta Control)*, Tyler the Creator, Eminem, Hopsin, Andre 3000, K'naan, Lauryn Hill *(I don't puff blunts so I always got my breath' – Nappy Heads)*, Lupe Fiasco, stic.man, Kid Cudi *('no drink no tree and I'm levitated' – Too Bad)*, Royce da 5'9", Ghostface Killah, Macklemore, Akon, Chuck D, Ice T, Pharrell… and most others do so only with balance and control.

'When I get bubbly I do it in moderation/'
– Common, Chapter 13

Many take it even further and are so focused that partying or going out at all causes anxiety because they know they're losing a bit of that focused energy. Like Drake said, "If I choose to go after this, and go kick it with a woman or go out for drinks, I know I'm potentially slipping because I have brothers like [Rick] Ross and Wayne that are working like nonstop."[18]

'I swear if ni***s put half of what they put in chasing ass/
Into a craft, by now you'd be famous and rich/'
– J Cole, Is She Gon' Pop

Of course we need to enjoy life, but the important thing is to think about tomorrow, and not let any potentially negative things we do today affect tomorrow i.e. our future.

It's a mark of genius to postpone reward today for a greater reward tomorrow.

Meditation

'So I just meditate at the home in Pompeii/
About how I could build a new Rome in one day'
– Kanye, Clique

Focus is about muting (or at least quieting) the distractions around us so we can concentrate only on the task at hand. This is how the mind thinks, learns and performs at a higher state. It's 'in the zone.'

Meditation is the practice of focusing the mind – the gym where focus muscles strengthen. Meditation is about living in the present and 'detoxing' from the constant overstimulation all around us. It helps us stand above the noisy, frantic, chaos of our day-to-day thoughts and experience the world with clarity. Then, from a clear, still, stress-free space, we can direct the mind however we want. As Russell Simmons says, "Meditation is the practice of touching stillness."[19]

Russell's book 'Success through Stillness' illustrates dozens of scientific studies showing the benefit that continual practice of meditation has on almost all areas of a person's life. For example physical benefits like decreased blood pressure, and lessened risk of cancer. Mental benefits like increased creativity, and decreased stress. And emotional benefits like increased feelings of compassion, gratitude and happiness.

Most names in this book use forms of meditation (i.e. quieting and focusing the mind) in their daily lives and will credit it as a major reason for their success. For example Russell says of Jay Z:

"Jay might be the coolest person I've ever met. I believe what makes Jay so unflappable is that he's able to live in the moment. In the recording studio, in the streets, in a boardroom, onstage, wherever he's at, people might be going crazy around him, snapping pictures, slapping his back, or scramming his name, but you sense Jay never gets caught up in it. He's always connected to, and content with, what's happening in his own head."[15]

The calm, controlled aura people often comment on after meeting Jay comes from living 'in the zone,' 'in the present.' We admire and want to be around that type of charisma, but it's not an elusive, godly quality. We can condition that same calm, focused aura in ourselves through meditation.

'Stepped it up another level, meditated like a Buddhist/'
– Jay Z, Can I Live

Meditation doesn't have to be about sitting cross-legged under a tree for hours trying to reach nirvana. Anything that involves focusing your attention in the present, on whatever you're doing, is using your mind-fully – and mindfulness is, in essence, meditation.

There are countless 'meditation snacks' that can be just as powerful and easily applied to your everyday life. Then, with practice, just like push-ups condition physical strength, meditation conditions mental strength and we can take that focus into all areas of our life.

How?

Russell recommends the following technique: [20]

1. **Sit** somewhere free from distractions. You could sit in your living room, stairwell, toilet or car, but don't think of noise around you as an obstacle preventing you form meditating. Instead of getting frustrated accept the noise as part of your world. "Let go of the negative emotion toward noise and realize it can't touch or affect your stillness, and it will fade away," says Russell.

Whether you sit on a chair, cross legged on the floor, (or in the lotus position if you can: right foot over left thigh, left foot over right thigh. Or half lotus, with only one foot on top of a thigh), keep your back straight (imagine a tight string through your spine towards heaven), shoulders dropped and chest open.

> 'Kept his mind focused, meditation position half lotus/
> Abbot's sword novas couldn't match his magnum opus/'
> – RZA, Samurai Showdown

2. **Mantra**. Russell recommends using the universal mantra 'rummm' as a tool to focus the mind. Repeat the word gently over and over to yourself while sitting quietly. The mantra is the only thing you will focus on.

(Although note that there is no right or wrong mantra, so do whatever feels right. Some Christians use 'Jesus,' some Muslims use 'Allah.' 50 Cent says he got his mantra 'I Am' from Deepak Chopra, the author of '7 laws of spiritual success'.

"I ask myself who I am," says 50. "It makes me conscious of me in a different way…then I go through my grandparents and say their name out loud so it makes me reflect on how they feel about me….I ask myself 'who am I?' I'm my mother's child. Grandparents child, and I run through a list of things important to me…then when I run into someone with negative energy I know it's not mine."[21]

> 'They thought I'm going down, now look I'm levitating/ I'm with Deepak, meditating/'
> – 50 Cent, United Nations

Or instead of a mantra many people just focus on breathing. They sit and just think about the sensation of air moving in and out of the lungs.)

3. **Maintain**: When you get thoughts about anything other than the mantra recognize them, let them go and bring the mantra back to the forefront of your mind. No matter how many thoughts come, don't engage or try to fight them. Just notice that the mind has wandered and gently bring the mantra back to focus. No matter how loud the distractions are at first, like an unruly child demanding attention, if you don't engage the thoughts and keep focused on the mantra (or breathing) they will leave you.

4. As you meditate you'll go through **stages**:

'Beginning Phase,' where the mind settles in and begins to focus. This is the hardest part, when the most distractions will come.

'Taking Inventory Phase,' with less distracting noise and where creative ideas may come to you – you can examine the ideas for a moment and then come back to the mantra.

'Pure Consciousness Phase': where "thoughts subside and you can access limitless pools of stillness inside you," says Russell. "This is the phase where the physical healing properties of meditation come from."

When your mediation is over gently come back to the real world. Sit for a minute and slowly breathe and listen, soaking up the energy around you. Then bring the feeling into your day.

Russell recommends doing this for twenty minutes in the morning and twenty minutes in the evening, every day. (Use a gentle alarm to mark twenty minutes.) Practice every day and eventually the serene 'in the present' focus will be a natural part of your life.

This practice turns us from a slave to the noise and distractions around us into the master of our mind – the root definition of success (*pg.14*).

Other Ways

Again there is no right or wrong way to do it. Meditation is a form of mindfulness and anything that gets you focused 'in the moment' can be called meditation.

For example, Kendrick Lamar doesn't necessarily use a mantra or focus on breathing, but meditates in his own way by starting each day staring at himself in the mirror for ten minutes:

> "It started when I was nine years old. Talking to myself in the mirror I saw something a little different than just what the eye can see in the physical form. I saw my soul in the mirror. It's scary to realize you can take your mind somewhere totally different…what it does for me is lets me know who I am and who I always will be and where I came from and what I'm trying to do with myself and the people

around me as far inspiring others and continuing to be positive...it's a tricky thing but it works. It lets you know who you are for real."[22]

RZA also meditates in his own way:

"To me, reading is meditating and playing is meditating. You have meditation and you have meditation in action. When Bodhidharma went to teach Buddhism, to help spread Buddhism in China, the monks were tired. Their bodies weren't strong. They would meditate good, but they'd fall asleep. So Bodhidharma gave them Kung Fu, a physical way to meditate. Then, with a strong body and a strong mind, they could reach this nirvana or phase of enlightenment that their heart was yearning for.

In my own personal life, I meditate both ways. At the top of my property there is this little pagoda-type structure. I go up there and sit for hours. Sometimes I sit with my eyes closed in a meditative position. Sometimes I sit with my eyes open. Sometimes – and I don't suggest this to others – I smoke my little bit of weed and relax. But the main thing I am doing is calming my heart and body and letting myself speak to myself. That's one of the main goals of meditation, I think. To have yourself speak to yourself."[23]

Russell Simmons's partner in founding Def Jam, Rick Rubin, is also a devote mediator (and cites it as a large reason for his long-lasting success in music). He describes some of the meditating exercises he does before getting out of bed in the morning:

"[Firstly,] pull your fingers on your forehead and then pull hard [and slide down your face] until your hands are placed kinda hard on your windpipe... [Another one is called] 'galloping horses,' and you start tapping on your head, working all the way back, from top to back."[34] (Whilst doing these exercises your only focus is on the feeling of your fingers on your skin.)

Here are some more short 'mindfulness/meditation snacks' you can take throughout the day:

• When you wake up take three deep breaths, and then listen to sounds around you. Listen to the traffic, the birds, the neighbors. Just listen.

Wake up give thanks for another day/Take a little time and meditate'
– Blu, Wake Up

162

- Try shorter deep breathing exercises when the mind gets cloudy or anxious: Take a deep breath through your nose for four seconds. Hold for eight seconds. Exhale for six seconds. Hold for four seconds. Repeat. Your only focus is on your breathing. This clears the mind as the body goes into 'survival mode' and blocks out the unimportant. You can then find it easier to refocus on your 'Higher Purpose'.

> *'I felt the panic when they locked me in that cell again/I had to pray and meditate, control my breath again'* – T.I., *Hallelujah*

- When feeling overwhelmed take a walk at night and look up. Think about space and the infinite universe and remember how small (in comparison) we and our problems are, and how ultimately:

> *'The world it seems so very small/cause nothing even matters, at all'* – Layrn Hill, *Nothing Even Matters*

- Meditation can also be about taking a break from the noise of everyday life. Once a week, or month, it can be useful to go into nature or somewhere peaceful, to clear the mind and assess what is important and where you want to be. Kanye moved to Hawaii for six months after the 'Taylor Swift incident,' and the subsequent media and public onslaught. "It was the first time I stopped since I had 'made it'. It was time to take a break and develop my thoughts as a person and a creative. Time to focus my thoughts on what I want to bring [to the world]."[24]

> *'I just need to clear my mind now, it's been racing since the summer time'* – Kanye, *Blood on the Leaves*

- Finally an exercise from entrepreneur and Hip Hop fan James Altucher: "Surrender. Spend sixty seconds completely dedicating this day to whatever higher power you want to believe in (The Force, God, the Tao, The Supreme Alien Intelligence from the Black Hole that's at the center of the Milky Way Galaxy, etc). They are going to take over your body and mind and do their thing today. Hand over the keys to your body and mind during those sixty seconds and know that today will be dedicated to doing their mission. You are just the vehicle."[25]

The 'Surrender' concept is a similar idea to how Pharrell lives his life:

"You know, we are vessels, we are straws. We are not the juice. And anyone that believes that, those are the people that end up losing their minds later on in life or not happy. I don't have to be the juice. I don't have to be the glass. I don't have to be the coldest part of the whole entire thing, which is the ice. You could be that. I am just happy to be a part of it."[26]

Maintaining Headlights 1

As people or businesses experience success it's tempting to branch out to different sectors and work on exciting new projects. But this can mean we're no longer as focused on the 'thing' that initially started us, the thing we're known and loved for, and so the quality of our original product gradually deteriorates.

This is a common issue for rappers who move into acting. "Movies have killed more rap careers than bullets," jokes Chris Rock. "If you're doing a record on the side it's not gonna be a banger. You gotta live it. Eat it. Breathe it…You gotta drop a verse, sit on it a few days, then come back and say, 'I don't like that, let's do it again.' That's advice for anything, writing jokes, music, whatever."[8]

Those who can work successfully in different sectors do so because they focus solely on one project at a time. "A lot of time when you're doing a lot of things you can't give it the proper attention," said rapper and actor Common. "The best music I made I had to focus on, so for me when I'm doing an album that's where my focus is."[27]

By the foes I was told, either focus or fold'
– Common, The Corner

Russell Simmons learned this principle the hard way. With the meteoric success of Def Jam in the late 80's, Russell diversified into a range of businesses from modeling to banking. Times were good and the team had visions of emulating Virgin Group with a diverse global brand. But Russell soon realized he had too many plates (or vinyl shall we say) spinning and could not commit the resources to make each venture a success. Not only were these offshoot businesses failing, but Def Jam Record label, the cornerstone of this empire, was also deteriorating. Russell had created Rush Association Labels, which tried to mirror Sony's structure by creating several labels under the mother label but "all of them were unsuccessful," Russell admits. Def Jam didn't have the financial or human resources needed and at its financial worst was $17 million in debt.

Russell took the positive lesson, "to focus on what we do best and master one craft at a time."[28]

Instead of doing two things with half an ass, Greats use their whole ass to focus on creating one great thing, and then move on to the next.

Maintaining Headlights 2

Another reason many will fall from the top is they lose focus and neglect the little things. They see themselves as 'Mr. Big Shot' who deserves to be on top, and thereby lose humility. When they lose humility they lose their connection to the marketplace – the people who've made them who they are. This is practically a guarantee that failure is close.

Look at the story of Dame Dash after he left Roc-A-Fella in 2006. Dame walked away from the company with around $20 million and was living the high life. His payroll of staff included: a personal assistant, executive assistant, chef, bodyguard, butler, chauffeur, barber, full time photographer ("to capture his every move"), as well as on call architects and other professionals. He told NY Mag in 2006: "Not many people understand how important having a butler is, but it is. I need somebody to help me get everything I'm going to wear for the day all set up, know what I'm saying?" (Incidentally, all Dame's T-shirts and socks were always brand new as he'd wear them only once before donating). Dame had properties around the country, one of which in downtown New York had three bedrooms devoted to clothes, "where the dressing room and the sneaker room each have their own bathroom."

Dame saw himself as a king entitled to his position, "in the motherfucking hall of fame," and now viewed the actual work he'd done to get there as beneath him. He told a group of his employees in 2006: "Now, it would be hard for me to hit the street looking for talent. I'm 35. I go to operas and shit in Milan. I want everything different now," referring that he would not be the one scouting and pushing new music signings. "After you made history once, it's like flying first class: You can't go back to coach."[29]

Just a couple years later his properties were foreclosed, he's divorced, owed millions in back taxes and travels by coach. Success was his falling. He distanced himself from his customers in luxury homes and offices and lost the connection with the streets.

In the corner office you can't spot and act on the cultural changes that a guy hustling on a street corner can. One day he will replace you.

'Arrogance bring the fall of many'
– Talib Kweli, Palookas

Now compare that story to Sean Combs, (after all Dame and Sean were the right hand men of (in many people's opinions) the world's two greatest rappers, Jay Z and B.I.G). Sean broke into the industry obsessed with 'the detail.' Working with Uptown and then Bad Boy he would involve himself in everything from the way an artist looked, to their production, video, makeup and marketing copy. Yet he's been able to retain that obsession after over twenty years and hundreds of millions of dollars of potential distractions. He told VH1: "If I have to jump in my car and go shopping to style a video, to this day, I will do things like that. If I have to button your shirt or tie your tie, I will do that."[30] He stays immersed in the culture.

'The word's on the street so keep your ears to the concrete/'
– AZ, Rather Unique

That mentality unites all Great people and companies who stand the test of time. Russell Simmons writes: "The President of a company also has to be a good servant. He has to provide a service to his people to make them feel good about what they're doing. You become a great leader by being a great servant. There's not much difference in that sense between being an intern and being the top leader."[30]

The reason Apple, (predicted to be the world's first trillion dollar company, (although Kanye thinks he'll get their first with 'DONDA'[31])), continues to grow is because it's run like a small local business. As the late Steve Jobs said, "Apple is the world's biggest start-up." The company pays attention to all the small details that might seem insignificant to outsiders. Every button, every pixel, every curve, every font, every word on every advertisement, is given serious attention and no (literally NO) corners are cut. It means no matter how big they get, every customer is important and they continually push to delight, never just satisfy, each and every one.

Cyhi Da Prynce sums up Kanye and the GOOD Music system similarly:

"Working with 'Ye is not a traditional rap environment, its run like Apple – the actual brand. It's strenuous work, sound for sound, word for word. Everything has to mean something. He's in there not trying to impress you, He's trying to put out a message."[32]

'Keep your nose out the sky, keep your heart to God
And keep your face to the risin' sun/'
– Kanye West, Family Business

There's numerous ways to remain focused on the core, the most important, the 20%, and not slip into 'entitled king' mode with success.

For example, Jay Z hangs artwork in his home, like Basquiat's 'Most Kings Get Their Heads Cut Off' as a "warning"[15] that *'success is like suicide'*, and David Hammons' 'Untitled,' which shows two panels of ominous grey shades with broken bricks scattered beneath, to remind Jay of his roots.

T.I. wears expensive jewelry on one wrist, and three rubber bands on the other, to keep his feet grounded and character humbled.

While in Russell Simmons' multi-million dollar, eleven bedroomed, Swarovski crystal chandelier furnished, mansion, hangs an old sign reading *'Waiting Room for Colored People.'*[33]

The
Infinite
Semester

'Had to play with fire and get burned/
Only way the boy ever gon' learn/'
– Jay Z, My First Song

Fall 1995 and a 17 year old Kanye sat alone in his bedroom. A messy pile of clothes lay in a heap on the floor alongside a stack of GQ magazines, while a keyboard and computer monitor took up all the space on two walls. Tupac's 'California On' was playing on repeat for over an hour, as Kanye desperately tried to understand how Dr. Dre had created such a multi-dimensional beat.

For days Kanye studied the beat, struggling to recreate the intricate sounds on his $500 Omega computer. But he persisted through the frustration, and sometimes boredom, in the learning process, and eventually 'got it.' Now he's able to create beats in minutes that 17 year olds sitting in messy bedrooms marvel at.

Like all Greats, Kanye started out knowing nothing, but committed himself to years of focused learning. Perhaps more than any other principle, that is the most essential quality that has made him who he is today, and who he will become tomorrow. In his own words:

"There's nothing I really wanted to do in life that I wasn't able to get good at. That's my skill. I'm not really specifically talented at anything except for the ability to learn. That's what I do. That's what I'm here for."[1]

The brain has evolved to learn best in two ways: by doing something first hand, and by watching other successful people.

Combining the two is the most effective way to learn anything.

Most Greats develop their unique style this way. After years of emulating their idol's technique they come across a unique style, which combines all their idols with their own distinctive 'voice,' to form something special.

'To every young man this is the plan/
Learn from others like your brothers Rae and Kanye/ '
– Raewkwon, Gorgeous

This is exactly how Kanye developed as a producer, rhymer, and now fashion designer, film maker, architect...

"My beats were wack at one point. I learned how to make hot beats."[2]

"I used to attempt to produce beats like Bad Boy," he told The Source in 2002. "The reason why I got so nice is because I'd be at home trying to be Stevie J, Nashiem, D–Dot, Ron Lawrence – all them combined. I finally came to New York and people were blown away. Like, 'Damn, dog you program your own drums? You find your own samples? Damn! You play your own instruments? Damn! What're you doing man? You're putting in too much work!' I learned. I was in the crib by myself, trying to make it sound as close to a BIG or a Ma$e beat as possible. Sometimes it would take me five days to make a beat."[3]

Pharrell and the Neptunes also applied this technique when learning how to produce. They were "obsessed with A Tribe Called Quest," and would spend days trying to understand how the trio made their beats, then try to recreate them.

Ronald "Slim" Williams, CEO of Cash Money, one of the most successful black owned record labels, did the same thing when setting up the label. "We studied people who came before us, and learned how to expand and take it further."[4]

Jay Z learned how to make the transition from the street corner to the corner office the same way. As Kevin Liles says: "Jay Z leaned how to up his game by watching other people and interacting with executives in the mainstream business world."[5]

J Cole analyzed the raps of Greats to understand how they connected with the listener. *I used to print out Nas raps and tape em' up to my wall'*. As well as studying the business and political side of the music industry. "I studied the game and I studied the Greats and I studied people's movements and the mistakes they made and the pitfalls."[6]

Even people who are far from icons, whose names you won't find anywhere else in this book because they violate most other principles, are astute, never ending learners. For instance, Death Row Records co-founder Suge Knight. "He was a clever student, soaking up each and every experience or encounter and then throwing out the stuff he didn't need," writes Suge's former bodyguard McKinley Malik Lee.[7]

"I find any great man, black or white,
I'm gonna study him, learn about him, so he can't be great to me no more."
– Tupac

Find the people whose work you admire most in your field, study what they do and how they do it. Once we can recreate the work of masters we have the skills to create great original work.

But a lot of people are eager to do it 'their way' from the get-go. They try to create original work before mastering skills to a high level and just end up producing bad products. Those who have first mastered skills and then 'did it their way' will surpass them.

So while in the learning, 'work experience' phase it's essential to shut-up and listen. Just listen. Absorb as much as possible. As opposed to spending their time trying to look smart or get one up on their co-workers, Greats start each day as an empty note book ready to be filled with wisdom.

Sean Combs became a vice president of a record company at 22 because of his single minded desire to learn. "I knew [interning] was the start and I took advantage of every opportunity and I learned so much just from being a fly on the wall…[my success came] from 'being patient, and being the guy people felt comfortable being in the room with. I never spoke I always listened. And if I did speak I picked and chose a private time to pull [CEO] André to the side after really thinking my ideas out. People got comfortable with me being in the room and learning."[8]

As well as learning directly from our own experiences and from observing others, books can be a great cheat-sheet to learning. It's like the best minds in history have condensed their 'Best Bits' onto page, and we can implement their wisdom into our work.

Hopsin's best advice to up-n-comers is: "I recommend all you guys that are fresh out of high school who plan on getting a deal to just read your books. People say that but you only know how important it is until you're in my situation and you're like 'damn I should of read that, I should of known this.' It won't take that long. Just spend a few hours out your day just reading about the industry. It will benefit you in the long run."[9]

Nipsey Hussle applied lessons learned from the book 'Contagious' to market his music more effectively. He sold a mixtape for $100, after reading how the technique brought attention to a cheesesteak restaurant in Philadelphia. True enough, Nipsey gained enormous publicity across the web and made a lot of money from this stunt.

Angel Haze started learning how to rap in 2008 by "doing a lot of reading up on, metaphors, wordplay, everything," she told HipHopDX. "I spent a lot of time on the forum RapBattles.com, where they teach you these things so it was really a learning process – just cultivating and crafting completely [from scratch]."[10] Three years after first educating herself she signed to a major label and is one of the prominent female rappers.

When Jay, Dame and Biggs were building Roc-A-Fella they learned a lot about the inner workings of the music industry through books like *'Hit Men: Power Brokers and Fast Money Inside the Music Business'*.

But make sure you're not just reading motivational books and watching inspiring people to feel good, (studies show inspirational material releases endorphins 'the feel good chemical' in the brain). Lessons must be actively applied to your life and the way you interact with others.

To really master skills or change habits, lessons need to be applied with repetition, repetition, repetition. Something Lil Wayne understands:

"Repetition is the father of learning. Intelligence comes from repetition. Awareness, preparation, all that comes from repetition. Record sales, radio spins, repetition. TV spots, awards, repetition."[11]

Not blind repetitions, where we repeat the same thing over and over, make the same mistakes, get the same results over and over – that's not learning, that's wasting time. We need to repeat intelligently. Actively analyzing our past performance and thinking, *'how can I do it better?'*

'Knowledge reigned supreme/
The ignorant is ripped to smithereens/ '
– KRS ONE, You Must Learn

No End

Greats have absorbed knowledge like a dry sponge dropped in the ocean. But there is no end. The main thing separating people who stay on top from those that come and go is they are always learning with that same intensity.

As Pharrell says, "Learn learn learn learn. I appreciate all the accolades I got but more than anything else I am a student still to this day. I'll be a student till I die."

The same is true of Eminem – the biggest selling musician of the last decade. His right hand man, Mr. Porter, observes: "Em will tell you himself like, he's still learning certain stuff. And that's funny 'cause I tell him like 'yeah you got it' and he'll tell me 'nah I'm still learning.'"[12]

Greats studiously analyze their previous work to understand how to improve. Like Lil Wayne revealed: "I listen to myself all day. Only because I'm trying to critique what I should have said."[11]

Many fall from the top because their years of work have made them believe they know it all. They think through their ego (which means from their past experiences and memories), and get defensive, even offended and angry about learning from anybody or anything 'beneath them.' *'I did it this way before so I'm doing it this way again'.* Their mind will tighten and decay.

30 years of experience can either work with or against you. If you're using past experience as a guide moving forward, it's like driving while looking through the rear view mirror. All good when the road ahead is flat, but when it bends, which it will, you'll fall off the cliff.

'Even the genius asks questions/'
– Tupac, Me Against the World

Hiphopsite.com was the leading website for Hip Hop news in the late 90's (it's the site Eminem sold the Slim Shady EP through). It was an innovator and one of the first of its kind to market. Now it looks like an amateur job in comparison to the hundreds of Hip Hop sites and blogs. They failed to keep learning and keep up with the times.

The reason Dr. Dre has spent 30, yes 30, years making hit records in an industry dominated by the young, is because his motivation to continually improve means he is always learning. He's always studying the industry, what others are doing, and what people are listening to. He's an eternal student. That is how you stay relevant.

"I listen to everybody's shit…even RnB, classical music, heavy metal, I listen to everything….really I listen to the whack shit more, cause I wanna know what not to do… it's easy to pick up a hit record and know what people are buying."

Dre is like a music consultant. He'll listen to music and think, 'What would I change?' 'How would I do it differently?'

As well as learning from others, Dre challenges himself to learn and master completely different music genres. He said in 1997:

> "I started studying music theory, learning how to read and write music...I definitely want to get into scoring movies [but] I have to have the knowledge [first]. I'm not even going to attempt to do something if I don't think I'm going to be great at it...
>
> That's almost like learning a new language. I have to really understand what I'm doing. It takes a while, and I want to be the best at it, so I'm going to put the time in."[13]

This comes back to why you are doing what you are doing. What is your driving motivation? If it's about the materials and the money that come with the job, are you going to spend hundreds of hours learning a completely new way of making music, when you could spend your time making sellable Hip Hop records and getting paid?

No. Dre's motivation comes from setting himself difficult challenges and evolving his skill to overcome those tests. Just like Dre loves working out and feeling himself getting physically stronger, he loves exercising his passion for music, learning and feeling himself getting better. This is why he will go down as a legend.

'One more CD and then I'm packin' up my bags/
And as I'm leavin' I'll guarantee they scream/
"Dre, don't leave us like that man!"/'
– Dr. Dre, I Need A Doctor

(Arguably the only other producer in the same league as Dre – in terms of longevity and influence – is Rick Rubin. He abides by the exact same principles. "It's always intuitive, but over time, the craft becomes better. In the beginning, I was a complete novice, and now I'm a complete novice with 30 years of experience."[14])

Always learning is essential in fast moving industries like music, where the Internet has completely disrupted the landscape in less than a decade. When legendary rapper Talib Kweli was asked what advice he'd give upcoming artists he responded:

"This might sound strange, but I think upcoming artists are in a better position to give me advice." After talking about the changes in music over the last decade he continues, "Your history doesn't matter in this business anymore, and there's no more money being spent on it. So at this point it's like the Wild Wild West. It's like a gold rush. You have to challenge yourself to find new avenues to make money...now it's even harder and I look towards younger artists, whether it be Wale or Odd Future or whoever. I look see what they're doing and apply that to what I do."

'Later played a fly on the wall on the side of the industry'
– Talib Kweli, Never Can Say Goodbye

Jay Z has been able to lead the way in breaking new ground in the entertainment business in large part because of his habits of always learning from the world around him, no matter how successful he becomes. Author of the Jay Z biography, 'Empire, State of Mind,' Zack Greenburg writes: "One of the things reiterated by most people who've worked with Jay Z – be they lawyers, record label executives or other musicians – is that they can't help but notice his thirst for knowledge. He constantly absorbs information from people, books and situations."

Jay demonstrated this thirst for learning even as a teen playing ball, as childhood friend DeHaven remembers: "He'd do a lot of studying before he'd make a move."[15]

The 'Always Learning' state of mind manifests across Jay's life. You can see it through the evolution of his music. He went from rapid–fire rhymer in the 80s/early-90s, to the lyrically sophisticated don of Reasonable Doubt. Then he learned to make songs more musical with a slower flow based on quotables and hidden wordplay, to appeal to a broader range of people, and he continues to learn, adapt and evolve today.

This is one of the biggest secrets to Jay's success:

> "I'm hungry for knowledge. The whole thing is to learn every day, to get brighter and brighter. That's what this world is about. You look at someone like Gandhi, and he glowed. Martin Luther King glowed. Muhammad Ali glows. I think that's from being bright all the time, and trying to be brighter.
>
> That's what you should be doing your whole time on the planet. Then you feel like, 'My life is worth everything.' And yours is too."[16]

'Next time you see the homie and his rims spinnin',
Just know my mind is working just like them...the rims that is'/ '
– Jay Z, Moment of Clarity

The
Hustle

A piece of rock floating through space with humans on it.[1]
That's our world. And that's it.
All 'rules' and 'boundaries' are artificially created by us.
A hustler knows this, so creates his own rules.
A hustler, creates his own world.

"Two types of people don't amount to anything.
Those that don't do as their told and those that do nothing else."
– Napoleon Hill

Hustling is about starting with what you have – however little – and growing. It's about finding a way-in, a way to gain access to resources, a way to connect with key people. It's about doing whatever is necessary to 'make it'.

Hustlers don't wait for a golden opportunity, they don't follow the herd, or follow rules to the letter. They don't get embarrassed by putting themselves 'out there' or get upset when rejected. They just make *it* happen.[2]

'I don't wait, I marinate, variate erryday/'
– Big Sean, The One

Hustlers like Sean Combs who went from an unpaid intern at a top record label, to vice president with his own label imprint in just two years.

19 year old Sean's passion was music. He dreamt of working in the industry but all his job applications to record labels were flatly rejected. Then he noticed friends in his Howard University business major class applying for internships with banks, and decided to approach record labels with a similar proposition – at a time where the concept of an intern did not exist in the music business. He pitched his services to Def Jam (the biggest Hip Hop label at the time) but was rejected once again after interview.

Still determined he looked for another way in. Because of the successful parties he hosted at Howard, Sean had developed some connections in the industry. One of these (rapper Heavy D) agreed to introduce Sean to Andre Harrell, CEO of Uptown Records – a rising force in urban music.

During their telephone interview, Sean passionately pleaded with Andre: "I'll come in and I'll wash your car, I'll get you coffee, I'll run the tapes for you. I just want to learn from you, you're a genius, you're the best."

"When can you start?" was Andre's reply.[3]

Sean would rise before dawn to catch the train from his dorms in Washington DC to Uptown's Manhattan office twice a week. Always in full suit, he'd run (literally *run*, tie flapping and all) errands for the office. He'd be doing typical intern tasks like delivering mail, while learning as much as he could about the record business. "He absorbed everything he could in the office and at the recording studio," writes Dan Charnas in 'The Big Payback'.

Sean impressed Harrell as, "the hardest working intern ever"[4] and was soon given more responsibility in the studio. By now he had dropped out of Howard University and moved into Andre's New Jersey home. Here he had the unrivalled opportunity to continually learn from an experienced mentor. (Interestingly Andre got his start in the music industry in 1984 when he lived in Russell Simmons's home while interning for Def Jam.)

While working with Uptown artists like Mary J Blige and Jodeci, Sean developed an original sound, putting smooth RnB vocals over hard Hip Hop beats, which soon became his chart-topping 'niche' style.

Aside from working in the studio, Sean also hustled to get his artists noticed. For instance he'd send squads of teenagers to popular nightclubs to pack the floor when a Jodeci song was played, (the 'fake it till you make it,' or 'look large to be large,' principle). He also hustled to build his personal brand by making cameo appearances on vocals and videos. He organized hugely successful 'Daddy's Room' parties in Manhattan, and even put together a charity all-star baseball game.

When Sean's direct boss left Uptown for another job in 1993, Sean took Andre to lunch and persuaded the CEO to give him the vacant 'Head of Artist Development' position. "You're making music for young people," Sean passionately pitched. "I am the demographic, I am the person you're making music for. Every time you want to know info on a record you play it for me. Just give me the chance, give me the opportunity, give me a trial period to do this."[3]

Sean became the youngest A&R in the music business. By the time he was 22, Vibe had written a 7,000 word article on him and he'd set up 'Bad Boy Entertainment' to take in artists who did not fit with Uptown's RnB image (like The Notorious B.I.G).

Although Sean was subsequently fired for lacking Social Intelligence (*pg.198*), he kept on hustling. When camping outside Andre's home failed to get him his job back, he focused on building Bad Boy Entertainment and was soon offered the 'Head of Black Music' role at major label EMI, if he could bring Bad Boy with him.

During his interview with EMI Sean's confidence was clear. Referring to himself in the third person he told the executives: "When you get in the room where you decided what you're gonna pay Puff, just when you got to that number that you think is gonna make Puff happy, get ridiculous on top of that."[5]

Convinced, EMI offered Sean a $700,000 starting salary, $15 million for distribution rights, $1m a year in overhead expenses for artists and a $1.5m loan for a studio. Of course Sean went on to prove his worth – in its first four years Bad Boy grossed more than $100 million, he has started a number of hugely successful businesses, and is as relevant today as he was then.

'10 years from now we'll still be on top/
Yo, I thought I told you that we won't stop'
– P Diddy, Mo Money Mo Problems

Hustlers like Kanye, who on his come-up would relentlessly promote himself at any given opportunity. "He has a camera follow him round all the time," said Dame Dash in 2002.[6] As an unsigned artist Kanye would visit influential companies unannounced to rap on tables for employees, and would rhyme in studio sessions when he was supposed to be producing, until the other artists complained.

When Kanye wants something to make a project better he'll never just accept a 'no this can't be done,' but will keep trying to find ways to get to 'yes'. For instance to get a Lauryn Hill sample cleared for the song 'All Falls Down,' he drove around Miami looking for her. "We were so by any means necessary. 'Oh, she lives in Miami? We'll just go find her,'" remembers manager John Mononpoly.[7] They got close (an email address from her partner Rohan Marley) but no cigar. They then tried sending her a check, but nothing. So they hustled, by not depending on anybody, and found a voice probably more suited for the song than Lauryn's.

For another song on The College Dropout, after being denied use of a sample, Kanye hired a musicologist and a band to recreate the sample with just enough difference to be legally used.

Then, before the album's release, when The Source magazine asked him, "What happens if the album doesn't go gold?" he responded:

> "Oh, that's not going to happen, because I won't let it happen. I know you can't control everything, and everything is in God's hands ultimately, but I'm going to fight, go out and perform for everybody. I don't care, I'm going to every school I can, colleges, I'll make waves, I'll charge less, I'll stop charging 10 G's a show, I'll charge maybe two thousand dollars a show but everyone has to have a copy of The College Dropout in order to come, [I'll] do venues that hold 1,000 people. If you do that 30 times, that's 30,000 records."[8]

And he wasn't joking. A month before the album's release he went to the Virgin Record store in Times Square and noticed the album wasn't on the store's 'New Release Schedule,' so demanded to speak to the manager.

"MY NAME IS KANYE WEST, AND MY ALBUM COMES OUT FEBRUARY 10, AND IT'S GOING TO BE NUMBER ONE!" he barked at the started shop assistant.[8]

"Y'all don't know my struggle/ Y'all can't match my hustle/
You can't catch my hustle/ You can't fathom my love dude/
Lock yourself in a room doing 5 beats a day for 3 summers/ "
– Kanye West, Spaceship

('The College Dropout' went onto sell over four million copies worldwide.)

Hustlers like J Cole, who on his come-up tried strategy after strategy to get noticed. Cole would hang around places where he had a chance of running into 'industry people'. He snuck into Baseline Studios in 2005 to try and meet anyone from Roc–A–Fella. He went to music executive L.A. Reid's son's sweet 16 birthday party in 2006 wearing a custom 'Producer for Jay Z or Die Tryin' T shirt with a beat CD in his pocket because he had a chance of running into "someone." He tried to get internships at studios and contacted every A&R he could through MySpace – he even called A&R's and executives to leave rap messages on their answering machine. He was ready to do anything and everything. So how could he lose?

'Hustle hard, yeah it really ain't a game mane/'
– J Cole & 50 Cent, New York Times

Hustlers like Jay Z, Dame Dash and Karem Biggs, whose Roc-A-Fella empire was built by capitalizing on commercial opportunities. "I can sell broken buttons, fried eggs, sour milk, I can sell anything, I'm a hustler," jokes Dame. "If we had the opportunity to cut out the middle man it didn't make sense for us not to do it because we already had the customer."[9]

This is how Rocawear was formed:

By the late 90's Jay had released three albums and would regularly tour the country (and internationally). His wardrobe consisted mainly of Iceberg branded clothing (a European sports wear designer) and the team noticed people in the concert audience would often wear the same brand. "It became clear to us that we were directly influencing their sales," Jay recalls.[10]

'Cop Iceberg and yell out 'Jigga'' – Kanye, Big Brother

So Dame set up a meeting with Iceberg to negotiate an endorsement deal. The team spoke about the power of Hip Hop as a marketing medium and how associating with Roc–A–Fella would boost Iceberg's credibility with urban youth. But just like when they were pitching their music to Lyor Cohen a few years earlier, *(pg.224)*, their dreams were too big for the people across the table to understand. "The executives looked at us like we were speaking a different language," remembers Jay. "They offered us free clothes, but we wanted millions and use of their private jet. We walked out of the office realizing we had to do it ourselves."[10]

The crew started slowly with a lot of stumbles. "We didn't know business yet, but we knew how to hustle." They learned from mentors like Russell Simmons, got other partners on board, and launched their own brand. Less than ten years later Jay sold the companies licensing rights for 200 million dollars and still retains ownership.

"I sell ice in the winter, I sell fire in hell
I am a hustler baby, I'll sell water to a well"
– Jay-Z (U Don't Know)

Access

Grandmaster Caz and crew were deep in battle. The local neighborhood had gathered at Slattery Park in The Bronx for an event pitting two local DJ heroes head to head. As usual, they had hijacked electricity from the nearby street lights to power their ever more sophisticated stereo equipment. The two crews were playing records back and forth, and with the battle reaching a climax, Caz loaded up his trump record. It boomed from the speaker system. The crowd screamed and Caz smiled.

Suddenly the vinyl stopped spinning. The sound muffled out and the park went quiet.

Frustrated that he'd overworked the street light's power, Caz set about restarting his system. But then the light bulb above the park cut off, setting the crowd into darkness. Like an invisible force travelling at twenty miles an hour, street lights down the block began turning off one by one. Poof, poof, poof.

Caz and his DJ partner Disco Wiz smiled at one another. *'Did we do that?'*

Their names would go down in legend if their DJ set had blown out the power for the entire street.

Moments later, lights in the apartment buildings around the park all shut off, and a confused hush came upon the crowd as they analyzed the reason for the darkness. It was the sound of nearby bodegas hurriedly slamming shut their entrances that confirmed what most now suspected. One word rang out: 'BLACKOUT!'

With that the crowd transformed into wild animals. Inhibitions switched off with the lights as they ran towards the nearby shopping district with the same state of mind. There was going to be some action tonight.[11]

By morning July 14th actions from the previous night had cost the city of New York 300 million dollars. 1,616 stores were damaged in looting and rioting, 1,037 fires were responded to and 3,776 people were arrested, (the largest mass arrest in New York history – there were so many arrests police resorted to transporting two people in trunks of squad cars).[12]

Even Grandmaster Caz admits to participating. "Yes I did sneak in [Sound Room Electronics Store]. I helped crash the gate down, crawled in and pulled out a Clubman Two mixer... But, like I said, you couldn't just say 'I'm gonna be a DJ' you needed equipment, and that's all I really wanted. I wasn't trying to loot everything I could find."

Hundreds of people across the city had the same idea as Caz. Electronics and hi-fi stores were the most looted, and DJ equipment was the most sought after. That meant from the reckless chaos of the night came an unexpected positive.

"The very next day sprung this whole revolution of DJ'S," Caz says.

"Before the blackout [The Bronx] had maybe five legitimate DJ crews," adds Disco Wiz. "After the blackout there was a DJ on every block…The blackout made a big spark in the Hip Hop revolution."[11]

An impoverished community hungry to express itself now had access to equipment it would otherwise not have been able to afford, and the art of Hip Hop rapidly developed.

Two years after the blackout, the song 'Rappers Delight' paved the way for the commercial dominance of rap music for the next several decades.

This story in no way condones theft or any other activity that violates universal principles. It is just an example to show how important access to resources is. Access is what will often separate two people of equal talent. As Sean Combs said, "Anyone can do what I have done. Kids just need a chance to succeed."[3]

Consider Bill Gates. (In a survey, marketing company Alloy Access found Gates to be the famous figure 'Urban Hustlers' most admired.) As Malcom Gladwell writes in 'Outliers,' a major reason for Gates' success with Microsoft was his early access to computers. He had accumulated around 10,000 hours of computer coding experience by his senior high school year, at a time when computer access was reserved for only the wealthiest schools.

Gates hustled to gain access. For example, yes having wealthy parents allowed him to attend one of the few private schools in the country that could afford a quality computer, but when the money for buying computer time ran out he hustled to get a job with a local computer programming company. He also lived close to the University of Washington, which happened to have free computer time in the early hours of the morning. So he hustled again, sneaking out of his parents' house to stay up all night coding at the university, before sneaking home a few hours before school started.[13]

Gates would also hustle in other ways with friend and future Microsoft cofounder Paul Allen. For example they'd go night-time dumpster-diving to find source codes that their employer wouldn't give them access to. They even obtained access to an administrator password and used it to hack the companies accounting system to get free computing time.[14]

Hustlers like Gates find a way to obtain access by working in the grey area between legal and illegal. In that two letter difference lie the codes to jumpstart ventures and careers. But as stated before, in our heart we know where the line is and when we are violating universal principles. There are ethics to hustling.

'That goes against all my hustling ethics/ '
– Lupe Fiasco, Around My Way

Street Lessons

The reason many street hustlers have been successful in the music industry, (think Eazy-E, 50 Cent, Pusha T, Wu-Tang, B.I.G, Jay Z etc.), is because they've applied the same 'street principles' to the boardroom.

The 'streets' represent the base of societies pyramid – the pyramid of power, wealth, influence etc. There's an abundance of people at the base aiming to reach the small number of lucrative jobs at the top. So, as Jay Z stated, "You learn something you never could at McDonalds. You learn to compete hard, even when you lose, because you can't settle for second best as a hustler. It's not worth it."[10] Applying the same mentality to the mainstream world has enabled them to live the 'hustlers dream' legitimately.

'They making they plans, dusting they guns off/
And wondering, what I need to do to be boss?/
Or who I need to fight? / Or who I need to kill?/
Or push back on the climb to the top of the thrill?/ '
– Yasiin Bey, The Tournament

But it is executives in the music business who are the ultimate hustlers. 50 Cent says even selling drugs didn't prepare him for the sharks of the music business, who are "ten times more manipulative."[15]

For example, look what happens when labels release a new album. Executives will send employees to stores across the country to buy several copies of the CD. They then take those records to another store and scan them to look like real sales. Then they give the CD's to another store to resell. Each CD is counted as 'sold' three times. Why do record companies do this? Because they know that when a record looks like it's selling well, we, the consumer, will think it must be good and will buy it. They understand the human mind and how to brainwash it. (Note that all those multi-purchases get charged back to the artist.)[16]

In order not to get used and abused in this viciously manipulative industry it's mandatory to have hustle skills.

Master P demonstrated this when he partnered his 'No Limits' label with Warner Brothers in the mid 90's, and was cheated out of millions of dollars. Instead of sulking he used his Hustle. P formed a new company, 'New No Limit Records,' and this time received money upfront from Warner. He took the cash and left the industry – "I'm gone." When others asked why, he said "I took my money back." That is the reality of the music industry. "You gotta almost cheat it," says rapper Chamillionaire.[17]

As we enter a new era where entrepreneurial, independent artists and labels will become the norm, Hustle is more important than ever – (see 'Business + Art' pg.238).

The Warning

Finally understand that 'hustling' has led to many people's downfall. Those who think of 'hustling' only as an obsessive purist to maximize profits – *'I need to make the most money/get the most views/the most likes…'* – will often fail because the quality of their products is given second thought.

For example, most classic albums have very few, if any, famous features and producers (see Illmatic, Miseducation, Ready To Die, Nation of Millions, 36 Chambers, Reasonable Doubt, Good Kid…), because the artist is thinking about what is best for the work, not *'who is the hottest out now, that can increase my sales?'* Whereas albums that boast about famous features on every song are almost certain to be forgotten within a few years.

Also consider the example of Dame Dash. When he split from Roc-A-Fella in 2006, he told MTV: "I'm a business man; I have no emotional attachments to any of my businesses. I'm a hustla, I flip things."[4]

How did that mentality work out for Dame? He tried developing businesses from boxing promotions, to TV shows, alcohol to fashion, but his pursuit was always *'all about the Benjamin's'* and that led to bad products, which couldn't compete with existing products made by people with a deep emotional attachment to their work. Creating things with no emotional attachment is noticeable and people don't get attached to them either. (See *'Do You'* pg.272 for more on this principle, and *'Maintaining Headlights'* pg.165 for more on Dame.)

Never forget that the cheapest, lowest forms of hustling are lying, stealing and manipulating to get your way. This violates all other natural principles. It may bring some short term results but will not lead to long term success, as your foundations are not built on trust.

Hustling is critical to getting noticed and staying relevant but it must be balanced with 'Pursuit of Greatness' and other principles for long term success. Like Jay *'I'm a hustler baby'* Z said: "I believe in karma and doing the right thing even if it may not advance you as far as you want."[18]

The
People

Most of the lessons in this book focus on what we can do to ourselves to live a successful life. But we're not alone. We live in an interdependent world, where our lives are interlinked with others. Understanding the art of people and relationships is fundamental to success in any calling.

LA FAMILIA

Summer 1973 in one apartment of a 102 unit building in a derelict district of The Bronx, Clive Campbell was contemplating whether to bring his DJ passion into the public eye. He had been practicing since coming to America from Jamaica six years previously but was nervous about performing in front of crowds of neighborhood kids. If it were not for his sister, Cindy, encouraging Clive, aka DJ Kool Herc, and organizing the venue and promotion, Hip Hop would not have been born that day.

Since then Hip Hop has been about, "creating mental and social wealth by helping, encouraging and raising one another higher," says KRS–One.[1]

People around you are the cast in your life's movie. That means you are the casting director and pick the people who create the movie you will live.

'Love me or leave me alone/'
– Brand Nubian

The people you surround yourself with will either push you higher into excellence or pull you down from your potential. That's why it's essential to surround yourself with positive, loving people who want you to succeed and achieve your purpose, and to 'cut of' those who do not contribute to your evolution.

'I'm tryna surround myself with people that inspire me/
Or at least inquire similar desires/
To do what it T.A.K.E just to reach the T.O.P/'
– Kendrick Lamar, cut you off

50 Cent has been living this principle since hustling in the streets of Queens in the late 90's. "My grandfather taught me, 'you'll be as successful as the people you talk to for no reason.' If you spend your days talking to a person with nothing going on what kind of information can he offer you? Can he teach you something in a conversation? Can he help you learn?"[2]

'Opinions are like assholes, not everybody fecal matter/'
– Talib Kweli, Art Imitates Life

On a journey to Greatness even friends and family may be the ones holding you back. They may try to force their idea of 'success' onto you and will cast doubt on your own beliefs. Many people come to believe the naysayers, as they see themselves as a reflection of what 'others' think. But Greats have a solid 'core belief' in themselves and their purpose, which enables them to overcome naysayers and do what they really believe in.

Chance The Rapper faced this in his relationship with his father. Chance had a vision for his future from an early age that his father could not understand. "I remember I used to be saying, like, 'I'm gonna be famous one day,'" says Chance. "I remember saying that when I was in fourth grade. My dad used to just hate that."

His father wanted to force his idea of 'success' on Chance. "I thought I was gonna run him for mayor someday. When I tried to push Chance to go right into college, he pushed right back – this is what he wanted to do."[3]

After Chance graduated High School, and told his father that he would focus on music instead of going to college, the tension was so serious they didn't speak for months.

'Even betters what my uncle did/
I pop my demo tape in start to beat my head/
Peaked out my eye, see if he was beating his/
He might as well say 'beat it kid', he's on the list/'
– Jay Z, So Ambitious

Dre understood the importance of surrounding yourself with the right people in the mid 90's when he made the difficult decision to leave the record label he co–owned, Death Row, because he realized the energy there was preventing him from being successful.

"There were fights in the studio, engineers getting beat up, just senseless things going on. It got to the point where I couldn't take it anymore… Still, it was difficult to leave. It was like a divorce."

Dre took the advice of mentor and music veteran Quincy Jones, to reflect on where he wanted to be in the future.

"I finally had to sit down and try to picture myself 10 years from now and imagine which people I wanted around me, which people were really a positive force in my life. That list turned out to be very small. But the list of people around me at the time could have filled the Forum [arena]."

Dre learned an important lesson, "that once you get successful, everyone wants to be your friend…But a lot of those people don't have your best interests in mind."[4]

So he left. He didn't take anything with him, no money or royalties, he just left to start a new life.

Dre would take lessons from his experience with Death Row to put a new team together with Aftermath Entertainment, and he recognizes the importance of this team in contributing to his success since.

"I am a perfectionist, but it has a lot to do with the people that are around you. They have to have the same vision, the same motivation. It takes a while to get the right people around you; it takes a long time. But I think I've finally done it, I think this is going to be my crew for a while."[5]

'Fuckin' backstabbers, when the chips were down you just laughed at us/
Now you bout to feel the fuckin' wrath of Aftermath/'
– Dre, I Need A Doctor

Most other names mentioned in this book live by this same principle, and their whole team is made up of people with similar dreams and motives. As DJ Sway said, "Jay Z and Kanye are really smart. I think they surround themselves with people who can serve as a muse to them, so to speak, that they can be inspired by."[6]

True indeed, and Kanye says that he sees himself as a combination of "Steve Jobs, Walt Disney, and Michelangelo."[7] He surrounds himself with images and quotes from these extraordinary people, to take inspiration from every day and *'any pessimists I ain't talk to them' – Touch the Sky.*

The reason Jay Z may appear to outsiders to 'discard' people he previously worked with (from Jaz-O to Dame Dash, and more recently John Meneilly and other executives) is because he lives this principle:

"I have to really look at it for the next three years and say, 'Am I doing it for the right reasons?' cause all I want to do is make history at this point – They got to pay me to make history of course – But that's my goal. I want to sit there with people really into making history. I mean everybody. I don't mean just artists [even] the interns. If everybody's not committed to making history every time I go into a meeting, and if I can't look into their eyes and I don't see the fire, then I gotta move on."[8]

'Don't listen to your crew/Do what works for you'
– Jay Z, Anything

Common realized *'you can't fly with eagles, if you cluck with chickens'* in 1995. By then he had already created a few good albums, but was feeling frustrated by the lack of commercial attention they received. At the same time he felt artistic frustration for not being able, or not feeling comfortable enough, to express himself freely.

At the time Common would roll with 15 childhood friends everywhere he went, whether on tour or in the studio. The feedback from these peers was the most important thing to him. While recording 'I used to Love HER,' Common could see his crew looking disappointed, and as he was laying down the final verse, he says one of his boys, "looked like he was about to punch me" for talking "Teddy P. turn–off–the–lights lover–man"[9] about a girl, (of course the song is not about a girl). Common thought to himself 'what's wrong with expressing my love for a woman,' but he still wanted the approval of his peers, so he suppressed the feeling and laughed about it.

Eventually though, Comm understood that in-order to use his full potential he needed to express himself without regard to the opinion of others, even 'friends.' He had to stop living in dogma. After that realization he changed his music style to reflect his true feelings. He moved to New York and hung out with artists, poets and creatives – a world away from thugs in Chicago he would usually associate with. He went on to create more 'socially conscious' music, starting with 1997's 'One Day It'll All Make Sense,' which would touch the lives of millions and take his career to new heights. He had to let go of people to achieve the life he wanted.

'I used to write shit to please ni***rs/ Now I write shit to freeze ni***rs/ '
– Common, Electric Wire Hustler Flower

Not only do Greats seek to surround themselves with people of the same mindset, but they seek competitors. They welcome competition because they know that tough battles make them greater – whereas being around people who don't challenge them only results in mediocrity.

Kanye says he always tries to compete with classic albums (like Midnight Marauders, Miseducation of Lauryn Hill and Bizarre Ride II the Pharcyde), by judging his work against them.

TDE's whole plan to dominate Hip Hop is based around their members competing with each other. As Kendrick's manager Dave Free said: "The way we keep Kendrick hot and relevant, is to make people around him just as good, cause that's gunna push him to do better. Schoolboy Q, Ab Soul and the others are not gonna let Kendrick out do them."

If you ever feel in a slump try to stay around people who challenge and push one another. Go towards the competition.

'Competition is good it brings out the vital parts/ '
– A Tribe Called Quest, Vibes and Stuff

Some people use a 'Make or Break List.' It's basically two columns, one with names of people who can improve their lives, and one with the names of people who drag them down. They then spend as much time as possible around people in the first column, and make a rule to not spend more than five minutes at a time with unavoidable people in the second.

Or taking it further:

Interviewer: *"They say you the average of the five people you spend most time with, do you believe that?"*
Eric Thomas 'The Hip Hop Preacher': *"Absolutely. That's why I try to spend as much time alone as I can." [laughs]*[10]

CIRCLE OF SUCCESS

'All right stop, collaborate and listen/'
— Vanilla Ice, Ice Ice Baby

Two or more people working in harmony towards the same goal can accomplish more in one year than any single individual could accomplish in a lifetime.[11]

All people in this book, and practically all successful people in any industry, understand this point and work as part of a team. This 'support network' combines, focuses and synergizes each person's unique experience and intelligence to achieve a common goal. A strong team in harmony is a Master Mind Alliance, (or "Power Circle," as Rick Ross says,) capable of so much more than any individual. As former Roc–A–Fella CEO Dame Dash said to his team, "Don't do everything on your own. If you do, by the time you do it, you could do 30 other things if you had help."

'Teamwork makes the dream work'
— Dizzy Wright

Teaming up with people with complementary skills means everyone can focus on areas they're passionate about, and good at, and combine to create something no one person could do alone. Like Pharrell said: "You are only as good as your team. When you envisage success, you should see all the people you work with, in addition to yourself. When I look at that picture, I see giant angels who are much smarter than me, who can oversee the things that I don't know shit about."[12]

'Creation is a package/
Generate together and we increase the wattage/'
— Damien Marley, In His Own Words

Kanye's GOOD Music clique, Jay Z's Roc–A–Fella crew, Kendrick's TDE family, Eminem's Shady circle etc., are fundamental reasons for the success of all these artists.

Before signing with ROC Nation, J Cole was far from on his own. His team consisted of business partner Mike Rooney, road manager Mike Shaw and A&R/DJ, Ibrahim, who were all working to get Cole's music into the right hands. Then Mark Pitts, President of Urban Music at Sony, decided to manage Cole (after hearing his assistant play 'Lights Please' in the office – "It's like I smelled some food," Pitts said[13]). All of this BEFORE Jay Z, and without it Cole's music would not have reached Jay.

Similarly without a record label Chance the Rapper has become one of the most talked about new artists in music. He has toured the world, had countless magazine covers, reached millions with his mixtapes and is helping redefine what an independent artist can do. All with a team of four:

- Pat Corcoran, 23 year old former promoter and blogger acts as de facto manager. Began working together April 2012 after '10 Day mixtape'.
- Dan Weiner: Publicist – Met at SXSW concert in 2012 when Chance was doing a show with a band Dan works with. (Dan also introduced Chance to Childish Gambino and others.)
- Carol Lewis: Legendry industry Booking Agent – Met in August 2012, introduced to Chance through Dan.

Aside from this core team, Chance's support network is made up of several other rappers, producers, DJ's, filmmakers and artists. The 'Save Money Crew,' who joined forces in high school after performing individually at parties and open mics, are able to combine their creative strengths to make each member stronger. Just like the GOOD Music Team.

Getting Out Our Dreams

Kanye officially formed GOOD Music in 2005, but before that, and prior to releasing his debut album, he had a stronger team than most established artists. His skill is in recognizing talented people, envisioning how working together can benefit everybody, and persuading them to come on board.

Promoter Olskool Ice–Gre, remembers Kanye asking him to work together in 2002: "He was like, 'How much do you get paid doing this promotion? I like how you move in the studio. I'll pay you to stay with me and help me out while I do all this stuff… I know you're a star yourself but I'm about to be the biggest star in hip hop and I need your help.'"[14]

In those early years Kanye's team included, Gee and Hip Hop, (A&R's for Roc–A–Fella and Vice Presidents of Atlantic Records, who managed him and did more promotion work than Roc–A–Fella [Kanye's label]), he had Jon Monopoly ("one of the greatest hustlers I've ever met in my career ever"), Don C and Benny Medina, (who managed other aspects), Devo Springsteen, (his cousin, producer and assistant, who also connected him with John Legend (his college roommate), XXL/Source magazine editors and renowned artist booking agency, William Morrison (both through business school friends)), Plain Pat (who was well connected with magazines and other artists), and others. This was all totally independent of Kanye's official label. The team would create mixtapes, organize promotional activity and arrange shows and features.

"Ultimately I make all my own decisions and I take full responsibility," Kanye said in 2003. "But the reason why I have a management team is I try to get really intelligent people around me to suggest things when I don't know shit and also to make things happen…We are so similar in the arrogant thing: we can make it happen, we can make it happen."[15]

On the music front, Kanye established close friendships with a number of producers and rappers from across the music spectrum, from 'socially conscious' to 'street'. "I got this Roc–A–Fella piece on my neck, but I'm on stage with Talib Kweli. How I ain't got best of both worlds and shit? Every audience looking at me."[15]

Today Kanye has assembled a team at GOOD Music that produces exactly that. GOOD is a collective of rappers and producers who collaborate and create friendly competition, to push one another higher. "If you see someone really hot, really talented, you take that energy, you use them," Kanye said, when the label was formed in 2005.

Jeff Bhasker who has been producing with Kanye for several years says: "I think everyone who gets around [Kanye], he pushes and gets the best out of them. If you wanna be good at something, you have to be around the best people. He's not gonna settle. Once you realize he's not gonna settle then there's nothing left to but deliver something great."[16]

"That competition just sparks something in you. It made me excited about music again," ads producer No I.D.[17]

In these environments Greatness blossoms. As rapper Big Sean admits, "I had to rewrite several times. You always got to make it better than the last time. If others set the bar here in history, you gotta set it one notch above."

The crew pushes one another to perform at the very best of their abilities. "Kanye nitpicked our verses so much, my goal is write a verse he's not gonna say anything about," adds Sean. "Now I know the level of excellence needed, songs can take three months to finish."[18]

This is something Kanye has always been doing, even before his first album release. As Common remembers from when they worked together in the early 2000's: "Kanye is the first producer I've worked with that would say 'man change that verse' or 'leave that.' Once I got ego out the way and listened, I learned from it. It makes everything better, when you have someone like 'nah this could be better,' because it's hard for eye to see itself."[18]

'As I look around they don't do it like my clique/'
– Big Sean, Clique

…though one crew that does 'do it' is *'GOOD music's drug dealing cousin'* *(Jay Z, Clique)*, who built a similar culture in 1996.

ROC–A–FELLA

'All I need is the love of my crew/
The whole industry can hate me/
I'll thug my way through/'
– Jay, All I Need

The original Roc–A–Fella team were all totally focused on the goal of being the biggest, most respected Hip Hop label and lifestyle brand in the world. And for a moment in time they achieved it.

The heads of the original team were: Jay Z, the public face of the company who created the music, Dame Dash, who managed the business with a relentless hunger that would blow down doors, and Kareem Biggs who brought in finances: talent, hustle, money.

Everyone had their own lane and they were all crucially important. Without Dame the world would never have heard of Jay Z and vice versa.

"We're a family here at Roc–A–Fella so there's no 'yes men'... that helps play a part in the success we've had," says Lenny S,[19] who was part of the original team.

The team looked out for one another. As Dame remembers: "I'm always secure that my friends that I love are alright. So if [somebody] don't have something [they] can take a little from each of [us] and be alright. We used to live by that code; we called it the 'Circle of Success.'"[20]

The code was to always put the interests of the group before the individual. If something was good for you but bad for The Roc it would not be done. This simple principle affected the whole company culture. For example, in an argument nobody was allowed to leave the room feeling angry. The problem was settled there and then so not to contaminate the group.

The bosses also lead by example, (the most important leadership quality for inspiring others), in their work ethic, loyalty and focus, which trickled all through their growing company, and eventually made them all multi-millionaires.

'Everybody round me rich or will be/'
– Jay Z, La Familia

The team's early success goes to show just how important a strong united crew with complementary skills is in building something remarkable. But...

Business X Family

The original Roc–A–Fella Records collapsed less than a decade after its birth. Conflicts in decision making, control and power caused a divide at the top of the company and the original 'Circle of Success' split.

Ego, greed and maybe envy, played a part in the downfall. Some would also argue that the management structure was doomed to fail: the Roc was run more like a family than a business.

Businessman and musician 50 Cent commented: "I think Jay has good intentions but I think the only place he really went wrong was saying 'La Familia,' like we [the Roc–A–Fella artists and Jay Z] are family…I understand that transition into the corporate space [from the streets]. [But] Jimmy Iovine doesn't say to me, 'we family,' so I know that I got to be on my P's and Q's with him 24/7, because if you are no longer generating interests there will be that new thing that works [to replace you]."[21]

Mixing family and business can lead to problems with both. Family relationships revolve around familiarity, a common belief and loyalty, whilst business relationships require discipline, a focus on the bottom line and consequences for under performance.

This is probably why Jay's new music empire ROC Nation operates from a very different perspective. In Jay's successive leadership team the role of Dame Dash or Biggs was replaced by people like John Meneilly, a professional lawyer, Lyor Cohen, a former banker, and other seasoned executives like Jason Iley and Michael Yormark, who are far more focused on performance than building a loving family.

Artists like J Cole are not treated on the same cozy level as previous signings. On making his album 'Born Sinner' Cole said, "Jay and I bumped heads on very few occasions." Jay is leaving artists to make their own mark.

"This rule is so underrated/
Keep your family and business completely separated/
Money and blood don't mix…/"
– Notorious B.I.G, 10 Crack Commandments

Still, without the support of the original 'Circle of Success' Jay Z would not exist today. But it was thanks to people he admired before forming Roc–A–Fella, that he was able to build that family in the first place. His mentors.

MENTORS

Early in life, as Jay Z was developing his craft and learning about the industry, he had been described as a 'sponge,' soaking in the wisdom and experience of those around him. From a child walking the streets of New York with his father and learning how to observe the world, to indirectly learning about rap from Rakim & Slick Rick then directly from Jazz–O & Big Daddy Kane, *(pg.216)*. Similarly he's developed in the business world by learning from experienced execs like Russell Simmons and Lyor Cohen. Jay's never been afraid to ask for advice and seek guidance from the best people around him.

'A closed mouth don't get fed/'
– Jay Z, Anything

If you have less than 10,000 hours experience in anything there are many people, living and dead, who are more knowledgeable than you and have already discovered the best way of doing whatever it is you're doing.

For centuries people have been repeating the same mistakes that others have made over and over again. How much more efficient would it be if we used their experience instead of trying to learn everything first hand?

Learning from other people's mistakes is like using cheat codes to life. Experienced mentors on our team, who can guide and warn us about potential pitfalls on the journey, save so much time, energy and money.

As Diddy says, "If somebody came before you and showed you how to do it, you should be able to learn from their level of excellence and take it to the next level."

With an experienced mentor on your team you learn things that books can't teach. Like their work process, body language, social skills and subtle ways of doing things that would otherwise take years to learn independently.

All people in this book have used the experience of others as a learning platform. Instead of starting their journey completely 'death, dumb and blind,' they stand on the shoulders of giants with years of experience.

'They say a midget standing on the giant's shoulder can see much/
Further than the giant/'
– Jay Z, Hovi Baby

Greats use past and current Greats as a template for where they want to be. Kanye wants to be a creative, culture-changing icon like "Walt Disney or Steve Jobs." No I.D, wants a long, balanced career like "Rick Rubin or L.A. Reid." These are their mentors. They don't try to imitate their lives, but emulate their genius.

Immortal Technique, one of the most respected independent artists in Hip Hop, says artists from Hip Hop's Golden Era, like Chuck D and A Tribe Called Quest, told him stories about getting financially extorted so that he wouldn't go through the same, saving him hundreds of thousands of dollars.

Jam Master Jay, from Run DMC, was 50 Cent's musical mentor in the late 90's. "He taught me about song format," recalls 50. "I could rap but I didn't know how to put it in song format and the melodies and cadences, I didn't even know how to count bars till I got around Jam Master Jay."[22]

When that relationship ended 50 found others mentors, like Eminem and Dre, who taught him more about music and the music business. (Em himself has some seemingly unlikely people as his mentors, like Elton John who helped him recover from addictions and "gives me career advice."[23])

When Kanye started trying to make beats he didn't have the equipment or knowhow to re-create songs he heard on the radio. So through 'connections' he hooked up with one of the few people in Chicago with that equipment and knowledge, No I.D., and enthusiastically learned all he could about production from him. (Rapper Grav remembers No I.D commenting on Kanye's enthusiasm: "ah man, he be on me like a bug!"[24])

As Kanye was moving forward he hooked up with D-Dott Angelettie, to learn how to produce for major artists. Then as he was developing as a rapper he spent a lot of time with other rappers he admired like Dead Prez, and of course Jay Z, who he still looks up to as a mentor to this day.

When making music Kanye thinks from the perspectives of his mentors. For example in making 808's & Heartbreak he would ask himself, "What would Jeezy do,"[25] or in making 'The College Dropout': "I was most inspired by the Miseducation of Lauryn Hill and I listened to that album everyday while working on my debut."[26]

Now as Kanye established himself in the fashion industry he surrounds himself with mentors he admires, to learn from in the same way. "Marc Jacobs is my fashion idol because of the way he merges all worlds, the way he's big in the hood and the head of the No. 1 fashion house in the world," 'Ye said in 2008. "For me, Jay Z's my big brother, but what he was to me in rap is what Marc Jacobs is to me in fashion – the feeling I get when I look at him is exactly what I got when I'd look at Jay Z in the studio."[27]

A big part of the reason Kendrick Lamar is where he is today, instead of dead or imprisoned like many of his friends growing up, is because of mentors. He was fortunate to grow up with a father figure, unlike most of the young people around him, who from an early age constantly reminded Kendrick 'not to make the same mistakes as him.' He then found mentors in Terrence 'Punch' Henderson and Top Dawg Entertainment CEO, Anthony 'Top Dawg' Tiffith, who expanded on his father's teachings, and who Kendrick learned the importance of focus and discipline from.

'Now Punch is my mentor, Top Dawg is the coach/'
– The Heart Part 3

When you find a person you admire as a mentor contact them sincerely. Say why you admire them, and why you want them as a mentor. Illustrate your genuine enthusiasm and what you can do for them, (for example you could be their personal assistant of intern.) If they agree, the key is not to play any games, try to superficially impress or pretend to know everything. Just be authentic and open, and show how strong your work ethic is. Like Eminem said: "With Dre I was like a sponge, learning the tricks of the trade."[23]

Also mentors don't have to be people directly guiding you. They are often iconic figures admired from afar. For example, people in books, films, or global leaders. Think about people you admire most in the world. What are their best qualities? What can you learn from them?

You could make a collage of their faces to keep them in mind, (like the cover of this book). And when working on a problem think: *'What would _____ do in this situation?'*

Napoleon Hill's advice is to hold "imaginary meetings" before going to sleep, where you picture sitting at a table with your mentors and you talk to them about an issue, and each speaks their mind. With continual practice this technique is supposed to become extremely realistic, with mentors giving you helpful wisdom on their own accord.[28]

The names in this book can be great indirect mentors. They all have impressive character traits we can work to model ourselves on. For example:

From Jay Z: *"I will develop your calm, Zen–like, poise. Your ability to think through all the possibilities before making a move."*

From Dr. Dre: *"I will emulate your work ethic. Your ability to focus on a project till it's the best it can be."*

From Kanye: *"I will strive to have your confidence to 'think it, say it, do it'. Confidence to express yourself to the fullest and not be controlled by fear."*

From Nas: *"I will always seek to maintain your humility, balance, respect and living by a code."*

'Follow my moves you wanna make it to the top/
I'm on star for new born stars/'
– Jay Z, Go Hard

Finally remember two things:

First mentors aren't our masters, and their advice isn't scripture. Like Jay Tweeted when asked 'What's the biggest entrepreneurial tip you've learned?': *"Don't listen to anyone, everybody is scared."*

Secondly, know that mentors can't be 'mentors' forever. Continuing a cozy mentor–mentee relationship when you're ready to move on is detrimental. Yet often people either become scared to leave the security of the relationship or do not want to upstage the mentor, so always work in their shadow.

But we have to surpass our mentors and take their teachings to a higher level. Then in time the next generation will surpass us, and so the chain of evolution continues as it has for billions of years.

As Kendrick Lamar says, respectfully, of his mentors Dre and Snoop, "I can't be looking at them as big hommies for the rest of my life."[29]

'To be number one I'm a beat my brother'
– Kanye West, Big Brother

CONNECTIONS

So many people get their 'big break' from their personal relationships.

"Everybody blew up basically the same way," said Biggie, "behind who you knew and what they could do for you at that time."[30]

Now although BIG's words are less relevant now than they were in the 90's – because of the internet and the increased power people with fewer connections have – his comment still holds weight.

Connections is the reason Big Sean was discovered by Kanye West. In 2005 Sean had been persistent enough to secure a job at a local Detroit radio station co-hosting a Friday afternoon show. One day he was in line at the bank when a friend called saying Kanye was on the radio station, and he should go down to the studio to give him his demo-tape. Sean thought this was a crazy idea but the hustler in him wasn't going to let the opportunity slide. So he drove to the radio station and was able to get past security, to the back office, because of his relationships at the station.

As Sean was walking through the building Kanye walked passed on his way out. Caught in the moment, like a deer in headlights, all a star–struck Sean could say was that he was a fan and hosted a show at the station. Kanye replied, "That's good, keep it up," remembers Sean. But as Kanye was walking away, Sean stammered, "Wait wait! Can I rap for you?"[31] He did and the rest is history. Sean's connections allowed him the opportunity to access people in positions of power.

J Cole tried to get signed by Jay Z in 2007, but didn't have any relationships with people around Jay. So when he uninvitedly approached his idol *(pg.127)* he was quickly turned away. Cole realized the importance of networking and (after a long series of events) connected with Mike Rooney, who was more established in the industry and acted as his business partner. He was able to get Cole's music into the hands of several influential people. Mike also got Cole access to studio time and more established producers. Eventually, after a "year and a half of us trying to get our foot in the door and trying to get somebody to pay attention," remembers Cole, a connection Mike had met played 'Light Please' for Jay Z and Cole met his idol soon afterwards.

Forming and maintaining relationships opens us up to so many opportunities. That's why it's important to show respect to everyone you connect with, from directors to interns. People who make tea one day are running companies the next and will remember how people treated them when they were struggling. Show respect to people and they will want to work with you again. As someone observed of Pharrell, "He'll treat a doorman and Bill Gates the same way…If you want people to have your back, you need to appreciate them."[49] It's also just the right thing to do – (see 'Who Benefits' *pg.318*).

It's also impossible to predict who connections can introduce you to, and where the chain will lead. Jay Z's relationships with neighborhood rapper Jaz–O started a chain that would lead to all the people who made Reasonable Doubt and Roc–A–Fella successful:

Jaz–O → Big Daddy Kane → Mister Cee → Clark Kent → Dame Dash → Biggs…

Finally, it's important not to hold grudges or to lash out because of perceived mistreatment. Why burn bridges with potentially valuable connects?

'Dry your eyes, never let up/
Forgive but don't forget…'
–Tupac, Keep Ya Head Up

But this is easier said than done. That's why we need to develop high SI.

SOCIAL INTELLIGENCE

'Shake hands, make friends…'
– Jay Z, 1-900-Hustler

Reasonable Doubt marked the culmination of 10 years of rapping for Jay Z, and the Roc-A-Fella team were focused on creating a product that would catapult them to the forefront of the industry.

'Can't Knock The Hustle' was planned as the lead single and featured the hottest rising star in R&B, Mary J Blige. (Because of Dame Dash's relationship with her before she 'blew up,' Mary agreed to sing the song's hook for "$10,000 in a brown bag.") Convinced that the song would be a hit, Dame put out a full page ad in The Source magazine, as well as advertising the song on posters across New York.

But according to Roc–A–Fella's lawyer Reggie Osse, "Mary's record label MCA/Universal did not want her associated with some unknown 'Jay-Z' rapper dude."[32]

Image is everything in entertainment (*pg.260*), so to maintain Mary's image as 'Queen of Urban Music' she couldn't associate with unknown artists who may lower her status. Universal ordered Dame to remove all Mary references from Reasonable Doubt.

But the Roc team are hustlers, they weren't just going to just accept 'No.' So Reggie used his years of networking and relationship building to negotiate with a Universal executive colleague. They came to an agreement that seemed to satisfy both parties, and let Mary remain on the album but not on a single, video or on any advertisements.

But the hustler in Dame still wouldn't take 'no' for an answer, so Reggie set up a conference call between Dame and the Universal executive.

"On the call, as my connect was explaining to Dame why Mary could not appear on a single, Dame lost it and asked dude if he owned Universal," remembers Reggie. "When dude said he didn't, Dame laid into him (and me) about how I had him dealing with 'peons.' My heart dropped and I immediately dropped Dame from the call."

Dame would continue his career with Roc–A–Fella trying to blast through people who stopped them doing exactly what they wanted. That attitude certainly knocked down doors for the team, (especially early on when guerilla promoting and negotiating deals), but it also burned a lot of bridges (especially once they established themselves and needed productive, workable relationships with others).

Eventually too many bridges were burning, too much bad blood was spilled, and The Roc–A–Fella empire collapsed.

Having a personality that people want to deal with often trumps knowledge or experience. In practically any industry to be successful in the long run: People skills are more important than technical skills.

Even in highly technical fields like engineering, Social Intelligence, or knowing how to deal well with people, is shown to determine about 85% of a person's income over their life, yet it's a skill not taught in schools.[33] This skill makes people want to work with you. It makes money chase you.

Social Intelligence is a large reason why Glacèau, makers of Vitaminwater, struck a deal (worth $100million) with 50 Cent in 2004.

Glacèau executives were initially hesitant to meet with 50, as based on his 'gangsta' image they expected an ignorant, aggressive thug. Instead though, they found 50 to be "thoughtful, calm, respectful and deliberate."[34]

On the flip side, Sean Combs almost ended his music career prematurely because of his poor Social Intelligence. Having just been promoted to an A&R position at Uptown Records, and seeing success with his production for Mary J Blige and Jodeci, Combs felt he deserved the number two position in the company. (He was already wearing a diamond-studded medallion representing Lazarus, a saint who had been reborn, perhaps because Sean felt his own powers 'Godly'.) But when CEO Andre Howell hired somebody else, Sean did not take it well. He was arrogant, aggressive and refused to co-operate with the new manager, even shouting and swearing at him in front of other staff. Unsurprisingly Sean was fired.

"I was getting caught up in my success. I was in a castle that had a King and I was running around with a crown butt naked," Sean later reflected. "I'm so passionate about music [that] I'm not understanding the politics or protocol of business…I lost the level of respect I should have had for the people above me. I did not understand how to massage relationships, I wasn't really a team player. I was very immature."[35]

(It was Sean's willingness to learn and change, and of course his hustle, *(pg.175)*, which saved his career).

Kanye West has a very similar personality to Sean and Dame, but he recognises this weakness and actively works to develop social intelligence. For instance, he says one of the main reasons he did the 'Watch The Throne' album with Jay Z was so he could spend time around his mentor. "Jay Z has the best social skills of anyone that I know, and I wanted to learn from him."[36]

'Show em' how to move in a room full of vultures/'
– Jay Z, Izzo

199

Hugely successful books have been written on the importance of having a 'pleasing personality,' like Dale Carnegie's influential *How to Win Friends and Influence People*. In essence, it's about first accepting the fact that every aspect of your personality is under your control. Your emotions, temper and mood are all controlled by you – either consciously or not.

'Nobody built like you, you design yourself/ '
– Jay Z, A Dream

Most of us, most of the time, don't think when we act. Everything is instinct and emotion. Social intelligence is about regaining control and acting with the rational brain, instead of reacting and being bullied by emotional, irrational responses.

The most effective way to 'take control' is: *To get out of our own head and see things through the mind of other people, by truly understanding their perspective.*

By doing this we can imagine what others are thinking and feeling. We can understand people on a deep human level. When we stop seeing the world only through our own eyes, we stop seeing the world from our own insecurities. We don't take everything personally. We're calm, understanding and able to influence people because we empathize with what's important to them.

Simply put, not constantly thinking about yourself, 'I...', and showing sincere interest in others, (by listening and trying to understand the way they see the world), makes people like you. If people like you they want to be around you and will share opportunities with you. Instead of learning a list of artificial tips to improve S.I. (like 'smile & nod!'), this one principle will naturally lead to all other 'quick-fix techniques.'

'Actions have reactions, don't be quick to judge/
You may not know the hardships people don't speak of/ '
– Gang Starr, Moment of Truth

Taking the 'God Perspective,' by rationally observing and understanding people on a deep human level, means you are mastering social intelligence. From this perspective you can't get insulted, defensive and aggressive by somebody you don't like, because you empathize with them and their situation. You understand that under similar circumstances you would behave just as they do. By really understating others you can also make most interactions advantageous because, whether you're trying to negotiate a deal or persuade somebody to act, when a person feels understood they feel comfortable opening up and are more willing to cooperate and to give.

The biggest obstacle to the 'God Perspective' is ego.

Ego

'I love hip hop music/
I just hate the ego/
The politics that follow it/
Getting caught in it can be lethal/'
– Macklemore, Ego

To an outsider looking in at Hip Hop, it can seem that ego – hyper-inflated feeling of self-importance – is practically a synonym for the culture. Brags, boasts and taunts do certainly make up a large proportion of the music's content, but even though the icons profiled in this book all have songs that belong in that category, they also know how destructive ego is. Those with the strongest social intelligence work to defeat ego.

Ego is all about 'I' (the word literally comes from the Latin word 'I'). Ego is part of our 'reptile brain' *(pg.81)*. Ego means to see the world as revolving around you. As discussed in 'The Core' chapter, *(pg.93)*, there is nothing wrong with loving and believing in yourself, in fact it's essential for success. But when that so called 'love' is coming from a place of ego, it separates you from the world around you. Working through ego means working solely for personal self-serving goals and is the exact opposite to what is required to work effectively in a team. Ego means 'Me' not 'We'. Ego shuts down teamwork by taking focus away from the purpose of the work and into petty personal quarrels, (just look at most episodes of 'The Apprentice'). Ego closes you off to empathy with other views and often results in defensive, aggressive and vindictive thoughts and behaviors. Instead of team members focused on creating the best possible work, they're focused on creating the best possible work *for themselves*. Adding those two words makes a big difference to the final outcome.

'Why throw everything away over ego? /'
– Jay Z, Trouble

Greats can deal with anybody – people with large or no ego's – as they try not to see the word through 'I' or 'Me,' so they don't let anyone else's ego affect the work. Interactions aren't a battle over who's the most important person in the room. Like No I.D says, "I'll come in the room, and I won't even say who I am, much less what I've done. I'm just Dion. I'm in the room, 'Hey, how's it going?'" 37

"True Greatness," writes Stephen Covey, author of 'The Seven Habits of Highly Effective People,' "True Greatness will be achieved through the abundant mind that works selflessly with mutual respect and for mutual benefit."

Jimmy Iovine (the legendary Interscope Records Chairman and cofounder of Beats by Dre), learned this lesson as a 21 year old sound engineer on Bruce Springsteen 'Darkness on the Edge of Town' album.

Whilst recording, the production team moved to a different studio with different sound equipment and Jimmy could no longer re-create one particular drum sound Springsteen was adamant on including. After weeks of trial and error, with Jimmy working hard to get the sound right and growing more and more frustrated with every failure, another member of the team suggested hiring a friend who could achieve the desired sound. Hearing this Jimmy became "mortified and insulted," and stormed in to meet with Bruce's manager. "I quit. Fuck this," Jimmy blurted, offended that somebody else was taking his job. To which manager Jon Landau replied:

"Let's just talk for a second. I'm going to try to teach you something now, at what could be a crossroads in your career. This is not about you. This is about Bruce's album and making the best album we possibly can. I want you to go in there and I want you to say to Bruce, 'I'm going to support you no matter what.' Bruce will remain your ally throughout the rest of your career. You don't just walk out because you think someone has insulted you and your pride has been hurt."

Taken aback by the sense in Landau's words, Jimmy took the lesson to heart. Refocused on the bigger picture he got back to work. The team found the elusive drum sound and released a successful record. Then because of their new positive relationship, a few weeks later Springsteen let Jimmy produce the hit song 'Because the Night' with Patti Smith, and his career was officially 'launched.'

"The rest of my career I approached [with that attitude]," Jimmy later recalled. "I just take a step back, don't buy my own bullshit. Just look at the work. That lesson is the most powerful lesson I ever learned. It goes against human instinct."[38]

NEGATIVES

Negative people are inevitable in any walk of life. People who put you down and hold you back from reaching your true potential. It's so important not to let them distract your focus from your mission. Life is too precious to be held back by others and the mind is too important to waste occupied with thoughts of them. Even masters of social intelligence, who practice understanding and work against ego, know it's foolish to engage with the negatives.

Often people you start with will be the ones who put out negativity or 'hate' most when you become successful. They feel that they deserve part of your success, or feel envious because you went on to better things and they didn't.

Eminem's original crew, 'Basmint Productions,' all turned against him when he signed to Dre. They spread vicious rumors in magazines and supplied The Source with supposedly 'racist' songs Em recorded when he was fourteen years old.

Or look at the tragically hilarious example of Esham, the underground rapper who, in fairness, was a Detroit Hip Hop pioneer. In every interview Esham seems unable to keep Eminem's name out of his mouth. In every interview he accuses Em of stealing his style, calling him and "all the other white artists that blew up," racists. He's almost insanely deluded:

"Instead of embracing the greatness that is Esham. A lot of people chose to steal and pretend to be the nucleus that is me, to this Hip Hop thang. Marshall Mathers was a made to be Esham MC by the corporate machine…They then went in and spelled his name with a 'E' made sure it ended with an 'M' to subconsciously take the buzz we built up for the city 10 years prior to him even coming out. But even hoe ass Marshall knows he is Ne-Yo to my Micheal Jackson. And it is written in history."

Every question Esham is asked comes back to Em. Like when AllHipHop asked: "Over 20 albums deep don't you ever feel burned out?" Esham responded: "I reckon Eminem feels burnt out cause he has nothing to say, but Esham. I got too much game. They get it from me. When I put a album out, everyone studies it so they can come up with dope shit."[39]

Esham seems to be so desperate for Em's attention he even cusses Em's daughters and ex-wife in songs and interviews.

This is the sad reality of spiteful miserable haters whose existence seems to stem around an angry deluded resentment toward somebody successful. Em, or any other having this negative energy put out towards them, shouldn't feel angry. These haters, let's call them 'fools' or 'losers,' are ruled by their ego and insecurities. Their life revolves around drama and politicking. They achieve little and want to stop others achieving too. A loser's objective is to lower you to their level. They fantasize about getting under your skin and bringing you into their battle. You can't win an argument with a fool because they don't care about rationality and results. Trying to fight fire with fire – negative with negative – just creates more negative.

'A wise man told me don't argue with fools/
Cause people from a distance can't tell who is who/'
– Jay Z, Takeover

We have to accept these people as part of life. We all have the same emotions when we think through our ego, (jealously maybe evolved in our DNA). It's human nature so we have to accept it in others.

'If you had it like me and I was in your shoes/
I'd probably hate on me too/'
– Chamillionaire, Good Morning

To deal with fools you can use three strategies:

Wish You Well:
Understand the person that 'hates' you is just trying to get by as best they can. There is pain in their life that has caused them to do what they did. (Hate is often, if not always, a by-product of fear. I may fear that I'll never be as good or as respected as you, which leads me to feelings of envy or hate towards you.) So whatever they're going through, (money problems, identity issues, loneliness, feelings of self-hate etc.), sincerely wish them well. Hope they get through it and become the better person that they want to be.

'You hate it before you played it. I already forgave ya/'
– J Cole, Villematic

Ha Ha:
Fools want to be close to you, they just do it in hateful ways. They're like attention-craving kids, and when we see them as silly toddlers, how can we get upset? Instead of getting angry all we can do is laugh at their antics. We just smile, blissfully ignore them, and focus on our own goals and the most important '20%' *(pg.155)*. When they receive no attention the kids will find something else to do with their time.

'Hatin' on your happiness you hit 'em off with laughs/
Smile 'til they surrender, then you kill 'em off with Glad/'
– Lupe Fiasco, Strange Fruition

Thank you:

You get what you give (*pg. 322*), so fools putting out negativity will bring about their own demise. Their objective is to lower you, so to 'beat' them, separate yourself even more by becoming greater. Like a sumo wrestler using an opponent's energy against them, Greats flip hatefulness into positivity. For example, by using fools as motivation to work harder, by analyzing their own behavior and making sure not to make the same mistakes as fools, or by using fools as material for work.

> *'But I want you to doubt me, I don't want you to buh–lieve/*
> *Cause this is something that I must use to succeed/'*
> *– Eminem, Survival*

By tuning negative energy to your advantage you're practicing the principle of 'Love Life' (*pg. 324*). It's part of loving the very fact that you're alive and comes from knowing that everything you deal with, (for some reason perhaps we cannot yet fully comprehend), is there to teach you lessons about life. To give you the character you need to achieve whatever Greatness you were meant for.

Finally, recognize when you yourself are acting like a fool towards other and correct it – it's the opposite of Greatness.

> *'I don't hate 'em, I congratulate 'em/'*
> *– Nas, Make The World Go Round*

ON NO ONE

'Nobody that I could just depend on/
Until I touch down in the end zone/'
— Nicki Minaj, Last Chance

The support of other people is no doubt important, but to depend on others for achieving anything, to think 'I can't do it without them,' is likely to result in failure.

To feel like 'I need him or her to progress' is a weak position. With 'The Hustle' and 'The Pursuit' there is always a way to do it without 'them'.

When we feel in control of our destiny, that, 'it's in my hands,' and feel that we will do it 'with or without you,' the people we need will sense our confidence and actually want to work with us. A person who knows where she/he is going is a magnet.

'Nothing handed out I'm about to take mine/'
— Kanye, Big Brother

After TDE had their negative experience with Warner Brothers in 2006 *(pg.114)* they learned, "Don't depend on nobody else to do things for you," CEO Top Dawg told Vibe. "The label is there, but they don't know shit 'cause they not in the streets. Spinning out of the WB situation, we realized that the internet was becoming big and that became our focus."[40]

And since then that has been the whole teams' attitude. TDE were set on going to the top without the help of any of the 'Big Boys'.

"I always had the mentality that I can always do this, even without [Dr. Dre]," Kendrick told HipHopDX. "Even if I go into a situation with Dre, I'm still gonna have the mentality that I'm gon' push with or without you. And he respects that, for me to have that type of grind and that type of hunger to go get it and not wait on a Dre beat, or however it comes."

'Everybody heard that I fuck with Dre/ and they wanna tell me, I made it/
*N****I ain't made shit, if he gave me a handout/ I'mma take his wrist and break it/'*
— Kendrick, The Spiteful Chant

"I actually sat down and told him what I said in one of my raps," Kendrick continues. *'Do I need a co-sign from Dre or Jigga / It could make it much bigger / But do I need 'em though?'* And he was like, 'Yeah, that's dope. That's how you supposed to think young man.'"[41]

ROMANCE

In April 2008 Jay Z and Beyoncé inked the Roman numeral 'IV' on their ring fingers, to symbolize their commitment to each other in marriage *for*ever. They had been together since 2002.

Why did Jay choose a long term monogamous relationship instead of living many people's ultimate fantasy – a bachelor life sounded by models?

The same can be said for practically every successful person you can think of, in and out of Hip Hop. Dr. Dre has been married since 1996, Snoop since 97, same with Will Smith, Spike Lee, and world leaders like Branson, Zuckerberg, Gates, Obama, Jobs etc. Even many successful people who choose not to get married, like Diddy or Common, have long term partners.

There is no one rule fits all but most successful people understand the power of long term intimate relationships.

Napoleon Hill studied hundreds of the world's most successful people and concluded that: "No man is happy or complete without the modifying influence of the right woman. The man who does not recognize this important truth deprives himself of the power which has done more to help men achieve success than all other forces combined."[28]

If Hill's statement did not cause you to think a little please read it again: *"the power which has done more to help men achieve success than all other forces combined."*

Quick science: The chemical Oxytocin ('the love hormone') is found to be higher in the brains of people in long term intimate relationships. Oxytocin is responsible for the feeling that 'all is right with the world,' which leads to calmness, accuracy of judgment, and balance – the perfect platform for courage, imagination and drive. That's what's behind the saying "behind every great man is a great woman," and why Jay rapped *'All I need in this world of sin is me and my girlfriend'*.

As with many of the principles in this book, this is something Kanye discovered naturally.

"Any woman that you're in love with or that loves you is going to command a certain amount of energy. It's actually easier to focus, in some ways. When you're uncertain about love, it can be such a distraction. It infects all the other areas. That's what I mean when I say like, 'Yo, I'm going to be super Zenned [when I get married].' I'm the type of rock star that likes to have a girlfriend, I'm the type of soul that likes to be in love and likes to be able to focus. And that inspires me."[42]

'Even in your lowest days when you no longer Superman/
At least you know you got Lois Lane'
– J Cole, Runaway

Choosing the Right One

The reason superstars typically always get together with other superstars is they are looking for partners to lift them higher.

Years before Kanye met Kim Kardashian, he knew the type of partner he would settle down with.

"I feel like the type of girl I would be with is a fellow superhero," he said in 2009. "So we get that 'already flying and now we're just flying together' thing." [43]

In the same way, superstars Jay Z and Beyoncé share the same values, ambitions and aspirations and can elevate each other to new heights. They also helped each other access whole new markets, with people whom they may not have been able to reach on their own. Their superstars combined to 'upgrade' into an ultra–super–power couple.

But why do many people in marriages not feel like this? Why do so many in long term relationships end up feeling trapped or like they're two singles under the same roof?

One natural core idea, (as oppose to superficial magazine advice), comes from 'The Celestine Prophecy,' a book Jay Z "lives by."[44]

Most of us feel incomplete, like a semi-circle, and we go through life looking for other people to 'complete us,' to make us happy. When we find 'The One' the first encounters are euphoric. It's the 'love at first sight' feeling. We come together to create a whole circle. The other person becomes the center of our lives, and we depend on them for our sense of "security, guidance, wisdom, and power."[45]

But this is an unstable creation and will erupt. The couple is made up of two incomplete beings forcefully fusing into one artificial 'circle' through a relationship, so eventually power struggles develop as each person wants to control the new creation.

'It's so insane 'cause when it's going good, it's going great/
I'm Superman with the wind at his back, She's Lois Lane/
But when it's bad it's awful, I feel so ashamed I snapped/ '
– Eminem, Love the Way You Lie

The bitterness and hurt an unstable relationship can cause often scars people for years, even life. Like Eminem, who said after his divorce, "I would rather have a baby through my penis than get married again."[46]

"I don't ever want to experience that again. I learned my lesson and I've seen what it is and what it can and can't be and I feel like I've learned enough from my first mistake. Let that be the last one and keep moving forward. Relationships? No."[47]

Of course there is no black and white answer, and this may be the best decision for Em and others. But the experience of the majority shows the overwhelming positive impact of a loving personal relationship.

So how can we create these relationships?

When we're able to feel the same high of the first moments of a relationship on our own we can form a whole circle with ourselves. Then we can connect with someone else to create a 'super circle,' like Kanye describes, where we grow individually and as part of a 'super couple.'[48]

The key is to not look for others to 'complete us' but to deal with the reasons for our own incompleteness first. The key is to love ourselves.

'You want a certain type of guy, gotta reach a certain point too/
At the destination, a king will anoint you/ '
– Common, Ghetto Heaven

Wiz Khalifa said, "Being single doesn't necessarily mean you're available. Sometimes you have to put up a sign that says 'Do Not Disturb' on your heart."

This is exactly what Jay Z did before his relationship with Beyoncé.

Agnes Reeves walked out on the family when Jay was eleven years old. Jay carried the resentment and bitterness he felt for his absent father from that moment on and it affected his relationships with everyone around him.

"[I felt] anger at the whole situation," he told Oprah in 2009. "Because when you're growing up, your dad is your superhero. Once you've let yourself fall that in love with someone, once you put him on such a high pedestal and he lets you down, you never want to experience that pain again. So I remember just being really quiet and really cold. Never wanting to let myself get close to someone like that again. I carried that feeling throughout my life, until my father and I met up before he died."

Jay's mother recognized his 'incompleteness' and set up a meeting between him and his father, 20 years after Agnes deserted the family. Their long conversation brought out all of Jay's pent up emotions. He was able to look directly in the eyes of the man who had caused him so much hurt and tell him exactly what he had done. His "stubborn" father came to understand how much his actions had affected Jay and accepted it. This was a massive event. "Reconnecting with my father changed me more than anything."[44]

It helped Jay open up to people, and be open to love.

The Story Of

Jay Z

Growing up in a world where death and imprisonment are a normal occurrence will shape a person in a unique way. Sean Carter compared the environment he was raised in to a game of boxing. "In these games where winning is close to impossible and losing is catastrophic, you learn how to compete as if your life depended on it."[1]

It is those learnings that have enabled him to become the number one entertainment–entrepreneur in the world. This is how he did it.

Sean Carter was born on a somber 4th December, in 1969 New York City. 21 year old Fred Hampton had been the latest black leader to be assassinated by government forces that day, in the effort to prevent a cohesive African–American political movement forming. Since the murders of the great civil rights leaders, Martin and Malcolm, the black community were feeling more disenfranchised and dejected from the land they called home. How could you feel a sense of belonging to a country that discriminated against you in work, school, service provision and now was actively trying to divide and deteriorate your community? Black neighborhoods like Marcy Housing Projects, Brooklyn, New York, were a different country.

Sean Carter was raised in, and by, Marcy. It was a landscape built to locate the poorest in the city, where bad schools and meager access to public assistance were the norm.

"Our self-esteem is low," says Sean, "because in these neighborhoods we're taught we're less than, we're not equal to everyone else in the world."[2]

Though this would also be the perfect breeding ground for Hip Hop.

The neighborhood was calm, where as a child Sean could play with his friends on their bikes or on the abandoned boat that for some reason lay in Marcy playground, as if someone had once dreamed of making it out 'by any means' via the Hudson River.

But when the calm was broken, the neighborhood erupted.

From the mid 70's the area was becoming a hotbed for drugs and gangs, which inevitably brought violence. "There could be people shooting outside at 12 noon on Sundays," Sean remembers.[2] As a nine years old he witnessed his older friend Benny fall to the ground in a pool of blood. Executed in the hallway outside his apartment.

The view overlooking Marcy Housing Projects, Brooklyn, New York. The bleak concrete buildings resemble prison walls.

The Carter family, (Gloria, Adnis, two daughters and two sons), were six of the 4,300 residents that filled Marcy's 1,700 apartments. Their government subsidised, 5C, home played an important role in the community. Sean's parents loved music and their extensive record collection, which included the first 'rap' records by King James the Third and The Sugar Hill Gang (1979), was continually playing in the apartment.

"Both my mom and dad had an afro. We lived in a supercool house," Sean remembers.[1] "They had the biggest record collection in the neighborhood. Everyone in the neighborhood came to party."[2]

In an otherwise bleak environment, music came to represent 'good times'.

"My early days shaped my musical vocabulary. I remember the music making me feel good, bringing my family together and being a common passion my family shared."[1]

As a boy, Sean would mimic performances seen on late night television shows with his sisters – singing and dancing in a family living room band.

Aside from the direct musical influence his parents had on him, growing up Sean also learned skills that would become indirectly applied to his future career. As a boy his father taught him how to closely observe life as they travelled around New York and when they visited aunts and uncles in other cities. Sean would have to lead the way, so would need to pay close attention to his surroundings.

"[My dad] taught me that life was a giant chessboard where you had to be aware in the moment, but also thinking a few moves ahead."[1]

Intimate observation is at the heart of any art. The ability to look closely at the world and make connections, then describe and communicate them in creative ways is the spirit of rap, and any serious art form. As poet Wallace Stevens said, *"A poet looks at the world, the way a man looks at a woman."*

All these childhood experiences: the unfiltered project environment, his parent's musical influence, and his father's teachings, laid the foundation for Sean's future. But he needed to first find the thing that would enable him to put all the pieces together. Luckily, it would soon find him.

My First Song

In the early 70's Hip Hop was birthed in a Bronx housing project twenty miles from Marcy and by the late 70's had spread across deprived neighborhoods throughout New York. This new youth 'kulture' had four forms of self-expression: graffiti, breaking, deejaying, and when Sean was nine years old he witnessed emceeing for the first time.

"I saw a guy in neighborhood freestyling about what everybody had on. It was fun...I was mesmerized...then I thought 'I can do that.'"[2]

With a few paper-clipped pages he began writing lyrics that night.

"I would practice from the time I woke in the morning till I went to sleep...I filled every blank space on every page of a binder with rhymes. Everywhere I went I'd write. I'd spend my free time reading the dictionary, building my vocabulary for battles."[1]

The creative process entranced him and he only wanted to get better.

"He worked on his flow every day," remembers cousin B–High, who lived in the same neighborhood. "He'd look in the mirror, zone out and rhyme to himself."[4]

At school, at home, on the streets, Sean's mind was constantly turning the world around him into rhymes.

"Late at night we'd hear banging on the table and mumbling," Sean's sister Michelle says. "'What are you doing, we're all trying to sleep' I'd say, 'I gotta get this out' he'd tell me."[4]

'Kitchen table where I honed my skills'
– Momma Loves Me

Sean would analyze the lyrics of major rappers in the early 80's like Run DMC, Kurtis Blow and especially Slick Rick. "Slick Rick taught me that not only can rap be emotionally expressive, it can even express those feelings that you can't really name – which was important for a lot of kids who couldn't always find words to express their feelings."[1]

"He'd rewind tapes until he knew [exactly] what they were saying," Michelle remembers. Sean studied hard and would then apply what he was learning in the street. "You'd always hear about him battling in the neighborhood or in high school."[4]

In Hip Hop Sean found an identity. He was a shy child but through Hip Hop he could confidently express himself, whilst having fun with friends.

Then came the day Superman walked out of his life.

'I wanted to walk just like him/
Wanted to talk just like him'/
– Where have you been

One day an eleven years old Sean woke up to a house without a father. "He just bounced" with no explanation. Sean's role model was gone. The move would massively change Sean's life and in time the music he would make.

"It made me not express my feelings as much. I was already a shy kid, and it made me a little reclusive," he told Oprah. "But it also made me independent. And stronger. It was a weird juxtaposition."[3]

"Jay closed down for a minute" recalls Michelle. "He wrote more and more rhymes, as a way to vent and get his feelings out."[4]

Following his father's departure, and his mother working two jobs and rarely home, life at home was becoming "dysfunctional"[3]. At the extreme there would be stealing, drugs and even shooting in the house.

A young boy will emulate role models closest to him, and with his father out of the picture, Sean found other male mentors in his environment: drug dealers.

During the crack epidemic of the 1980's drugs became a major form of employment for inner-city youth with little parental guidance Sean couldn't see a reason not to partake in the world. If the 'fiends' were going to buy drugs anyway, why not be the one selling it? So at thirteen he started dealing drugs with other kids in the neighborhood. "In my mind, that wasn't risking a lot. You think, 'If I'm living like this, I'll risk anything to get more. What's the worst that could happen?'"[3]

'Hustling' came to dominate his life and although he loved the expression Hip Hop provided and continued writing rhymes, he never saw music as a viable potential career path. That is until he met-up with another mentor.

The Jaz

Big Jaz, or Jaz–O, was one of the most respected local rappers in Brooklyn and was introduced to Sean through mutual friends in 1984. Sean looked up to Jaz like an older brother (Jaz is five years older) and partly like the father figure he no longer had. They would spend hours together reciting lyrics, battling and exchanging rhyme styles.

"We'd lock ourselves in a room with a pen, a pad, and some Apple Jacks and Haagen–Dazs," remembers Sean.[1]

Because neither Sean nor Jaz had naturally gravelly voices suited to rap, (like a DMX, Tupac or CyHi), they had to compensate with more advanced lyrics and flows, inventing words and shaping the voice into an instrument.

They had few life experiences to rap about at this stage, so the focus was purely technical. "We would work on the craft all the time. The goal always to rhyme perfect," remembers Jaz.

The duo's friendly competition is at the heart of Hip Hop. Since anyone with a voice can rap (to some level at least, as oppose to the few born with a natural singing voice), there is always competition to push the craft further and further. For example technically through complex rhyme schemes, compound syllables, double entendres, or through the richness of the stories told. Competition sharpens poetic steel and in-time would push Sean to make his first album extraordinarily lyrical. As Sauce Money, another rapper who grew up with Sean remembers of the time they recorded together some years later: "It was a war in the studio. You watch your friend put it down and you had to step up!"[5] – (see 'Circle of Success' *pg.187*).

(This is also the point where Sean adopted the rap moniker Jay Z – a combination of his childhood name 'Jazzy' and a reference to the J/Z subway line that has a station at Marcy Avenue.)

Like a guiding mentor Jaz took a teenage Jay Z under his arm and in 1986 Jaz got a sixteen year old Jay involved in the Brooklyn rap crew 'High Potent.' It was Jay's first time in the studio and they recorded 'H.P. Gets Busy'. The song talks about the standard braggadocio 'I'm the best' subject matter of Hip Hop, and demonstrates Jay's early 'speed rapper' style. In the ten years between the song and Jay's debut album his style would evolve unrecognizably.

17 year old Jay Z with Easy L.B from the group High Potent, 1986.

Jaz was growing his reputation as an emcee, by networking and getting his demo heard, with Jay watching and learning by his side.

In 1989 Jaz signed a deal with the major record label EMI – one of the first rappers to do so. "I was shocked," Jay remembers, "'they're giving you money to do that?!'"[3]

The label gave Jaz $300,000[22] and two months to record an album in London, covering expenses including an upmarket apartment in Notting Hill. Jaz took Jay with him to England, at a time when most people in the neighborhood had never been outside New York. "I was a kid from Marcy projects, and I spent two months in a London flat," he gleefully remembers.

It was at this point Jay saw rap as a viable career option. "It wasn't until Jaz got a contract that I was like, 'Wow, this stuff is going to happen.'"[3]

Jay also featured in Jaz's lead single 'Hawaiian Sophie,' a comical story of Jaz's attempt to seduce a tropical girl, by playing a cameo role in the video.

The pair also featured in a twenty second freestyle on 'YoMTV Raps,' where Jay appeared wearing almost a ton of jewels on his neck and arms.

Jay Z, Jaz and friend Chase in their cameo appearance on Yo! MTV Raps 1989

All these experiences gave twenty year old Jay the invaluable opportunity to learn about the music industry first hand. "I was like a sponge when I'd sit in on Jaz's recording sessions and meetings."[1]

"That one experience taught me about the whole rap business. That was an important time for me."[6]

However, a few months after returning from London he came to view it as a very negative experience.

When 'Hawaiian Sophie' did not sell well EMI quickly dropped Jaz and shelved the album, in search of the next 'hot thing.'

The way labels could smile and tell you 'you're the best, you're gonna to be a huge star' one day, and not answer your calls the next, was a shock wake up call to the realities of the music business. Jay became disillusioned with the idea of a music career. He saw the reality of the industry and the type of people running labels – accountants, lawyers and managers who follow trends and chase money with no connection to the culture that the music comes from – and felt revolted.

The executives told Jaz what he would rap about and how he would present himself. They were following the Fresh Prince blueprint, trying to emulate Will Smith's success in the soft family friendly rap style, even though Jaz was the exact opposite of this – having come from one of the roughest housing project in the country. "It was like telling a tiger 'you're a rabbit'," says music exec Irv Gotti[4].

After Jaz was dropped, Jay was offered a record deal by the same people at EMI, but his loyalties were with his friend. "Jaz was the one who'd brought me in, and I felt that signing wouldn't be loyal to him. So I told them no. I didn't want to be involved with those record guys. They weren't stand–up people."[3] (Remember this is a person whose income comes from hard drug sales, an occupation many see as the most morally corrupt imaginable, and *he* is disgusted by the character of music industry executives.)

That's when Jay stopped trying to pursue a music career. He had dropped out of high school some years prior to go into business with his friends selling drugs on street corners, and that became his life.

(Incidentally his high school was ranked as the worst in New York, with 15% dropout rates, 30% reading at grade level[8] and major anti-social problems like muggings in unlit bathrooms. It was shut down in 1988, though it also 'educated' other superstar rappers of the 90's like Notorious B.I.G, AZ and Busta Rhymes.)

Dreams of being an artist were shut down, and his focus turned completely to the street.

'The streets robbed me I wasn't educated properly'
– Never Change

Future in the Balance

The sound of police sirens screaming through the night became a regular soundtrack to Sean's life. After the EMI experience he went months without recording, instead using his time to cook, cut and sell crack in the streets of New York and further down the East Coast.

As he got more involved in 'the streets' and saw the realities the life involved – the practical certainty of death or imprisonment – he went through the same symptoms of the drug users he served. On the one hand, wanting to escape from the street life and not live with the constant paranoia and distrust of others, but on the other hand addicted to the excitement of living on the edge and of course the money that came with it. For several years Sean would go through this mental limbo, balancing his two lives, trying to decide what he wanted from life.

'I felt like life was cheating me, for the first time/
In my life I was getting money but it was like my conscience was eating me/
Was this a lesson God teaching me?'
– Streets Is Watching

One thing he knew for sure was that he still loved rap, and standing for hours idly on street corners, combined with all his exciting new life experiences, meant rhymes kept coming. "I was getting a ton of knowledge in the street. I had to write, I had so much to say."

This is where his memory developed to the almost photographic one he has today. "As I was moving further away from home I had to memories the lines. So I'd do memory exercises, first 8 bars then 16, then a whole song and more."[2]

With the help of cousin B–High and Jaz–O, Jay was persuaded to once again pick up the microphone. He independently recorded the song 'Originators' with Jaz in 1990, where they were free to rap in their own style, without label manipulation. The duo showed off their super-fast rhyming skills, which were far more developed than the 'HP' single in 86. (The song was Afrocentric influenced, in line with the black conscious style popular at the time. It begins with the line, *'It is indeed a pleasure / to see so many Nubian faces, so many original faces here tonight'.*)

But rap was very much a sideline, an independent hustle Jay did when he took a break from the streets. "I was almost embarrassed to say I want to be a rapper," he admits.[9] In truth a major reason was Jaz's failure still haunted him, and would prevent Jay from fully focusing on music, his real passion, till he could let it go, (*pg.80*).

Meanwhile, although spending most his time in the streets, Jay was still close with Jaz–O, and being around a more established rapper meant Jay was introduced to many people who would come to play an vital role in his rise.

Long Live The Kane

Big Daddy Kane has his name in Hip Hop history books. In the early 90's he was the most successful rapper from Brooklyn. He was Jay Z's idol. The two met at friend Fresh Gordan's house, where Kane and Jaz–O had organised a battle, but instead ending up recording a mixtape together. Jaz asked if Jay could be featured on the tape too and Kane agreed.

Whilst recording the tape Jay was so impressed by Kane's raps and the way he could invent slang like *'put a quarter in your ass cause you played yourself,'* he didn't see how he'd be able to compete: "I thought I'd never be heard."

But Kane was also impressed with Jay. As he remembers, "Afterwards on the ride back home, Shirt Kings was like 'Jaz isn't with EMI anymore. We're trying to get him a new deal. You think you could [help out]?' And I [responded] 'To be honest with you, I kinda like the skinny, light skinned n**** better. Can you plug me with him?' And that's how me and Jay got cool and we started rocking."[10]

Some months later Kane wanted Jay to perform on his tour and picked Jay up from Marcy projects in his "batmobile." "[That] was the greatest moment of my life so far," Jay recalls.

On tour Jay was a side–act, alongside Bronx rapper Positive K, and would demonstrate his double/triple time rhyming technique for the crowd in between Kane's songs. The experience was an apprenticeship, and from watching Kane perform Jay learned about show pacing, how to play with the crowd's energy, how to appeal to girls and guys in the audience without alienating either and more. Jay credits Kane with many of the techniques he uses to this day, over twenty years later.[1]

Kane also helped Jay develop musically. "Jay could spit and I was basically trying to show him how to put lyrics in a song format, watching with his puchlines and the set up for it," he says.[10]

Kane tried to use his influence to get Jay signed to a label. In the early 90's they recorded the song 'Show and Prove' and tried to sell it. "We took these songs to people. Benny Medina, Lyor Cohen, I took it to a broad I was [having sex with] and she still wouldn't sign him," remembers Kane.

Record Executives were saying 'he doesn't have a look,' 'he can rhyme but can't make a record' and all doors were closed.

Though in truth even Kane at the time couldn't see Jay going very far:

"I'm gonna be honest with you, I always thought Jay was an incredible emcee and I thought that he could make some great records but I never saw his career going as big as it did, but I'm so, so happy for him."[10]

With so many doubters and naysayers in the industry saying he couldn't get a deal and not understanding his style, Sean questioned his future.

"At this point he doubted himself, saying 'maybe I can't do this, maybe I'm not good enough'" remembers his sister Michelle.[4]

Once again he returned to the streets, where he'd work in Maryland for six months at a time, and once again he came close to ending his music dream.

MC JZ, WHO USED TO BE THE JAZ' RAP PARTNER, HAS NOW JOINED FORCES WITH BIG DADDY KANE. DURING A BREAK IN KANE'S SET, JZ TREATED THE CROWD TO HIS NON-STOP RAP-FLOW, WHICH, JUDGING FROM THEIR REACTION, THEY CAN GET USED TO.

Left: 'JZ' in a Hip Hop magazine following his performances with Kane.
Above: Jav with some of his street partners. His two worlds.

Statistics show that on an average day in the mid 90's, more black male high school dropouts aged 20–35 were in custody than in paid employment.[11] Jay witnessed this first hand and spending so many idle hours on the streets gave him a lot of time to think about his future and what he really wanted.

"I started seeing people go to jail and get killed, and the light slowly came on. 'This life has no good ending.'"[3]

"I had a feeling deep down that no matter what success I had on the streets, I would be a failure for not chasing my dreams to be an MC."[1]

The internal feeling was amplified by positive people around Jay who would not let him quit. Cousin B–High would not talk to Jay for months as he felt he was ruining his life on the streets. B–High and DJ Clark Kent (who Jay meet on tour with Kane) would be on him "all the time" to get back to studio. Clark played a vital role in changing Jay's perceptions of himself from 'street hustler who happened to memorise rhymes' to an 'artist'. And in his mind Jay began to make the transition from one life to another.

"I started to realize that I couldn't be successful until I let the street life go. My mom always taught me that whatever you put into something is what you're going to get out of it. I had to fully let go of what I was doing before for the music to be successful. That was a leap of faith for me. I said, 'I have to give this everything.'"[3]

Whenever Jay came home from working out of state, Clark would call him for Open Mic nights at local clubs, and tried to use his influence to get him signed. The pair would record songs at Clark's home and take them to labels, but only to face rejection after rejection. Clark remembers: "It was one of the most hurtful periods in my life. Going to A&R meetings with great music and an unbelievable rapper, and people going 'I don't get it.'"[4]

For Jay to permanently move into the life he wanted, he needed to overcome the brick door blocking his entry to the music industry. He needed a character who refused to take 'no' for an answer, who wouldn't just knock down unopened doors, he'd tear down the building. So Clark introduced him to his friend Damon Dash.

Connecting the 'Circle of Success'

Dame Dash, a "Harlem dude through and through," lived with an immense hunger to "take over the world." His drive took him from sweeping barber shops and paper rounds in Harlem to attending private school, through scholarships, to promoting parties and managing artists.

Twenty years old in 1992, he was managing the rap group Original Flavor, which he signed to East/West Records through Clark Kent who was A&R for the company – Dame earned around $150,000 from the deal.

Clark had already tried to sign Jay to East/West, but as Reggie Osse, lawyer for Roc–A–Fella in the mid 1990's recalls, "back then NO ONE was feeling Jay, not even Clark's then boss, Sylvia Rhone."[12]

Clark did however manage to use his close relationship with Dame to get Jay a cameo appearance on Original Flavor's single, "Can I Get Open" in 1994, where Jay again displayed his rapid fire rhyming technique, (which he would later learn to modify to reach a larger audience.)

'Can I Get Open' marked the start of Jay's relationship with Dame Dash, who also managed other key players from Roc–A–Fella's early days, like producer Ski, Tone Hooker (the Original Flavor MC turned Roc A&R who also named the label), and the group's DJ, Chubby Chub, whose mixtapes would play a key role in pushing Jay's music to the streets.

"Dame and Jay clicked like they twin brothers in afterlife," Tone Hooker remembers.[4] The pair shared similar aspirations, and Jay admired Dame's almost uncontainable enthusiasm, backed up by a clear vision. "He projected bullet proof self-confidence," Jay remembers[1], so Dame became Jay's manager.

Dame set up all kinds of promotional activities like underground radio appearances, club performances and mixtape features. He would take Jay around the city to battle or just rap on pool tables in crowded back rooms. Jay became a local sensation. "People didn't want be on stage against him," remembers Tone. All of this was time spent building his name, his brand, learning about the industry and sharpening his saw till it was ready to slice through the industry.

After recording 'Can I Get Open,' Dame put Jay on an East Coast "makeshift tour" with Original Flavor (O.F.), to keep Jay focused on music and away from his 'other' life. O.F. became the third rap act Jay 'interned' with. He remembers some shows in North Carolina "with maybe 20 people in the audience." But regardless how small, each experience saw Jay grow as an artist. (Dame's friend Kareem 'Biggs' Burke also joined the team at this point, acting as a sort of tour road manager.)

Dame arranged more record label meetings for Jay, but again was met with unanimous rejections. Labels appreciated Jay's talent but couldn't comprehend the pairs' vision.

Jay believes he couldn't get a record deal as, "what I was saying was slang and coded, and on top of that has deep metaphors that most didn't get…I don't think everyone really understood it or got the emotion behind what was being said. They just heard regular words."

Although the team were growing their underground buzz, they were not experiencing major breakthroughs and were at risk of fizzling out, like so many up'n'coming artists. That is until necessity meant it was 'Do or Die'.

Dame was hit with major tax problems following his work with Original Flavour. The IRS was coming for him and he could no longer afford to keep the Pathfinder Jeeps that he was proudly transporting the team in on their East Coast 'tour'. With bankruptcy near, the team did everything they could to secure Jay a record deal. Again though, all to no avail.

"We must have shopped Jay to every label under the sun," remembers lawyer Reggie Osse.[12] "They had me up in all types of meetings, selling, pushing, damn near begging the record execs to give Jay a deal. Nada. One exec even told me 'why the fuck should I sign Jay Z, I have Black Sheep on our roster, Jay ain't fucking with them'... I remember specifically sitting in Def Jam begging Lyor Cohen for a shot. He passed."

Lyor, who would eventually form a partnership with Roc–A–Fella, later recalled the reasons he passed: "People in the music industry no longer dream, they are scared to death, only talking about what can go wrong. Jay Z is a dreamer, that's why the music business people didn't get him."[4]

But dreams don't feel so special when you can't lift them off the ground. At the time West Coast artists like Pac and Snoop were reigning, Nas stunned the world with Illmatic, Bad Boy Entertainment dominated New York, and Wu-Tang ruled the underground. The competition was intense, and Sean's feeling of hopelessness was real.

> *'It's like '93, '94, bout the year/*
> *That Big and Mack dropped and Illmatic rocked/*
> *Outta every rag drop, and the West had it locked/*
> *Everybody doing them, I'm still stretching on the block/*
> *Like 'Damn, I'mma be a failure'/*
> *Surrounded by thugs, drugs, and drug paraphernalia/ '*
> *–This Can't Be Life*

Sick of the rejection in New York, Dame took Jay to the 1995 Gavin Convention in San Francisco. The event allowed unsigned artists to promote their music to college radio stations across the country and also served as an important networking event, where unsigned musicians could meet potential managers, record label A&R's (who are responsible for discovering new talent) and other artists to collaborate with.

One morning at the conference, Jay and Dame were having breakfast in McDonalds when they met Loud Records A&R executives Matt C and Schott Free. (The A&R's had already heard 'Show and Prove' almost two years earlier.) When Jay gave them his recent demo tape, which included the song 'Reach the Top,' they were keen to sign him to Loud.

However, just like the team had experienced with countless other labels, Loud's CEO Steve Rifkind blocked the deal. "The chemistry wasn't there with all parties involved," says Matty C.[13]

All the while Jay was getting older in a young man's game.

Going Alone

After that rejection they were done. Jay, Dame and Biggs decided to sidestep the labels and do it alone.

"Roc–A–Fella came about out of frustration, through [unsuccessfully] shopping deals," says Jay. "A&R's can't really feel what I feel. My music wasn't something really simple. It was something people had to really sit down and listen to. So with the record company being the bridge to reach the people, I was like 'Man, we gonna build our own bridge.'"[14]

The team studied and were inspired by the four dominant independent Hip Hop labels of the time: Death Row, Bad Boy, Cash Money and No Limits. These companies had been built from nothing and in a few years were dominating urban music. 'If they can do it, we can too.'

They put together a simple plan to get the ball rolling. "'Let's just press up some vinyl, shoot a video, create some energy, and see where it goes" said Dame, and so an early version of Roc–A–Fella Records was formed.

The founding trio were "crazy hungry" to prove all the naysayers wrong. "We stepped away from industry, we don't need the industry for nothing," said a determined Jay at the time. "If you don't play my stuff on the radio it's [still] gunna be heard."[15]

Being involved in and having ownership of an actual record company made the decision to live the streets easier for Jay than if he was just an artist on a labels rooster. Unlike Jaz–O in 89, he had control of his work.

'Homeboys own your masters, slaves/
The mentality I carry with me to this very day/'
– No Hook

Also reading books like *'Hit Men: Power Brokers and Fast Money Inside the Music Business'* and learning more about how exploitative label contracts are, made the decision to go independent a lot easier – through it wasn't really a decision, more a necessity.

Jay locked in on overdrive with producers Clark, Jaz–O and Ski Beatz (from Original Flavor) to create product. Reggie Osse remembers: "24/7, they was producing records left and right outta Clark's crib. Jay was swimming in a pool of beats to sharpen his rhyme play."[12]

Jay soon began evolving his rhyme style. He was influenced by ground breaking artists of the time like Nas's Illmatic, and slowed down his rapid-fire tempo, while stuffing his flow with sophisticated metaphors, entendres and poetic imagery. At first listen rhymes might sound simple, but they would take many people literally years to fully decipher.

The 'genius' rhymes were a direct result of all the pressures the team were under — evidence that 'necessity is the mother of invention.'

Birthing a Dynasty

In 1995, 25 year old Jay and 23 year old Dame officially formed Roc–A–Fella Records. It was important for Jay to begin this new life with a clear conscious and so no 'dirty' money from hustling was used to establish the company – (though this claim is not proven). Instead Karem 'Biggs' Burke was brought in as a silent partner after investing $16,000. The new label's first songs released were 'Can't Get Wit That' and its B side 'In My Lifetime.'

They spent $5,000 shooting a video for Can't Get Wit That in Marcy projects, with the goal of getting it played on New York's number one video music show 'Ralph McDaniel's video music box' – a show Jay Z's mother said "he watched everyday"[16] growing up.

Operating on tight budgets, the team had to come up with innovative ways to get noticed. One tactic was to make 'goodie baskets' for DJ's. Jay's cousin B–High would make baskets with two copies of vinyl, a bottle of Moët, party favors (like chocolate), decorated intricately with Easter basket lining, and send them to DJs – both underground mixtape and mainstream radio DJs. (Though Jay says the tactic "didn't really work." He remembers, "standing outside radio station at 4am to catch [Funkmaster] Flex. And Flex just walking by 'yeah yeah yeah hommie, I'll get back to you.'"[9])

An important difference between Roc–A–Fella and many other boot-strap companies was their laser focus on the clear goals they set for themselves. "In order not to get stuck at low level hustling, we had a plan. A clearly written business plan with short and long term projections," said Jay. "This was as important as visualization in realizing success."[1]

Because radio stations weren't playing 'Can't Get Wit That' or 'In My Lifetime' the team had to play it people themselves. They would distribute the music directly, selling tapes from the trunk of their car and at shows, and would also work with record stores, like Fat Beats, to distribute CD's on consignment, (giving the stores free CD's and only getting paid when customers purchased). "We would be politicking with retailers and building relations with DJ's. It was Do or Die," remembers Jay.[1]

Though the team had big dreams and knew that to reach a larger audience they couldn't sell the records themselves. Not only did they have no experience in the production, distribution or marketing of music, they didn't have the money or man-power to reach a large audience in New York, yet alone around the country. They wanted to partner with another label that could provide the nationwide distribution networks and marketing power to promote Jay to the masses.

A year after pressing up the original, Ski–produced version of 'In My Lifetime' and selling it themselves, Jay and Dame had achieved enough underground buzz to negotiate a record deal with "the only label on the bloc biting" according to Reggie, Payday Records – the Hip Hop imprint run by

Patrick Moxey, who had a production and distribution deal with the larger Polygram Records, and acted as a go between for them and other independent labels like Death Row.

The Roc were able sign a distribution deal as they had already built momentum and achieved some grass roots buzz, like: underground radio play, good press, local touring and a growing audience. Reggie remembers negotiating the deal: "Moxey signed Jay for like 25–30K, and had Jay locked in for a couple of singles and several albums."[17]

Payday would receive 30% of record sales and were supposed to split some overhead expenses.

(In hindsight it seems UN-BE-LIEV-A-BLE that a label would sign Jay Z for only 30,000 dollars for even one album, let alone several. – Jay would go on to sell over 50 million albums in his career.)

In 1995 Pay Day re-released Jay's first official single, 'In My Lifetime,' a laid back 'hustlers dream' track, questioning 'what's the real meaning of life?' The team recorded the song's video on a luxury Caribbean island using Biggs's investment money. No other underground rapper portrayed this 'playboy living the life' persona. They were standing out.

The single was launched with minimal marketing support. "Payday gave us a box of flyers to promote," remembers Jay.[1]

"They were acting shady the whole time, like they didn't know how to work a record. The things that they were setting up for me I could have done myself. They had me travelling places to do in-store promotion, and my product wasn't even available in the store. We shot one video, but when the time came for me to do the video for the second single I had to be cut out."[18]

Because Jay was largely unknown, and Payday did a poor job promoting and distributing, the record sold poorly. The Roc were unhappy and wanted to cancel their deal. Pay Day was unhappy too and obliged by *dropping* Jay.

Imagine working hard for years, making numerous records and visiting every record label in New York begging them to sign you. You've given up a life of riches on the street for rejection after rejection after rejection. Still you pick yourself up again and again and again. Then when one small label eventually does give you a chance, they quickly DROP you. Imagine.

The vast majority would take this as a sure sign that 'enough is enough,' take a bow and quit. But this goes to show the level of hunger, and self-belief the team had. Their business plan was firmly ingrained in their mind, which meant they weren't derailed by the lack of support from Payday. They stayed focused. (After all, this is the same Sean who as a kid would lose basketball games in Marcy but keep returning to challenge the opponents till he won.)

Getting dropped from Payday was the straw that broke the camel's back. They were now completely finished begging the industry for support. It was time to blow the industry to smithereens. The trio pooled their collective recourses, including Payday's advance money, and went all in.

Roc on a Misson

Jay, Dame and Biggs set up a low rent office in a downbeat part of New York's Financial District. "I remember rats," said Omoyele Mcintosh[4], one of the first employees. But Jay and the bosses had their eyes on the long term and saw no problems with the space.

"I don't mind being down here in this area, because this is just a starting point for us," Jay said at the time. "I like being away from everybody right now, because I can get all my stuff together, then I can move uptown with all those other n**** when everything's straight. No sense in spending a whole lot of money on office space and moving employees round if your product isn't bringing in any money yet – that's a mistake executives make. I used my money to get this label off the ground and that was the right decision, yaknowhatI'msayin."[18]

From the beginning the bosses understood that they were selling more than music; they were marketing a lifestyle. The brand 'Roc–A–Fella' represented the luxuries of the 'rock-star life,' with a street spirit at its core. The name is based on oil tycoon John D. Rockefeller, the richest American of all time (net worth of $340 billion), and the famous Brooklyn drug dealer named 'Roc–A–Fella,' who street hustlers idolized, as well as the literal meaning 'we will 'roc a fella' if he gets out of line.'

The team embodied the Roc–A–Fella brand in everything they did, said and wore.

"We always aspired to have the best," recalled Dame. "And that name just, it just meant so much too American society, for aspiring to have finer things, an affluent lifestyle. That name represents the best for us."[19]

Their strategy was 'to look large to be large' so they started a fan club (fan–fam) before they had any fans and the whole crew would wear matching Jay Z jackets and ride in limousines with 'Jay Z' number plates. "Anything to make noise and get attention" recalls Dame. They'd uninvitedly bumrush other people's rap shows and throw thousands of dollars into the audience at their own shows. They represented the picture perfect 'Hustlers Hustler,' even while partying they'd be promoting the brand. People who saw them aspired to the Roc–A–Fella lifestyle.

Their marketing strategy was to constantly remind the streets who they were, and show them they were 'It'. They build alliances with local and underground DJ's, they offered record stores their singles on consignment, and they hired a street team of promoters who would be handing out flyers and putting up posters across the city. Jay & Dame ran the street team like a crew of drug runners, putting a man on every corner of the neighborhood they were canvassing, with promotional posters, flyers, and CD's.

They even secured the cover feature of independent New York Hip Hop magazine 'Stress,' summer of 1996 (before Reasonable Doubt's release.) It's likely (but unconfirmed) that the Roc 'incentivized' stress editors, by offering to cover the cost of printing of the entire issue – another example of their 'by any means' hustle (*pg.174*).

All this activity was building the buzz around Jay Z to higher and higher levels, but the most important element to determine the new companies' success would be the quality of their product – the music.

Reasonable Doubt: Prepping

While all this promotion was going on, Jay poured his 15 years of life experience since releasing 'HP Gets Busy' into his debut album. "We didn't sleep for weeks at a time," he remembers, "just living off adrenaline."[5] He had all the beats he needed from connections with other artists like Original Flavour, Jaz–O, Clark Kent and DJ Premier. He also had connections with some superstar rappers. Jay's relationship with The Notorious B.I.G (introduced through Clark Kent) brought about the song 'Brooklyn's Finest.' Given that Big was of the hottest rapper in the game at the time, this was a big deal and the planned single release would have achieved major attention.

However, when the team tried to get clearance from Big's record label, Bad Boy Ent wouldn't authorize the release of a single as they didn't want Big over exposed before his second albums release, especially with an unknown rapper. (Most record contracts prohibit established artists from working with non-gold or platinum artists.) As Roc lawyer at the time Reggie Osse says: "I remember being on the phone begging for Puff to let Big rock on a single and video, and Puff asking me, 'Yo, what the eff is a Jay Z? I can't get Clive Davis [head of Arista Records] to clear Big on some unknown rapper's record.'"[17] The team couldn't promote Big or release a single, although they did manage to keep the song on the album.

Plan B. The album's first single was then intended to be 'Can't Knock the Hustle' featuring Mary J Blige. Dame had a close relationship with Mary before she 'blew up' and persuaded her to sing the hook (for $10K cash). However before the single's release, Mary's label, Universal, also said they did not want her associated with 'some unknown Jay Z.' By this time Dame had already spent a lot of money advertising how the song featured Mary. There was even a full page ad in The Source magazine. He was frustrated, but eventually after pooling all their contacts, they were able to keep Mary for the album version of the song, though again no promotion and no single.

Although infuriating, to the team it was just another barbed wire fence they had to maneuver. (See more on this story *pg.198*)

Plan C. The album's first single was now going to be 'Dead Presidents'. (An anti–hero Scarface type song about dead–end material pursuits. The track features Nas's classic line from 'The World is Yours,' and marked the beginning of the infamous Jay Z/Nas feud, as Nas may not have been properly compensated. (Although Dame remembers Nas declining his many invites to rap the hook live and preform in the music video.[20]))

The team's goal was to get 'Dead Presidents' played on Hot 97 – the biggest urban radio station in New York. Due to Payday's advance money (and other sources of investment) the team were in the unique position of having money to promote, but not the experience or radio politics needed to get the song played on mainstream media outlets. They tried calling

Funkmaster Flex to request the song but found it impossible to get his attention. However, the years Jay spent networking once again paid dividends, and they used a connect with Irv Gotti, who was close to DJ Clue, who worked with Flex, to break the record on air.

To promote the single they took out ads in Hip Hop magazines, would pay DJ's to play songs in clubs and would pay to get on some radio stations. Irv Gotti introduced Jay to Kevin Liles, a senior figure at Def Jam, who had the connections to get the song played on the radio. Kevin remembers Jay coming to his office with a bag of money in his hand. He told Kevin: "'This is to help you get our songs on the radio. We don't want nobody to do anything for free."

(It turns out Irv told Jay to bribe Kevin as a practical joke, knowing Kevin wouldn't accept.) "That's not how we do things here," Kevin calmly replied, but still helped the team with radio connections.[21]

By this time the album was almost complete but the team felt it was still missing that one single that could infiltrate clubs and mainstream urban radio. The one song that would bring the masses in and get the other songs noticed – (see 'Play the Game' *pg.286*).

Whilst recording the album, in mid–late 1995, Clark Kent's fifteen year old cousin Inga Marchand, better known as 'Foxy Brown,' was making noise as a rapper and started a bidding war between Def Jam, Bad Boy, Elektra and several other labels. On the strength of her buzz, Clark reached out to her to feature on what would end up being the single that skyrocketed Jay's popularity – 'Ain't No Nigga'.

The team were hugely excited about the record. They believed this was the song that would make Jay's album stand out from all the other quality street rap records out at the time. And right they were.

Dame leaked the record to club DJ's, and once clubbers and record execs heard it, 'Aint No' became the season's biggest club hit. DJ's had it on repeat in practically all clubs in New York. It got constant airplay on Hot97 and even with international radio DJ's like the UK's Tim Westwood.

Meanwhile CEO of Def Jam Russell Simmons was producing the Nutty Professor movie, and agreed to use the song on the movie soundtrack – in part because Foxy Brown was now a Def Jam artist. Dash also convinced Def Jam to fund the music video and it received heavy rotation on MTV.

Just when it seemed failure was a taunting inevitability, all the pieces started falling into place. As Reggie Ossee says: "Inga single handedly, in my opinion, saved Jay Z's career. Without her on that record, and Reasonable Doubt being Jay's last shot, the world at large might have never heard of Shawn Carter."[12]

With the single out the stage was set for the album.

Reasonable Doubt: Serving

'Aint No' was the record that got major labels sniffing around Roc–A–Fella. The same people who flatly rejected the team a few months prior now started to see potential in partnering with the trio to release an album. All however were quickly put off by Dash's demands to retain full ownership of the music. Kevin Liles remembers Jay stating in their first meeting: "I don't rap for a record company, I own a record company."[21] (After reading music industry bible 'Hit Men' the Roc were adamant on retaining ownership of their product, so not to get financially exploited like countless artists before them.)

Only one company agreed to Dash's requests.

The beat to 'Ain't No' used the same 'Seven Minutes of Funk' break as Will Socolov's first hit record, 'It's My Thing,' with the group EPMD. As owner of 'Freeze Records' he set up a meeting with Dash and agreed to distribute and promote Reasonable Doubt. As with Payday, Freeze Records was the 'middle man,' and had its own distribution deal with the larger Priority Records. In the Priority-Freeze deal, Freeze brought in the artists and received 4% of a records retail price, whilst Priority distributed and promoted the artist nationwide and took 20% of the retail price.

However, in the negotiations with Freeze the Roc's lawyer misunderstood Dash's '20 and 4%' offer, and gave an extra 24% of the sales away – now 44% of retail price went to Freeze and Payday.[25] A furious Dame learned the importance of not depending on others to handle the business of your art *(pg.238)*.

On the positive, now with wider backing the album was ready for release. Following the radio play 'Aint No' was receiving in early 1996 they saw a three to four month window of opportunity in which to release Reasonable Doubt.

Left:
Original
Pressing of
Reasonable
Doubt, 1996

Reasonable Doubt sold 34,000 units in its first week and within a year it had sold 420,000 copies, peaking at No. 23 on the Billboard's album chart – a great accomplishment for a new artist independent of major label support.

Freeze Records were shocked. They owed Roc–A–Fella close to one million dollars but when Dame came to collect on the agreed date the small label wasn't ready to pay. Jay & Dame did not appreciate this treatment. Their contract was already deemed exploitative and now they couldn't even collect the money owed to them. They cancelled the agreement and retook control of the record. Dame's insistence on keeping 100% of the rights to the product came in useful.

They went in search of another partner to distribute Reasonable Doubt on a larger scale, but this time partners came to them. Off the success of the album's sales they orchestrated a bidding war between Epic Records, Def Jam and others for the rights to sell and distribute Reasonable Doubt and future albums.

In these situations record companies usually offer artists "the n**** deal" as Dame Dash calls it, (others call it a 'vanity label'), where they appear to 'give' you your own record label, and allow you to sign new talent, but in reality they own the rights to it, including masters recordings. Well aware of this the Roc team demanded a joint venture. "I knew I was going to be successful and the equity would be worth something down the line," Dash says.[22]

Meanwhile Def Jam Records were facing serious financial and credibility problems and were desperate to acquire an imprint or artist who could reconnect them with the streets. They wanted their own 'Bad Boy' or 'Death Row' label, or they feared the company, like so many other labels, would lose relevance and die. So, impressed with Roc–A–Fella's success and Jay's now obvious talent (he had written most of Foxy Brown's own platinum selling debut album that same year), they made a compelling offer: A joint venture where Roc-A-Fella would earn 50% sales income and keeps ownership of their masters, while 25% of sales would go to Def Jam and 25% to their parent company Polygram (who would be doing the actual record distribution). The deal included a $1m advance on profits and another $1m to cover overhead costs. Dame made it clear from the start that Roc-A-Fella would operate as an independent island and needed to be consulted on all decisions Def Jam made.

As part of the deal Jay Z committed to releasing five to seven more albums, a difficult promise for him to agree on.

"In my heart I wanted someone else to do it, I wanted to be the businessman," Jay later said. "[But] I never waited for anybody to give me anything. Opportunities didn't come my way. I had to chase them. I finally caught one."[18]

Because Reasonable Doubt was the only album Jay intended to make (before going 'behind the desk'), he gave it his all. It was 26 years in the making and told his life story: a biography with bounce.

Jay could only make the album because he was independent. There were no labels executives or A&R's imposing their ideas of what's hot, so he was free to create something purely from the heart. There was no trend chasing, no shock value, no bombast or trying to appeal to teens with explicitness. It was real emotion – regret, remorse, jealousy, betrayal – based on raw, real life experiences.

The story of the anti–hero, underdog, bad guy's rise. The story of a person trying to chase their dreams without regard to judgment from others. The story of a crab escaping the bucket. The story of survival. The album was cinema, like Scarface or Goodfellas, through sound. It was the first album to give a mature, honest and open portrayal of the hustlers mind – his demons, his conscious, his inner battles.

Every listener felt like it was an intimate personal conversation. It connected. We felt it. People who had no affiliation with street life related, because as Jay says in his book Decoded: "The deeper we get into those sidewalk cracks and into the mind of the young hustler trying to find his fortune there, the closer we get to the ultimate human story, the story of struggle, which is what defines us all."[1]

It took a while for Reasonable Doubt to receive the attention it deserved, but in time many would come to see it as the best Hip Hop album ever recorded.

For Jay it took ten years of building and overcoming countless obstacles. But it is exactly that struggle that became the solid foundation he and the Roc built their empire into a legendary chapter in Hip Hop's story. Twenty years later the writing hasn't stopped.

KEY LESSON:

"BELIEVE IT when nobody else will"[24]

How It All
Got Started

Part III

Practical

Lessons

'Step one in the process....'
– Jay Z, American Dreamin'

This section looks at more practical lessons we can directly apply to our lives right now. It includes:

- The daily routines of Jay Z and other Greats.
- What it really means to be a celebrity.
- The simple principle of 'Creative Genius' and how Kanye, Pharrell and others make millions of dollars using it.
- *The* most critical element to living a 'successful' life and creating remarkable art.

Business

+ Art

People who feel a deep desire to work in creative industries (actors, artists, musicians, designers, comedians, writers...) mostly get into it because they love the art. They love the creative process.

That often means they put the 'business' side to one side, and that can be great for the art – as art is about expressing self in the purest form, and mixing it with money can cause compromise. But the lesson learned from many of the creatives in this book is it's vital to: Handle Business and Art.

Dr. Dre learned this the hard way. "The record business is just that; record–business. You have to take care of both worlds, or they won't take care of you," he said in 1997. "I got into it just wanting to make music, I didn't give a dam about business. I trusted people to handle the business, and I got fucked."

Dre would urge all creative people to understand the numbers themselves and not rely on others. "Don't trust managers [or] record execs. Know it yourself...9 times out of 10, people are not concerned with the business and just want to make music...90% of artists don't know when, how much or what they're supposed to get paid, but they can tell you how much a Mercedes costs."[1]

Most creatives get taken advantage of because of this. They get paid what they accept, not what they 'deserve.' As 50 Cent observed: "In business there's people who have talent and there's people whose talent is to take advantage of people who have talent...the guys behind the scenes get a lot of money."[2]

'Industry Rule number 4080/
Record company people are shady/'
– Q Tip, Check the Rhythm

Having financial matters secure creates peace of mind and means artists can focus on creating quality work. Like Dre says, "you can't make your best music if [the] business is not taken care of."

The Artpreneur

Making sure financial matters are in order is the simplest most basic element of being an artist and entrepreneur; an 'Artpreneur.' But being able to think like a businessman and manager is a vital skill to take your work to higher levels. It's something which the Hip Hop Greats, the names mentioned most in this book, naturally embody. They have the soul of an artist and the instincts of an entrepreneur.

They care about the art/product/culture and at the same time have just as much interest in the 'business side' as their record label, and make sure they got a fair cut of the cake – which is why Hip Hop has done more than any music genre to stop the exploitation of recording artists.

"What advice would I give to rappers....take control of your shit...watch your money," said The Notorious B.I.G (which stands for Business Instead of Game). "I mean, soon as I got in the game I got a lawyer to watch my lawyer. That's just how it's supposed to be played."[3]

Perhaps the person who embodies the Artpreneur combination best is Kanye West. Former Rock–A–Fella CEO Dame Dash, described Kanye as a combination of Jay's artistic talent, and Dash's business acumen.[4]

In 2003 while working hard to create a quality album, he was also relentlessly building his own buzz by promoting himself and his music, largely without label support. As Dame said, "He's an entrepreneur; he's promoting himself as we speak. Every time I see him he has somebody with him, like a program director, or publicist or camera and he does really good music that comes from a good place."[5]

(In fact since Kanye was 18, film maker Coodie Simmons had been recording him make music, as he believed Kanye would 'make it', and wanted to make his own version of the documentary 'Hoop Dreams'.)

Kanye understands the importance of remaining in the public eye to stay relevant. His business mind sees the opportunity in the worst of circumstances, like his near fatal car accident in 2002. He is, he says, his own best manager in that regard:

"After the accident when I went into the studio to record 'Through the Wire,' it was like me as a manger saying, 'Hey, you nearly died, go in there and capitalize on it.' I'm everything in my career. I have people who are way better at certain things and I get them in to help me out, but I'm the first stylist, the first video director, the first manager, the first writer and the first marketing guy."[6]

It's easier for a creative to learn business elements than the other way round. The internet is flooded with quality resources to learn about accounting, marketing, law, and other essential sides of the business. If you're in college you can look out for classes which teach some of these subjects. For example J Cole took public relations classes which enabled him to see the music business from a different perspective. For instance he wrote a long thoughtful letter apologizing for an inappropriate autism lyric before any of his PR team took notice.

By no means become an expert, you should be working with others who are more experienced in these areas, but it's important to have a basic knowledge too, so you're not fully dependent on anybody.

Balance

*'I've seen a lot of kids come and go with marketing gimmicks/
But without balance you don't last more than a minute/'*
— Immortal Technique, Positive Balance

Jay Z's daily routine consists of a run in the morning, weight training, listening to and learning from other people's music, thinking of new songs, marketing and business expansion ideas, spiritual reading or meditation, family time, and working on the numerous businesses he's involved in. He is healthy, wealthy and wise because he knows how to balance the four areas of life:

- **PHYSICAL:**

Daily, goal orientated, exercise. At least ten minutes of sweating a day. Without it the body eventually breaks down and the mind gets sick. Nobody can work or live happily like this.

- **MENTAL:**

Doing exercises every day to work out the mind. That could be analytical/problem solving exercises, for instance Jay plays vertical chess, practical exercises, like memory training, or creative exercises, like challenging yourself to come up with fresh ideas (see *pg.253*).

- **SPIRITUAL:**

Jay reads inspirational and Zen related books like 'Seat of the Soul'. Common reads the Bible and Quran before recording. Others like Russell Simmons meditate several times a day. They all do this to keep their life centered and focused on 'the bigger picture.'

- **EMOTIONAL/SOCIAL:**

This means only staying around people who uplift you, and keeping away from those who drag you down – the emotional baggage. Like Kanye told DJ Semtex: "I judge people off of 'are they a nice person, and can I see what is this persons intent?' My amount of time I spend around them is based off of 'oh, does this relationship make sense, do I need to be around this person?'"[1]

Being emotionally healthy also means always being honest with ourselves and others – see 'Do You' *pg.272*.

Success isn't about working hard to focus on one area of life, like your business, while letting all other areas deteriorate. As the many people who have achieved great financial success after years of hard work but have poor physical and mental health and no meaningful personal relationships, come to realize when they reflect, *'was it really worth it?'*

> *'I celebrate life for nobody else/Mountains of wealth ain't really shit without health/'*
> *–Xzibit, Meaning of Life*

The one and only path to long term wealth, health and happiness is to balance the four areas of life. You'll find that if these accounts are out of balance, all other principles described here become difficult, if not impossible, to live. Vision, focus, ambition etc. can quickly disintegrate if even one account is neglected. But when body/mind/spirit/emotion is in balance you create a great foundation for creative thinking.

Creativity

Every new idea is a combination of two or more old ideas. They have sex in a person's mind and give birth to something fresh.

Nas is partly right when he raps, *'no ideas original, there's nothing new under the sun,'* but the process of bringing together different existing ideas does create something original – like a newborn is an original product of two existing people.

"People told me when I did the Fabolous beat [My Life] like 'man that's so unoriginal,'" Kanye said in 2008. "I'm like 'ummmmmmm, did you notice that none of these beats are original, they're all old records, they're all jacks. Now they're original!'"[1]

Creative Greats, like the ones in this book, understand and practice the process of creativity. In essence it's about being able to combine their child and adult mind. Being able to combine the playful exploration of a child with serious tasks of adult work, to create 'serious play'[2].

Imaginative Exploration X Practical Knowledge = Ultimate Creativity

---

Before exploring this principle further, we should understand why 'Creativity' is one of the most valuable chapters in the book. A person can master all other principles: they can be totally focused, hungry, work with good people and follow universal principles, but without creativity they will always be doing 'it' the hard way.

'Fuck the harder way, we're doing it the smarter way/'
— Talib Kweli, Going Hard

Our society has gone through the agricultural, industrial and technological revolutions. We are now in the ideas age. Ideas are the powerhouse of the economy. With more accessible funding and production resources than ever before, a creative mind is incredibly valuable. Creativity allows you to find innovative solutions to problems and bring about huge financial reward by uncovering commercial opportunities. One idea can change your life.

Children's imaginations are brilliant because their brain continually questions the world around them and makes connections. This is the brain's natural state; a hunter for links and patterns between ideas. But children's creativity doesn't result in anything useful because they haven't developed practical knowledge or skills.

On the flip side, adults with years of experience in a subject have far more practical experience and knowledge for the brain to explore, but most don't have imaginations anywhere near a child's because their mind has 'tightened' and lost its natural flexibility. Whilst some adults do retain their childlike spirit, but because they haven't the patience to develop skills in their field of interest, like children, they don't come up with anything practical or useful.

Combining the adult and child brain (that is combining hours of learning and experience in areas that interest you with a child's natural mental fluidity), creates a huge ocean of knowledge for the brain to explore and make new, creative and practical connections. This is using the brain's power to the fullest.

'And I still won't grow up, I'm a grown-ass kid/'
– Kanye, Through the Wire

This is Kanye's 'secret' to creating amazing art which connects with people around the globe. His mother remembers him drawing 'outside the box' figures as a toddler, like purple bananas, and telling ducks how they should quack in Lake Michigan, "that's not how they're supposed to quack, it should sound like this…," remembers Donda,[4] who always tried to nurture this creativity, and Kanye maintained that mindset as an adult.

"I just close my eyes and act like I'm a three year old," he said in an interview with director Steve McQueen. "I try to get as close to a childlike level as possible because we were all artists back then. So you just close your eyes and think back to when you were as young as you can remember and had the least barriers to your creativity."[5]

Kanye also told Fader magazine: "I always think about it like a four year old, how's a four year old gonna react to this? Never lose your childhood, never lose that innocence. Like, people will say, 'Oh he's a big baby,' and it's like – exactly. In all the bad ways but in all the good ways also."[6]

Ask any great artist and they will likely say the same. Independent rapper and mogul TechN9ne explained: "I feel like this kid in the body or in the brain of a dude that writes this crazy music, and this TechN9ne guy is taking me all over the world. I'm just excited, ready to go!"[7]

Once again it all goes back to the foundations of passion/

We find it easiest to be creative when we're working on a project that connects with our deepest interests. Because we're deeply interested in the work, we're motivated to focus more on problems, we're more patient, persistent and learn faster. We have a desire to discover something new, so we work. With years of experience we develop a mastery of our subject and sit on a volcano of potential creative energy.

But what do most people do with this creative potential? Nothing.

For most, the more they work within the boundaries of a subject the more their thinking becomes limited to the established rules, and they become prisoners of their own experience. They become too comfortable with their knowledge, and fear trying something different (*"if it fails I'll look like an idiot"*). They only follow the 'normal' way of doing things, and the mind doesn't explore different spaces or connect different ideas. They will always come up with the same unoriginal responses that become more and more rigid and defensive with age, as the creative muscles weaken. These are people who end up with years of experience working against them, which is why they eventually fall off and get replaced by younger, fresher minds (– see Maintaining Headlights *pg.165*).

What's more, our society's idea of an 'adult' is all about practical knowledge and leaves no space for imaginative exploration. "Society has put up so many boundaries, so many limitations on what's right and wrong that it's almost impossible to get a pure thought out," Kanye explains.[6]

We're taught to segregate the adult and child in us, using the adult-brain for work and letting the inner child out only in free time. Segregating the two tightens and decays the creative muscles and we lose the felling of childhood wonder with age.

'My childlike creativity, purity and honesty/
Is honestly being crowded by these grown thoughts/
Reality is catching up with me/
Taking my inner child, I'm fighting for custody/ '
– Kanye, Power

Some people find it so hard to get their brain making connections that they give it extra stimulation through drugs. But highly creative people, like most in this book, don't need drugs for extra stimulation. Their mind is always open to new connections, new ways of thinking, of doing things, because they've learned how to keep the fluid, original 'child mind' and combine it with their adult experience.

'You telling me the kush make you think on level four?/
I'm on five you saying I can level more?'
– Kendrick, H.O.C.

How?

"They say your brain's most creative in your sleep, see they say in the sleep state the brain thinks much more visually and intuitively. As dream chasers, we accomplish that wide awake." –DJ Drama, Ready or Not

The key to maintain mental fluidity with increasing knowledge is to not (subconsciously) limit yourself to think only within the normal boundaries of your work, so:

1. Don't rush.

Most of us are insecure, anxious and uneasy in unfamiliar situations, like when others say things we don't agree with, or when faced with a new problem. So to sooth the anxieties we rush to form conclusions. We immediately label the person without trying to understand their point of view. We try to solve the problem the same way we solved a past problem. Above all, our ego tells us *'we must be right'* because it worked in the past, or because it doesn't want to admit it's wrong, for fear of appearing weak or dumb, so we hold on to our ideas tightly.[8]

But creative greats work against the ego and its anxieties. They play with problems for longer before trying to resolve them. When coming up with creative ideas, or in unfamiliar situations, they feel discomfort and anxiety but they tolerate it. Unlike most people who make quick decisions to get rid of the uncomfortable feeling, they're not in a rush to come to conclusions. As Pharrell, who calls this process 'tapping in' said, "People call you a genius but all it is is being open to other things in the world."[9]

Their mind is open to entertaining ideas while just observing. Just observing, not judging. By being open to other possibilities they allow more neuron connections to occur in the brain and are then often able to come up with a more creative solution.

"If you don't interrupt [your subconscious] with the ego, or are like, 'No, it's gotta be like this,' then a lot of ideas will come," Pharrell adds. "Once you start judging it and editing it, then you're no longer tapped in. You've moved it over to your mind before you even realize. So I spend a lot of time just standing in the [shower] with a blank stare ['tapped in']."[10]

Look at Dr. Dre who began learning how to orchestrate classical music in the mid 90's. At first he was afraid that learning this completely different style of music would spoil his Hip Hop production, but he overcame that anxiety and worked hard to master the genre. Now his mind is able to roam around in a much larger ocean of knowledge to look for connections between new sounds and his production skill has evolved and diversified.

When trying to solve a problem creatively, it's important to not just accept the first solution you think of. These are usually obvious, easy solutions – the low hanging fruit. Creative greats tolerate the 'mental search' for longer. They sit with the problem and stick at it. The mind will be agitated and anxious but by sticking with the problem it will quiet down again and eventually is more likely to come up with something more original.

Some call this process meditation or prayer. Like Kanye said to The Source magazine in 2003, "My definition of genius is not being that person, the actual human 'genius', but it's a person that just allows God to work through them…I definitely couldn't have come up with a lot of that music I have out on my own. A lot of that is just me sitting back and praying."[11]

(Meditation is a form of prayer, and scientific research demonstrates exactly what Kanye is saying – that meditation/prayer helps connect neurons in the right (imaginative, child), and the left (practical, adult) sides of the brain. See Russell Simmons book 'Success Through Stillness' for more on the science behind meditation and creativity.)

The principle of 'Don't Rush' can be practiced daily by trying to communicate with people and not judge or put them in a box immediately (the ego). Instead keep your mind open and move inside their perspective. See into their mind and seek to understand. With time it makes the mind less anxious, judgmental and open to different ways of thinking.

'Unless you was me how could you judge me?/'
– Jay Z, Momma Loves Me

2. Think like an outsider.

Tourists' often spot things in a city that a person living there for twenty years hasn't noticed. 80% of major inventions of the 20th Century were made by outsiders to an industry.[12] (Like Maurice Ward, a hairdresser with no scientific training who invented Starlite, a material which could withstand the heat of seventy atomic bombs and still remain cool to the touch. A material NASA and the world's top scientists – 30 years later – have no idea how to recreate (he died without revealing the 'recipe')).

Why?

Because they have experience in other areas of life they ask different questions and make connections in unique ways.

Look at Grandmaster Flash who in the 1970's pioneered many of the innovations DJ's use today. Flash's two passions were music and electrical engineering, which he studied at high school. One day he was walking in his rundown neighborhood in South Bronx thinking of a party he had attended with DJ Kool Herc at the turntables. It was one of the first Hip Hop shows ever, and although Flash loved the new music style he noticed that when Herc switched between songs there would be a short silence as one turntable was substituted for another.

As Flash was walking past a dumpsite near his building he spotted a used light switch on the ground. Because he had spent so long developing his craft for electrical engineering and music, his brain made a connection: 'What if I could re-wire this light switch, to shift between two turntables at parties so there would be no pause in the music?' After a lot of trial and error he invented the crossfader and is now credited as being one of the three founding fathers of Hip Hop.

To think like an outsider, expand your knowledge base from the standard industry-related material. Read, understand and experience different topics which interest you. Start each project with a blank canvas and open mind, not limited by boundaries of what worked in the past or other people's safe 'trends'. Force yourself to think about a problem from a different set of questions, from a different perspective. Like Tupac said, "Sometimes I sit and look at life from a different angle."[13]

Some creatives will think how people from completely different industries would handle the issue. They ask themselves: 'How would Steve Jobs solve this?' 'What questions would Tarantino ask?' 'What would Napoleon choose?'

Kanye got the idea for his breakthrough 'Through the Wire' music video after seeing an unrelated Adidas advertisement in BlackBook magazine. "I don't like gettin' ideas from direct shit, I like to pull ideas from all the way over here. Sometimes my vision can't be explained in words cause I couldn't have told you in words how I envisioned that video ending up."[5]

Above all don't get too cozy in your way of thinking.

Pharrell

Pharrell's process in making the song 'Happy' for the film 'Despicable Me' illustrates the two techniques ('don't rush' and 'think like an outsider') perfectly. After being briefed by the film's producers, Pharrell got to work on a song to fit the themes and mood of the film. He made nine full songs and each time he presented them he'd get the same response from the movie producers, "No, it's not good enough," he said in an NPR interview.

"I went through everything that I thought was possible in my mind based off of what I understood about Gru and what I thought the studio was looking for, and none of it was working."

Pharrell was working through his ego; that is, working through his previous experience and memory of what worked in the past. But he persisted through the rejection and eventually got himself into a place where he could see the problem through fresh eyes, free from ego.

"It was only until I was tapped out that I had to ask myself the fundamental question: they're asking for a song that's happy. They're asking for something where Gru is in a good mood, and that's when I realized that everything I needed was right there. I began to ask myself, 'What does feeling like a good mood feel like?' That's where 'Happy' came from.

"All the 'no's' brought me to a place of zero, and that nirvana, that place of that stillness of nothing is when you can ask yourself a clear question and get a clear answer back...when you feel like you don't have any more answers, I want you to know that you're the closest to the best thing you'll ever do in your life. There's no ego in it, and you're just asking a clear question. You don't know where the answer's gonna come from, and that's when the answer comes."[13]

Workout Exercises

The 'secret' to coming up with creative ideas in all area of your life, from conversations with friends to business strategy's, is to exercise the creative muscle every day. Exercising the creative muscle regularly will develop imagination into a powerful creative force. Studies have shown that over time neurons across the brain become better connected, allowing you to come up with more 'flashes' of inspiration as disparate ideas are linked. You'll also feel less anxious when faced with problems so won't rush to conclusions, and by practicing creativity your personality also becomes mellower, less stressed, you even age more slowly – just look at Pharrell.

Many creatives make a daily commitment to writing ten or fifteen ideas based around things they're interested in. It could be: businesses to start, people to meet and why, ways to help other businesses or people, ways to improve as a person, ideas for TV shows or books, solutions to problems in the newspaper, etc. It's helpful to start by asking yourself, 'What If...'

Make this a commitment to do every morning as part of your '20%' *(pg.155)*. You don't start your work day until you have written those ideas.

Here are some techniques to come up with ideas for your list and to exercise creativity every day. (Ideas don't have to lead to anything real, they are just exercises to work out the creative muscle)[14]:

- Combine ideas. Many successful ideas are just a blend of existing ones, for example:
    - Slamball=basketball+trampolining
    - Dr. Dre's G Funk = 70's oldies music+synthesizers+deep base
    - Muesli=oats+fruit+grain+milk,
    - Instagram=photos+geo–location+filters
    - Duffin=jam filled muffin+doughnut mold
    - This book=Hip Hop+Life Lessons

There's millions to be made from clever combinations.

- Think how something can be applied somewhere else. Alan Sugar's first business was when he figured out that left over tar from road works could be reused as lighter matches. Robert Chesebrough created Vaseline out of wax built up on oil machines, and marketed it as a medical product for skin problems. The lawn mower was invented by a guy who repurposed an industrial velvet cutting machine to cut grass.

- Make something. Use your hands to actually make something – painting, drawing, writing, collage, music... You'll be strengthening a part of the brain that's otherwise decaying. Drawing well is also a useful skill to help communicate your ideas.

- Run away. Leave your house. Go somewhere new. Take a break. Turn your mind off for a day. Refresh. Re-energize. Refocus. Take one afternoon off every two weeks or so. Call it 'Inspiration Time'.

- Seek inspiration. Quality newspapers are sprinkled with gold dust for new connections and ideas. You could make it a habit to go through one each morning, actively making connections and coming up with solutions. Also many websites are steaming with creative ideas that could be a good source of inspiration. You might find these interesting:

springwise.com interesting ideas from around the net	99u.com vids and articles on creativity
swiss–miss.com interesting links from around the net	good.is all sorts of creative inspiration
boingboing.net interesting links from around the net	instructables.com 'How To's' to create stuff and get the brain stimulated
core77.com fresh interesting product design	hello.bauldoff.com nice artwork
extragoodshit.phlap.net interesting links from around the net	itsnicethat.com creative art and design
brainpickings.org interesting articles on a number of topics	psfk.com interesting stories

(Warning: Some of these sites are highly addictive!)

- Experience different things. Things you wouldn't normally expose yourself to like different radio stations, foods or books, getting to work a different way, even brushing your teeth differently. You'll be keeping your senses stimulated and feeding the mind with new experiences.

- Freestyle. Freestyle rap stimulates areas of the brain linked to creativity. So practice improvised rhymes to a rhythm. It doesn't have to make sense, you're just connecting words and flowing with your mind.[15]

- Know your history. We often think our problem is unique in the world and forget that millions of people have faced and overcome similar problems before us. Understanding the history of your field of interest (through books, the internet or museums) means you discover ideas most have forgotten about and puts you in a position to combine the old with the new to create something unique.

- Be silly. To maintain the childlike fluid mind do things a kid would do for fun. The number one thing is laughter. Children laugh hundreds of times more than adults every day. Laughter releases endorphins, stimulates the brain and is just a healthy thing to do. So you might want to watch stand-up comedy or a funny movie every day.   You could also maintain that 'inner-child' by doing silly things for the sake of fun. For instance, I (the author) was feeling disheartened midway through writing this book. So I took a run across some fields and ended up on an overpass of a fast-moving freeway. I got the idea to 'moon' oncoming cars, but years of living 'how an adult is supposed to live' had made me nervous. Eventually though I thought 'screw it,' waited for a little gap in the cars and mooned away. It was only for a second but afterwards I continued running feeling elated. On the way home I came up with a great idea for restructuring the book and had completely lost the feeling of 'UGGHHH' I had in the morning.

- Humility. Staying humble and not stuck in a 'this is how it's done,' or 'I know this' state of mind keeps you open to possibilities and allows you to flow with change. You'll be able to see connections and relationships others can't spot. So NEVER feel smug and superior to others or other ways of doing things. For example, you can "imagine everyone you meet is enlightened except you," so you have something to learn from everyone you meet.[16] Or when somebody disagrees with you, instead of arguing to justify yourself, sincerely say, '*Good, you see it differently. Help me understand your view.*' You don't have to accept what they say but you're open and secure enough to let yourself be influenced in order to fully understand another point of view.[17]

Interesting Diversion: Synesthesia

Synesthesia, means 'joined perceptions.' It's when one sense (like sound) is perceived at the same time by other senses (like sight). For example, seeing a letter or number and experiencing a certain smell or color at the same time.

Interestingly, its relativity common among artists, and it's possible that it can be helpful for creativity – as creativity is essentially about strengthening neural connections in the brain.

Synesthesia comes from 'crossed–wiring' in the brain, where neurons that are 'supposed' to be contained within one sensory system cross into other sensory systems. Nearly everybody is born with these 'crossed connections,' but most lose them as babies. Those that don't have synesthesia.

Many musicians, like Kanye, Pharrell, Mary J Blige and Hit-Boy are visual-auditorial synesthetes i.e. they see sound as color. For them the visual nerve ending and the auditorial nerve ending are still connected and send 'ghost images' to one another.

"It's the only way that I can identify what something sounds like," says Pharrell. "I know when something is in key because it either matches the same color or it doesn't – it doesn't feel right."[18]

Synesthesia happens to affect a number of other artists, authors, and designers, even some famous computer scientists, mathematicians and architects, and the 'condition' is a fundamental part of their creative process.

So far though there is no concrete scientific evidence that synesthete's are more creative than others. Anybody who regularly exercises the creative muscles will have the power to create great work.

The
Break-In

'And FUBU was on Jamaica Ave. giving away hats for free'
— Sticky Fingaz, I Don't Know

Great artists, billion dollar companies, drug dealers, politicians, and religious leaders understand the importance of Free. Countless Greats have found this to be the most effective way to get a foot in the door of any industry they wish to work in.

Looking at some of the artists in this book, whether working within organizations and starting as an unpaid intern (like Diddy), a ghost producer (like Kanye), or working independently and giving their product away in the form of mixtapes (like every rapper/producer you know), all gave themselves away for free so they could:

- Get noticed by people in positions of power.
- Establish trust.
- Create a buzz.
- Build a fan-base.
- Learn from feedback how they could improve.

Rick Ross built his Maybach Music Group in Miami off of this principle.

"As long as the music gets where it's supposed to and people embrace it, they are going to find ways to financially reward me," he says.[1]

Kanye says that while trying to break into the music industry he "was doing beats for free 99% of the time,"[2] *(pg.40)*.

Before forming Roc–A–Fella, Dame Dash built a rep organizing parties in New York. He rented prestigious venues like the Cotton Club, and would get noticed across the city by giving away a free bottle of Moët & Chandon to the first hundred ladies through the door each week. Soon famous rappers and athletes were spending their nights at his parties.

At 19 Chance The Rapper preformed in clubs and schools for free, and pressed up 4,000 CD's of his debut mixtape, '5 Day'. "I was giving 'em out for free all over Chicago," he remembers. "It got me a decent fanbase."[3]

50 Cent was able to sell eleven million copies of his debut album in large part because he had given so much product (over 4 mixtape albums) away for free in the years prior.

After his infamous shooting in 2000, 50 was dropped from his label and given back his publishing rights as well as his $150,000 advance. He could have put out an album then, but instead choose to put out mixtapes until the right distribution deal came.

"The only business model I had was from selling drugs, so that's how I marketed my products. I knew that the only way to get into any market is to give away free samples. I had to build up a clientele before I could see a profit. I had to invest in my brand," he writes in 'From Pieces to Weight'.

The mixtapes built 50 a strong fan base who trusted him and his music – they knew they weren't going to get an album with two singles and ten fillers. He'd also been continually testing songs on the audience. "I treated the mixtape circuit like a chemistry set. I got to see what the consumer would react to, what they got excited about, and what they wouldn't."

50 actively worked to make the mixtapes as good as a real album, using a professional photographer for cover art and with quality packaging so CD's

stood out even on bootleggers' shelves. "I'm not mad at the bootlegger 'cuz as long as I'm reaching people, even if they don't buy this record they'll buy the next one. They'll feel like 'you know what I'm gonna get that and it's worth me spending my 16 dollars' eventually they'll catch up and buy it."[4]

(In the years since, 50 has continually used the 'power of free' principle. In fact he earned a nine figure check from giving himself away for free:

In a 2004 Reebok print ad, 50 was pictured drinking from a bottle of glacèau Vitaminwater. He hadn't consulted or charged the beverage company for the promotion but his manager, Chris Lightly, made sure glacèau executives saw the add and understood the potential of partnering with 50. The two sides agreed to sign an equity deal and when Coke-Cola bought the company out in 2007, 50 earned an estimated $100 million.)

Aside from mixtapes, even for their first official album many artists don't expect to make much money. Their goal is to get the music to as many people as possible and build an audience so they can make money from their second album (or from touring). For example, Eminem doesn't make a penny from writing his breakthrough single 'My Name Is.' The person who created the song's sample owns 100% publishing rights. But without the song Em would not have had a crossover radio hit, and who knows where he would be now.

'I give away this music and make double back in shows/'
— Nipsey Hussle, Forever

Many companies do the same thing. They give their product away for free, and so: "establish yourself as the best at what you do and people will come to you for it," says Pharrell (who started as an intern at a local studio). It means playing the long game. Taking a loss in the short run because you believe in your product and know the long term gain will be worth it.

Pharrell adds, "You have to know that [giving away] this one thing will get [you] in the door that will allow people to see [your] perspective and from then on they'll say, 'Hey, if I want a slice of this reality I've got to go back to this guy.'"[5]

It's all about proving your value upfront, and then being rewarded. Sowing the seeds, then reaping the fruit.

Just because Devo Springsteen is Kanye's cousin doesn't mean 'Ye was going to 'put him on.' It was only after Devo proved his value in the early 2000's, by getting Kanye magazine coverage and meetings with important booking agents, that Kanye offered him an assistant job (for $200 a week). Devo accepted and continued 'giving before getting' which enabled him to eventually become a Grammy winning producer and now successful technology entrepreneur.

We live in an age where giving digital products for free costs nothing, (see the thousands of blogs started by aspiring and renowned writers), (Amazon's Createspace is also a great tool for independent authors, musicians and film makers to distribute and market their digital products).

Giving physical products away will need more investment, but if the product is right for the market surely it's worth it.

To give products for free most effectively, think about the 'Key Opinion Leaders' (KOL) or 'Gate Keepers' for the audience you're trying to reach. These could be magazine editors or people with a large social media voice.

Drug Dealers were KOL's for early Hip Hop artists. To young people living in poor inner cities in the 80's-early 90's, drug dealers represented the American Dream. They were people who escaped the poverty around them to live life seemingly to the fullest. They had the best cars and would drive through neighborhoods loudly bumping Hip Hop tunes. Youngsters aspired to be like them and would eagerly buy the music they heard.

Of course drug dealers are long out of fashion, but the same principle applies when companies hire a 'Brand Ambassador' on college campuses. They look for the most popular person, the 'go-to-guy/girl,' and use them to attract others to events sponsored by the company.

Other companies and artists give part of their product away for free and then make it easy for people to pay for more. Tim Ferris partnered with BitTorrent to give away two gigabytes of content related to his book 'The Four Hour Chef.' He included a link to the book telling people to 'support the artist' or 'read more' and 60% of people clicked through to buy the book – a ridiculously high percentage in the marketing world.[6]

This is an example of the 'freemium' business model many tech companies use to grow a large user base quickly while earning income.

On another note, good artists understand how important it is to create a quality portfolio to showcase their work. It allows them to prove their value before asking a buyer to trust them. If you don't have real work to fill your portfolio then make some. Videographers can make videos for their favorite songs, producers can remix classic tracks, designers can reimagine iconic brands. Nobody is stopping you from creating.

Giving your services away for free is usually cheaper than giving products for free. You just need to contact the person that would effectively be your boss, for example head writer or marketing manager, and pitch them your skills explain and what you can offer. Then *ask for advice* on how you could work for them, offering services for free if need be. When you prove your value first the money will follow.

'Ask for money, and get advice/
Ask for advice, get money twice/ '
— Pitbull, Feel This Moment

Getting Noticed

'Gotta work every day gotta not be clichéd/
Gotta stand out like Andre 3K/'
– Lil Wayne, Dr Carter

Getting noticed is the biggest challenge for artists and businesses – up'n'coming and established. When we can overcome this obscurity problem, and if the product is right for the market, the money takes care of itself.

The only long term effective way artists or businesses get and stay noticed is by making remarkable products that connect with their audience.

Create your art/product/service and share it with ten people around you. If you deliver something truly remarkable – 'worth making a remark about' – that these people each share it with ten others, then that's it. You're going to 'get noticed.' Your offering will spread organically.[1]

Again, look at Chance the Rapper, for a recent example. He released his first official mixtape '5 Days' locally in Chicago, by just handing it out for free around the city. People shared it with their friends because his music connected with them in such a strong way. Eventually Chance's music went all the way to radio and record label offices just through word of mouth. Soon he was touring the country, collaborating with major artists and turning down offers from record labels.

But, it's naive to think that the 'best' people/art/products/services all get noticed organically over less-good stuff. In reality, marketing plays a huge role in getting noticed.

"Album sales aren't based on how good your album is. It's about the push and hype behind it," Kanye said before releasing The College Dropout.[2]

The ability to use marketing to your advantage, to distinguish yourself from the pack and be recognized as the best in your field, means customers come to you. Look at Donald Trump, who is in a league of his own compared to other real estate developers, or Richard Branson, or Steve Jobs, even professional lawyers like Thomas Mesereau. Learning how to get noticed is important whatever your occupation.

Let's look at four key areas:

- Superstar – how to become a 'celebrity'.
- Shamelessness – how to maximize your exposure.
- Surprise – how to stay relevant.
- Stories – the most powerful way to connect with others.

Superstar

People consistently in the public eye understand how to get the spotlight on them. They know how to be celebrities.

Why are the masses captivated by celebrity? A girl can stroll down the street unnoticeable from the hundreds of others walking by, then a week later, after appearing on television alongside a famous person, she can't walk the same street without crowds staring and following. Why?

For most people life is mundane. Our environment and routines are repetitive and predictable (wake, work, eat, sleep), so we are fascinated by different, mysterious, or 'larger than life' characters who stand above the 'ordinariness' that surrounds our lives. We fantasize about their life and follow them.

That means the key to celebrity or getting noticed is to appear larger than the humdrum everyday lives of 'normal' people – for instance someone like Jay Z can't walk without security because people don't see him as a normal human.

Once people's eyes are on you, you gain a special legitimacy, and 'crowd mentality' means more and more people take notice, like ducks to bread.

The first step is about understanding and mastering your image.

'Image is everything I see it got a lot to do/
With the way people perceive, and what they believe/'
– J Cole, Chaining Day

We all project who we are all the time. Just glancing at a stranger you will form an impression of who they are, how they think and what they do. We are always putting people in boxes based on the image they project.

Those who understand how to 'get noticed' take control of the image they project. They define their own space. They understand who they are and express it as best they can, from the way they tie their shoe laces to the way they handle business.

A superstar/celebrity/'larger than life' persona can be achieved by creating an unforgettable image that sets you apart from the ordinary.

Way back in 2002 Kanye was already scheming on how to project this 'larger than life' image. "People told me, when you get on TV you got to personify something more than what you are."[2]

'I need to separate myself to stand out/'
– Kendrick, The Heart Part 3

We can project our image through the way we present ourselves – our unique style – and our distinct personality quirks. Here are some examples:

Charismatic style:

-   Eminem: came to mainstream notice with immediately recognizable bleach blonde hair and a white tank top for the 'don't give a fuck' trailer trash look. The exact opposite of the mainstream Hip Hop image at the time – braggadocio gangsters flaunting everything. (Even before getting signed in the early 90's when Em went by the name 'M&M' he understood the importance of branding to get noticed and would paint M&M sweets on his stage clothes.)

-   Pharrell: The 'Mountain Hat' he wore throughout 2014 has featured on numerous fashion websites, has its own Twitter account and, as blogger Perez Hilton says, "Made him larger than life"[3]. Similarly Nas's beanie hat (worn high up his head), and Jay Z's Yankees cap are immediately recognizable, unique (and natural) aspects of their brand.

-   Rick Ross: carries his overweight body with the confidence of a king. His other distinctive features include: every inch of skin covered in tattoos, thick bushy beard and slow, raspy voice.

-   Slick Rick: signature English accent, eye patch, gold teeth and chains.

-   Run DMC: Synonymous with leather suits, Porkpie hats and gold chains. They were pioneers of 'Hip Hop branding,' at a time when other rappers tried to look like Rick James, with glitzy costumes, platform shoes, and disco curls.

-   Hopsin: wears eerie white contact lenses to distinguish himself from other performers on stage.

-   50 Cent: The name itself is a great brand identity for Curtis Jackson. First it refers to a stick-up kid from New York, so reflects a part of 50's background. Secondly, it's one of the most memorable names around. Whenever you're holding change you think of him. Third, since the beginning of his career, 50 felt it was broad enough to lend to different products and promotional items. For example in the late 90's, he would wear a gold chain that had a quarter and five nickels arranged like a cross. He also made stickers of a 50 cent coin with his face on it and the phrase 'In God We Trust'. Finally, the name is a clever metaphor for 'change,' to represent moving from one metaphorical life to another.

-   Nikki Minaj: enough said.

Outside of music:

- Richard Branson: Long hippy hair, tieless, open collar shirt and jeans, reflects the youthful and adventurous nature of his companies.
- Steve Jobs: The now iconic black turtleneck sweater, round glasses, and casual jeans represent simplicity and elegance, like his products.
- Donald Trump: Wavy golden forward–sideways–comb–over hair (which has its own Twitter @TrumpsHair), orange skin, television appearances and political comments, all completely differentiate him from other real estate developers.
- Thomas Mesereau: lawyer for Michael Jackson, his shoulder length snow–white hair and round specs differentiate him from other lawyers.
- Seth Godin: One of the world's most-respected marketing experts wore distinct round yellow glasses for years before 'switching it up' to round burgundy specs. It's part of his memorable look.

Personality quirks:

- Eminem combined his distinct look with an over the top 'don't give a fuck' personality in Slim Shady. In early interviews he'd be swearing, giving the finger, goofing out, even pissing on the street. Many viewers had never seen such an unrestricted personality and were fascinated to follow his moves.

- Snoop Dogg's characteristic laid back, Cali, pimpish, charisma and vocabulary has enabled him to stay relevant for twenty years and lend his name to all types of products without damaging its value.

- Dame Dash epitomized the aspirational playboy lifestyle Roc–A–Fella represented – going so far as not wearing the same clothes (even socks) twice. People who sought that lifestyle connected with him.

- Immortal Technique the 'revolutionary rapper,' only wears clothes with political meaning and speaks on the most important social, political and economic issues in interviews. The rebellious and 'revolutionary-minded' love him for it.

But image doesn't have to be wildly flamboyant and imposing. It can be a subtle part of our day to day behavior. For instance it can be about exuding professionalism by: grooming well, standing straight, making eye contact, being courteous, saying please and thank you, returning calls and emails, honoring your word, treating others as they want to be treated, delivering when promised, overall just seeking to do everything as best it can be done.

Important to note is the most successful 'celebrities' have their unique image flowing through them naturally, (see 'natural vs. artificial' *pg.14*). It's not an act. They have overcome the fear of exposing themselves and authentically express the part of themselves that sets them apart from others. (Or they take their core 'truth' and push it to 'the edge' – *see pg.276*.) Their confidence attracts people and, on a local or global scale, creates 'celebrity'.

Very few people who create a fake, artificial or counterfeit brand based on something they're not last for long. Either their work doesn't match up to their image so the audience senses duplicity and doesn't connect, the entertainment factor wears off, or the person finds it's too much effort trying to keep up with a phony persona.

Style X Substance

Getting noticed through your distinct image is the first step, and there are two types of people who can do it: Greats and Clowns.

Greats (by in large – there are a few exceptions) are successful because they back up the attention they receive with quality work. Substance matches style. (Whereas clowns do whatever they can for attention but are soon forgotten because their work doesn't deserve to exist.)

Eminem embodies the 'Style X Substance' combination. Following the release of his debut album SSLP, he became the most publicized celebrity in the world. Condemning reactions to his 'shocking lyrics' by groups from ministers to the FBI, insisting on preforming a live duet with Elton John while LGBT campaigners protested outside, public trials with his on/off wife and estranged mother etc. etc. all shocked and surprised and kept him in the public eye. But the substance of the music surpassed the hype surrounding him. Lyrically few MC's could compare, and tailor made production by Dre made songs appealing even to people who just enjoyed the beats and hooks.

Em's entertaining personality combined with his multi-syllable-next-level technique, meant he received mainstream and underground love, and on his debut album's release became, according to Newsweek, "the most compelling figure in pop music." He knocked on America's door with 'My Name is', and when they answered, he followed it with real, emotive, skillful raps, which now could get attention.

Shamelessness

Once an unforgettable or even controversial image is established, celebrities welcome all the attention that comes with it; good and bad. They often make shamelessly bold, amusing gestures and actually welcome scandal because "it's better to be slandered than ignored."[5] As Snoop said when he was being criticized for his lyrics in the 90's, "controversy sells."

Dr. Dre went out of his way to thank the FBI, who sent his label a letter urging them to stop making songs like 'Fuck the Police.' The letter caught headlines around the world, and as Dre said, "made us a lot of money."

It's vital not to be afraid or embarrassed about shamelessly promoting yourself. It's part of the hustle of getting noticed. We need to overcome the common fear of saying 'this is who I am, this is what I made,' and shout about our work.

When Jay Z said "Kanye, you're a genius" on the song 'Lucifer,' Kanye literally put that quote on every song in his mixtape 'Kon Louis Vuitton Don' in 2003, and used it to raise his beat prices. He also started saying 'Kanye-to-the' in all verses he featured in, so people remembered his name – though he stresses this needs to be done "eloquently".

Part of 'shamelessly' promoting yourself effectively is to understand how to craft your words to have the biggest impact. Like how to use quotables.

Kanye is a master of quotables. So is Richard Branson, Michael O'Leary, and many other CEO's of adventurous, boundary-pushing companies.

To get a serious point across in a revealing, fun and shocking way is the holy trinity, which journalists love to write about and people remember. It gets you noticed.

You can take a look at Kanye's Twitter feed for numerous examples of quotables. His songs and interviews are also filled with them – in interviews as far back as 2002 he consciously talks about "trying to speak in bites."[2] For instance:

- "I am Shakespeare in the flesh" – Sway, 2013
- "My apartment is too nice to listen to rap in" – Semtex 2008
- "I'm just the espresso, the shot in the morning to get you going" – Lowe, 2013
- "Sometimes I get emotional over fonts" – Twitter, 2010
- "I'm like a soldier of culture" – Ellen, 2010
- "I put my anonymity, put myself in the line of fire. It's straight up the kid in Tainan square in front of the tank. I'm in front of the social the media tank." – Fader, 2008
- "I will go down as the voice of this generation, of this decade, I will be the loudest voice." – AP, 2008
- "I am God's vessel. But my greatest pain in life is that I will never be able to see myself perform live." – VH1 Storyteller, 2009
- "I will be the leader of a company that ends up being worth billions of dollars, because I got the answers. I understand culture. I am the nucleus." – NY Times, 2013
- "I wanna marry a pornstar" – Semtex, 2008

Surprise!

Another reason people with less talent than others often get more attention, is they understand the power of surprise, of mystery.

Interesting people or art today can soon become dull – fame is like fruit, what's fresh today is stale tomorrow. Like most things in life that are too regular they become ordinary. So an important part of maintaining a 'larger than life' image is mystery. Mystery intrigues and can make the average appear remarkable.

Great artists are like great con-artists. They understand the link between mystery and attention. They never make it obvious what they're doing or what their next moves are. That mystery heightens their presence and creates anticipation. It creates a power over their audience who eagerly watch, and talk about them and their next moves, amplifying their voice further.

Great businesses use this tool as much as Great artists. For instance Apple, especially under Steve Jobs, has this mastered. Their secrecy in developing and releasing products creates excitement. They will often defy expectations and the surprise it causes gets them noticed by almost every person on earth.

"I've been so quiet, I got the world like 'What the fuck is he planning?'"
— *Drake, Versace*

Kanye's name is always in the public eye because he is the master of re-inventing himself and doing unpredictable things people can't help but talk about. In his own words:

"[I try] to go out and buy some shit where motherfuckers is like, 'Ohhh!' Or say some shit where n**** be like, 'How did you fucking think of that!? Nobody said that before! Nobody sampled that before! Nobody made a song about that before! Nobody's video looked like that before!'"6

Some examples of Kanye and the Power of Surprise:

- In 2002 an unheard-of 'Ye first created mainstream buzz by rapping with his jaw wired shut, and as The Source wrote, "he used the element of surprise to his advantage."
- He filled 'The College Dropout' with unexpected surprises, from back to back skits to special guest features.
- For the album 'Graduation' he changed the release date to go head to head with sales giant, 50 Cent and staged a heavily publicized beef.
- He built anticipation for 'My Beautiful Dark Twisted Fantasy' by releasing a freshly made free song every Friday ('G.O.O.D Fridays'), with some of most seemingly unlikely artists, like Bieber and Raekwon, on the

same track, and started the 'Rosewood Movement', which seemed to be about always dressing his whole crew in fitted suits.

- He released 'Yeezus' with almost no marketing, notice, or even any cover art, just a Tweet saying that a song from the album would be projected at 66 locations around the world simultaneously.

- Overall he's totally changed the direction of his music, from a 'backpacker/street' rap mix on his first two albums, to inspiring stadium rock–rap on his third, to singing–rap on his fourth, to maximalist production on his fifth and total minimalism on his sixth. He never lets people grow too familiar with one type music so always stays fresh.

The important thing to note about Kanye is, he is (for the most part) not intentionally trying to create 'mystery' or manipulate people for attention. He is simply expressing himself as purely as possible and this naturally leads to mystery and attention – (see 'Do You' *pg.272*).

'Don't do no press, but I get the most press kid'
– Kanye, Mercy

Switching It Up

Especially at the beginning of their career, people (and businesses) with little to lose may try to 'surprise' and get attention at all costs, like aspiring rappers who attack the most visible people in the culture to try and draw attention.

(50 Cent did this to perfection in 1999, when he was just another lowly new signing to the giant Colombia Records, with the song 'How to Rob' – a witty and direct track about robbing over 50 relevant artists, at a time when most rappers were afraid to mention names because of Biggie and Tupac's deaths. "I knew if I didn't make a record that made people ask 'Who is 50 Cent?' then I was wasting my time," he said.[7]

The song achieved the target of making 50 stand out from other artists, but also major rappers like Big Pun, DMX, Wu-Tang, and Jay Z acknowledged (by dissing) him in songs and interviews, and immediately 50's credibility was put on the same level as these superstars. He was doing interviews on major radio, and had people across the country talking. "The response helped put me in the game. The more they reacted, the bigger my name got. I couldn't pay for that kind of publicity." The buzz eventually led to 50's deal with Shady/Aftermath.)

But as Greats rise higher and achieve celebrity and notoriety they need to adapt. Fresh becomes stale soon enough, and a person's once 'mysterious' actions may begin to seem predictable and expected. So to stay 'hot' and keep the attention of fickle fans in search of 'the next thing,' we must constantly re-invent ourselves, renew the method of getting attention and go against what's expected. Artists with staying power are ones who have continually switched up their brand.

On the flipside artists, entrepreneurs or people in jobs who try to court attention for the sake of attention, often signal insecurity. Like the rapper Gravy, who literally had a friend shoot him in the ass in the parking lot of radio station HOT 97, then went in to his interview bleeding. Playing games like this and trying to gain attention artificially may get some notice in the short run, but it's risky, as the façade is built on a falseness which is not only difficult to maintain, but it's easy to be replaced next season by someone younger and more extreme. And more importantly, as 50 Cent said, "Controversy doesn't sell records, it just gets attention. Once I had the attention I had to make sure the music could live up to the hype, because nothing sells more records than good music."[7]

Power of Stories

Something about a compelling story gets the human mind engaged in a way no other form of communication can. The reason Oscar Pistorius, the South African Paralympian who killed his girlfriend, received infinitely more news coverage around the world in 2014 than thousands dying in Syria, is because people connect with the emotion of the story and are attracted by its drama. To millions his lengthy trial was a soap opera, with 24 hour live coverage.

The 2009 Iranian protests only really caught worldwide mainstream attention when student Neda Soltan was killed on camera. Her dying face transfixed people around the world. Same with the couple who died in each other's arms in the collapsed Bangladeshi factory in 2013. They gave the otherwise distant and abstract events a personal, emotionally-relatable story.

When people understand your story, they emotionally buy into you. Through stories you connect with people and move them to act; whether to sign a petition, donate money, or buy a song.

Every artist in this book has a story that others relate to. These are the stories interviewers talk to them about (check any of their early interviews online). Jay Z: the 'anything is possible' hustler turned rapper turned mogul. 50 Cent: the crack dealing, nine-bullet-hole-survivor. Eminem: the abused kid with a vengeance on the world. Kanye: the car crash survivor, 'getting out my dreams' fighter:

> "I turned tragedy to triumph, I flip positive in from the negative. I almost died. So I flipped it around and made my first single, 'Through the Wire'. People have to feel that single. It's definitely a blessing that I'm here, but the fact that what I went through gave me a story – a true-life story that people can cling on to – they can hear

that and be like, 'OK, we fuck with Kanye more than just on the beats – as just a real person that goes through the exact same shit that we can go through.' When you can feel like a person like that, when they speak, what they're saying holds more weight."[6]

As Kanye says, the key to an effective story is to form an emotional connection with the listener. The way to have an emotional connection is to sincerely (and creativity) display that emotion, live that emotion. A story can be about the emotion of 'turning tragedy to triumph,' 'loss,' 'fear,' 'luxury,' 'feeling a boss,' 'me against the world.' A company can tell a story based around 'reliability,' 'efficiency,' 'quality,' or any emotion which resonates with your 'niche' market.

Niche

'Life's a journey you gotta find your niche/
I'm leaving this tight space because I don't fit/'
— Hopsin, caught in the rain

In late 2011 MC Hammer announced the launch of Wiredoo, an online search engine he envisioned as 'the next Google.' In early 2012 it was dead.

A successful business fills a hole in a market. It has a unique way of satisfying a need. A business won't be successful if it wants to be the 'next something,' because there's no room for the 'next something,' when that something is still here. The problem has already been solved and usually the market isn't big enough for two dominant players.

The most successful businesses are usually the first of themselves. The same applies to the most successful artists. They carve out their own territory. They drive down their own lane.[1]

'I drove by the fork in the road and went straight'
– Jay Z, Renegade

Your niche is your unique voice/sound/solution/brand/story that nobody else can duplicate. It means you are regarded amongst the best in the world at a particular topic.

Finding your niche is not something most can do when just staring out. People will often spend years learning and experimenting before they can see a gap they're going to fill or before they find their own unique expression.

For example look at Kendrick Lamar between 2003 and 2009, when he went by the moniker 'K.Dot.' His music, he admits, was largely an imitation of his favorite rappers, and he was following the typical 'Compton Gangsta' style. It was only after some difficult character building experiences *(pg.111)*, that he found his own identity, his niche, and since then his career has skyrocketed. He explained:

"[Now] I try to stay as original as possible, and have my own sound that nobody can really duplicate. Nobody can really make sense of doing [my style of music] easily. It's really my niche and I think everybody in the game should have their own niche."[2]

J Cole recognizes his unique niche as a major reason for his success:

"From North Carolina with an East coast flow, but still repping the South and having all the culture of the South in my music, that set me apart so much. If I was from New York, I probably wouldn't have gotten as far as I did because, it's hard. People these days are less likely to pay attention to a New York rapper."[3]

Being an expert in your own niche means you're one of the only people who is trusted to deliver a particular thing. That's why people can have large commercial success in obscure industries like 'Chinese slippers,' '12th century battle ships,' or 'styles of knitting.' It takes years of practice, which is why loving what you do is so important – (see 'The Re-finding' *pg.58*).

When a person has found their niche and is successful in it, there will be imitators who try to follow in your success – look at 'Beats by Dre' which revolutionized the luxury-headphone market in 2008 and now every artist from 50 Cent to Swizz Beatz has their own brand of headphone. Eventually your once unoccupied niche can become saturated, so it's important to not become complacent, but keep 'switching it up' and evolving. ('Beats' for instance, continues to stay ahead of the competition by adapting its product range to include speakers, a music streaming service and 'Beats Audio' built into cars and computers.)

A final point is, like every chapter in this book, 'niche' is a natural principle. Every living thing exists because it has found a unique niche in its environment. There are plants that have evolved inner toxins to stop animals eating them, sloths that have evolved a four-stomach digestive system to be able to eat those toxic plants, as well as algae covered green skin to camouflage from jaguar predators, who have themselves evolved shorter arms to climb trees and hunt for monkeys, who have evolved to…

In ecology if you don't occupy a niche you don't survive. Just like in business. Just like in art.

How do you find your natural niche?

By 'Doing You'.

Do
You

'You can't stop my glow/
I been born to be what I am/'
– Yasiin Bey, Casa Bey

Robert Diggs had been rapping around project neighborhoods on the East Coast since he was 11 years old. In 1991 he turned 21 and landed a record deal where he went by the moniker 'Prince Rakeem' and made songs, on the guidance of his record label, portraying himself as a black-family-friendly-Casanova-Will Smith type character, hoping to follow in the Grammy winning footsteps of The Fresh Prince.

Diggs hid his own personality (like his love of Asian culture), and turned himself into a bubble gum caricature to try to fit into a box that was successful at the time – but he wasn't successful. The audience could detect his 'falseness' and didn't connect. He was dropped from the label after one song.

For the next two years Diggs reflected on why he had failed and how he could break back into the music business. He decided to stop imitating others and to be real to himself – to represent his core emotional truth. The result was something totally unique: gritty, authentic Hip Hop, combining influences from Diggs' environment with his deep interests. He changed his name to 'The RZA,' recruited a team of warriors and devised a five year plan *(pg.122)*, that would bring the Wu-Tang Clan to the forefront of Hip Hop.

'Express Yourself'

Few people are honest. Our world is overloaded with political correctness and inauthentic imagery where everybody tries to show off their best, not their true, self.

'And everything on TV a figment of imagination/
I don't want a plastic nation, dread that like a Haitian/'
– Kendrick Lamar, HiiiPower

Most people hide their failures, fears, weaknesses, and true thoughts deep inside themselves, so they can fit in or pretend to be perfect. Those things represent a part of us, the real part of us, that, like a fragile candle flame, we keep hidden for fear exposure will extinguish the delicate light.

But the Great artists (writers, rappers, marketers, painters, poets, chefs, comedians, actors, speakers...) have the courage to openly and honestly express the things that make others uncomfortable. They expose their authentic self. They take their candle out into the world.

'Shine the light up!'
– Common, the Food

(Again, 'artists' doesn't just mean painters and poets. Whether you're a publicist or marketer, your work can be art, and so these principles apply. Using the definition set by Seth Godin[1]:

"Art is a personal act of courage, something one human does that creates change in another."

"An artist is someone who uses bravery, insight, creativity, and boldness to challenge the status quo. An artist takes it personally. An artist takes a stand, and doesn't care if someone disagrees. His art is part of him, and he feels compelled to share it with you because it's important, not because he expects you to pay him for it."

Or like Kanye said, an artist feels on some level that: "I need to express this or I'll die inside."[2])

What is the result?

The masses are drawn to them. We are all made of the same thoughts, feelings and emotions so we relate to them on a deep human level because they are expressing what we are feeling. Expressing emotion honestly jerks the same emotion out of the audience. As 50 Cent understands: "People love me because they think like me. We're the same."

'People addicted to me/
Because they addicted to real/'
— Big Sean, Memories

Their honesty and intimacy exposes vulnerability. Vulnerability (as long as it's not coming from a place of neediness) is probably *the* most compelling human quality. We're drawn in. We want to learn more about their success, failure, glory and pain because the best artists get inside of us.

They become a voice of *their* people. They tap into and represent the 'collective consciousness' of their community. We see ourselves in them. We become them. (That is the definition of 'swag': how much you make other people want to follow or be you.) We insist on sharing their work because it says something we weren't brave enough to say. As psychologist Carl Rogers wrote, *'what is most personal is most universal.'*

'I never woulda dreamed in a millions years I'd see/
So many motherfuckin' people, who feel like me/'
— Eminem, White America

So in this world flooded with makeup, honesty is like a deep breath of pure oxygen: Refreshing.

Something Kendrick Lamar understands. "It's the connection I got with the younger generation. They need something they can hold on to that's organic, not coming and going quickly....it's really about tapping that emotion that they're scared to express...For people trapped in a shell, I express myself through music to help you express yourself. That connection is what I'm here for."[3]

Kendrick is describing the difference between leaders and followers: Leaders do things the masses are uncomfortable doing.

On 'New Slaves' Kanye raps: *'You see there's leaders and there's followers/But I'd rather be a dick than a swallower'.* A 'dick' meaning, to speak the truth no matter the consequences,' instead of a 'swallower,' who silently accepts something they believe is wrong because they're afraid to speak up.

The great MC's (Jay, 'Ye, Nas, Pac, Em, BIG…) shape their personal experiences into rhyme. They're real to their inner self. There is a core emotional truth in their songs.

'Athletes today are scared to make Muhammad Ali statements/
What's up with your motto?/ Will you lead? Will you follow?/ '
– Nas, My Generation

Most artists don't get this. The Greats do.

Director Quentin Tarantino understands, which is why his movies connect with so many:

"I'm all about the day. I can write a script nine months before. Then on the day of shooting, say Tuesday, to me Tuesday is the most important thing about the scene now. It's not about what I was thinking about before. It's about today. What happens today? How do I feel about it today? If one actor hits a dog on their way to the set, that needs to fit its way into the scene else he's denying what's really going on."[4]

20 years after Tupac Shakur's death he's still regarded by many as either 'the realest,' 'the most influential,' or simply, 'the greatest' of all time. Quotes like this (spoken at the height of rap's *I'm a stone cold killer gangsta'* phase) help explain why: "To me, I am the hardest n**** out there cause I am real – I cry when I need to but I am real."[5]

To 'Do You', to come from the heart, to be credible, is the only way to put your soul into your work. It's the only way to make "Christmas Presents,"[6] that is, making things that are so emotionally connected to people they're excited to buy it, and say 'Wow!' when they get it.

"[Working through my instincts has] only led me to complete awesomeness at all times. It's only led me to beauty, truth, awesomeness. That's all it is," said Kanye.[7]

(Kanye is such a testament to the principle of 'Do You,' that people want to emulate him to the extent where, recently, the shirt a random boy wore in a photo with him sold out hours after the picture was posted online.[8])

'The more emotion I put into it the harder I rock/ '
– OC, Time's Up

Being yourself is about being self-aware, not self-conscious. I can't 'Do Me' if I have no idea who I am. I can't 'Do Me' if I see myself as a product of what others think of me.

'It's hard to correct yourself when you don't know who you are in the first place/ '
– Cee–Lo, G.O.D

To 'Do You' is to tap into your soul, your individuality. To 'do you' is to understand what brings you happiness and a sense of balance. "You give off positive energy when you let your soul shine," says Kevin Liles.[9] When you aren't 'faking it' you're in tune with your instincts and can react to the moment in a way that's real.

'It ain't what you know it's what you feel/
Don't worry about being right, just be for real/'
– Parliament, Ride On

As mentioned in 'Getting Noticed' chapter, the honesty or realness that we're talking about can't be faked. Many try to grab attention in artificial ways, and it may work for some time, but longevity comes only from authenticity. Being unique is only effective when it comes from a deeply personal place, when it is a natural extension of yourself, your character, your soul.

Trying to be different for the sake of being different will likely lead to making art or products which are not personal and have no emotional connection with your audience.

'I never could see why people reach a/
Fake ass facade that they couldn't keep up/'
– Kanye West, Everything I Am

Importantly, 'Doing You' doesn't mean art has to be 100% 'real.' The best artists (from comedians, to rappers), use their creativity to take their core truths/emotions/lives and amplify them to be more dramatic/exciting/provocative, in order to live on the edge.

The Edge

'Don't, push, me, 'cause, I'm, close, to, the, edge'
– Melle Mel, The Message

The most impactful artists push boundaries by living on the edge of their comfort zone.

They are honest with themselves and although they might still think like most of us, *"If I say X, everyone else might think Y,"* or *"If I do Z, I might get embarrassed or fail,"* they don't let the fear or discomfort stop them from doing it. They are the pioneers who lead the way in pushing boundaries further and further out – (see 'The Enemy' *pg. 78*).

You know you're living on the edge of your comfort zone when you worry what others might think of you, or the things you are creating.

It starts small, every day pushing boundaries a little by being honest to ourselves. In doing so we find we care less and less about what others think of us and eventually we will reach a level of maturity where our sense of security doesn't come from other people's opinion, but from within. An unchangeable inner core of strength.

'Living my life in the margin and that metaphor was proof'
– Kendrick, Poetic Justice

Like most principles, Kanye illustrates this point well:
"I think that's a responsibility that I have, to push possibilities, to show people, 'This is the level that things could be at.' So when you get something that has the name Kanye West on it, it's supposed to be pushing the furthest possibilities."[7]

Music executive Lyor Cohen tweeted: "Kanye West is incredible. He has a ton of courage; he never plays it safe. For those who do, know this—you'll soon be forgotten."

A sentiment echoed by Jay Z: "Whether it's accepted by everybody or not. I'm supposed to be pushing that envelope and trying new things. And people are supposed to say, 'Hov, you might have went too far.'"[10]

Only those who live a life of boundary pushing honesty feel true freedom. They are the ones who get noticed and push culture forward. They break boundaries and others follow.

The pattern throughout history is a few innovative people push the envelope, many call them 'radicals,' then 'liberals,' then most eventually follow. Over time their contribution becomes the norm, as others feel safe imitating, and eventually seems old-fashioned, even conservative.

(Like rappers never in a billion years considering talking about gay marriage to Macklemore. Or what about in other areas of life, like women's dress: from it being 'radical' to show a bare ankle a century ago to short skirts today? Or in movies from being 'scandalous' to depict kissing a few decades ago, to the naked orgies of 'The Wolf of Wall Street' today. And what about Politics and Religion? Thousands have been persecuted as 'radicals' because of a belief humanity ended up accepting as standard, like Galileo who was punished as a heretic because he claimed the earth revolved around the sun.)

The question is, will you be a boundary-pushing leader, or wait till it's safe enough to follow?

The Value of Honesty: Trust

Most of us are fortunate enough to not live with a shortage of food. Our physical needs are met. Now though, many people live in a famine of emotional needs, like trust. Trust is scarce.

How many people or companies do you completely trust?

There are millions of people in every industry who want to sell you stuff, but there are very few who offer trust. Economics says that making something scarce pushes the price up (like designer brands making 'limited editions'), so because there is little trust in the world, its value is high. If it were a commodity its price would be up there with Californium 252.

That means authenticity is the most valuable currency and people who can achieve high levels of trust *will* be rewarded massively.

You are the product. If we trust and believe in you, we will believe in what you create. This is what separates winners and losers in an age with thousands of entertainment and lifestyle choices.

When your behavior is not based on what you want to gain or avoid losing, but rather comes from the desire to express yourself honestly, you are seen as legitimate, as trusted.

Immortal Technique has built his career as an independent artist by selling trust. "People follow integrity and follow loyalty," he says. "They want to believe in you. And if don't provide that as an independent artist you don't have a foundation for people to build any trust with you. And that's what they buy now: Trust – buying into who you are."[11]

Leaders who represent their people from a base of honesty can attach themselves to products their audience will buy because the trust between them is strong and we feel they are part of our shared culture.

But, as KRS-One teaches, people who just try to sell things and operate at a 'product level,' not on a 'collective conscious level,'[12] have no trust with the tribe. They might be successful for a short time (because the audience likes the entertainment factor, see below) but not for long. Humans can't connect to duplicity and dishonesty.

'You know you real you don't say it/
You know you real, we gon feel it'
– Wale, Ambition

When you (as an artist or business) have built a reputation around honesty and integrity, people know your actions are coming from the heart, not because you're trying to get something out of them or sell something for a fast buck. This is why artists like Kid Cudi can drop an album independently (Satellite Flight) with no promo and sell 84,000 copies in its first week – that's more than Schoolboy Q and Rick Ross who released the same week, with a record label marketing machine behind them.

Whether you're an artist, a manager or team member, honesty leads to trust. And trust leads to love.

'Cause you just, did the impossible, gained my trust/ '
– Eminem, Space Bound

Honesty is also attractive because it's entertaining. It's captivating to watch and follow someone who seems free from the social constraints that bind most of us. We want to know what the person will do next, so we follow their work like a 'Stan.'

One of the most honest rappers is Eminem. In his rhymes he talks openly about major problems that have, and are, affecting him, like being bullied as a child or his negative relationship with his mother. Millions of people around the world can relate this pure honesty to their own life, which is one of the reasons for his immense success.

Em's first album 'Infinite' (1996) completely flopped. Why? Because he was imitating others; trying to be the next Nas or AZ, whose style was 'hot' at the time. The problem with trying to be someone else, is the very best you can be is a copycat second, who will soon be forgotten as trends change. There are literally hundreds of rappers who latched onto a hot trend, like Gravy with his Jay Z and Biggie clone mixtapes, but are now unheard of. Eminem is different.

After Infinite, Em went through a difficult period which made him lose his inhibitions, *(pg.302)*. He no longer cared about following trends but just wanted to create something that represented him and that he could be personally proud of. He found his unique expression and developed the Slim Shady persona. This fresh voice turned the music industry on its head.

'Flipped rap on its ear like I dropped corn' – Evil Twin

His style was 100% real to himself. He was big and ballsy. He rapped about things never heard before on record. He unashamedly belittled himself and others. He was funny, rude and offensive.

'Cause I'm talking about things you joke about with your friends inside your living room/ only difference is I got the balls to say it in front of ya'll/ and I don't got to be false or sugarcoat it at all' – Real Slim Shady

At the same time Em was deeply honest and expressive. He cut himself and bled over the microphone. He spoke about his deepest thoughts, like his traumatic childhood, feelings towards his father and his relationship with his spouse. For him it was a therapeutic healing process. He said the music allows him to, "get shit off my chest and walk out of the studio booth relieved."

Listeners are made of the same emotions, feelings and thoughts that Em expresses and can relate to his songs on a deep personal level.

'I can relate to what you saying in your songs/ so when I have a shitty day I drift away and put em on' – Stan

In fact Eminem has the most diverse fan base of any artist. Interscope's research showed his fans age range goes all the way up to people in their late 60s, early 70s. You can find teenagers in Egypt with Eminem tattoos or radio stations in Korea that host Eminem marathons. His music transcends age/race/culture/language. It connects directly to our universal core.

When 'The Slip Shady LP' was released in 1999, Hip Hop was in the 'shiny suit era.' The line between pop music and the Hip Hop that was receiving radio and TV airplay was non-existent (Puff and Ja Rule were dominating the charts). But when Em dropped SSLP he went completely against the grain and tapped into a vein of people feeling the same way about the state of their culture. His style couldn't be categorized, he was an: asshole, loving father, woman-hater, victim, hyper-sensitive, bully, lyrical genius, underdog, indecent, decent. He was human.

"Whether I'm the best or not I'm one of the most personal rappers. That's why people relate to me, because people feel like I show so much of myself. That's why random people call me Marshall… The reason why I put so much out there in the first place was because I had no idea I'd be famous."[13]

Over 15 years after SSLP, Em remains one of the most trusted 'celebrity' figures, because everything he does is done with authenticity. He is not considered a 'sell out' when he partners with companies because what he is advertising is connected to who he is. (Like driving through Detroit for Chrysler [with 17 million YouTube views], or a Brisk ad where he repeatedly says 'I don't do commercials'.) Em never tries to bank on his name. Since '8 Mile' he's been offered hundreds of movie scripts, but won't do anything unless it's "authentic, with a reason to be out there."[14]

Em gives the advice to 'Do You' to the people he works with, like singer Skylar Gray. "All the people in the industry try to force their ideas on you," she says. "Em is the opposite, he just says 'be yourself' and he makes me feel more confident in my own instincts."[15]

Evolver

To 'Do You' also means to continually adapt. As an artist develops as a person, so should their art. Greats don't try to stick to one particular style that worked in the past, or get caught up in what their fans want, they just do what feels right to them at that time. Look how Eminem has matured and not tried to artificially stick with the 'Don't Give A Fuck' attitude that defined his first album. Like Nas said about recording 'Life Is Good': "I felt like I couldn't lose. How can you lose when you're being you?"[16]

'If you speak what's on your mind you can pass the test of time/ '
– Nas, Make Nas Proud

Jay Z is another prime example: "I've never looked at myself and said that I need to be a certain way to be around a certain sort of people. I've always wanted to stay true to myself, and I've managed to do that."[17]

"My thing is related to who I am as a person. The clothes are an extension of me. The music is an extension of me. All my businesses are part of the culture, so I have to stay true to whatever I'm feeling at the time, whatever direction I'm heading in. And hopefully, everyone follows."[18]

Jay's 20+ year music career reflects his personal development. Take the subject of female relationships; the evolution of his state of mind is clear to hear in his songs: Ain't No N**** → Big Pimpin → Girls Girls Girls → Song Cry → 03 Bonnie and Clyde→ Venus vs. Mars → On the Run (Part II).

People might voice their anger, saying they like the 'old Jay,' but Great artists don't let other people's perceptions get in the way of their personal development, (though they are open to feedback and constructive criticism).

This is true of businesses as well. In order to remain competitive companies must continually innovate and improve their offering, even though customers may not at first appreciate these changes. When, for example, Facebook is updated, many users complain, but eventually love the new features more than the old.[19]

*'Hov' on that new shit, n****s like 'How come?"*
*N****s want my old shit, buy my old albums/ '*
– Jay, On To The Next One

Do It For You

This book is written for the author. It's for me to use as reference throughout my life. It's taken a while to write because if I'm going to use it for years to come, it needs to be to my satisfaction. If no one else agrees, I'll still be happy in the work created.

This is something learned from the best artists and entrepreneurs, who first and foremost create art/products for themselves. Their own feeling about their work is the main compass, the litmus test, it's judged by.

'I came into this game with nothing to prove/
You never stop a n**** in that type of mood/'
– Jay Z, Dead Presidents 3

In the words of Kanye: "When I made [College Dropout] no one thought that I would get played anyway. So I just made the songs I wanted to hear the most, because I figured at least I could play them in my car if they never blew up or anything."[20]

A few years later he told Fader: "I'm not worried about what I'm supposed to be doing or what I think people want. All I'm gonna do is put out what I want… (The reason why that works for me, is that I actually do have a really pop ear. I kinda have good taste, so it works for me to just put out stuff that I like, as opposed to putting out shit I think other people gonna like.)"[21]

Or as Eminem said: "I make my music for me and how I want to sound. I don't think 'is everyone else gonna like this.' I listen to it and make it for me so that I'm satisfied with it. Because I feel if I am satisfied with it then everybody else is gone like it."[22]

Run DMC pioneered the connection between Hip Hop and corporate America by striking a million dollar endorsement deal with Adidas in 1986, but it all came about from natural 'Do You' principles. "We weren't trying to sell Adidas at first. I wrote a song about what was in my life. We were doing what we loved, and the money followed," says Reverend Run.[23]

Most of the best entrepreneurs, writers, product designers, comedians, actors, and other artists, will say the exact same thing. They create things that solve a problem for themselves, something they "can play a million times and not find fault with," as Eminem said, then they share it with the world.

That means there are no 'genres,' no 'rules,' no 'this is how it's done.' If they feel like using completely different sounds that are labeled as 'hard rock' and 'opera' together, they'll do it. If they feel it's right to write a book with detailed biographies in between a series of interrelated principles, using hundreds of quotes and lyrics, they'll do it.

'I did exactly what I wanted that's what made them checks fly/
In my direction, you never questioned when I said I/
Would be a mogul before I visit 2Pac and Left-Eye/'
– Dr. Dre, The Recipe

Embracing what makes you unique, what makes you weird, and following that, will mean you naturally create something only you could have done. It naturally makes you stand out from the masses. It's your natural niche.

J Cole learned this by watching people who came before him, and has vowed not to make the same mistakes. "Some of my favorite artists refused to step out of their box so never made it far…But someone like Jay Z or Kanye follow no rules, they go here and there. Don't put rules on yourself like, 'gotta keep it real,' just be pure."[24]

'I won't succumb to all the stereotypes/won't sacrifice me for what the stereo hypes/
They told me get in where you fit in, this is what's in demand now/
So I told em why try to fit in when you a standout?/'
– Joe Budden, Just to Be Different

'Doing You' then naturally leads to the essential qualities Kanye describes in being a Great artist: "charisma, originality, and believability."[24]

Or like the poster you'll see in Top Dawg's office on 'Rules of Success' in order of importance:

1.Charisma/personality/swagger. 2. Substance. 3. Lyrics. 4. Uniqueness. 5. Work Ethic

This is a natural principle we already know, deep inside, but have to keep reminding ourselves of because the social pollution and busyness of everyday life can often make us forget who we are – (see 'Re-Finding' pg.58).

Similarly, many people are afraid to 'Do You' because, as Kanye says, "society has broken us down to not really feel what we feel any more." We must remember our time is limited and we only make the most of it when we 'Do You.' "There's only a few characters, not so much that are geniuses, but are dreamers, and bring their dreams to life constantly," adds 'Ye.[25]

You can choose to be one of those characters.

The Deepest Level

To make art that reflect all sides of your self – light and dark/Yin and Yang – is the essence of 'Do You.' Portraying oneself as a human – with flaws and good intentions – connects with universal human emotion. Then when you make more intelligent or emotive art people connect with you in a stronger way than if every song or piece was like that. Like Dame Dash said, "the only way to talk to people is to be one of the people…then you can lead people and show them the way..."[26]

'Power to the people/ when you see me, see you'
— Jay Z, Murder to Excellence

The most successful artists/leaders in any industry epitomize that quote. It's why 'The College Dropout' was so well-received. It was from the perspective of a rounded human, not a pop culture dumbed down character. Kanye depicted a real person, expressing the part of him that wants to brag and the part that wants to cry, someone who prays and checks out girls, someone who likes jewelry and reads books. In doing so he reflected how we all (to some extent) think, and what it means to be human.

For his second album, 'Strictly 4 My N.I.G.G.A.Z,' Tupac released two singles. There was the fun party anthem about chasing girls, 'I Get Around' and the introspective, somber track about respecting girls, 'Keep Ya Head Up'. Some were puzzled how these two seemingly opposite singles could come from the same artist at the same time. But Pac was just poetically, and unashamedly, expressing himself as a real human. Fans loved his complexity and both singles were Billboard Top 20 hits.

'I'm a loser, I'm a winner/
I'm good, I'm bad, I'm a Christian, I'm a sinner/
I'm humble, I'm loud, I'm righteous, I'm a killer/
What I'm doing, I'm saying that I'm human/'
— Kendrick, Kush & Corinthians

This principle is why a line like, *'smoking my Kush reading Corinthians'* in a Kendrick Lamar song is so powerful. He's not advocating drugs, or religion/spirituality, he's just expressing his struggle between wanting to be better and the temptations around him. The listener feels the authenticity.

"The best thing is to let people know that you a human just like them," Kendrick said. "I think that's why a lot of motherfuckers fuck with me because the shit I put out on my music is me not knowing everything. It's me trying to figure out the world just like you."[27]

"[My success] is because people perceived me as a human being rather than an action figure that can't be touched."[28]

What's more, the best artists can make the exact same product appeal to a broad audience. They get mainstream love and underground/professional respect. From comedians (see Dave Chappelle) to authors (see JK Rowling), they appeal to the masses through the emotion in their characters/stories, and to the pro's through their intelligent social commentary, imagery, juxtapositions, etc. They are the most successful, the most loved, the G.O.A.T.'s.

Reality I: Negative Backlash

When you 'Do You' to the fullest all the positive things above will happen, but there may also be a backlash from those closest to you. Some might be offended, some turned off, some may hate you. In fact most people who decide to walk their own path are initially ostracized by those around them.

"Revealing the truth is like lighting a match, said Wiz Khalifa. "It can bring light or it can set your world on fire."

Greats do not let potentially negative backlashes affect their art. They express their truth no matter what the outcome of the honesty is.

"Thinking twice about what's really in my heart because of what people's reactions might be is me selling my soul to the devil," Kanye told Rolling Stone. "Sometimes the truth isn't modest. People ask me to apologize for my greatness."

Others might label Kanye's statements as an 'aggressive asshole' but he doesn't let it affect him or his work. Like Dame Dash observed, "I realized that he was going to make it happen [because] he didn't mind being an asshole. If you don't mind being an asshole, you're not going to lose."[26]

For instance, when Kanye interrupted Taylor Swift at the 2009 MTV VMA awards a lot of people, including the US President, labeled him a 'jackass.' But to Kanye it's the complete opposite:

"You know, to be a visionary, all you have to do is make decisions based off of your eyes instead of your ears and your memory. So at the moment of the MTV awards, I made that decision off of my eyes. I was like, that's not correct. That is invalid. Completely invalid. And everybody else don't move, that's off their ears. 'Oh, he gon' get in trouble,' that's off their memory. They don't move. They're enslaved. They're enslaved to what could possibly happen. We're constantly enslaved."[29]

Those who have a problem with you, you're not trying to appeal to anyway. By 'Doing You,' even though some will hate, many will connect with you and truly, deeply love.

Eminem is another prime example. He told Rolling Stone in 2000: "I don't believe in talking behind nobody's back or being fake…When I write something I don't hold back, there's no holds barred. And whatever the consequences may be, if I offend anyone or whatever, I'm saying it so I'm willing to deal with it…If I'm feeling it, then I'm gonna say it. Flat out."

A sentiment shared by most leaders.

"Never apologize for what you feel. It's like being sorry for being real." Lil Wayne says.[30]

Or as No I.D told Complex: "You can never be in trouble telling the truth. If you're in trouble for telling the truth, then that's not trouble. That's just dealing with the truth. I am the guy that if you catch me saying something, I don't do the, 'Don't tell anybody I said it.' If I said it, I said it. I'm gonna stand right here and say it again to whoever – the end. What's the trouble? Where's the problem?"[31]

When you can stand strong on your honest opinion, with no fear of 'I might lose this if I say this,' your credibility goes through the roof. You're not a 'Yes Man,' with no backbone saying what 'the master' wants to hear. People will trust you, want to work with you, and your success will last longer (but might move more slowly at first), than the oceans of phonies.

BUT, although honest opinions are important, they are just opinions and not everybody needs to hear them all the time. Often opinions reflect part of us rather than the situation so we shouldn't speak out of place.

A mature person knows how to balance the courage of honestly expressing themselves, with consideration for the feelings of others. This is why if Kanye's VMA outburst is going to be criticized, it can only be for lacking maturity. He had the courage to stand up for what he believed in, but not necessarily the consideration to understand Taylor's point of view.

However, when asked, we must speak our truth. Not because we are forcing anyone to agree, but because 'Do You' is essential to success. When need be, we are confident expressing ourselves to anyone, anywhere.

Reality II: Play The Game

A lot of 'advice' (including what you've just read) says *'just be yourself, do you'*, which is well and good, but the reality is that even the names mentioned here, like Em and Kanye, understand that being '100% you' all the time may not be the right move. It may not get you the voice/reach/power you ultimately want, especially when starting out.

It depends on what the artist wants. If they want to be heard by the most number of people or earn the highest record sales, they have to understand the tradeoffs that are going to have to be made between 'Doing You' and compromising to meet a certain expectation. They have to learn to play this game. Or like J Cole's mentor and manager told him, "play the game to change the game."

It's extremely difficult to 'change the game' when just starting out – without power, relationships or realistic knowledge of how your industry works. These all need to be first established, and then can be manipulated to your desires.

"Learn the rules like a pro, so you can break them like an artist"
– Picasso.

Naive newcomers who think they can change the game from the beginning and refuse to compromise on any principles, refuse to play along to some industry customs, are unlikely to have a major voice. Like some rappers labeled as 'conscious,' find they can't escape that box and won't have platinum number one records. But that may not be their goal so it doesn't matter to them. It's about what makes sense to you.

'If skills sold, truth be told, I'd probably be/Lyrically Talib Kweli/
Truthfully I wanna rhyme like Common Sense
But I did 5 mill' - I ain't been rhyming like Common since'
– Jay Z, Moment of Clarity

The people mentioned most in this book know how to 'play the game.' They know how to balance the principles of 'Do You' with 'commercial realisticness'. They know how to create art that's true to themselves, whist deeply connecting with their audience on a large scale.

"I'm an artist," said Tupac. "It's not like I have to tell the truth. I have to tell a story and reach you and get some kind of feeling from you. And then try to get the moral across."[32]

Kanye acknowledges the ability to balance 'Do You' with maximum exposure as one of his most important skills.

"I'm acting off of 'this is what I want to do,' but I realize that I want to be popular, so let me balance how much I push the envelope and how much I take back. I say I'm the Steve Jobs of rap, it's like I'm not gonna give people too much at one time."[33] [In the same way for example Apple has the ability to release a years of product upgrades at a time, but chooses to space them out for higher profits.]

"It's always going to be 80 percent, at least, what I want to give, and 20 percent fulfilling a perception."[21]

"I sit and think about what I'm doing. Like, 'I wanna express this message' but, maybe I might have to get another artist on it and place it like this and put it in this vein. I'm not just gonna step back and just be like, 'Yo just look at everything I have right now' and then the world not accept it. I gotta put in in a way that the world will accept it *and then* develop it into being an artist."[34]

Eminem is another classic example. He could focus on only making honest, heartfelt music, but knows that wouldn't get him the voice he wants. So he makes 'compromises,' cleans up records for radio *("I cringe every time I gotta do it")*, and makes mass appeal songs like 'My Name Is.'

He told Rolling Stone in 2002: "The shit that I really like, that I put my heart and soul into, I don't get recognized for, like 'The Way I Am.' There's a difference between me being funny and me being real. I feel like I don't get recognized for my best shit, the shit that's my true feelings and emotions."

So, because he wants a large voice he plays the game and, "makes songs that appeal to everybody to get people to listen to my realer songs."

It worked out for him…

287

The Story Of

EMINEM

Marshal Mather's life story is one of the most remarkable, not just of any Hip Hop artist, but of any human being. Growing up, everything seemed to be stacked against him. Everything seemed to point towards failure.

- A dirt poor childhood, living on welfare in a broken home.
- Moving home and school almost every six months as a kid.
- The victim of violent bullying, at school and at home.
- No father figure, no male role model, no footsteps to follow.
- A white guy trying to set the precedent as a serious Hip Hop artist.

This man's early life had the kind of immense pressure that either breaks a person down, or builds a diamond. Marshall found a way to channel all these experiences into an art that has made him the most successful musician of the last decade.

Source[20]

Marshall Mathers III was born in 1972 to a 17 year old mom and a father who would leave the family six months later. As a child he and his mother lived on welfare and moved constantly, so Marsh would attend many different schools in one year. Inevitably he found it difficult to make friends and would be bullied as 'the new kid' or because he was small and often mistaken as retarded, (for instance because he'd do things like hum melodies not realizing he was loud enough to be heard by others).

He retreated away from the outside world and into comic books, drawing and eventually Hip Hop. This fantasy world provided an escape from the harshness of reality. In this new world the otherwise shy Marshall could excel at something, he could affirm himself. In this new world he had father figures he could relate to. Here he could dream about a better life than the sad one he was stuck in.

In 1984, 11 year old Marshall starting hearing rap on the radio, with songs like 'Jam on It' by Newcleus, but it was his uncle Ronnie who gave him a proper introduction to Hip Hop. Ronnie owned many early rap records and would record himself rapping in his trailer home with makeshift equipment. He played Ice T's song 'Reckless', and Marsh was captivated.

After memorizing all the words to the song, Marsh explored other aspects of Hip Hop and in school learned about breaking.

"I went to a mixed school in fifth grade, one with lots of Asian and Black kids and everybody was into break dancing. They always had the latest rap tapes – Fat Boys, L.L. Cool J's Radio – and I thought it was the most incredible shit I'd ever heard."[1]

After learning to dance from other kids in the school library, Marsh would carry a boom box on his shoulder and cardboard under his arm and go to parks to blast rap songs and bust moves. But when he realized he couldn't dance as well as some of the other kids, he went back to explore emceeing. As a kid Marsh listened to Prince and Michael Jackson, but found it hard to

289

relate to them. Their dress, behavior and 'rich–people–problems' were a different world to the gritty, working–class Detroit he called home. Whereas rappers came from and represented similar neighborhoods to the ones Marshall lived in. They were raw, direct and confrontational. He could relate to them and naturally they became his role models, his teachers, his fathers.

"Growing up I wanted to be LL Cool J, I wanted to be Run, Ad–Rock, Big Daddy Kane, a lot of people. Me and my friends used to stand in front of the mirror and perform. The kids from the neighborhood would come around to watch."[2]

Dreaming is common in children, they fantasize about being fire–fighters, astronauts and rock stars, but Marshall is one of the few whose childhood dream would eventually come true. First though, he'd have to go through hell.

A year after first tasting Hip Hop, when Marshall was 12, he and his mother settled down on the east side of Detroit. But his shy awkwardness followed, and he was the victim of regular bullying and beatings. Once he even suffered a brain hemorrhage from a pounding that put him in a coma for days.

"Where I was growing up, everybody tried to test you," he remembers.[2]

'I get my ass kicked damn near everywhere/
From Bel–Aire shopping center just for stopping in there/
From the black side all the way to the white side/'
– Yellow Brick Road

Yet despite the consequences Marshall would stand up for himself. Like when a gang drove by 'flipping him off,' he replied with the same gesture.

"They got out of the car. One dude came up, hit me in the face and knocked down. Then he pulled out a gun. I ran right out my shoes, crying. I didn't know how to handle that."

One of his bully's at school (now an unemployed laborer) remembers:

"There was a bunch of us that used to mess with him. Sometimes he'd fight back – depended on what mood he'd be in."[4]

Although these were traumatic experiences, what Marshall didn't know at the time is how useful they would be to him in the long run. Marsh's tough adolescence built up his character to get through the ruthlessness of the music business. It would eventually sprout his 'Don't Give A Fuck' attitude that catapulted him to stardom. Everything from the domestic feuds with his mom, to the bullies he faced almost daily, would be his fuel to win in life and show 'them' what he could become.

For now though the abuse pushed him deeper and deeper into Hip Hop.

Hip Hop began in the 1970's as a tool for expression, a voice for a group of marginalized, exploited poor people living in a place they didn't feel they belonged. This was Marshall to a T, and Hip Hop consumed him.

"As soon as my mom would leave to play bingo, I'd blast the stereo."[4]

He was carving out a new world.

9th Grade

Ninth grade marked a major point in Marshall's life. In the three years he retook 9th grade he'd find his passions, meet people who would help launch his career, and go through experiences that would define him as an adult and an artist.

Marsh began seriously writing rhymes aged 14 (the first time he sat 9th grade classes). He would often skip school to stay in his room lip-syncing to songs, or rapping his own lyrics with friend Mike 'Manix' Ruby.

The two young white rappers formed a duo, 'Manix and M&M' (short for Marshall Mathers), and would practice writing and rapping in Manix's parents' basement. The support from his friend was important for Marsh to have the confidence to begin performing publically.

They also formed a rap and production crew, 'Basmint Productions,' (because they were literally recording from Manix's basement on ultra-basic equipment), with Chaos Kid, and Manix's twin brother Matt 'DJ Buttafingaz' Ruby – (see *pg.203* for more on these guys).

The group would practice rhyming together and recorded regularly, though Marsh admits the first couple years he was "wack." "I didn't know how I should sound. I didn't know barely anything."[5]

Marsh committed himself to critically studying other artists, regularly practicing freestyles, and even reading the dictionary to expand his vocabulary. He wasn't born with a God given talent. All his "Guinness Word Record" skill came through learning. Continual, never-ending learning.

Rap became the dominant part of life. Marsh loved the feeling of getting better. He loved the affirmation from friends and the respect he got from onlookers. As a shy kid he loved just having a voice and being able to express himself through rhyme in a way he couldn't do in normal conversation. He loved the escape rap provided.

"Rap music kept my mind off all the bullshit I had to go through."[6]

Marshall identified so closely with Hip Hop culture that he adopted the style of his rap idols. He wore black and green colored clothes, Nubian medallions and even Flavor Flav style clocks around his neck, during Hip Hop's Afrocentric period in the late 1980's, to "show off," not realizing that these were symbols of the black power movement.

He recalled one experience to Rolling Stone:

'Me and my boy are in matching Nike suits and our hair in high–top fades, and we went to the mall and got laughed at so bad. And kinda got rushed out the mall. I remember this dude jumpin' in front of my boy's face and bein' like, 'Yeah, boyyyeee! What you know about hip hop, white boyyyeee?!''[7]

'We was being laughed at, "you ain't even half black!"/ '
— Yellow Brick Road

Marsh loved Hip Hop but the culture didn't seem to want his love. When albums came out he would rush excitedly to the record store to spend the little money he had. But when he heard the tracks his enthusiasm could sink:

> "I loved the X Clan's first album [1990]. Brother J's delivery was so confident. But he also made me feel like an outcast. Callin' us polar bears. Even as militant as Public Enemy were, they never made me feel like, 'You're white, you cannot do this rap, this is our music.' The X Clan kinda made you feel like that, talking about 'How could polar bears swing on vines of the gorillas?' It was a slap in the face. It was like, you're loving and supporting the music, you love it and live it and breathe it, then who's to say that you can't do it?"[7]

Teenagers go through 'identity crises' anyway, but with Marshall this was compounded by his love of Hip Hop, yet feeling unwelcome in any culture.

"Walkin' through the suburbs and I'm getting called the N–word, and walkin' through Detroit I'm getting jumped for being white. And goin' through that identity crisis of, 'Am I really not meant to touch the mic? Is this really not meant for me?'"[7]

XClan members: (from Left) Paradise, Brother J, Professor X, Sugar Shaft

Also in 9th grade Marsh met several people who would play an important part in developing his career. 'Bassmint Productions' would perform at school talent shows and Gary Kozlowski, aka Goofy Gary, would help Marsh promote the shows. On one occasion (in 1988) they were outside Osbourne High School handing out flyers for a talent show at Marshall's own Centerline High, (flyers that the Detroit rap group ICP accused him of using their name on to attract more people), when they meet a student named Deshawn 'Proof' Holton.

'I had told him to stop by and check this out sometime," Em raps in Yellow Brick Road. *"He looked at me like I'm out my mind/ Shook his head, like 'white boys don't know how to rhyme".*

But when Marsh demonstrated his complex compound syllable rhymes, the two connected. "What made us become great friends was we both rhymed 'first place' and 'birthday,' and we've been tight ever since," remembers Proof.

Marsh would skip school and attend Proof's Osborne High school, to battle in lunch rooms. Proof organized a scheme where he would bet on Marsh while everyone else bet against him. "It was like White Men Can't Jump," remembers Proof. "Everybody thought he'd be easy to beat, and they got smoked every time."[4] Proof and Marsh would split the winnings.

Proof saw potential in Marshall; something not even Marsh saw in himself. Also, as Proof was one of the most respected people in Detroit's underground scene, by hanging around him Marsh stopped getting bullied.

"He was my ghetto pass,"[3] admits Marsh.

The duo would practice rhyming with exercises like seeing how many words they could rhyme with a random word, or making a rhyme out of five random words in one minute. (All good 'Creative Workouts' – *pg.250*).

9th grade was also the time 15 year old Marsh met 13 year old Kimberly Scott at a youth home. "I'm standing on top of their coffee table with my shirt off, with a Kangol on, mocking the words to LL Cool J's 'I'm Bad.' And I turn around and she's at the door smoking."[7]

It marked the start of their love-hate relationship, and without that encounter its possible Eminem would not exist today, as the child they would later conceive provided much of the motivation for Marsh to overcome the difficult barriers on the journey through the music business.

This was also the time he first heard three Jewish boys from Brooklyn rap. The Beastie Boys, 'License to Ill' was a phenomenal influence on Marshall. They would help erase the doubts X Clan and others put in his mind about his chances of making it.

"That's what really did it for me. I was like, 'This shit is so dope!' That's when I decided I wanted to rap."[1]

"I liked the Beastie Boys because they were themselves – they weren't fronting. Millions of kids around the world could relate to where they were coming from….It was them being themselves that helped me figure out how to relax and be me. Made me feel I could rock mic and rock millions."[3]

Meanwhile Marshall's performance at school was bad and he dropped out at 16 after failing the 9th grade three times. At school he was a failure. (Something his teachers and most of his family keep reminding him.) But humans are not meant to be failures. We all want to do well, better ourselves and be great at something. Marshall was slowly finding this 'something' in music.

'Compelled me to excel when school had failed me/
Expelled me and when the principal would tell me/
I was nothing, and I wouldn't amount to shit…'
– Revelation

After dropping out he held down several odd jobs while continuing to hone his craft. He worked as a cook and in a factory, sweeping floors and cleaning toilets, whatever a boy with no qualifications could get, all the while building a dream in his mind of where he wanted to be.

The Space between Dreams and Reality

When Marshall turned 17 he had been rapping for 3 years, continually working on his flow, lyrics and learning from the best. "I was like a sponge, studying the techniques of Kool G Rap, Naughty by Nature, KRS1." "These rapper were my teachers and I was a fulltime student."[3]

While people his age were studying math formulas, Marsh studied the techniques of great rappers. He studied how they put words together and flowed with the beat. "I studied what everybody did, and developed my own sound." (Just like Kendrick, Jay, 'Ye and countless other Greats, *pg.167*)

At this point Marsh believed he was "good but not great"[3] and was unsure if a career in Hip Hop was really practical – Vanilla Ice, the gimmicky 'Ice Ice Baby' guy, had made it near impossible to get respect as a white rapper.

Meanwhile, Proof had been working with Marsh at Little Caesars restaurant but quit to work on rhyming full time. He formed the crew 'Five Elements,' and was getting interest from New York record labels. One night he and Marsh, who by now had adapted his moniker 'M&M' into 'Eminem,' played each other their songs in Caesar's parking lot. "That was a defining moment for me, as it made me feel I could keep up," Marsh recalls.[3]

As well as realizing his rhymes were on a similar level to Proof's, he noticed that his raps were lyrically better than many established rappers out at the time. *'If they can be successful, why can't I?'*

Believing he was a good rhymer, seeing from the Beastie Boys that it was possible to be a popular white rapper, and having the support of friends like Proof, (who was giving Marshall constant affirmation and reinforcing him in the belief he was good and had the potential to be great, "people need to hear this!" he'd say), made Marsh decide rap was what he wanted to do.

"This is it."[3]

But believing he could win just because his lyrics were technically better than other rappers was a naive mistake that he'd soon discover. For example, Em would hang around street corners where kids rapped in ciphers, but when he tried to join he'd often be dissed – usually for being white and having the nerve to attempt rap.

Em remembers one of his first public performances at a venue called 'The Rhythm Kitchen': "The first time I grabbed the mic, I got dissed. I only said, like, three words, and I was getting booed. I started getting scared, I started getting scared, like, is this gonna happen? Am I gonna make it or not?"[6]

'Backstab the Kingpin', another white Detroit rapper performed on a set with Em in this period. He faced similar challenges:

"I was the first to take the stage that night. When I came out, the crowd instantly started booing me. The music hadn't even started, and they were booing. I hadn't even grabbed the mic yet and they screamed racial remarks at me. It was apparent it was because of my color.

"By the end of my show I was escorted off stage for throwing things back at the crowd. The promoter said 'man you better go out the backdoor, unless you wanna get your ass beat to death.' I was rushed out the back. I never got to see Em perform that night but I heard from his manager after seeing me he got real drunk and fell all over the stage and skipped his music alot. He was most likely scared. He showed up only with his girl and another couple. He had no fan base at all."[8]

Experiences like this could have easily made Marsh curl up into a shell, consumed by fear. Instead, with the help of the support group, he chose to work on his craft, to evolve as a lyricist, to overcome his anxiety and come back to demand the respect of the people who booed him. Friends like Proof would persuade a reluctant Marshall to keep rapping in public, and to perform at Hip Hop clubs in Detroit, like the Ebony Showcase Lounge and Saint Andrews Basement aka The Shelter.

'I been chewed up and spit out and booed off stage/
But I kept rhyming and stepped right in the next cipher/
Best believe somebody's paying the pied piper'
– Lose Yourself

The handicap of being white in a black dominated culture meant Em had no choice but to display super advanced technical skill to get any respect.

"I had to work up to a certain level before people would even look past my color."[1]

So he continued honing his craft, writing rhymes everywhere he went – at home, on buses, at work. The manager of the restaurant Marsh worked in recalls: "He was a good worker, but he'd be in the back rapping all the orders, and sometimes I had to tell him to tone it down. Music was always the most important thing to him."[4]

After The Rhythm Kitchen, Em's next big public performance was when Proof, who hosted The Hip Hop Shop's Saturday Open Mic event, persuaded Em to come along.

Em had yet to receive a positive public audience reaction to his rhymes, and the Shop's crowd was infamous for being notoriously harsh on bullshit, so, he initially refused to perform. It was only after Poof suggested Em arrive 20 minutes before the end of the show, when there were less people in the crowds, that Em eventually agreed. He arrived as people were leaving and, despite the fear, spat his rhymes. He remembers the reaction well:

"People were quiet first. Then I heard a couple applause. Then it got louder and louder…That was the first time I got any kind of respect when I grabbed the mic."[3] "It made me believe I could do it."[9]

The crowd's reaction was like a hit of heroin, and an addicted Em started preforming every Saturday – arriving on time – and scheduling his whole week around the open mic event. He built his confidence there and eventually entered into the Hip Hop Shop's infamous quarterly Rap Battles.

"He was kind of a mystery man because he would only show up when there were battles," remembers Bizarre, who would later form a band with Em. "He would come with his hat brim real low and kill everyone in the battle, then come back three months later [for the next battle]."[10]

Em was earning respect. He'd get props and use it as motivation to work harder. The better he got the more respect he earned, the more respect he earned the more confident he became, the more confident he became the more he worked, the more he worked the better he got…This positive cycle is the reason Em went from writing as well as any random person, to become the best technical lyricist in Hip Hop history.

At this time Em would also go to the Detroit radio station 96.3 WDRQ for their Friday Open Mic Nights. DJ Lisa Orlando explains:

"We basically let 'em call, and they'd rap for us on the phone. If I thought they had some talent, we'd bring 'em down and put them in the production room. It was all live on the radio. You'd point to the kid, and this street kid would have to just start doin' his thing."

Eminem made the cut and he and his crew became regulars on the Open Mic Night. But, although Em clearly had rhyming talent, his style was so different to what Hip Hop typically represented, that most people couldn't see him 'making it.' As DJ Orlando remembers: "He was different, but he was shy. He was a little more timid when he was doing the show. At the time, he wasn't the one that I thought would make it. But he'd come down, and his raps would always be funny. The other guys would all talk about some girl or getting into fights, your typical gangsta rap stuff. And he'd come in talkin' junk– he was unique."

Hanging around the radio station also brought networking benefits. For instance after performing one night Em met the group EPMD in the building elevator. He spat some rhymes and received positive feedback. "This was a huge moment for me. It gave him a vital energy boost to keep at it."[3]

Em would record songs with Bassmint Productions during the week and take them down to the radio on Friday evening to try and get a chance to perform. One night listening to Em perform 'Crackers and Cheese' on air was Mark Bass, a local music producer for FBT Productions (Funky Base Team). Mark called the station and spoke to a teenage Marshall over the air, inviting him to come to their studio and make some songs. This seemingly 'chance event' only happened after Marshall had been attending the Open Mic night for months, constantly working to improve his art in that time.

After meeting, the FBT brothers signed Em to their independent label, Web Entertainment, to create a demo tape, in the hope of getting it picked up by a major label.

This was the early 90's, and the energy in Detroit's underground Hip Hop scene was bubbling. Hip Hop clubs, street ciphers, competitions and demo tapes circulating, were the ingredients for something ready to blow.

'Don't ever say this is a ghost town/
One million rappers in this bitch, they need to slow down/'
– Hush, We Shine ft Eminem

But still nobody from the city had broken into the national elite, (with Dre, Snoop, Wu, BIG, Pac, Na etc.) New York and L.A. dominated the global Hip Hop charts, and as Em says, "everyone felt they would be the first person to make it from Detroit."[3]

Mark and his brother Jeff Bass had connections with Electra Records, so to make his three song demo Marshall was able to cut studio quality songs to present to Electra. He really believed he would be offered a deal then and there.

However Electra quickly turned him down, and he and the Bass brothers went their separate ways.

Once again, many people may have accepted defeat and found something else to do with their time, but Marshall chose to reload and shoot again.

A recent photograph of one of the several homes Marshall lived in growing up in Detroit[19]

In 1992 Marsh moved into small house on Novara Street, East Detroit, with his girlfriend Kim. Denaun Porter (aka Kon Artis/Mr Porter) also lived with them (and worked at Little Caesar with Em). Porter rapped and made beats. He set up his turntables in Em's bedroom while Em slept on the couch.

Marsh continued to work minimum wage jobs, from dish washing to factory sandblasting, to pay the bills, whilst using his free time to develop his craft. Porter made beats, and they'd go to studios like Mo Master to record for $40 an hour. Every hour in the studio represented eight hours washing dishes or sweeping floors, so they made sure to use their precious time wisely.

In 1992 Em also made his first video appearance in Detroit rapper Champtown's 'Do–Da–Dipity' video.

By now Em was stating to perform more in clubs around the city (often for no money), and he was tightening his mic skills – improving technically and making sure all his lyrics were purposeful punch lines.

With his reputation growing, Em partnered with other rappers like the New Jacks, then formed the group Soul Intent, with Chaos Kid from the now defunct Basemint Productions crew. Recorded on the proceeds of a tax refund, they released the single 'Fuckin Backstabber' in 1995 when Marsh was 23. The song is about hunting down an evil lunatic with 'green hair,' and ends with a positive message, *'dealing with backstabber's there was one thing I learned/they're only powerful when you got your back turned'*. Marsh made his own cassette tapes, drew the covers, and put the song (along with 'biterphobia') out on consignment in records stores.

"It sold maybe 3 copies" Em says.[3]

Still with nothing else going for him he journeyed on.

Soul Intent, with Eminem (far left)[21]

By 1996, at 23, Marsh had been rhyming for nine years, and it was four years since first working with the Bass brothers. In that time he had developed his rhyming skills and Mark Bass once again heard him on a local radio station. He again called the station up and offered to give Em another chance.

This was the only way Em could record an album, as he had stopped working with Basmint Productions over personal differences, and didn't have enough money to pay for studio time on his own, let alone buy beats.

He needed an album, or at least a demo, to put out on the streets and present to record labels.

Meanwhile in his personal life the relationship with his mom soured, his uncle Ronnie committed suicide in 1991, which devastated Marsh: "I didn't talk for days after…For a whole year I stopped writing,"[3] and his girlfriend Kim became pregnant. Through these difficult times he found the greatest motivation imaginable: providing for his soon–to–be daughter, Halie. A few years later he'd frankly state: "My family is all I have ever fought for and all I ever try to protect. I did this so I could be family to Haile, and raise her in the right way, not cut on her like my dad did to me…the only thing I'm scared of is being taken away from my little girl."

Friend MC Hush remembers: "By summer of 95, Em was like, 'Man I got a baby on the way. I gotta do something, I gotta make some money or there's no way I can take care of this shit.' He just seemed overwhelmed…"[11]

Eminem and FBT recorded Infinite a few months before Halie's birth.

Infinite Hope

Since splitting from Basmint Productions Em had developed his production skill and made some of Infinite's beats himself along with Denaun Porter, Proof, and the Bass brothers.

In winter 1996 FBT pressed up 1000 copies of the album. The outcome?

"It sold maybe 5 tapes" recalls Marsh, "we couldn't sell em for shit around Detroit"[5] – though they really managed to shift around 50 copies.

Critics labelled him a Nas and AZ clone, and Detroit DJ's left the record virtually un-played.

"When [radio DJ] Billy T. did finally play it, he actually faded it out just when Em's verse came up. [Em] was crushed," remembers MC Hush.[11]

'Hope, I just need a ray of that, 'cause no one sees my vision/
When I play it for 'em, they just say it's wack/'
– I Need a Doctor

Although at the time Em was angry that no one was showing him love, he later agreed with some of the criticism.

"Infinite was me trying to figure out how I wanted my rap style to be, how I wanted to sound on the mic and present myself. It was right before my daughter was born, so having a future for her was all I talked about…It was way hip–hopped out, like Nas or AZ – that rhyme style was real in at the time."

Marsh admits to always being a "smartass comedian" but he didn't show any of that on the album. It had none of the pent up range or alter-ego that would define his later work. He was following others instead of expressing himself, and that's why he says "it wasn't a good album."

Still he took it as a positive learning experience on his journey. "It was a growing stage. I felt like Infinite was like a demo that just got pressed up."

Though aside from the quality of the album, another reason for the record's poor reception was probably because the underground Hip Hop community was not ready to hear a serious white MC. Here was Marshall respecting the craft and working every day to improve, yet he was being immediately dismissed because of something he could not control. Of course it affected him.

"After that record, every rhyme I wrote got angrier and angrier. A lot of it was because of the feedback I got. Motherfuckers was like, 'You're a white boy, what the fuck are you rapping for? Why don't you go into rock and roll?' All that type of shit started pissing me off."[4]

Marsh was simmering inside. He was getting ready to take vengeance with his next work.

Rock Bottom

In early 1997 Eminem performed at Scribble Jam, an annual Hip Hop festival in Ohio. Just like when Proof first urged him to perform at the Hip Hop Shop, Em was initially hesitant but his manager Mark Kempf, (who Marsh met through Proof at the Hip Hop Shop, as Mark was editing local Hip Hop magazine 'Underground Soundz'), persuaded him to go and paid his expenses – Em was flat–broke.

Seventy of the best MC's from around the country competed and Marsh battled into the semifinals before losing to Rhymefest.

Rhymfest then backed out of the final, as he did not want to go against his good friend MC Juice, so Eminem took his place. He went four extra tie–breaker rounds with Juice, before being deservedly beaten.

"I choked," Em admitted. "I went back to Detroit depressed and totally broke."[3]

He was dejected, though his situation would get worse before it got better.

Less than two months after the disappointment of Infinite, Marshall hit rock bottom. He had already seen the deadline he set for himself to 'make it' come and go, and was now working as a minimum wage cook in Gilberts lodge for up to sixty hours a week, trying to keep up with rental payments and providing for his new born daughter. Then just days before his daughter's first birthday (Christmas Day), he was fired.

Marsh dreamed of being able to provide a better life for Hailie (who he'd inked a tattoo of on his shoulder), unlike his own father. But he was tormented by the reality of surviving on government handouts and not being able to provide even basics. "That was the worst time ever," he recalls. "I couldn't afford to get Haile diapers…I wrote 'Rock Bottom' right after that…it was a cry for help."[12]

'I'll never forget that Christmas I sat up the whole night cryin/' – Mockingbird

'Hallie and Marshall' by Lilian Pimentel de Abreu: talenthouse.com/lilianbreu

Ironically, while recording the song Rock Bottom, Marshall received more bad news that added to his depression and made him seriously doubt whether he would ever make it in music.

"We had just found out that this guy who was saying he was gonna get us a major record deal was working in the mail room and he was nobody... A bunch of other personal shit was happening in my life, and I just thought I wasn't gonna get a deal no matter what, shit is not going to work out."[2]

In a *'what's the point anymore?'* state of mind Em used drugs for the first time, swallowing several Tylenol 3 pills, thinking "this will be the last song I record."[3] He came close to death but his body was not finished and puked the pills before they could do damage.

And still the bad news kept compiling. Marsh lived with Kim and Halie in a small run-down house in a dangerous neighborhood, which only added to their troubles. Firstly, there was the racial tensions of being the only white family in a black neighborhood. "Little kids used to walk down the street going, 'Look at the white baby!' Everything was 'white this, white that.' We'd be sitting on our porch, and if you were real quiet, you'd hear, 'Mumble, mumble, white, mumble, mumble, white.'"[1]

Though as an 'outsider' in one of America's crime hotspots he had to deal with a lot more than mumbling.

'And at the time, every house that we lived in/
Either kept getting' broken into and robbed or shot up on the block'
– Mockingbird

The family were victims of frequent burglaries, and even a stray bullet once flew through the house while Kim was doing dishes.

"I went through four TVs and five VCRs in two years," recalls Marshall. "After cleaning out the first of those TVs and VCRs, plus a clock radio, the guy came back one night to make a sandwich. He left the peanut butter, jelly – all the shit – out and didn't steal nothing. Ain't this about a motherfucking bitch. But then he came back again and took everything but the couches and beds. The pillows, clothes, silverware – everything. We were fuckin' fucked."[4]

The constant pressure almost broke the camel's back.

"I caught a guy breaking into the house for the 5th time, I was like 'fuck this it's not worth it. I'm out here.' That day, I wanted to quit rap and get a house in the fucking suburbs. I was arguing with my girl, like, 'Can't you see they don't want us here?' I went through so many changes; I actually stopped writing for about five or six months and I was about to give everything up."[1]

'My daughter wants to throw the ball but I'm too stressed to play/
Live half my life and throw the rest away/'
– Rock Bottom

It's important to understand just how close Em was to completely giving up here, and if Haile had not been born he likely would have quit. However, there was a force within that compelled him to continue. He refused to allow his daughter to live in this poverty-ridden environment, and vowed to buy a house in the suburbs where she could have a better life. No matter how far-fetched his music dream seemed, to him it was the *only* way to escape this unhappy life.

"When Hailie was born, it was the reality of 'I have to do this.' I had nothing else. I had no high school education."[13]

He made a promise to himself so he pushed through the hard times, sucked up the abuse and channeled his frustration into music, writing songs like 'Rock Bottom', and 'Just the Two of Us.'

"I just couldn't quit. I'd keep going to the clubs and taking the abuse. But I'd come home and put a fist through the wall."[1]

When a man makes a decision to do something, a definite, no–turning–back, *Do or Die'* decision things start to happen.

The coldest hour is always before the dawn, and little did Marshall know that soon things would become a lot, lot hotter.

Unstoppable

In 1996 Proof had been going back and forth to New York, because Tommy Boy Records were interested in signing him. On one journey back he had an idea for a better way to get signed. Instead of everybody trying to come up on their own, why not unite and work together?

So came the Dirty Dozen.

"I want the twelve best MC's in Detroit to do our own version of the Wu-Tang Clan," he told Em.[3] But Proof only found 6 MC's suitable for the group, so his other idea was for each member to have an alias.

Proof was in part influenced by other underground Detroit and New York rappers like Esham, who's Horrorcore 'Acid Rap,' lyrics turned him into the biggest selling independent rapper in 1990s Detroit – (in 'Still Don't Give a Fuck,' Em describes himself as *a cross between Manson, Esham and Ozzy'*).

The idea was to create a 'dark side' that would rhyme "about the illist most ridiculous shit,"[3] like drug overdoses, family homicides and other 'shock rap' subjects. But what differentiated 'D12' from those other 'shock tactic' rappers was their serious lyrical acrobats.

They formed a pact in Em and Proof's makeshift basement studio that if one of them got signed he would come back for the others, thereby multiplying the chances each of them would 'make it.' Most members believed that Proof would be the one to blow up first. Em was seen as the least likely, since everything about him, from his race to his quiet demeanor, was so different to the loud and proud personality typical of Hip Hop artists at the time. Em himself still described rap as a "pipe dream"[3] at this time. (The group's first release was 'The Undergroup EP' available at HipHopTeaches.com)

Within a few weeks most of D12 had decided on their alias identity, but Em was still searching. He developed and experimented with his style and sound, listening and learning from those around him. Friends like DJ Rec remember advising Em to step away from the tongue twister double time style of Infinite and "get a gimmick, get more metaphors and not just syllables…and be [more] humorous."[11]

All the different ideas came together while Em was sitting on the toilet, and inspiration struck him with the name 'Slim Shady'. "Boom, the name hit me, and right away I thought of all these words to rhyme with it."

Slim Shady was more than just shock rap, it was based on a core of truth of who Marshall Mathers is. "Part of me is coming out too," he says. "Like me being pissed off at the world." People already labeled him 'white trailer trash' so he decided to embody that to the fullest and vent his "anger at everything" in his life through Slim Shady.

"I put my personal feelings on wax in a creative way instead of really doing it," he said in 1998.[14]

The new subjects he rhymed about came with a distinct high pitched voice, which came to him after he picked up the mic following his time off after Infinite's flop. The Slim Shady transformation also came with a 'Rot in Pieces' tattoo and friend Rec remembers, "He used to get really pissed when we'd call him Marshall."[11]

"We created a monster!" Bizarre joked to DJ Hush.

With nothing to lose, Em recorded as his new alter ego.

Slim Shady Is Born

The Bass Brothers decided to give it one more go, and record one last EP with Marsh. They had already lost money on Infinite and couldn't afford any more flops. This was probably Marsh's last shot to try and make it. If this album failed he would need to find work to support his family. He told friend Hush, "Man, if this record doesn't hit, this is it, I quit."[11]

With the experiences Em had been through in the last few months and the Slim Shady alter ego revelation, he came in determined, like a gladiator fighting for his family's freedom. He was going to create an album that he could be personally proud of, not trying to imitate any 'hot styles' at the time but being completely true to self. Instead of trying to sound like the East

Coast rappers he accepted the image in the mirror.

So in the spring of 1997 he recorded his eight track Slim Shady EP.

"I had nothing to lose, but something to gain," Eminem says of this defining moment. "If I made an album for me and it was to my satisfaction, then I succeeded. If I didn't, then my producers were going to give up on the whole rap thing we were doing. I made some shit that I wanted to hear."

The Bass Brothers (WEB Productions) provided the money, studio and some production, while Mr. Porter, DJ Rec, Hush, and Proof made beats, which were far more advanced than those on Infinite.

"With Infinite I was rhyming big words but not expressing myself, not putting my life into music. Whereas with Slim Shady LP I reached a point when my daughter was born, I didn't give a fuck anymore. It seemed as soon as I stopped giving a fuck, other people stated giving a fuck and caring about my music."

They say the most dangerous man is one with nothing to lose and by finding his unique style and presenting himself as himself, Eminem's career begun to take off.

Meanwhile Paul 'Bunyan' Rosenberg was working in a New York Law firm after graduating from the University of Detroit. Paul's passion was music. He originally dreamed of being an MC, but when he accepted that he wasn't as good as others in the underground, he pivoted and decided to become a music lawyer. However, after discovering how difficult it is to work at a respected music law firm if you don't have an Ivy League school diploma, or have the right personal connections, he ended up as a personal injury lawyer in New York.

Unsatisfied, Paul decided to pivot again around his interests and explore artist management. He reconnected with rappers back home in Detroit, like Eminem, (who Proof had introduced him to in 1995 after Em won a battle at the Hip Hop Shop), searching for somebody he could represent and help establish in the music business.

Em sent Paul a demo tape with the bones of the SSEP, and Paul got excited. "He had really figured out what he wanted to be as a rapper," Paul remembers. He called Em from a Manhattan phone booth and asked if he could be his lawyer and promote his music.

The Slim Shady EP, released December 1997, was a world away from Infinite. It combined witty, lyrically ferocious, sometimes sadistic lyrics (the Slim Shady – like the song 'Low Down Dirty'), with deep, introspective and emotional personal stories (the Eminem – like the song 'If I Had'). Em and his team would sell the CD at shows and offer it to record stores on consignment, (where the stores only paid them if it sold), and it soon gained a respectable local underground following.

In New York, Paul also booked Eminem for gigs. Em was completely unknown, but used the small shows to begin building a name in the birthplace of Hip Hop.

The core team consisted of Marsh, Paul and Mark Kempf, however Marsh was finding it difficult to trust Mark as he felt Mark didn't really care about him. Marsh ended their relationship when in Queens for a show and Mark ordered a Burger King without inviting Marsh, knowing he was broke. "What kind of manager are you?" Marsh said. "I thought to manage someone you're supposed believe in them. You invest. It's a gamble. Like roll of a dice."[3]

Paul took over management duties and moved to Detroit with Em. Though they both knew that they would have to leave the D to make it big, and travel to one of the two main spots on the Hip Hop map. They choose to go West.

Olympian

Wendy Davis started the Rap Coalition because she was disgusted by the exploitative contracts rappers signed. The not-for-profit coalition would work with top lawyers to get rappers out of bad record deals. Because Wendy didn't charge rappers, she had to foot all the admin and lawyer fees herself, and of course soon her bank account started shrinking. She urgently sought a way to sustainably fund the coalition.

'Necessity's the mother of everything that's invented/'
– Talib Kweli, Hard Margin

Around this time, Wendy was introduced to Gregory Thomas who had been running an East coast three–state rap competition since 1993 called the 'Rap Olympics'. It was a place where unsigned MC's could battle for recognition, and artists, managers, sponsors, and label reps could network. Impressed by the event's potential, Wendy decided to organize one in Los Angles, and got to work promoting.

She attended a music convention in Chicago to advertise the event when her friend, rapper Rhymefest, pointed out a white boy reciting lyrics in a cipher outside the Atheneum Hotel.

Marshall had made his way to the Windy City with the hope of running into people who could help him get on. He stood outside the most exclusive hostel opposite the convention and rapped and rapped and rapped. A cipher formed and Wendy spotted him.

Wendy was initially very skeptical about a white rapper, and actually threw the tape Rhymefest handed her on the street. But after Fest insisted on playing the music she was intrigued. The lyrics, tone, beats and subject matter were unlike anything she had heard before. Not only did she invite Em to attend the first L.A. Rap Olympics in 1997, she also tried to land him a deal with Interscope Records.

Although talks with Interscope went nowhere, at least respected people in Hip Hop were now showing an interest, and Em was going to the Olympics.

At this time, following the numerous burglaries at their 7 Mile road home, Em was living with friends, while Kim lived at her mother's house with Halie. "I didn't have a job that whole summer," Em recalls. "Then we got evicted, because my friends and me were paying rent to the guy on the lease, and he screwed us over." The night before he headed to the Rap Olympics Em came home to a locked door and an eviction notice. "I had to break in," he says. "I didn't have anywhere else to go. I was so pissed. There was no heat, no water, no electricity. I slept on the floor, woke up and went to L.A."[4]

The Rap Olympics was raw Hip Hop. Competitors would be pitted against one another, each with thirty seconds to deliver witty rhymes, whilst flowing to a random beat. The crowd of several hundred instantly reacts to what's hot and what's not.

Em first participated in the team round, but his crew didn't get far. So it was up to the solo competition to really showcase his skills.

He appeared to effortlessly eat up all challengers on his way to the final. The standard was lower than Scribble Jam, and Em had been battling nearly every day for years, so he was comfortable on stage. He'd pour out complex multi–syllable rhymes like:

"I got so many ways to diss you that I'm playful with'chyou/ I'll let a razor slit you 'til they have to staple stitch you/ and everybody in this fuckin' place'll miss you/ If you try to turn my facial tissue to a racial issue."

He was on fire and in videos of the event its clear his opponents were nervous, to say the least, about going up against him.

But in the final things didn't feel right. The rapper Em faced, Overdose, was a local favorite, who had relatives organizing the event. When Em was spitting his verse, Overdose walked behind the stage living Em rhyming with nobody in front of him. He was trying to throw Em off, but it didn't work, and Em didn't choke like he had done at Scribble Jam.

Still, amid boos from the crowd, the judges gave the trophy to Em's opponent. Many thought he should have won, like Interscope rep Dean Geistlinger who recalls, Em "was so far ahead of competition it was embarrassing." (Although some criticized Em for using the same 'freestyle' punchlines he used in Scribble Jam.)

Em was crushed. He needed the first–place prize, $500, but more importantly he felt "robbed." "He really looked like he was going to cry," Paul Rosenberg remembers.

At the event Paul and Marsh did some networking and gave the Slim Shady EP to Geistlinger – though Em had been made false promises by record labels in the past so wasn't expecting anything of it. He was too busy contemplating his future. "All I kept thinking was 'what the fuck am I going to do?' Because I was going home to nothing."[3]

Although Em was feeling depressed, most people in the audience were impressed. His performance had the city talking and the following evening he was invited on 92.3 The Beat's Sway & Tech Wake Up Show; his major radio debut. Realizing that this was the opportunity of his lifetime, he went all out in his freestyle for the hosts and the nine million listeners.

"I felt like it's my time to shine. I have to rip this. At that time, I felt that it was a life or death situation."

His performance (available on YouTube) impressed the audience so much, he beat more established MC's (like Craig G, Mos Def and The Dogg Pound's Kurupt) to win the coveted '1997 Freestyle of the Year' award.

When Em and Paul returned to Detroit from the Olympics they focused on moving the newly finished Slim Shady EP. The single they released 'Just Don't Give a Fuck' was a hit at shows and Em's buzz was building. "When I walked into clubs people knew who I was."[3]

The plan was to sell the record independently, while also reaching out to larger labels for distribution and marketing support. They attended and networked at industry conferences like 'How Can I Be Down,' 'Mecca,' and 'VIBE.' Em was also one of the first artists to make the EP available to buy online, at hiphopsite.com and Sandbox Automatic. "Online sites couldn't keep it in stock. I was getting calls about shows," Em writes in his book 'The Way I Am.'[3]

That same year (1997) Em performed with the rap group 'Outsidaz,' in New York. (D12 member Bizarre had met Outsidaz member Young Zee in 1994 when Zee performed with The Fugees in Detroit, and the two built a collaborative relationship.)

The Outsidaz also brought Em with them when they opened for Wu-Tang Clan in Park Hill Housing Projects, New York. Em came out and was immediately booed by the crowd, but the sound soon turned to cheers when he opened his mouth. By now Em loved performing and was addicted to the crowd's reactions. He was getting noticed.

Following the SSEP, several underground artists approached Em to feature on their songs. He featured with Hush's group Da Ruckus on, 'We Shine' (Hush did some beats for the EP, and was Em's neighbor), MC Shabaam Sahdeeq's 'Five Star Generals,' Kid Rock's 'Devil Without a Cause,' and other songs. All of this shone the spotlight a little brighter on Em and helped him earn a spot on the January 1998 Lyricist Lounge Concert in New York, where he performed alongside Big Pun, MOP, Fat Joe, and others.

Em's hustle got him a valuable mention in the Source's influential Unsigned Hype column in March 1998 (Paul had sent the SSEP to the magazines offices). In that time he'd also been covered by other publications like Billboard, Stress and local Detroit magazines.

Underground Detroit was starting to show love, but still the team found it near impossible to get mainstream attention. "We were so big on trying to get on the radio at home but the radio did not mess with us. We did not have the support at all," remembers Dean Porter. "We were trying to make songs that may work but they still didn't play them."[15]

Detroit was also such a small location on the Hip Hop map that the team decided the best strategy would be to go back to L.A, and build a following there, which would then hopefully be picked up back home.

They went back out West in early 1998 (around three months after the Olympics) with the intention of putting the EP in every record store they came across and work back to the D.

Because of Em's growing underground buzz, the team were able to partner with Fat Beats, a distribution company that worked with independent artists (including an unsigned Jay Z in 96), to sell records on consignment in their nationwide stores. "For a totally independent artist, one without any distribution deal, getting your record in Fat Beats was the only way back then," Paul told the Village Voice.[16]

The EP was selling around 250 copies a week, an amazing feat for an independently released record. They would sell out and use the money to re-press more records, selling around 2,000 copies in total.[5]

The team hustled independently, without waiting for, or depending on, record labels, and were becoming locally successful.

There is a big difference though in being locally successful and being nationally known. In the late 90's, without the internet as it is now, artists had a lot of difficulty scaling up their local rep independently. Record Labels provided the much needed promotion and distribution support, and because of the team's local success, several labels like Rawkus, Duck Down and Fat Beats came knocking. Em was going to sign with these indie labels, but then an offer came that blew the others to smithereens.

Aftermath

Two months after Marsh and Paul gave the EP to Dean Geistlinger, it got into the hands of Jimmy Iovine, Interscope Records chairman.

Although impressed by the demo, Iovine was hesitant to sign a white rapper in the aftermath of Vanilla Ice. He had already rejected Eminem twice (when Paul Rosenberg then Wendy Day tried to represent him) and was having a hard time deciding whether to make it three. So he played the demo for Dr. Dre at one of their regular listening sessions, to get the legendary producer's opinion.

"Jimmy pops in the cassette and I was blown away," Dre told VH1. "There was a song called 'Bonnie and Clyde' that I really loved, I knew I had to work with him right then."

Em's energy, invention, cheek, lyrical acrobatics and original song topics were what attracted Dre to him. "He sounded like he had big–ass balls. He finds ways to rhyme words that don't seem like they should rhyme. I felt that."

Coincidently, shortly after first hearing the tape at Jimmy's house, Dre was driving through L.A, and Eminem came on the radio. It had been three days since Em and his team arrived in L.A. to sell the SSEP, and they made an appearance on Power 106's Friday Night Flava, (after his previous performance for Sway, few stations would turn him down). He freestyled for them over the 'Phone Tap' beat, as Dre drove through the city with a screwface.

Dre's label 'Aftermath' is a subsidiary of Interscope Records, which itself is part of the giant Universal Corporation. Like most large companies it is run by people trained in accounting, law and management. Every day they try to identify and follow trends in 'the industry.'

Now a highly technical white rapper was definitely NOT a trend they could see. The only white 'rapper' they could reference was Vanilla Ice, the joke of Hip Hop, so some advised against signing Em.

"I got a couple of questions from people around me," Dre said. "You know, he's got blue eyes, he's a white kid.'" But as an artist Dre saw beyond Em's color, and could appreciate his skill. "I don't give a fuck if you're purple: If you can kick it, I'm working with you!"

> *'It was YOU, who believed in me when everyone was tellin'/*
> *You don't sign me, everyone at the fuckin' label, let's tell the truth/*
> *You risked your career for me, I know it as well as you/*
> *Nobody wanted to fuck with the white boy'*
> *– I Need a Doctor*

Ignoring the advice of some at the label, Dre's camp called the Bass Brothers (whose number was on the SSEP cassette case), and Em had a meeting with Interscope two days later.

"Don't lie to me! Don't fucking lie to me!" Em exclaimed when Mark Bass told him who had called.

Aftermath's $400,000 advance payment offer was not the only one on the table, but Em knew without Dre's stamp of approval, which showed he had respect from the Hip Hop community, it was almost certain he would not have been accepted by Hip Hop mainstream. After Dre gave him legitimacy, then Em could take advantage of his race by appealing to suburban teens (who make up 70% of Hip Hop record sales).

"It's obvious to me that I sold double the records because I'm white," he told Rolling Stone. "In my heart I truly believe I have a talent, but at the same time I'm not stupid. I know, when I first came out especially, being produced by Dre made it cool and acceptable for white kids to like me. In the suburbs, the white kids have to see black people liking you or they won't like you. You need that foundation of legitimacy."[7]

Aftermath and Em got the paperwork signed March 9th 1998, and the next day they were in Dre's home studio.

There was no way Em could lose. This was his opportunity, which he knew would come once in a lifetime. He was not only fighting for himself and his daughter, but for Dre, who as Em said, "Basically put his credibility on the line for me. Because if I come out wack, it could destroy his career."

Em was in the gladiator mode. "I knew with Dre I had to give it everything. I had to go to tenth power when we worked together for the first time," he told Sway. "I would be ready to rhyme to any beat, writing new lyrics on the spot. There was so much to live up to. I needed to be the illest."[17]

"We came up with four joints that night and three of them made it onto his first album," remembers Dre.

They could feel something big was going to happen.

Slim Shady LP

The Slim Shady LP was cut in just two weeks of studio time. The work ethic was relentless.

"We'd give Em a cassette of the songs we'd worked on all day, he'd take it to his room that night, then come back with three or four raps and just bust 'em out," says producer Mark Bass. "The label was like, 'Don't you guys have a life?'"

This is the reason Em and Dre work so well together. They share the same work mentality in the studio – both on 'The Pursuit' (*pg.137*).

However executives at Interscope didn't all share the same mind state and were still trying to disassociate with the new white signee.

While Em was waiting for the album to be released Geffen and A&M Records were merging with Interscope and there was talk of dropping Eminem, because the album was deemed too controversial at an important time for the company. From his trailer payphone in Detroit, an anxious Em arranged a meeting with Interscope bosses where he and Dre pleaded their case and agreed to make some content changes. They got the green light.

In late 98/early 99 Em had also changed his appearance. High off ecstasy, he dyed his hair blonde and the next day went to meet Dre in the studio wearing a simple white T-shirt. "That's it' that's the look," Dre exclaimed. "This is your identify we've been looking for."[3] (See *pg.261* for more on 'the look').

When the album hit it flipped the script on Hip Hop. Till then the genre had been dominated with gangbanging, and boasting, so Em's 'Don't Give A Fuck' brutally honest self-expression combined with his sick South Park style humor were not just a different page, they were a different book written in a different language.

People could relate to his songs on a far deeper level than the 'Money Cash Hoes' gangster rappers. His lyrics about low self-esteem, mental breakdowns, killing people you hate and expressing yourself unashamedly, while giving a finger to the world, struck a chord with millions.

"I'm not alone in feeling the way I feel. I believe that a lot of people can relate to my shit – whether white, black, it doesn't matter. Everybody has been through some shit, whether it's drastic or not so drastic. Everybody gets to the point of 'I don't give a fuck.'"[18]

Millions of people bought into Em's lyrics because they either related to his honest emotional expression or they enjoyed the entertainment of the crazy world he created. Like a Hip Hop Seth McFarlen, Em sold a fun fantasy away from the normality of everyday life. He provided young people with an escape from the constant social pressure to conform.

Ice T and NWA sold similar fantasies to suburban teens, but Eminem took it to another level. Because of his technically advanced rap skills he was able to put words together like few before him could.

At the same time race played a significant part in his mainstream popularity. As Dre said when he first found out Eminem was white, "my wheels started turning. I thought he would be able to get away with saying a lot more than I would get away with saying. If a black guy said that stuff, people would turn the radio off. That's reality."

'If I was black I would have sold half/
I ain't have to graduate from Lincoln high school to know that/'
– White America

Em's technical genius (rhyming four or five more syllables in his lines than most MCs), on–point delivery, infectious voice, and over–the–top entertaining personality, meant he got respect from underground headz and mainstream audiences.

The album's first single, released January 1999, immediately took the country by storm.

A funny, explicit, introduction to Slim Shady, 'My Name Is' became the first rap song reach the top of MTV's Total Request Live (TRL), which meant teens and pre-teens devoured it.

"I had no idea 'My Name Is' would blow up. I just knew it was a catchy song," Em later said, almost in defense of the shallow song. "I didn't mean for pop success to happen, I didn't know it would catch like it did. I just put my stuff out there."[3]

Between the single and the album's release in late February 1999, the Slim Shady LP was causing major controversies. Its graphic depiction of drug use, sex, and violence as well as the most profane insults available in the English language directed towards his own mother, and songs about murdering his child's mother, horrified many for being a bad influence on children.

There were full page magazine editorials criticizing it, and politicians on TV calling for censorship. Em was described as "the most dangerous threat to children since Polio."

But all the controversy only served to increase Em's publicity around the world and make rebellious youngsters want to buy the album even more.

'Now I'm not the first king of controversy'
– Without Me

The buzz around Eminem was huge and demand for his album across the country was so great Interscope shipped more than one million copies to stores – extraordinarily rare for a first record. This all drove The Slim Shady LP to double–platinum–plus sales. It won Best Rap Album at the Grammys, and had rave reviews like, "contains some of the most memorable and demented lyrics ever recorded." The hype was backed up with substance.

By the end of 1999 Eminem's life was what he'd been fantasizing for a decade. The 'freshest voice in Hip Hop' had featured on major albums like Dr. Dre's Chronic 2001, covered almost all major music magazines, appeared on MTV so often it should have been called EMTV, and that summer was offered slots on practically every major tour, including Warped and Lyricist Lounge (where he performed alongside a young 50 Cent), often playing two or three shows a day. By the years end he had established Shady Records.

People wanted more, and in the coming decade he would sell more records than any other breathing musician.

KEY LESSON:

No Matter How Seemingly Unlikely, There is a Way
"You can do anything you set your mind to man"[22]

How It All
Got Started

Part IV
Universal
Principles

'King of the bars and I'm goin hardcores/
All my confidence comes from knowin God's laws/
— Talib Kweli, Listen!!!

No lasting success is ever achieved without living in harmony with Universal Laws. Universal laws are just like Physical laws (like gravity). They dictate the flow and balance of life.

What are some Universal Laws?

- Law of Attraction: When the mind is completely focused on something, you'll notice opportunities and people who can help bring the idea to reality.

- Law of Attention: Whatever you put your attention on will grow stronger in your life. Whatever you take your attention away from will fade away.

- The Golden Rule: Treating others as you would want to be treated. Or taking it further: treating others as they would want to be treated as unique individuals.[1] "That's the one piece of advice I would give everybody," says Kendrick Lamar.[2]

- Law of Karma: Every action generates a force of energy that returns to us in like kind.
  'What you do will come back to you' – *Dizzee Rascal, HYM*

Here are four more and how Hip Hop Greats live by them.

Who Benefits?

Sugar Hill Records was the first Hip Hop record label. In the 1970's mainstream and major labels either saw Hip Hop as a worthless fad, or didn't know it existed. It was up to this independent label to introduce the world to The Sugar Hill Gang, Kurtis Blow, Cold Crush Brothers, Furious 4, and other Hip Hop pioneers.

Sugar Hill Records should definitely be credited for playing an important role in the foundation of Hip Hop, but one of the main reasons the label quickly died was the owners violated one very simple universal principles. They did not value their people.

Wonder Mike, from the The Sugar Hill Gang, remembers: "We were waiting for our foreign royalty because we were number one or two in like 16 countries. We were waiting on a fat check, but they told us that we had been paid."

Another Sugar Hill Gang member, Master Gee, ended up as a door to door sales person a few years after selling millions of the hit single 'Rappers Delight.'[1]

Afrika Bambatta nicknamed the label co-owner Joe Robinson, 'Joe Rob-a-Nigger'.[2]

This is just another example that a negative attitude towards others can never bring success. All successful business and individuals know this.

The principle is woven into the fabric of capitalism. Though capitalism is about the pursuit of personal gain, the greatest gainers provided the most value to the greatest number of people.

We cannot win for long if we are exploiting the people around us, or the people we do business with (including customers). In the long run, if both parties aren't winning, we're both losing.

Our business will explode either from the inside, like key employees leaving (such as Dr. Dre from Ruthless Records), or from the outside as customers go elsewhere or changes are imposed on the industry.

As Napoleon Hill wrote: "Whatever your main goal in life it must benefit all it affects."

(Hill's groundbreaking book *Think and Grow Rich* is available free at HipHopTeaches.com. The book is credited as creating the most millionaires and billionaires of any in history.)

So when making decisions always ask yourself: *"Will this choice that I'm making bring long term happiness to me and those around me?"*

If the body sends a message of comfort, the answer is yes, so go ahead with that choice. If the body sends a message of discomfort, and you feel that choice brings pain to you or to those around you, then the answer is no, that's not the right choice. Simple.[3]

The Extra Mile

When Tarantino is writing a script for a movie, he literally writes a novel that he knows large pieces of will not be used. He writes it because it completes his literarily art. "It's more emotionally satisfying."[1]

Kevin Liles was promoted from the bottom to the top of Def Jam Records because he always went further than his co-workers. He spent two years as an unpaid intern constantly doing more than he was expected to. For instance he'd show up to meetings with concertina files crammed full of color coded pie charts analyzing artist's radio spins, record sales and other valuable information. Others would laugh at him, but the insights he provided the bosses made him stand out and he became indispensable.

"I was all about getting work done and asking for nothing in return...I did the stuff that nobody else wanted to do. I used to spend thousands of dollars out my own pocket on mail outs. I did whatever it took to make Def Jam a success."[2]

Kevin made it a commitment to get to the office before his boss, Lyor Cohen, every day. When Cohen stared arriving earlier and leaving later it became a friendly competition and soon trickled across the company. (Cohen started walking round empty tables in the mornings with post-it notes reading 'What makes you so good you can come in after me?')

Through example, Kevil helped turn Def Jam employees from acting like entitled prima donna's to hungry interns. The company's culture shifted. A good day was where your brain ached a little from hard work, and every decision was centered round the question, *'is it good for the logo?'*

The turnaround in performance was obvious. 50% of Def Jam was sold to Polygram in 1994 for $33 million. The other 50% was sole to Universal in 1999 for $135 million.

In the studio Dr. Dre and Kanye will use live musicians instead of samplers, just because they feel it fits the song better. They will edit songs hundreds of times, when others around them are thinking 'that's good enough.' They push hard to 'go the extra mile' from 'good' to 'Great.'

People around Jay Z frequently comment on his 'do more than is expected' approach to business. For instance he doesn't just mail important contracts in to partners; he hand delivers them.[3] He also doesn't (unlike the majority of artists) arrive late to functions and meetings. Even as far back as 1997, the photographer for Jay's first magazine cover remembers: "Jay Z was at least 20 minutes early, so he immediately gained my respect. That's a very rare thing in hip hop and always stuck out in my mind."[4]

Similarly in his rhymes Jay uses intricately clever lines that few people will understand because he wants to challenge himself. Could you identify the multiple meanings in these lines when you first heard them?

> *"Like short sleeves, I bear arms"* – Brooklyn's Finest
> *"My shit is butter, for the bread, they wanna toast me"* – Can I Live
> *"Young n****s that blast for me, no religion"* – Dear Summer
> *"I don't half-step on the 'caine"* – Hello Brooklyn
> *"Survive the drought, I wish you well"* – American Dreamin
> *"My track record speaks for itself, I'm so instrumental"* – Reminder

Developing a habit of going the extra mile, going further than expected, and doing it positively, makes you indispensable. Our compensation for work is based on the quality, quantity and attitude with which we do our work. By doing more than is expected you are promoting yourself in advance. In time the outside world will recognize and promote you. By that time you can promote yourself again, and the upward cycle continues.

One technique to 'Go the Extra Mile' is to treat your work as if you own the company, as if the company bears your name. Even if you're sweeping streets, waiting tables or working for the government, it's your company, bearing your name so the quality of your work reflects who you are.

That means you naturally arrive early, go further in the work, and do more than others expect. You do it cheerfully and positively, not necessarily expecting a direct reward. Soon enough though, the reward will find you.

Give
Before Get

'Then ask why is life worth living?/
Is it to hunt for the shit that you want?/
To receive's great, but I lust giving'
— Nas, Success

"The way to get that paper is to help somebody else get their paper,"[1] says Russell Simmons. Similarly the best way to get love is to give love, the best way to feel good is to make others feel good, the best way to achieve success is to help others achieve success.

No I.D., who mentored a teenage Kanye, is one of the longest running relevant producers in Hip Hop. He's worked closely with Common since 1990, and now has made hits for Jay Z, Big Sean, Nas, J Cole and more. A large reason for that success is because of his 'unconditional giving' mentality:

"I never felt entitled to anything. I always just gave," he told Complex Magazine. "The law of life is, you give and you receive. It didn't surprise me that I would receive. It surprised everyone that [Kanye] would give to me like that [e.g. shout out on 'Big Brother']. It's just the energy of the universe. Everything is what it is. I give to people when I don't even have a reason to give to people. I gave to him and never asked for anything… Anything I ever did was out of pure giving at the moment, never planned."[2]

(This view is opposite to the norm in society: 'Do this for me because I did this for you,' – like most 'principles of success' it usually involves doing the exact opposite to what most people are doing.)

But don't expect when you help somebody out you will directly get it back from them. You are putting the positive energy 'out there' with no selfish ego expecting something in return. Like Kanye said: "You never know how God gonna set it up for you. I helped people get whole demos and deals, and didn't get shit for me. Now look where I ended up."[3]

Kanye has lived this 'give before get' principle throughout his career, from the aspiring producer in Dion's basement asking every rapper he met to, "let me help!" (pg.25), to where he is now. Common remembers one such example when working with him in 2005: "I will be forever loyal to Kanye because I was in between labels when we started [working on the album] Be, and he produced the whole thing before he ever got a check."[4]

Before speaking with somebody you should be thinking, 'What can I do for them?' 'What value can I offer their life now?'

That mentality comes naturally to a person motivated by a higher purpose of contribution (pg.73). As Russell Simmons writes: "I want to contribute more to the earth than I take away…when you get up in the morning you should think, 'what can I give?' not 'what can I get?'"[1]

A practical example: If you want a blog or magazine to feature your work, instead of trying to take from the go, like so many others trying to get the magazine to 'check this out!' *GIVE*. Contribute something meaningful to a story, write for them, give them a free product to review, build a relationship over time, and eventually you'll get.

'Give Before Get' applies to practically all areas of life, especially in dealing with people. If you have a negative relationship with a housemate/friend/relative/business partner it may be because over time you're both only trying to 'take,' from one another. Flip it around and give. Do things for them. Start to build a positive balance in their view towards you. Give, give, give, before you try to get something.

Two additional notes:

First, for this principle to be effective you need to give wholeheartedly without the intention of *'I'm doing this for you because I want to take something from you later.'* That is manipulative and is obvious to see. Just give.

Second, and this is a point which needs further elaboration, you should practice this principle mostly with the 'right' people – people who don't live to 'leach' off of others. Continually giving to these 'takers' can lead to burnout – you're not Will Smith in '7 Pounds'. You need to prioritize 'giving' with your own goals and values and make sure the people you're giving to align. (See Adam Grant's book 'Give and Take' for more on this.)

Love
Life

In this game of life nobody knows what's going on. Our bodies are born from nothing and shrivel back into that a few decades later. Billions of years have passed before us and billions more will pass ahead of us. In the micro-cosmic moment in time we are breathing, we choose our own meaning of life.

On this journey, wherever we end up, we can either go through it seeing 'the bad,' angry and anxious, or just embrace, accept and love it.

Love is a good feeling, so it doesn't really make sense to do anything but love life. Love and appreciate the moments we are here. If you found out a loved one was going to die tomorrow, you'd love and appreciate all the time you had left with them. If your favorite food was going to stop being produced next week, you'd savor the last tastes.

A big part of loving the journey is loving all the supposedly 'bad' things we face. Loving the struggle, loving the negative, the competition, the hate. It's about the bigger picture of loving life so much that everything in life, the good and the bad, is loved the same. It's the motto Lil Wayne lives by: "Make jokes. No stress. Love. Live Life. Proceed. Progress."[1]

Love Fate

'If the game shakes me or breaks me/
I hope it makes me a better man/'
– Notorious BIG, Sky's the Limit

One of the books Jay Z lives by, The Celestine Prophecy, teaches that every event has significance and contains a message that relates to our purpose. This especially applies to what many see as negative experiences. The challenge is to find that silver lining amidst 'the bad'.

"The ghetto, the projects, is a real tough area to grow up in. A lot of learning experiences shape you as a person," Jay said in 1997. "You become a strong man if you can make it out of there. You can do anything."[2]

This is something most Greats have in common. They interpret all personal experiences as positive driving forces towards their goals.

In the word of Tupac Shakur, "I believe god put us whether we're meant to be at. Then it makes sense to put us in the ghetto. He wants us to work hard to get out, he's testing us even more."

Or as Common said in a lecture: "As you live your path, know you will experience challenges and disappointments. Challenges economically, spiritually, physically. These challenges are there for you to grow, to become a better human being. You turn obstacles into possible, so anything comes your way that you may not want, you have to see positive in it. There's something in there that you can get out of it that's gonna be good for your growth, your evolution to become a better person."[3]

Common experienced this first hand when his best friend and cousin 'AJ' died in a motorcycle accident. Common was distraught, but at the funeral seeing images of AJ's adventures made him understand the positive lesson for himself – to experience life to the fullest and not just focus on work.

Accept whatever situation you find yourself in. Whatever's happened to you, whoever's done whatever to you, know that it will be transferred into something Great for your future, if you choose to.

'It was clear why the struggle was so painful/
Metamorphosis this is what I change too/
And god I'm so thankful/ '
– Nas, Smoking

J Cole felt this when he was working near the poverty line in between graduating from college and signing with ROC Nation. "I always felt it was coming, even though I made no major moves. I always felt it was right around the corner…always had belief, that's why I kept going…even working menial jobs, you don't mind it because its temporary to you, you know what's coming, and will have this life experience that will be invaluable to you. It's a temporary sacrifice.

"Every day I thought, 'Today I'm closer than I was yesterday.' Certain things happen in life you have no control over, but life is about how you react and handle those things. I absolutely believe that you choose what you wanna be, where you wanna go and it's up to you to get there."[4]

(J Cole's song 'Love Yourz' is a great illustration of this principle.)

Kid Cudi reflected on his career beginnings after leaving Good Music in 2014: "I think about going to work [at a clothes shop] a lot, clocking in. I think about going on my lunch break, not being able to eat lunch because I didn't have no money, bumming cigarettes from people walking by me on the street. I think about sleeping on people's couches and not being bummed out about it because I knew I was on a quest and I knew God was testing me. I didn't mind it at all."[5]

This same way of thinking is what unites every long term successful person in any industry. Everything – the good, the bad, the ugly – serves a purpose to get you where you're going. Whatever happens to them they embrace and find a positive in it. No matter how seemingly bad something is, they find something to love or learn from it. Sure they may react emotionally to hard circumstances like most people, but they take control of their mind and think 'How can I turn this to an advantage?'

'Sometimes I want to drop a temper but no emotion from a king/ '
– Lil Wayne, Hustla Musik

Like Kanye said of Dr. Dre in Rolling Stone Magazine: "Dre feels like God placed him here to make music, and no matter what forces are aligned against him, he always ends up on the mountaintop."[6]

Kane himself has always lived this principle. Even back in 2002 he said:

"I feel like everything that anybody ever said in life would be a disadvantage to me, I'mma make it my advantage…I'mma use everything that people say I can't do and flip it to positive.

"I look at everything as glass half full. I don't hold grudges, like one of my best friends made a song dissing me and I looked at all the positives in the situation – I got my name out a bit more, he said sorry…

"10% of life is what happens to you, 90% is how you react."[7]

'I'm a champion, so I turned tragedy to triumph'
– Kanye, Through the Wire

Sure Marshall Mathers was bitter, even depressed when he'd be regularly beaten up as a teenager, but upon reflection without that he wouldn't be where he is today.

"I should be grateful. If I hadn't gotten the shit kicked out of me, I might never have started snapping [witty comebacks], then might never have started rapping. I'd probably still be in Gilberts Lodge, 5.50 an hour."[8]

'Cause I can't explain to y'all how dang exhausted my legs felt/
Just having to balance my dang self/
When on eggshells I was made to walk/
But thank you, ma, 'cause that gave me the/
Strength to cause Shady-mania/'
– Eminem, Guts Over Fear

Rapper Hopsin was signed to Ruthless Records (run by Eazy E's wife), and was put on the shelf waiting to release an album for three and a half years. During that time he received no finances, promotion or touring support from the label. He was just a product forgotten in storage. Hop could have been consumed by negativity, but instead chose to find the positive. It forced him to set up independently and now he's one of the most successful indie artists in music.

'When the storm comes then how should we address it?/
My situation with Ruthless turned out to be a blessing/
During the time it left every ounce of me affected/
But when it was done I swore I was bound to be a ledged/'
– Hopsin, Caught In The Rain.

When Sean Combs was fired from his VP A&R job at Uptown Records he was distraught and desperate – his dream job was gone, he had a baby on the way and bills he couldn't afford. "I'm 22 and I'm crying for days and days and days because I knew I disappointed [my boss] Andre and my mother." But he extracted the positive lesson. "It made me a better person. I needed something dramatic and drastic to change me."[9]

In 2005 Noah '40' Shebib (best known for producing most of Drake's music), was diagnosed with MS – a nervous system disabling disease. How did it affect his goals?

"I've got this disease I'm gonna live with it and I'm gonna win with it, and my story's gonna be that much better when I get there."[10]

Finally, artists more than any other group of people have to 'love fate' as often the 'realest' most-ground-breaking art comes from intense pain and struggle. Like Eminem admitted: "My worst fear is that if there's not drama and negativity in my life I won't be able to write, and all my songs will be really wack and boring."

Or Like Kanye told Fader Magazine at the time of '808s & Heartbreak': "I appreciate the bad, I appreciate when bad things happen. This album is very personal, and I just think that if I hadn't been through the terrible things that I've been through – that I was the victim or the cause of – that I couldn't deliver art on this level, and that's the good out of it."

(But of course pain and suffering – the 'tortured artist' stereotype – is not essential to create great art. They key is being able to creatively express emotion, but that's another chapter.)

Once more:

"Make jokes. No stress. Love. Live Life. Proceed. Progress."

Outro

A space for your thoughts and ideas on what you've just read.

How This All Got Started

It all started with a dream.

Well, maybe it did – a dream I have long since forgotten. It actually all started by accident.

A longtime Hip Hop fan, I was inspired by talks and stories on the history of the culture and started to write a book looking at the legacy and impact of Hip Hop. It was going to be as beautiful as Jay Z's 'Decoded,' as educational as KRS-One's 'The Gospel of Hip Hop,' and as entertaining as a browse through Complex magazine – lofty dreams I realize. It would include chapters like the origins of Hip Hop – how its roots go back thousands of years to Arab traditions, what Hip Hop today is like in cultures around the world, the evolution of MC's and DJ's, a hall of fame, a Hip Hop family tree, and one chapter looking at the 'success principles' that can be learned from the lives of Hip Hop icons.

The problem was the success chapter kept growing and growing. It got divided into sub-chapters, yet still kept on expanding. Eventually it dwarfed the other chapters and the idea to create an entire book around the concept seemed natural.

So why Hip Hop? Why has an Irish-Egyptian living in England spent countless hours writing about life lessons learned from Hip Hop icons?

As described in 'The Re-Finding' *(pg.58)* and 'Do You' *(pg.272)* I have just combined my two deepest interests: Entrepreneurship and Hip Hop.

Entrepreneurship – living a life around your interests, being the boss of yourself – seems to me to be the only rational way to spend the precious time we have on this earth. It's not easy, but we're lucky to live in an age with more access to resources than ever before. We, the 'common man/woman,' have more power than at any time in history to live a life based on what we love. And that's one of Hip Hop's core lessons. It's why Kanye's 'The College Dropout' (for better or worse) played a role in my decision to leave college after two semesters. All my time was devoted to I was working 10-12 hour days on my own projects and can remember attending two lectures the entire second semester.

Since leaving I have 'hacked' *(pg.63)* in a number of ventures, in industries from art to home appliances. I've created some value, and admittedly caused some embarrassing damage. I've tried to take lessons from every venture into each successive project, and this book represents many of the lessons learned. Lessons, or principles, are presented through the mouths of Hip Hop icons, largely because through all the projects I've been involved in, Hip Hop provided the soundtrack, and some of the motivation.

For me, and no doubt for others born with no silver spoon, the stories of Jay Z, Kanye, Eminem, Kendrick, Diddy, 50 Cent etc., are inspiring. Building something so deeply impactful out of nothing and living the 'Scarface' life (meaning living the life you want) legitimately (and ethically) is, to me, admirable, and I wanted to emulate some of the character traits of the Hip Hop icons – Kanye's passion, Nas's humility, Dr. Dre's work ethic for example.

Another reason for writing this book was being sick of the meaningless, uninspiring 'Hip Hop' that permeates culture and the airwaves. It is that which has given Hip Hop its ignorant reputation, yet for so many people it's the exact opposite.

So I set out wanting to create an inspirational but practical, educational but entertaining, book that I could personally re-read several times without losing interest. Something fun, which would also help me solve problems and develop as a person – while demonstrating to others just how much universal wisdom can be gleamed from Hip Hop

It began with organizing and fitting together different possible chapters and topic ideas, a literal jigsaw puzzle. Eventually after numerous hours of research came two dozen of the most practical and interesting lessons learned from the Hip Hop Greats.

I strongly believe that the information here, if practiced, has the power to greatly improve your, mine, anybody's, life. There's the practical information – like how to work out the creative muscle, or tools to maintain focus – as well as the motivating emotions I hope come to you from the stories told, like the awe inspiring work routines in 'The Pursuit'.

I personally will struggle to apply most of the principles discussed here. It's hard. But I do know that the people you've just read about are no different from you or me – that is to say they started out no different to you or me. So maybe someone will write an updated version of this book some years from now – perhaps unrelated to Hip Hop – and your name will grace its pages.

This book will have done its job if the advice, stories and examples of what Greats before you have done become just one stepping stone on your life's journey.

Take as you want. Live well. Make it happen. *The World Is Yours*.

Ramsey "Ramses M" Mullaney
HipHopTeaches.com

Appendix

Acknowledgments

This book would not exist without the work of several Greats.

Firstly the artists and entrepreneurs mentioned most throughout:
Jay Z, Kanye West, Kendrick Lamar, Nas, Sean Combs, Pharrell, KRS-One, No I.D, Common, Russell Simmons, Eminem, Drake, J Cole, 50 Cent, Talib Kweli, The RZA.

Several authors have also greatly influenced this book:
Stephen Covey, author of 'The 7 Habits of Highly Effective People' – one of the best 'personal transformation' books ever written.
Robert Greene, author of 'Mastery,' '48 Laws of Power' and 'The 50th Law,' particularly influenced chapters 'The Re-Finding' and 'The Enemy'.
James Altucher, a great blogger and author of 'Choose Yourself!' influenced chapters on 'Balance,' 'Creativity,' Do You' and more.
Seth Godin, a leading figure in 21century marketing, influenced several chapters including 'Break In' and 'Do You'. He has many great books, 'The Dip' is a good start, and a thought-provoking blog: sethgodin.typepad.com
Jay Z, his excellently produced book 'Decoded' tells the story of Jay and Hip Hop from the 80's to today, and has been useful throughout my research.
Napoleon Hill, author of 'Think and Grow Rich,' – the book that's responsible for creating more millionaires and billionaires than any in history.

Suggestions from friends have also greatly improved this book, namely:
Mike Green, Joshua Preston, Brian Kaufman, Nancy C.

Also huge thanks to **Leslie K** (smdesign.webnode.hu) for doing a great job on the cover design.

Finally, a special dedication to **Nehad Kamel** who provided many of the resources needed to get this book up and running.

The Source(s)

INTRO

1. Statistics from: Huffington Post article, 'The American Myth of Social Mobility' by Howard Friedman, 07/2012
2. Quote from NY Times article, 'Invisible Child' by Andrea Elliott, 12/09/2013
3. Referencing NY Times article, 'For Poor, Leap to College Often Ends in a Hard Fall' by Jason DeParle, 12/2012
   Note: Jean Paul's real name has been changed.
4. Quote from Robin Wright, author of 'Rock the Casbah,' interview with PBS News Hour, 07/2011
5. 'Raptavist' term coined by Aisha Fukushima
6. Davey D, hiphopandpolitics.com, 'Cuban hip-hop used to overthrow government,' 12/2014
7. Ben Horowitz interview with allthingsd.com, 07/2012
8. Ben Horowitz quote, 'The Legend of the Blind MC,' bhorowitz.com, 03/2014
9. Quote from Men's Health article, 'Not a Businessman--a Business, Man,' by Anthony Decurtis, 10/2010
10. 'Entrepreneurial Generation,' statistics by Kauffman.org, 11/2011
11. Mark Anderson quote, 'Ben and Mark explain practically everything' podcast, a16z.com, 08/14
12. Ben Horowitz quote, NY Times article 'Using Rap to Teach Pithy Lessons in Business,' by Claire Miller, 02/2012
13. Term coined by Abi Noda, article 'Why I listen to rap,' from abinoda.com
14. Urban Hustler quote from urbanmecca.net article, 'Twenty Million Young Americans Representing the New Definition of "Urban Hustler"' by Nolan Wilder, 06/2007
15. Hip Hop education organizations quote from stern.nyu.edu 'How Hip-Hop Education Programs Attain Legitimacy,' thesis by Yuxi Liu, 06/2013
16. businessweek.com article, 'The CEO of Hip-Hop,' by Susan Berfield, 10/2003
17. Quote from the book 'Hip Hop Inc,' by Richard Oliver and Tim Leffel, 03/2006
18. KRS–One '40 Years of Hip Hop' lecture, 2013
19. Quote from the book, 'Decoded,' by Sean 'Jay Z' Carter, 11/2010
20. Steve Stoute quote from Harvard Business Review, 'The Tanning of America,' 10/2011
21. Eminem, The Source magazine interview, 2001
22. Inspired by Duane Lawton's blog, bookothov.com
23. Common, University South Florida Lecture on Greatness, 2011

The Story of: KANYE WEST

1. Donda West's book, 'Raising Kanye: Life Lessons from the Mother of a Hip-Hop Superstar,' 05/2007
2. BBC Radio 1 Zane Lowe interview, 09/2013
3. Sabotage Times 'Breakdancing In China, Self Esteem Issues & The KKK,' interview by Chris Campion, 2004
4. Details magazine interview, 'The Unraveling of Kanye West,' 02/2009
5. The Fader '20,000 word' interview, 2008
6. Fox News 'Kanye West Knows Good' article, 08/2004
7. Men's Health 'Take it from Me Kanye West' article, 2008
8. VH1 'Driven' documentary, 2005
9. Billboard Magazine 'Kanye West's 'The College Dropout' an Oral History,' 02/2013
10. 'Watch The Throne' tour shout out
11. Complex Magazine, 'The Making of Kanye West's 'The College Dropout',' 02/2014
12. Rolling Stone quote from 'Dr. Dre, 100 Greatest Artists of All Time' feature.
13. MTV 'You Hear First' Interview, 2002
14. TheMostAccess.com No I.D. interview, 09/2007
15. Irish Times interview, 11/2004
16. Robocop Music Video Set interview, 2008
17. 'Kanye West in the Studio: Beats Down! Money Up!', 2006
18. RedefineHipHop Grav Interview, 03/2012
19. Noah Callahan–Bever interview from Complex, 2002
20. Common 'One Day It'll Make Sense', book 2011
21. D–Dotomen.com, Kanye 1996 performance, 01/2012
22. Donnie Kwak interview, from Complex Magazine, 2003
23. No I.D. Complex interview, 02/2012
24. Thomas Golianopoulos interview for The Source (posted by Complex Mag), 11/2003
25. Kanye Santa Monica High School Show speech, 12/2005
26. D–Dot, XXL mag interview, 06/2011
27. Craig Bauer, 'Recording & Mixing Kanye West' Sound on Sound interview, 02/2006
28. D–Dot Hot 97, Juan Epstein interview, 06/2013
29. Kanye West, 'Thank you & Welcome' book, 2008
30. Fake Shore Drive interview Mickey Halsted, 05/2008
31. Shade 45, Whoolywood Shuffle Just Blaze interview, 09/2013
32. 'DJ Lazy K Presents – Kanye West' Mixtape, 2009
33. Jo Whiley BBC Radio 1 interview, 09/2009
34. Kanye, radioplanet.tv interview, 2002
35. MTV 'You Hear First' interview on tattoos, 2002
36. 'The Art of 16 Bars' documentary, 2005

37. Complex 'Combat Jack Presents: True Stories Behind 25 Rap Classics, 09/2009
38. MTV, Kanye West, Kanplicated interview, 2004
39. MTV 'Kanye West: Greatness, Perfection, Gucci', 10/2005
40. New York Times, 'Kanye West Behind the Mask,' interview 06/2013
41. Vlad TV interview with Talib Kweli, 06/2013
42. Devo Springsteen interview with The Phat Startup, 04/2014
43. HardknockTV, Talib Kweli and HiTech interview, 2012
44. Just Blaze HOT 97 interview, 08/2013
45. RapGenius.com, Last Call annotations
46. Song 'Last Call,' from The College Dropout, 2004
47. DJ Whoo Kid Thisis50 interview with Young Jack Thriller, 01/2012
48. Quote from Live Wire Yahoo! Music interview 04/2004
49. MTV Road To The Grammys: The Making Of Kanye West's College Dropout, 02/2005
50. MTV, J Cole SOB's interview, 03/2011
51. Common, University South Florida Lecture on Greatness, 2011

PART I: FOUNDATIONS

THE RE-FINDING

1.   Jay Z interview with Forbes, September 2010
2.   Book, 'The Top Five Regrets of the Dying,' by Bronnie Ware (03/19/2012)
3.   Common, USF lecture, 2011
4.   Kanye quote on Dr. Dre from Rolling Stone, 100 Greatest Artists of All Time.
5.   Dr. Dre, Ice T 'Art of Rap' interview, 2012
6.   Dr. Dre Esquire 'What I Learned,' interview, 12/2013
7.   Benjamin Bloom research from 99u.com, Cal Newport talk
8.   Pharrell quote from Kidult Youth Leadership Conference, 07/2010
9.   Kevin Liles, 'Make It Happen' book, 2007
10. Kanye, VOYR Watch The Throne, 12/2011
11. Inspired by ideas from Robert Greene's book 'Mastery,' 11/2012
12. Jay Z, BBC interview with Andrew Marr, 09/2009
13. Quote from the book, 'Decoded,' by Sean 'Jay Z' Carter, 11/2010
14. Jamesaltucher.com blog

THE WHY

1.   Pharrell interview with Tim Westwood, BBC Radio 1, 2011
2.   KRS–One '40 Years of Hip Hop' lecture, 2013
3.   Kanye quote, Zane Lowe, BBC Radio 1 interview, 09/2013
4.   Rick Ross quote, Rolling Stone magazine, 'Ask A Boss,' segment, 05/2014
5.   Soulja Boy, Real Talk NY interview, 2008
6.   Russell Simmons quote from HOT 97 interview, March 2014
7.   Jimmy Iovine quote, Esquire magazine 'What I've Learned,' interview, December 2013
8.   No I.D. interview with Complex Magazine, February 2012
9.   Quote from book 'The World's Religions,' by Huston Smith
10. Quote from the book, 'Decoded,' by Sean 'Jay Z' Carter, 11/2010
11. Sean Combs quote from CNBC 'The Big Idea,' interview, 04/2008
12. Talib Kweli, Thisis50 interview, April 2009
13. Dr. Dre quote, Esquire magazine, 'What I Learned,' interview, 12/2013
14. Quotes from Men's Health magazine, 'Not a Businessman--a Business,' article by Anthony Decurtis, 10/2010
15. Russell Simmons quote from, 'Do You!: 12 Laws to Access the Power in You to Achieve Happiness and Success,' 04/2008
16. Common, 'One Day It'll All Make Sense', 2011
17. Kendrick Lamar, Hollywood Reporter interview, January 2014
18. Pharrell quote, 'Inspiration and motivation from Pharrell Williams (Get Your Focus up!),' video by Heru Duenas

THE ENEMY:

1.   Will Smith, Charlie Rose interview, 03/2002
2.   50 Cent '50th Law,' BBC interview, 02/2011
3.   Inspired by Seth Godin lecture on Fear.
4.   Kendrick Lamar, Guardian newspaper interview, 12/2012
5.   Jon Brion quote, USA Today, 08/2005
6.   Dame Dash quote, Complex 'Making of College Dropout' 02/2014
7.   Steve Stoute, SXSW interview with Nas 03/2012
8.   Drake interview with Rolling Stone, 02/2014
9.   Dame Dash, Combat Jack Show, 04/2013
10. Kanye quote, Minnesota Radio Station, 11/2010
11. NY income stats from loopnet.com and bber.unm.edu
12. Quotes from book, 'The 50th Law,' by Robert Greene and 50 Cent, 2009
13. London Real interview with Robert Greene, 12/2012

14. Kanye 'Take It From Me' interview for Men's Health Magazine, 2008
15. Dr. Dre quote, interview with STREETFUNKTV, 1999
16. Quote from the book, 'Decoded,' by Sean 'Jay Z' Carter, 11/2010
17. Inspired by Fast Company article, 'The ultimate motivator: adding your own death to your calendar', 11/2014
18. Jimmy Iovine quote, Esquire magazine 'What I've Learned,' interview, 12/2013
    + Credit to Seth Godin lectures and teachings on 'Fear' for partly inspiring this chapter.

THE CORE

1. Sean Combs, BET 'Black and White' interview, 10/2006
2. Kanye West, VOYR 'Watch The Throne' tour documentary, 12/2011
3. Jon Brion quote from Rolling Stone, West World, 02/2006
4. Common, 'One Day It'll All Make Sense', book, 2011
5. Dead Prez, The VillageVoice.com, 06/2013
6. Kanye 'Thank You and You're Welcome' book, 2008
7. Kanye quote, Zane Lowe, BBC Radio 1 interview, 09/2013
8. Talib Kweli, HardknockTV inteview, 05/2012
9. Will Smith, Charlie Rose interview, 03/2002
10. 'Jay Z and the Roc–A–Fella Records Dynasty,' book, 2005
11. Jay Z, Charlie Rose interview, 2010
12. Talib Kweli, DJ Vlad interview, 2010
13. 'How Hip Hop Changed the World' documentary with Idris Elba, 2011
14. MTV, 'Greatness, Perfection, Gucci,' 10/2005
15. Donda West, 'Raising Kanye' book, 2007
16. Fox News Article, 'Kanye West Knows Good', 08/2004
17. Michael Johnson, 'Gold Rush' book, 2012
18. Kanye West Guardian interview, 'The Cockiest Man in Rap', 08/2005
19. 'Kanye West Flippin Out' video on Youtube, by Theo Huxtable
20. Quote from the book, 'Decoded,' by Sean 'Jay Z' Carter, 11/2010
21. Jay Z, Juan Epstein Hot97 Interview, 2010
22. Punch interview with Homegrown Radio, 09/2013
23. KRS-One quote from book, 'The Big Payback' by Dan Chanras, 2011
24. J Cole, Complex 'In The Zone', 11/2011
25. Drake interview with Rolling Stone, 02/2014
26. Rick Ross, HOT 97 interview, 2010
27. Kendrick Lamar Google Play 'Life & Rhymes' interview, 10/2012
28. Crown Principle, adapted from '48 Laws of Power' by Robert Greene, 1998
29. Russell Simmons quote from, 'Do You!: 12 Laws to Access the Power in You to Achieve Happiness and Success,' 04/2008
30. Sean Combs quote from CNBC 'The Big Idea,' interview, 04/2008
31. Pharrell, Fast Company interview, 11/2013

The Story of: KENDRICK LAMAR

1. Complex, The Making of Good Kid Maad City interview, 10/2012
2. LA Weekly 'Born and raised…' interview, 01/2011
3. 'Railroad Hip Hop' interview, 10/2010
4. Spin 'Kendrick Lamar Not Your Average…' interview, 10/2012
5. Statistic from city–data.com
6. HipHopDX.com 'The West Coast Got Somethin' To Say', 01/2011
7. Google Play Hangout/interview 03/2013
8. Guardian 'the rise of a good kid rapper in a mad city' interview, 12/2012
9. Cam Capone News interview, 02/2014.
10. The Hollywood Reporter interview 01/2014
11. TDK Interview, 09/2011
12. Vibe magazine Top Dawg interview, 08/2013
13. Wild 94.9 interview 05/2012
14. NPR 'A New Hip–Hop Recipe' interview, 05/2012
15. Rap Rader TDE Punch interview, 06/2013
16. GGN News interview S.2 Ep.2, 08/2011
17. Nardwuar interview, 03/2012
18. Image from Beats by Dre commercial 12/2013
19. 'Kendrick Lamar Breaks Tradition' article by Antenna Magazine, 01/2012
20. Kendrick Lamar Goggle Play 'Life & Rhymes' interview, 10/2012

PART II: BUILDING

THE BLUEPRINTS

1. NPR, 'The Wu-Tang Clan's 20–Year Plan' article, 04/2013
2. '48 Laws of Power' reference.
3. Punch on Homegrown radio, 09/2013

4. Kanye quote, Rap City interview, 01/2004
5. Kanye quote, BET interview, 2004
6. DJ Hi Tech, Hardknock TV, 05/2012
7. Quote from the book, 'Decoded,' by Sean 'Jay Z' Carter, 11/2010
8. Inspired by 'Gold Rush,' by Michael Johnson, and '48 Laws of Power' by Robert Greene.
9. J Cole, ABC News interview, 09/2009
10. Kevin Liles, 'Make It Happen,' book, 2005
11. Tarantino, 'Hollywood Reporter Directors' interview, 2012
12. Donda West, 'Raising Kanye,' book, 2007
13. 50 Cent, AOL interview, from daveyd.com, 2002
14. 50 Cent, 'From Pieces to Weight,' 2005
15. Referencing, Harvard Business Review article, 'How to spend the first 10 minutes of your day,' 06/2014
16. Statistic from Forbes article '5 reasons 8 out of 10 businesses fail,' 09/2013
17. ABC News article 'Jay-Z Protege J. Cole Takes Unusual Path to Stardom,' 09/2009
18. Common, USF Lecture, 2011
19. Jamie Foxx Comic-Con 2012 article from hollywod.com, 07/2012
    + Credit to make–me–successful.com for inspiring an idea.

THE HUNGER

1. Tupac quote from tupac-thuglife.tripod.com
2. NPR, 'The Wu-Tang Clan's 20–Year Plan' article, 04/2013
3. Dame Dash, 60 Minutes interview, 2002
4. Dame Dash, my philosophy interview, 12/2013
5. New York Magazine article 'Why Damon Dash Hates Mondays,' 06/2006
6. Dame Dash, Black Electorate interview, 11/2002
7. Irv Gotti, Reasonable Doubt Documentary, 2008
8. 50 Cent, CNBC interview, 2009
9. 50 Cent Forbes interview, 'The 50 Cent Machine' 08/2008
10. Eminem Miami Times interview, 03/1999
11. Dr. Dre Dr. Dre Esquire 'what I learned,' interview, 12/2013
12. Kanye, The Fader interview, 2008
13. Kim Kardashian interview with BBC Radio 1, 09/2014
14. Lil Wayne The Carter Documentary, 2009
15. Pharrell, Rest in Beats, You Can Do It Too, 06/2009

THE PURSUIT

1. Ben Affleck, Hollywood Reporter, Directors Roundtable, 2012
2. Pharrell interview with Tim Westwood, BBC Radio 1, 2011
3. Eminem, 'The Way I am' book, 2008
4. Rick Rubin quote from BBC Radio 1 interview with Zane Lowe, 06/2014
5. Quote from the book, 'Decoded,' by Sean 'Jay Z' Carter, 11/2010
6. Will Smith, CBC 60 Minutes, 11/2007
7. Kanye, The Fader interview, 2008
8. 'Rick Ross – Words of Wisdom (How to be a boss)' video by mycomeup.com, 11/2012
9. Vibe magazine, 'The Original Hit Man', 08/2008
10. Michael Jordan, Richard Lawson interview, 1994
11. Dr. Dre, Rhythm and Rhyme documentary, 1997
12. Complex, Making of Good Kid Maad City, 10/2012
13. Mannie Fresh, Soul Culture TV, 08/2012
14. The Carter Documentary, 2009
15. Damon Ranger, Chicago CBS, 02/2013
16. Rick Rubin quote from Rolling Stone interview, 02/2014
17. No I.D, quote from Complex interview, 02/2012
18. Inspired by journalist Hannah Prevett's writings

THE HUSTLE

1. Line inspired by Hopsin song, 'What's My Purpose?'
2. In part influenced by therisetothetop.com 'What is Hustle…' article
3. Sean Combs quote from CNBC 'The Big Idea,' interview, 04/2008
4. Quote from the book 'Hip Hop Inc,' by Richard Oliver and Tim Leffel, 03/2006
5. Dan Charnas's book 'The Big Payback: The History of the Business of Hip-Hop,' 12/2010
6. Get Well Soon Mixtape, 2003
7. Billboard 'The College Dropout: An Oral History,' 01/2014
8. Kanye The Source interview 2003, republished by Complex, 02/2014
9. Dame Dash, My Philosophy interview, 12/2013
10. Quote from the book, 'Decoded,' by Sean 'Jay Z' Carter, 11/2010
11. Documentary on New York Blackout of 1977, JanicesSonHarpo, Youtube, 06/2013
12. Wikipedia article on 'New York City Blackout of 1977'

13. Malcolm Gladwell's 'Outliers: The Story of Success,' 06/2011
14. Business Insider article, '10 things you didn't know about Bill Gates,' 04/2011
15. 50 Cent, From Pieces to Weight, 2005
16. Lisa Fager 'Industry Ears' at Hip Hop Entrepreneurship Summit, Kansas City, December 2008, (credit to pyramidwest.tv)
17. Chamillionaire SXSW, 04/2011
18. Jay Z, Oprah interview, discussing 'The Seat of the Soul,' 2009

THE GUARANTEE

1. Pharrell quote, from video documentary, 'How To Become Successful by Pharrell Williams,' by amirrahman15, 09/2013
2. Positive Mental Attitude from Napoleon Hill's 'Think & Grow Rich,' 1937
3. RZA quote, from Westfest TV interview, 10/2012
4. Kanye, Rolling Stone 11/2007
5. Jeff Bhasker interview with WhiteLies 'The Secrets of Working with Kanye West' 03/2013
6. J Cole, Interview Magazine, 'Tales Out of School' 01/2013
7. Seth Godin blog post, 'But what if I fail?' 01/2014

THE HEADLIGHTS

1. KRS–One '40 Years of Hip Hop' lecture, 2013
2. Kanye quote from Complex "Honorary Degree", February 2014
3. Story from Jay Z, Charlie Rose interview, 2010
4. Quotes from Audra McDonals and Sanaa Lathan, found in book 'Hip Hop Inc,' by Richard Oliver and Tim Leffel, 03/2006
5. Diddy quote, from mycomeup.com
6. Diddy BET 'Black and White' interview, 2006
7. Pusha T, Fuse GOOD Music interview, 09 /2012
8. Sway in the Morning, Shade 45, Chris Rock interview, 08/2012
9. RZA, Red bull Music Academy, 05/2012
10. Stephen Covey book, '7 Habits of Highly Effective People,' 1989
11. Entrepreneur Magazine articles on productivity inspired
12. Study, 'Ego depletion and the strength model of self-control,' ncbi.nlm.nih.gov
13. Chain Game inspired by James Clear 'seinfeld Strategy' article on Quora.com
14. Quote by Albert E. N. Gray, found in book '7 Habits of Highly Effective People.'
15. Complex Magazine, Combat Jack stories, 09/2010
16. Kanye Crunch Time quote, from The Fader interview, 2008
17. Quote from the book, 'Decoded,' by Sean 'Jay Z' Carter, 11/2010
18. Drake quote from make-me-successful.com, 04/2012
19. Russell Simmons Hot 97 Interview 03/2014
20. Russell Simmons book Success Through Stillness, 2014
21. 50 Cent Katie Couric interview, 01/2013
22. Kendrick Lamar Grammy video interview 10/2013
23. RZA, Shamthda Sun interview, 03/2010
24. Kanye, 'Ellen' interview, 2010
25. James Altucher article 'Naked girls, astral projection, and achieving Nirvana in 60 seconds or less'.
26. Pharrell, Red Bull Magazine interview, 2014
27. Common, Sway in the morning interview, 08/2012
28. Russell Simmons book 'Life and Def: Sex, Drugs, Money, + God' 09/2002
29. Dame Dash, NYmag interview, 2006
30. Quote found in 'Hip Hop Inc,' by Richard Oliver and Tim Leffel, 03/2006
31. Kanye 'Trillion dollar company' quote from BBC interview, 09/2013
32. Cyhi The Prynce, 247HH Interview, 06/2013
33. Russell Simmons, BusinessWeek article, 'the ceo of hip hop' 10/2003
34. Rick Rubin interview with, Men's Journal magazine, 11/2011

THE INFINITE SEMESTER

1. Kanye, Guardian interview 'Natural born show-off,' 08/2005
2. Coodie Simmons video footage, 2003
3. Kanye, The Source interview 2003, republished by Complex, 02/2014
4. Slim, Hip Hop Wired, 06/2010
5. Kevin Liles, Make It Happen, book, 2005
6. J Cole, ABC News, 09/2009
7. McKinley Lee autobiography, 'Chosen by Fate: My Life inside Death Row Records.'
8. Sean Combs quote from CNBC 'The Big Idea,' interview, 04/2008
9. Hopsin quote from, indiehiphop.net
10. Angel Haze interview with Hip Hop DX, 09/2012
11. 'The Carter Documentary,' 2009
12. Hip Hop N More Interview With Mr. Porter, 04/2012
13. Dre, Rhythm and Rhyme Documentary, 1997
14. Rick Rubin interview with Rolling Stone Magazine, 02/2014

15. Zack O'Malley Greenburg 'Empire State of Mind…', 2012
16. Jay Z quote from Men's Health Magazine article, 'Not a Businessman--a Business, Man,' 10/2010

THE PEOPLE
LA FAMILIA
1. KRS–One '40 Years of Hip Hop' lecture, 2013
2. 50 Cent, Cocaine City TV Interview, 06/2008
3. Chance the Rapper interview, Chicago reader, 04/2014
4. Dr. Dre, LA Times, 10/1999
5. Dr. Dre interview from scratch magazine, 2002
6. Sway in the Morning with Chris Rock, 08/2012
7. Kanye West Paris Concert February 2013
8. Jay Z, XXL 'I'll Still Kill' Interview, 10/2007
9. Common, One Day It'll All Make Sense, 2011
10. London Real Eric Thomas episode, 05/2013
+ Dave Free quote, Superstar Magazine, 12/2012
CIRCLE OF SUCCESS
11. Inspired by Napoleon Hill, Think and Grow Rich, 1937
12. Pharrell, Fast Company interview, 11/2013
13. Hollywood Reporter 'J Cole premieres debut album' article, 08/2011
14. Billboard magazine, Origins of College Dropout, 01/2014
15. Kanye, The Source interview 2003, republished by Complex, 02/2014
16. Jeff Bhasker, WhiteLies Magazine, 03/2013
17. No I.D., Complex interview, 02/2012
18. FUSE TV, GOOD Music interview, 09/2012
19. Lenny S, PMP Worldwide interview
20. Dame, Vibe magazine, My Philosophy interview, 12/2013
MENTORS
21. 50 Cent, Power 99 Radio, 11/2009
22. 50 Cent AOL Music interview, 2002
23. Eminem , The Way I Am, book, 2008
24. Grav, FifthElementOnline, 03/2012
25. Kanye, Semtex interview, 2008
26. Kanye blog post responding to Entertainment Weekly's 'Album of the Decade' award, 12/2009
27. Kanye, Marc Jacobs, Details Magazine, 02/2009
28. Napoleon Hill, 'Think and Grow Rich,' 1937
29. Kendrick, US Rap News, 11/2012
CONNECTIONS
30. Biggie unreleased interview posted at rappingmanual.com
31. Big Sean, Vlad TV, 05/2011
SI
32. Combat Jack Story 'Can't Knock The Hustle', Complex Magazine, 09/2010
33. Statistic from Carnegie Institute of Technology (in Dale Carnegie's 'How To Win Friends and Influence People').
34. 50 Cent quote from, 'The Big Payback' by Dan Chanras, 2011
35. Sean Combs quote from CNBC 'The Big Idea,' interview, 04/2008
36. Kanye quote, 106KMEL radio interview, 10/2013
37. No I.D. interview, Complex, 02/2014
38. Jimmy Iovine story, Esquire magazine 'What I've Learned,' interview, 12/2013
NEGATIVES
39. Esham interview AllHipHop.com, 07/2011
ON NO ONE
40. Top Dawg, Vibe interview, 08/2013
41. Kendrick, HipHopDX interview, 01/2011
ROMANCE
42. Kanye West, NY Times interview, 06/2013
43. Kanye, Details magazine interview, 02/2009
44. Jay Z, 'Oprah' interview, 09/2009
45. "security, guidance, wisdom, and power" from '7 Habits of Highly Effective People', 1989
46. Eminem, Launch Magazine interview, 07/2002
47. Eminem, MTV interview, 2002
48. 'Circle' idea from 'The Celestine Prophecy', 1993
49. Tyson Toussant quote on Pharrell, from Fast Company interview, 'Get Busy: Pharrell's Productivity Secrets,' 11/2013

Story of: JAY Z
1. Quote from the book, 'Decoded,' by Sean 'Jay Z' Carter, 11/2010
2. Andrew Marr Show interview BBC, 09/2009
3. Oprah interview, 10/2009
4. 'The Rise of Jay Z' documentary

5.   'The Making of Reasonable Doubt' documentary
6.   VIVA Word Cup (Berlin) interview, 1997
7.   'Jay–Z and the Roc–A–Fella Dynasty' book, 2005
8.   New York Times article on Eli Whitney High School, 03/1986
9.   Juan Epstein Podcast with Ciph and Rosenberg, 2010
10.   Big Daddy Kane weuponit.com interview 09/2013
11.   Bruce Western, Princeton University article 'The Impact of Incarceration…'
12.   The Combat Jack Show, 03/2009
13.   Matty C quote, from Complex interview 12/2012
14.   Vibe Magazine 'Thinkin' of a Master Plan' interview, 08/1996
15.   Shades of Hip Hop, Jay Z interview, 1996
16.   dnainfo.com 'video music box' 02/2013
17.   Combat Jack 'stories behind 25 rap classics' for Complex magazine, 09/2010
18.   IYahoo music, Rockin' On A Roc–A–Fella interview, 05/1999
19.   The Combat Jack Show, Dame Dash episode, 04/2013
20.   Dame Dash and Biggs interview MTV, 10/2007
21.   Kevin Liles 'Make it Happen' book, 2005
22.   Dame Dash Black Enterprise Magazine interview, 12/1999
23.   MTV interview 'Jay Z explains his writing process' 04/2012
24.   From Jay Z twitter, @S_C_ 06/2013
25.   Dan Charnas book 'The Big Payback: The History of the Business of Hip-Hop,' 12/2010

PART III PRACTICAL LESSONS

BUSINESS + ART

1.   Dr. Dre 'Rhythm and Rhyme' documentary interview, 1997
2.   50 Cent interview with AOL music (available at daveyd.com), 01/2003
3.   'Unreleased Biggie Interview! Speaks On The Music Industry,' by iLLmixtapes, 03/2012
4.   Dame Dash, MTV 'Kanplicated' interview, 2005
5.   Dame Dash, 'Champions' song from 'Get Well Soon' mixtape (available at HipHopTeaches.com)
6.   Kanye West, Irish Times interview, 11/2004

BALANCE

1.   Kanye, DJ Semtex BBC Radio 1 interview, 2008

CREATIVITY

1.   Kanye, from DJ Lazy K, 'The Making of Martin Louis The King Jr Mixtape.' (Available at HipHopTeaches.com)
2.   'serious Play', an expression by psychologist Carl Jung
3.   Adult answers to 'how to make Melbourne better' question from: heraldsun.com.au, 06/2013
4.   Donda West, quotes from 'Raising Kanye,' 2007
5.   Kanye interview from interviewmagazine.com, 01/2014
6.   Kanye '20,000 word' Fader interview, 2008
7.   Forbes interview, 'Inside Tech N9ne's Midwest Empire,' 09/2013
8.   Creative process partly inspired by John Cleese Creativity Lecture and writings.
9.   'How To Become Successful by Pharrell Williams,' amirrahman15, 09/2013
10.   Fast Company interview, 'Get Busy: Pharrell's Productivity Secrets,' 11/2013
11.   Kanye, The Source interview 2003, republished by Complex, 02/2014
12.   John Jewkes book 'The Sources of Invention,' 1958
13.   Tupac quote, tupac-thuglife.tripod.com
14.   Pharrell, NPR interview, 12/2013
15.   Other techniques, partly inspired by James Altucher. Some website links are from venturevillage.eu and creativesomething.net
16.   Study from the National Institute on Deafness and Other Communication Disorders at the National Institutes of Health, 2012
17.   Richard Carlson's book, 'Don't Sweat the Small Stuff and It's All Small Stuff: …' 1997
18.   Stephen Covey's book, 'The 7 Habits of Highly Effective People,' 1989
19.   Synesthesia, inspired by Pharrell interview with NPR (12/2013), and Washington University online resources.

GETTING NOTICED

1.   Inspired by Seth Godin lectures.
2.   Kanye quote, MTV 'You Hear First' interview, 2002
3.   Perez Hilton article, 01/2014
4.   Bizarre quote, Ballerstatus interview, 2010
5.   Quoted from 'The 48 Laws of Power' by Robert Greene, 1998
6.   Kanye quote, Complex interview, 2003
7.   50 Cent quote, from his book 'From Pieces to Weight,' 2005

NICHE

1. Inspired by Seth Godin lectures.
2. Kendrick quote, from YouHeardThatNew.com
3. J-Cole interview with Complex 05/2009

BREAK IN

1. 'Rick Ross – Words of Wisdom' video montage, mycomeup.com
2. Kanye quote, MTV unreleased video interview, 2002
3. Chance The Rapper interview with XXL magazine, 09/2012
4. 50 Cent quotes, from AOL interview 2003, and book 'From Pieces to Weight.'
5. Pharrell, from Fast Company interview, 'Get Busy: Pharrell's Productivity Secrets,' 11/2013
6. From Joe Rogan Experience #320, 01/2013
7. Influenced by Jamesaltucher.com
8. Method Man raped a song about Sour Patch Kids candy in 2011

DO YOU

1. Definition of an artist from Seth Godin, 'Linchpin: Are You Indispensable?' book
2. Kanye quote, Rolling Stone interview, 2010
3. Kendrick Lamar, Guardian newspaper interview, 12/2012
4. Quentin Tarantino quote, from The Hollywood Reporter, Directors Roundtable, 2012
5. Tupac Shakur quote from thuglifearmy.com
6. "Christmas Presents" is a term Kanye West coined.
7. Kanye quote, from NY Times interview 06/2013
8. XXL article 'Shirt Worn By Pap In Photo With Kanye West Quickly Sells Out' 11/2014
9. Kevin Liles, 'Make It Happen' book, 2006
10. Jay Z, XXL 'I'll Still Kill' interview, 10/2007
11. Immortal Technique quote, from '15 Minute of Fame' radio interview
12. 'Collective Conscious' term from KRS-One '40 years of Hip Hop' lecture, 2012
13. Eminem quotes, from 'The Way I Am' book, 2008
14. Em quote, from Irish Radio DJ 'Dave Fanning' interview, 2001
15. Skylar Grey quote, from DJ Sway in the Morning interview, 2013
16. Nas quote, from 92Y Anthony Decurtis interview, 01/2012
17. Quote from the book, 'Decoded,' by Sean 'Jay Z' Carter, 11/2010
18. Jay Z quote from Men's Health article, 'Not a Businessman--a Business, Man', 10/2010
19. Partly influenced by The Phat Startup, 'Growth Hacking' article.
20. Kanye quote, BET interview, 2004
21. Kanye quote, from The Fader interview, 2008
22. Eminem quote, from 'Up and Coming' interview, 2000
23. Run DMC quote, Businessweek article, 'The CEO of Hip Hop,' 10/2003
24. J Cole quote, Harvard lecture, 02/2013
25. Kanye KDWB/Radio interview, 2010
26. Dame Dash quote, from Combat Jack Interview, 04/2013
27. Kendrick Lamar quote, from The Fader, 02/2012
28. Kendrick Lamar quote, from The Guardian, 12/2012
29. Kanye Quote from BBC Radio 1 interview with Zane Lowe, 09/2013
30. Lil Wayne quote from addictedtosuccess.com
31. No I.D. Complex interview, 02/2012
32. 'Tupac: Resurrection' documentary, 2003
33. Kanye quote, from NY Times interview, 2013
34. Kanye Quote MTV 'You Hear First' interview, 2002

The Story of: EMINEM

1. Spin magazine 'Chocolate on the inside' interview, 2000.
2. Music365 interview, 'Oh Yes, It's Shady's Night,' 04/2000
3. 'The Way I am' – Eminem's memoir, 2008
4. Rolling Stone 'Eminem blows up' interview, 1999
5. Eminem interview by D–Ex on Phatclips, 1999
6. The Source magazine interview, 07/2000
7. Rolling Stone interview, 11/2004
8. BackstabtheKingpin quote, from universalmetropolis.com
9. Launch 'Up and Coming' interview, 2000
10. Bizarre quote, from Ballerstatus.com, 05/2012
11. MetroTimes article 'The real Slim Shady,' 10/2002
12. 'Survivor Eminem' book, 2012
13. MTV interview, via eminemlab.com, 2002
14. Undergroundhiphop.com interview, 09/1998
15. Porter interview with hiphop–n–more.com
16. Rosenberg interview, Villagevoice, 09/2010

17.   Sway, MTV interview, 2004
18.   Published by Eminem Official, 1999
19.   Image source, mlive.com
20.   Image source, eminemphotos.tumblr.com
21.   Image source, ieminem.ru
22.   Eminem, 'Lose Yourself' outro

PART IV: UNIVERSAL PRINCIPLES
1.   Treat others as they want to be treated, inspired by Stephen Covey's 7 Habits of Highly Effective People.
2.   Kendrick quote from camcaponenews.com

WHO BENEFITS
1.   Wonder Mike quote and Master Gee, from thafoundation.com/wonmike.htm
2.   Quote from 'The Big Payback' by Dan Charnas, 2011
3.   Questions to ask yourself, inspired by 'The 7 Spiritual Laws of Success' book from peace.ca

EXTRA MILE
1.   Quentin quote, from Hollywood Reporter Directors Roundtables, 2012
2.   Kevin Liles quote, from his book, 'Make It Happen,' 2005
3.   Quote from Reasonable Doubt Documentary, 2008
4.   Complex article, 'stories behind-first covers of famous rap magazines,' 10/2013

GIVE BEFORE GET
1.   Russell Simmons, quote found in book 'Hip Hop Inc,' 2006
2.   No I.D. quote, interview with Complex magazine, 02/2012
3.   Kanye quote, from 'DJ Lazy K Presents Kanye West – The Making of Martin "Louie" The King Jr. Starring Kanye West,' 2009
4.   Common quote from Vibe magazine 'GOOD Music' interview, 07/2005

LOVE LIFE
1.   Lil Wayne quote from addicted2success.com
2.   Jay Z quote, German television interview, 1997
3.   Common quote from lecture at University of Florida, 02/2011
4.   make-me-successful.com ' inspiring words from J Cole' 12/2012
5.   Kid Cudi, Complex Magazine interview, 02/2014
6.   Kanye quote from Rolling Stone '500 Greatest Artists of all time' article.
7.   Kanye MTV 'You Hear First' interview, 2002
8.   Eminem quote, from 'The Way I Am' book, 2008
9.   Sean Combs quote from CNBC 'The Big Idea,' interview, 04/2008
10.   '40' interview with CNN, 04/2012

Made in the USA
San Bernardino, CA
20 November 2015